To Speak a Defiant Word

To Speak a Defiant Word

Sermons and Speeches on Justice and Transformation

Pauli Murray

Edited and with an Introduction by
Anthony B. Pinn

Foreword by
Michael Eric Dyson

Yale

UNIVERSITY PRESS

NEW HAVEN AND LONDON

Published with assistance from the Ronald and Betty Miller Turner Publication Fund.

Published with assistance from the foundation established
in memory of Calvin Chapin of the Class of 1788, Yale College.

Yale University Press books may be purchased in quantity for educational, business, or promotional use.
For information, please e-mail sales.press@yale.edu (U.S. office) or sales@yaleup.co.uk (U.K. office).

Designed by Mary Valencia.
Set in Fournier type by Integrated Publishing Solutions.
Printed in the United States of America.

Library of Congress Control Number: 2022948316
ISBN 978-0-300-26806-5 (hardcover : alk. paper)

A catalogue record for this book is available from the British Library.

This paper meets the requirements of ANSI/NISO Z39.48-1992 (Permanence of Paper).

10 9 8 7 6 5 4 3 2 1

We are called upon to be suffering servants,
but nobody said a suffering servant couldn't scream when it hurts.
And, brother, it hurts!
—Pauli Murray

I have never been able to accept what I believe to be an injustice.
Perhaps it is because of this I am America's problem child,
and will continue to be.
—Pauli Murray

Contents

ON THE STRIVINGS OF THE FAITHFUL

ON SUFFERING SOULS

GETTING CHURCH RIGHT

WOMEN AND WOMEN'S RIGHTS

Foreword
Murray Slaughter

Michael Eric Dyson

I confess that the title of my brief essay is a bit of nostalgia heated up in a skillet of sizzling paradox. I grew up in the sixties and seventies, and in 1970, right before my twelfth birthday, I was glued to the television set for the debut of *The Mary Tyler Moore Show.* I suppose the series about a single career woman working at a Minneapolis TV station was my introduction to feminism—well, to second-wave feminism at least—but with a big enough dollop of family values to make its progressive perspective popular. That is the nostalgia.

The paradox is that I aim to capture the complicated meaning of a professor and preacher who was vigorously nonviolent in her beliefs and activism. But here I am, for the sake of brevity, and with a nod to cleverness, pinching the name of a male character from a feminist sitcom to suggest how Pauli Murray slaughtered female stereotypes in her evolving identity.

Murray Slaughter was the head writer at the fictional television station WJM-TV, but there was nothing made up about how Pauli Murray rewrote the rules as a Black, iconoclastic, feminist lawyer turned priest who was both pioneer and prophet. She started with the law, then took to the classroom, and finally mounted the pulpit to say her piece in her effort to change the world. She often felt misgendered; she felt like a man inside and was undoubtedly what we now understand as nonbinary. This may redeem my choice of a male character to channel her furious dispute with the way things were.

The way things are now is tough, brutal even, calling for a figure of Murray's vision and complexity to name the whirlwinds that shake us to our core. As I write, the mortally battered body of Tyre Nichols, a twenty-nine-year-old skateboard enthusiast in Memphis, Tennessee, who was beaten to death by five Black cops, awaits burial in the same city where the greatest witness for justice in America met his violent end on a motel balcony nearly fifty-five years earlier.

Pauli Murray stood bravely against police violence and other forms of racism as a lawyer. Her unorthodox legal brilliance prompted Thurgood Marshall and his coterie of social engineers in the *Brown v. Board of Education* case to pivot from proving the inequality of "separate but equal" facilities to arguing before the Supreme Court that state segregation laws are unconstitutional. In this and other ways Murray's stirring voice echoed across the land in defense of vulnerable victims of hate and derision.

The nation's highest court could surely benefit now from Murray's tonic insight. Great segments of the nation are still reeling from the 2022 *Dobbs v. Jackson* ruling, in which the Supreme Court overturned *Roe v. Wade* and ended the federal constitutional right to abortion. Before there were any women in that once august collegium, Murray, in 1971, penned a letter to President Richard Nixon applying, with only part of her tongue in her check, to fill a vacancy on the court left by Hugo L. Black's resignation.

She knew this was not how appointments were made. At worst her gesture was futile, at best it was symbolic. But of course, Murray slaughtered convention once again. She argued to the president that it should "be of passing interest that I represent the largest group of minority status in the United States—namely, female." Murray contended that if Nixon appointed a woman, the Court would better reflect "the composition and interests" of the nation. That same moxie led Murray to name Jane Crow the evil twin to Jim Crow because she believed that sexism is just as lethal to the country as racism.

Murray carried that belief with her as the first ordained Black female Episcopal priest in the United States. Her very existence slaughtered patriarchal precepts preached from some of the nation's leading pulpits. Murray's theology hardly fed on doctrinaire anti-establishment ideology. She was decidedly Black and feminist, but she did not champion the sort of religious belief that wagged its ritualistic tongue and waved its liturgical finger at humanistic universalism. She was never enchanted by theologies rooted loudly in race and gender. She seemed to believe that some of these theologies of skin color and sex made the scandal of particularity more scandalous than necessary.

Murray's suspicion of the punishing exclusivity of the Christian faith meant that she was far more comfortable in ringing the chimes of interfaith accord than goosing the organ to cheerlead for "my-faith-is-better-than-yours." She favored dignity over dogma; she chose love rather than praise-the-Lording it over others. Her sublime skepticism is precisely what we need to fight the chest-thumping bravado of white evangelical bigotry and to resist the self-satisfied verities of social media and cancel culture.

This collection of Pauli Murray sermons and speeches should be greeted by a hearty amen. Anthony B. Pinn is the perfect intellectual and spiritual accomplice to Murray's slaughter of the sterile shibboleths of the cloth. A brilliant, and brave, thinker, Pinn is unafraid to challenge the religious status quo. He knows that too many religious folks go to worship with an indefensible vision of God. He knows that too many of us bow to a defective theism that is a thin cover for power and prejudice and the pernicious cult of personality.

If Pinn leaves God out of the equation, it is because he has seen the hurt and horror made in that God's image. He has glimpsed the suffering that follows when a God of moral convenience is created. He has witnessed the harm done in the name of God to those we should consider God's most precious children. But all is not lost; there is hope.

It often ends up, at least by my reckoning, that those who chide us for using Providence to justify base authority and to sanctify rank privilege are among the best friends of the faith. Pinn has justly kept us on needles as he punctures treacherous theisms with his strong humanism, just as Murray slaughtered detrimental religious belief with rigorous and reasoned faith. I thank God for them both as we face this untenable epoch: two of the brightest minds blended in battle against the enemies of truth, justice, and democracy.

Acknowledgments

Making available this collection of Pauli Murray's religious writings took a good number of years, and it required the help of many. Thank you to the Pauli Murray Estate for trusting me with the work of this tremendous preacher-activist and for granting permission to reprint the pieces found in this collection. I am grateful to Charlotte Sheedy, who contacted me seven years ago about editing what turned into this project. Without Jesseca Salky and her team, this volume would have remained a file on my desktop. Thank you for your sharp insights and tremendous skills that moved this project from my computer to Yale University Press! A special thank-you to my Yale editor Jennifer Banks, her assistant Abbie Storch, and the rest of the Yale team, as well as to my copyeditor Margaret Hogan. I must also thank Maya Reine, my friend and colleague at Rice, for editorial help preparing the manuscript for submission. Finally, as always, an energetic thank-you to my family and friends!

Note to the Reader

As my introduction to the volume will indicate, an effort was made to keep materials as Murray presented them. Notes were added in some places for clarification, and minor spelling issues, etc., were addressed. More challenging than these issues was the question of pronouns. From Murray's papers, it is clear that Murray thought deeply about issues of gender identity and sexuality—describing in some of these materials the feeling of being a man within a woman's body. Some commentators have identified Murray as a "transgender man." When we read across Murray scholarship, what surfaces is the fact that currently there are numerous ways in which Murray's gender identity is represented in scholarship and popular materials.

In more private correspondence, during this pronounced period of struggle (1930s–1940s), Murray often used "he/she" for a personal pronoun. Later, in published work and letters, Murray used the pronouns "she" and "her." In my introduction, I use "she" and "her." This decision follows on my effort to remain true to the historical context in light of the pronouns used by Murray during the time frame represented by this volume. I wrestled with this, and I understand that my decision will not satisfy all who read this book. However, because the sermons and speeches collected in this volume are drawn from the later materials, when Murray typically used "she" and "her," I made the decision to maintain that usage. My choice is not meant to dismiss other possibilities. Mine is one possibility that privileges what I understand to be the case based on my reading of the archival materials and in light of Murray's historical context.

To Speak a Defiant Word

Editor's Introduction

For some time now, many have witnessed deadly anti-Black racism, religiously fueled hate and xenophobia, and various challenges to the rights associated with democracy. While these forms of violent disregard are disturbing and appear out of line with assumed collective commitments, they do not represent practices foreign to nations such as the United States. They are not new. Rather, they are unfiltered, "raw" in a sense, and in this way they have challenged some basic assumptions concerning the promises made by a nation that has understood itself as a "city on a hill"—special and unique. All this has rocked the United States and has fostered a search into figures whose words and actions might offer a way forward. One of these figures experiencing a renaissance of importance is the Reverend Dr. Pauli Murray (1910–1985), the first African American woman ordained an Episcopal priest and a leading figure in the fight for race and gender equality.

While some specialists in the study of religion, women's history, and legal studies have given attention to Murray over the past several decades, a more general consideration of her writings and activism has been missing. However, fueled in part by efforts to better appreciate and reflect the impact of race and sexuality on academic inquiry, as well as a need to explore and explain the manner in which "difference" informs political practice, there has been a surge in research on Murray, particularly her political activities and relationship with key figures, such as First Lady Eleanor Roosevelt.[1] What is missing, however, from this new focus on Murray is substantial attention to her religious and theological development and perspectives.[2] Yet such a study enhances understanding of the role of women in religion in general, and African American women's religiosity in particular.[3] Murray sought to problematize existing conditions and thereby highlight the necessity of justice. She spent her life attempting to correct flaws and, through religious and social agitation, humanize life.

1

One can only imagine the extension of her religious influence had Murray had the time (and inclination) to bring her nonbinary sense of sexuality more forcefully into her theological thinking.[4] Still, the renewed interest in Murray speaks to her relevance beyond the years of her activism and ministry. In our troubled times, Murray's writings and sermons provide wisdom and insights that might serve to help bridge the distance between pain and prosperity—hard times and hope. We simply need to listen and reflect.

Pauli Murray was born in Baltimore, Maryland, on November 20, 1910, at a time when African Americans "reached the lowest ebb of their fortunes since Emancipation." She was the fourth of six children born to William Murray and Agnes Fitzgerald Murray, a school principal and nurse, respectively, who died while Pauli was young.[5] After the death of her mother in 1914, and in keeping with her mother's final wishes, Murray lived with her aunt Pauline in North Carolina. Sometime after her move to North Carolina, a guard at the Crownsville State Hospital (where William Murray had been placed due to a breakdown) killed her father. Murray described this event as an act of "racial antagonism."[6] According to Murray, these early years of separation and anxiety played on her psyche in lasting ways, shaping the manner in which she responded to situations. Years later she would write that "learning to be a Negro came later, but as I look back, those early shocks left me so sensitive and exposed that I reacted with double force to the vicissitudes of life which others seemed to take in stride. The burden of being a Negro was not the first crushing experience of my childhood."[7] In light of these family losses and circumstances of discrimination, Murray developed early on a strong sensitivity to and an outspokenness in response to injustice.

Growing up, Murray had a sneaking suspicion of the path she would take and the "cosmic" and historical events that might have conditioned her life. After all, she had been told by a bishop and family friend that she was "a child of destiny."[8] This sense of purpose shadowed her and informed her professional and spiritual development. And so Murray's life was dominated by two concerns: education and participation in religious community. School and church were extensions of her home life.

Education and Activism

After completing her final year of high school in New York City, Murray enrolled at Hunter College and received her degree in 1933. In retrospect, she considered the decision to attend an integrated school in New York as opposed to the segregated North Carolina College for Negroes her first act of defiance against racial segregation and discrimination.

It was the Great Depression when Murray graduated from college, and jobs were difficult to find. Fortunately, through the kindness of friends and strangers, Murray survived New York on very little. Two years of struggle ended with the organization of the Works Progress Administration (WPA) in 1935. Through the WPA, Murray worked as a teacher in the Remedial Reading Project at Public School 8 for a year, and this was followed by a job with the Workers' Education Project, training people in such areas as education, unemployment, and unions.

During the 1930s, she also developed contacts with important literary figures such as Stephen Vincent Benét and Langston Hughes, as well as Eleanor Roosevelt. Her relationship with Roosevelt and her later appreciation for Martin Luther King Jr. were probably two of the more significant influences on her sociopolitical sensibilities and activism, with the most prominent intellectual influence being Caroline F. Ware of Howard University. Murray argued for years that Ware extended the method of nonviolent direct action applied to the North American context and used by King. Murray noted that her nonviolent action as a way of life pushed beyond King's work for two reasons. First, it was based on psychic nonviolence as a life choice by committed individuals. And second, unlike King (and Mohandas Gandhi, for that matter), it was shaped by feminist sensibilities.[9]

From Eleanor Roosevelt Murray gained invaluable lessons on compassion and love.[10] Murray's exchanges with the First Lady highlighted her growing political perspective with regard to the deep-seated causes of racial inequality and her recognition of how both parties—Republicans and Democrats—had failed to make sustained and positive change regarding the race question. This situation, from Murray's perspective, made it unwise to sit back and assume that the established political process would work without nonviolent direct action or agitation. And this type of agitation had to be done in light of the manner in which the Western "will to power" impacted life across the globe.[11] These relationships, and a long-held interest in writing, were important to Murray—and included an array of endeavors such as poetry. For example, based on encouragement received from Benét, Murray eventually published a collection of poems titled *Dark Testament* that highlighted the ongoing struggle for equal rights. Benét also motivated her to write *Proud Shoes,* the story of her family.[12] At this stage of her life, Murray's goal was to become a professional poet, a creative writer who explored social conditions through the written word. But with limited success in this area and encountering a series of injustices, Murray gave more focused attention to direct social activism through the law, and she was influenced in her sense of activism by a range of figures. For example, Murray read Mohandas Gandhi and Krishnalal Jethalal Shridharani's *War Without Violence: A Study of Gandhi's Method and Its Accomplishments*.[13] This study of nonviolence inspired her to further develop nonviolent direct-action strategies.

In her life and work, Murray had several brushes with processes of social control—for example, the killing of her father, race-based restrictions on educational opportunities, and gender bias. However, none of these were more impactful than her arrest on March 23, 1940, as she traveled on a bus heading south to Durham to spend Easter with her aunts Pauline and Sallie. Changing buses in Richmond, Virginia, Murray and her travel companion and housemate, Adelene McBean, found that the only available seats for African Americans on this segregated bus were uncomfortable and positioned over the back wheels. The driver was unsympathetic, so in Petersburg they moved to the row vacated in front of them. The driver demanded they move back, although they were still behind the section reserved for whites. The driver threatened Murray and McBean with police action. A long conference between two police officers and the bus driver, however, resulted in only a warning. But shortly after that, when the driver only gave white passengers an "in case of accident" card, Murray had her say. She asked why the African American passengers had not received cards. The driver promptly got off the bus and came back with the officers, who placed the two under arrest for creating a "public disturbance."[14] Once in their cell, Murray and McBean made an effort to utilize Gandhian methods by issuing courteous demands for humane treatment. They also made a point of interacting with others being held in a way that spoke to the humanity and worth of all people. This struggle against racial injustice from their jail cell did not have national consequences, although NAACP attorneys on the case hoped it might. But it did deepen Murray's understanding of the infrastructures of racial bias as well as the merits of nonviolent direct action.

While this arrest and brief period of confinement were important in sharpening Murray's social justice sensibilities, she first demonstrated her activist spirit in her work toward increased visibility for African American students at Hunter College. It was further kindled when Murray became involved with the Workers Defense League, eventually becoming one of its field secretaries. While working for this organization, she came into contact with a sharecropper, Odell Waller, sentenced to die for the murder of his employer over goods he had been denied wrongly.[15] She made two trips, one with his foster mother, spreading his story and seeking to raise funds for his appeal. She also took this work as an opportunity to critique the poll tax that kept African Americans from participating in the electoral system because most could not afford to pay it. In spite of all efforts to the contrary, and regardless of the $30,000 raised for his cause, Waller was found guilty and put to death. This and other racist episodes, combined with conversations with Dr. Leon Ransom of Howard University's Law School, inspired Murray to attend law school.[16] She believed legal training would help her apply to public issues Christian social ethics and the demand for truth that marked the framework of her early family life.

Murray enrolled in Howard University's Law School and completed her studies in 1944 as the only woman in her graduating class. While at Howard, she combined her commitment to nonviolent direct action and detailed study of the law through student sit-ins and other activities meant to break the back of Jim Crow in Washington, DC.[17] As she began her final year of law school, Murray's experiences over the summer, including a riot in Harlem sparked by a police shooting of an African American soldier, combined with her new friendship with painter Betsy Graves Reyneau, served as important catalysts for addressing the combined injustices of racism and sexism. Murray moved from a collective sense of racism and a personal sense of sexism to a corporate and connected recognition of both as individual and communal dilemmas.[18] Murray also pushed for aggressive legal arguments to dismantle racist laws. For example, as a senior law student she wrote an essay in which she proposed a "frontal assault" on the constitutionality of segregation, rather than simply concentrating on a questioning of the unequal nature of facilities. While initially viewed as an impractical strategy by both students and faculty, it ultimately proved useful in that the NAACP legal team followed this strategy in *Brown v. Board of Education.*[19] Murray continued her legal training after Howard, earning an LLM degree in 1945 from the University of California at Berkeley.

The Law and Beyond

From 1946 to 1977, Murray held a variety of prestigious positions, including service as the first African American deputy attorney general of California and the only African American associate (and initially one of only three women) at the New York law firm Paul, Weiss, Rifkind, Wharton, and Garrison, a post she secured even *before* becoming the first African American to earn the Doctor of Juridical Science degree from Yale Law School. These career moves and the accompanying accolades did not distract her from her activism. Her continuing attraction to questions of justice and public policy remained clear throughout these years.

The intellectual and spiritual values instilled in Murray as a child influenced her activities during this period. Her successes and failures with dismantling inequality point to the merits of a particular type of struggle. In her words, "I do not intend to destroy segregation by physical force. . . . I hope to see it destroyed by . . . a power of the spirit, an appeal to the intelligence of man, a laying hold of the creative and dynamic impulses within the minds of men. . . . I intend to do my part through the power of persuasion, by spiritual resistance."[20] While all humans have a moral obligation to seek justice, African Americans are uniquely positioned to play a special role in these efforts, she believed. In making this assertion, Murray was ahead of her time and in line with late twentieth-century arguments concerning the unique status of African Americans, an argument forged in response to social Darwinism and persistent notions of manifest destiny and the "chosen people" paradigm of prevailing American ideologies. Yet while this might give rise to a type of epistemological elitism, Murray's philosophical sensibilities did not devolve into a cultural isolationist perspective or attitude of existential superiority.[21]

Murray made clear her devotion to democracy and human rights. In her work for justice and equality, all structures of power and authority were equal targets, even Christian churches. In 1969, Murray said the following concerning her "home" denomination, the Episcopal Church USA: "The history of Episcopalianism in the United States reveals a consistent policy of subordination, not merely of Negroes/Africans/Afro-Americans/Blacks, but also of women. . . . The Episcopal Church USA has begun to recognize its failure to fulfill its Christian mission in the case of Negroes; what it has not fully recognized is its equal and far more extensive failure to fulfill its mission with respect to half or more of the human race, namely, women."[22]

This critique was followed in 1970 by her participation in the development of a resolution that called the Episcopal Church to task, demanding change in light of the gospel of Christ and the values the gospel promotes. The resolution pushed for alterations to church doctrine and hierarchy that prevented the full inclusion of women and thereby promoted the dehumanization of all Christians as the body of Christ.[23] The resolution recommended the ordination of all qualified women, open admission to seminaries, focused recruitment of women, equal employment opportunities in keeping with federal law, and a program of education meant to bring congregations in line with full equality within the church.[24] From her perspective there was a profound link between activism and religious commitment, and the struggles of women exemplified this linkage.[25] She thought in terms of an ultimatum—change or lose a member. "I had been taught," she wrote, "all my life to revere the church and its teachings; now I could not condemn the church as sinful when it denied me the right to participate as fully and freely in worship of God as my brethren. If the present church customs were justified, then I did not belong in the church and it became a stumbling block to faith."[26]

Murray was torn: she had a desire for Christian fellowship, but all she had fought for over the years demanded that this fellowship grow out of equality. So, she wrote, "my feelings toward the church were ambivalent: I could neither stay away entirely nor enter wholeheartedly into Christian community."[27] The resulting frustration meant a brief departure from the Episcopal Church, a move that she described this way:

> These innovations [small gains in lay ministry roles] only whetted my desire to help do away with other restrictions, for they served to emphasize the male domination of the most elaborate and solemn service of the week— the Holy Eucharist on Sunday morning. . . . I do not know why this familiar spectacle suddenly became intolerable to me on Sunday morning in March 1966. . . . I remember only that in the middle of the celebration of the Holy Eucharist an uncontrollable anger exploded inside me, filling me with such rage I had to get up and leave. I wandered about the streets full of blasphemous thought, feeling alienated from God.[28]

In spite of continuing discrimination, she eventually returned—as a "Christian by conviction and an Episcopalian by choice."[29] She came back to her childhood denomination, but in what capacity changed as personal circumstances pushed her to think beyond the resources available to laity.

Responding to Her Calling

The death of Murray's partner, Irene ("Renee") Barlow, forced a reevaluation of her participation in the life of the church.[30] In her position as a layperson, she had been unable to provide for Barlow's spiritual needs—the last rites. This realization, combined with reflection on her "personal priorities," resulted in Murray's pushing for her own ordination as an Episcopal priest.[31]

Some suggest Murray's call to ministry really dated back to her childhood. That is, as Suzanne R. Hiatt, a leading figure in the women's ordination movement, speculated, "Though I never heard her say it, I have the impression that even as a young child she felt a call to ministry but quickly put it aside as impossible for a girl. She had dealt with so many 'impossibilities' in her life that when women as priests seemed a flicker of possibility in the late 1960's she naturally looked at the idea afresh. . . . When the issue of women in the priesthood came up, old dreams and a new fight began to stir in her."[32] In her autobiography, Murray suggested that the death of her aunt Pauline in 1955 and her reaction to it also pointed in the direction of ordained ministry. She "knew that Aunt Pauline's devotion to her church was central to her existence, and the thought that she might die without a priest to administer Holy Communion was terrifying." When asked by Aunt Pauline to lead prayers, as she lay dying, Murray remarked that "I was agonizingly aware of my inadequacy, for as a layperson, I felt I had no authority to give a blessing. . . . I kept asking myself why, in the ultimate crisis of a devout Christian life, I was called upon to render the service that I then believed was authentic only when performed by an ordained member of the clergy."[33]

What is interesting, however, is that this experience of inadequacy regarding the passage of Aunt Pauline did not immediately spark her fight for the ordination of women into the priesthood.[34] Instead, it served to intensify a challenge she could not resolve simply through her personal spirituality. In all other areas of her life, Murray had some degree of control, could map out legal and social possibilities, but death was a humbling reality.[35] It took away her ability to plot and plan, to exercise some control over circumstances. Her persistent drive for transformation confronted human finitude. "If I am mortally afraid to die myself," she wrote, "then I am not fit to give pastoral guidance to others who face death. In the working out of this confrontation with the reality of Death, I came closer to God, to Jesus Christ, and to the heart of our faith."[36]

She thought of personal and professional life not strictly in pragmatic terms, although the race and gender dynamics of her times would certainly have made that a reasonable approach. Nonetheless, for Murray life events were guided by a larger and more complex logic, one connected to the manner in which inner drive and inner self are sensitive to and linked to a larger, perhaps cosmic rationale and plan. In Murray's words, "I came [into the priesthood] because I had no other alternative. I fought death, God, and my own articulated plans—but the Call would give me no peace until I had made the decision."[37] It was not enough for Murray to discern the calling on her life; she wanted this recognized and acknowledged in ways she could not produce on her own, ways that might point to the cosmic trail of God working in her personal history. Hence, she offered the following statement reflecting on a comment from a seminarian, Tom Pike, who served at St. Mark's Church in Manhattan when Murray and Barlow joined in 1959, and who later officiated at Barlow's funeral:

> When it was all over [the funeral for Barlow], Tom Pike commended me on a beautiful service. I was astonished when he added, "You may not have realized it, but you have been acting as an enabler, a function of a deacon in our church. Have you ever thought of ordination?" Late that afternoon as I drove back to Boston thinking of Tom Pike's words, an exquisite sunset of gold, blue, pink, and aqua filled the western sky. It was as if Renee's spirit was smiling in approval as she bade me farewell.[38]

These various encouragements toward ordained ministry—her aunt's need for spiritual guidance in the face of death, the death of Barlow, or destiny—did not create an epistemological paradox or a conflict of emotion. Rather, taken together they suggest Murray's personal interest in ministry was not the result of a calling stemming from one particular event. Instead, this call was a deeply spiritual response to human frailty and finitude over time. She wanted to address this recognition, this existential angst, this basic human need for answers to ultimate questions beneath the surface of social problems. The mundane pointed to the "sacred," and the synergy among various events sent Murray in a new direction on her life journey. Ultimately, her call to church ministry grew out of a lifelong sense of purpose that reached beyond studying, teaching, or practicing the law.[39]

Leaving her tenured position as the Louis Stulberg Professor of Law and Politics at Brandeis University in 1973, Murray began studies at General Theological Seminary in New York City.[40] She reflected on this move as a radical and existential transformation, a redirection of personal religiosity toward the application of moral and spiritual forces to social problems.[41] This of course did not entail a break with her outspoken nature, her commitment to maintaining "voice," or her sense of righteous discontent with any perceived injustice. Murray's concern with voice as a dimension of freedom and equality was present in her response to fellow student Bob Godley, who requested her assistance in getting beyond the "apathy" that marked the seminary community. She noted that the school was clearly set up for white males, and she saw little reason for her participation in school governance (an odd assertion based on her efforts during the civil rights movement; one might assume this was a rhetorical device as opposed to a statement of policy). She concluded her letter with these words:

> Given this dim view of the institution and its direction, I am struggling with
> some major decisions. I had hoped that the student body would indicate a
> more hopeful future for the Church, but there are times when I look at my
> fellow Seminarians and say, "God, help the Church!" THIS DOES NOT
> HAVE TO BE. Individually, there is a treasure-house of talent, but leader-
> ship and followship are lacking. Perhaps you can supply that leadership, but
> as one potential voter I will have no interest in supporting you or anyone
> else unless I see a tangible program addressing itself to the needs I have
> articulated.[42]

The importance of voice, and the reluctance of a patriarchal environment to foster it in women, confronted her as a law student, and her battle to end this silence went on. Accordingly, she wrote, "it was not that professors deliberately ignored me but that their freewheeling classroom style of informal discussion allowed the men's deeper voices to obliterate my lighter voice, and my classmates seemed to take it for granted that I had nothing to contribute. For much of that first year, I was condemned to silence unless the male students exhausted their arguments or were completely stumped by a professor's question."[43] This di-lemma would not last long. Her outspoken critique of injustice, combined with academic excellence, meant leadership status and respect in campus activities.

She connected the struggle for voice in the context of race and gender is-sues to the work of ministry. Both required toughness and compassion, and she was not shy about naming these circumstances. In a letter, Murray responded to a student, Ernest Pollack, who was critical of her classroom approach. She wrote, "If I can't take your judgmental statements and your anger, I am in the wrong place. If you cannot take my methods of fighting for survival, then you have chosen the wrong vocation. In both instances, we are called upon to be suffering servants, but nobody said a suffering servant couldn't scream when it hurts. And, brother, it hurts!"[44] Murray not only fought to maintain visibility when dealing with other students. She also was quick to remind faculty and ad-ministrators of the significance of women in the history of faith practices and in

Christian thought over the centuries. And on more than one occasion she wrote to members of the General Theological Seminary faculty suggesting ways they might incorporate such recognition of diversity into the curriculum.[45]

Through the power of God and human talent, according to Murray, ministry bridged spiritual and physical reconciliation. A commitment to rights is only fulfilled through grace—an extension of this commitment beyond the physical to the inner life. Reconciliation in either form (spiritual or physical) has to involve a sense of proper relationship—humanity humble before God, and the development of human relationships based on compassion and respect.[46] This for Murray entailed ministry extending beyond traditional responsibility for a pulpit.[47] With family and friends, and under the authority of church leaders, Murray was ordained a deacon in 1976—a month after completing her Master of Divinity degree.

Shortly after her ordination, she addressed the issue of inclusion with passion, biting humor, and sarcasm. In this way, she pointed to her deep resolve to make social equality a moral and spiritual issue as well as a matter of mundane law: "Bearing pain for Christ's sake does not mean that I shall participate in my own degradation. It means that I must witness to the equality of all humanity before God in words as well as deeds. Or would you prefer 'all *huwomanity*'?"[48]

Murray believed issues such as sexism and racism were fundamentally moral and spiritual issues that could not be addressed strictly through mundane means of jurisprudence. Theological training and ordained ministry only enhanced her commitment to nonviolent direct action as a way of life, one with deep moral and ethical implications.[49] Murray was committed to an activist faith, a recognition that religion at its best is "this-worldly," committed to the application of the gospel to historical change, salvation as the transformation of societal existence. She framed this understanding when saying, "All the strands of my life had come together. Descendant of slave and of slave owner, I had already been called poet, lawyer, teacher, and friend. Now I was empowered to minister the sacrament of One in whom there is no north or south, no black or white, no male or female—only the spirit of love and reconciliation drawing us all toward the goal of human wholeness."[50]

On one occasion she summed up her experience and her position as her "pixie-prophetic (poetic) background," a context she felt put her in good company with "those scrappy 8th century B.C. prophets Amos, Hosea, Isaiah and Micah and with Paul, the Apostle, whose name I bear."[51] This statement was not the only indication that Murray felt her push for a spiritually and morally based nonviolent way of life was a calling bordering on the prophetic.[52] Murray thought of herself as possessing a special mission, perhaps similar to that of the prophets she named in the quotation above. It involved a task that required sacrifice and aggressive attention to justice and righteousness. She believed her life experiences and professional development gave her an important chance to enhance the church's response to women and their vision for Christian community. This opportunity was particularly pertinent with respect to women of color, as well as, in a more general sense, all who felt alienated from the church. In a letter to Reverend Franklin D. Turner, staff officer of Black ministries for the Episcopal Church, she hints at this perspective when writing, "Perhaps in no other field than the field of religion do we people of color, as clergy, have so rich an opportunity to demonstrate to our White sisters and brothers that Black people have something to teach them and they shall be the richer for it."[53]

Although there were initial questions concerning the practicality of ordaining someone of Murray's age (sixty-two at the time of her inquiry to Bishop John Burgess of Massachusetts), she became the first African American woman ordained an Episcopal priest in 1977—having been ordained a deacon the previous year.[54] After ordination, Murray ministered in the Episcopal Church of the Atonement in Washington, DC, and the Church of the Holy Nativity in Baltimore, Maryland, before retiring in 1984. While formal ministry might have ended at this point, informal ministry continued until Murray passed away on July 1, 1985, in Pittsburgh, Pennsylvania.

Murray's Theology

Murray's preaching was not marked by Pentecostal fervor in delivery but was thoughtful and reasoned out—appealing to a respect for and safeguarding of human dignity as Christian duty. She celebrated the moral and ethical virtues of the Christian faith and critiqued its shortcomings. And this was done without great or exaggerated gestures, as she noted in her General Ordination Examination. In terms of worship style, she "would tend to lean more toward the Quaker's 'listening in silence' than toward the charismatic's 'speaking in tongues.'" From her perspective the expending of such energy within the church's four walls was not an indication of a concern for social justice, a commitment to those in need, and such a concern was for her the true test of Christian faith.[55]

Her theological orientation strongly resembled a combination of Martin

Luther King's personalism (i.e., a philosophical position that privileges human and divine personality because, the argument goes, reality is available only in relationship to the conscious mind), the Social Gospel (and its social and humanizing efforts), and liberal theology growing out of the midcentury thought of philosopher of religion and theologian Paul Tillich.[56] A critique of white supremacy as it plays out theologically also was part of Murray's consciousness and was reflected in her politico-theological thought as early as the 1930s and 1940s. Yet the sense of Black consciousness and cultural nationalism that influenced so much early social activism and Black religious discourse—for example, the "The Black Manifesto," a document read at New York's Riverside Church in 1969 calling for reparations from religious organizations—troubled Murray.[57] From her vantage point, such efforts damaged the integrity of humans, reduced human dignity, and attacked the sense of unity or inclusiveness that marked the best of the Christian tradition and the best practice of social protest.

Albeit less than effectively, Murray attempted to avoid some of King's Christocentric tone through her theology. This theological position entails an appreciation for the religious devotion of others. While an outspoken Christian, Murray argued that the religious impulse behind each tradition had a shared source, and this divine spark is the basis of mutuality, dialogue, and understanding across religious lines.

She proposed a theological perspective that was pro–African American and pro-woman yet concerned with the dangers of particularization as they related to a limited perspective on the nature of oppression and righteousness.[58] She believed that human dignity and progress could be achieved through nonviolent direct action and persistent critique of social ills. In many ways Murray was opposed to what she considered the generally exclusivist agenda and tone of Black theology of the early 1970s as articulated by theologians James H. Cone and Albert Cleage.[59] She considered the anger shadowing such work as an unnecessary strike against its utility and creativity.

The ontological significance of "Blackness" presented by theologians such as Cone ran contrary to Murray's own sense of identity formation as complex and thick. What she seemed troubled by was how this sense of Blackness gave it paradigmatic and symbolic significance beyond its standing as an "accident" of history and nature—a social construction without any verifiably deep biological (genetic) significance. For Murray, while Black theology's rhetoric gained some attention (if for no other reason than the shock value it had during the 1960s when it developed), the lack of a clearly defined and organizing ideology did major damage to its push for social justice. Social justice had two platforms from which it developed for Murray: nonviolent direct action and universal human rights. But Black theology did not fully recognize the web of oppression and spoke only a limited (and limiting) word to suffering humanity. This limited word was based on the Christ event, which demonstrated God's primary commitment to those who are suffering.[60] What was missing from this stance, according to Murray, was attention to universal issues of human rights. It was much too focused on African Americans to the exclusion of a realization of how the plight of African Americans connected to the misery of the oppressed across the globe.[61]

Despite her disagreement with thinkers such as Cone and Cleage, Murray held a strong appreciation for theologian J. Deotis Roberts, another major figure in early Black theological discourse, but one whose push for simultaneous attention to liberation and reconciliation mirrored her sense of how human dignity is best developed and nurtured. This approach—liberation *and* reconciliation—was in keeping with nonviolence as a way of life. In opposition to this perspective, some of the more "radical" voices in Black theology refused to denounce the possibility of violence as a legitimate tool in the struggle for freedom and to consider reconciliation as worth discussing prior to the achievement of liberation. It was also Roberts's work, particularly *Liberation and Reconciliation,* that first fostered Murray's concern with developing a theology blending the best of feminist and Black theological theories and methods.[62]

Murray made an effort to ease unhealthy tension between what many white and Black Americans understood as competing interests. Recognizing the weblike nature of oppression, she suggested a *theology of relationship* through which the formation of complex and democratic community became the goal of ministry and social activism. From her perspective, a proper response to God is inseparable from attention to human need. In either case, one is required to engage fully, to risk oneself through connection to others. The Christian's obligation involves fostering healthy and harmonious relationships within all spheres of existence. Christians are able to accomplish this task of right relationship through a recognition of "transcendent power" above and beyond us that works within the context of human history. And this force fosters the ability to "project ourselves beyond our present circumstances, to envision a better world and to call upon our latent resources in the struggle for survival of the good life and in the adjustment to rapid change." This is the rightful consequences of the Christian's understanding that humans are made in the image of God, with certain rights that must be respected and protected.[63] Exclusionary tendencies troubled her, regardless of the form they took. Murray pushed beyond history as the framework for theological thinking, and in its place suggested sensitivity to "her-story." This effort to look behind patriarchal constructions of meaning also involved rethinking the church in order to recover its more justice-minded elements. This theological synergy must have seemed obvious to her because over the course of her life, tension and paradox had allowed for creative possibilities, for fruitful engagement.

The agendas for both feminist and Black theologies spoke to a need for humanization and an understanding of the oppressed as subjects of history with whom God identifies.[64] Although they were vital movements toward religious and social betterment, neither feminist theology nor Black theology spoke sufficiently to the experiences of African American women, who suffered because of their race, gender, and class. Black male theologians approached "women's issues" with suspicion, and feminists held a rather provincial conception of the community of women. In both cases, theological thinking was devoid of creative tensions and complexity, and for Murray this was deeply problematic in that it entailed a misconception of life and the struggle for full humanity. Keeping to this narrow agenda, both forms of theological discourse missed the uniqueness of African American women.[65]

In essence, Murray took the critique of racism from Black theology, the critique of sexism from feminist theology, the general appeal to the gospel as an agent of social change from the Social Gospel (i.e., Martin Luther King's theological orientation), and her life experience to foster a theological platform that was pro-Black, pro-woman, and concerned with the dangers of particularization. In her theological formulations as in her life activities, Murray avoided the simple route. Instead, she celebrated complexity, acknowledged paradox, and pushed publicly for a continually expansive understanding of and space for the life well lived.

Murray for Our Times

Murray kept very good records of her thought and activities. Both formal and informal reflections—research papers and holiday letters to family and friends—offer glimpses into the unfolding of her praxis. It was her goal to reflect on her religious development, to present to the public her spiritual story and the vocation that summed up her presence in the world.[66] Several of her letters, gathered in the Pauli Murray Papers at the Schlesinger Library at Harvard University, from which the following sermons and speeches were gathered, speak to this interest, as does Caroline F. Ware's epilogue to Murray's autobiography: "During her later years Pauli continued to write, contributing articles to theological publications and, through 'confrontation by typewriter,' as she put it, challenging newspapers and public officials on a wide range of issues that mattered deeply to her. In whatever time she could spare, she worked on this memoir, drawing on her memory and on her voluminous records. If she had been granted the time, she would have followed this volume with another devoted to her calling as an Episcopal priest."[67]

This book, *To Speak a Defiant Word*, seeks to provide some resolution to Murray's unfulfilled plan by using sermons and other writings to construct the contours of her avocation—her years in the priesthood and her theology and sense of activism inside and outside the church. Although it is not in the autobiographical tone intended by Murray, this collection of primary documents—sermons and lectures—does give readers access to Murray's voice through her own reflections on what it meant to be religious in the context of the troubled United States. The goal is to provide the general public and scholars with documents that exemplify her activism in light of her life in relationship to the church and what it seeks to represent.

Of course, these documents do not represent all of Murray's religious and theological writings. There are thousands of pages in the Murray Collection at the Schlesinger Library. What I gather in this volume, through the generous cooperation of Pauli Murray's estate and Charlotte Sheedy, are what I have come to view as some of her most representative pieces. These are the documents that graphically frame the ideas and commitments expressed during the last decade of her life—providing the most detailed or textured response to theological issues and themes she considered central.[68] I have arranged the documents into six themes that reflect rich components of Murray's religious thought and sense of ministry as they developed over time. Regarding the documents, readers will find my editorial notes numbered and presented in the back matter of the volume. The majority of my notes are meant to provide context, and when possible, I have also worked to finish Murray's incomplete citations. In addition, I have made an effort to provide reference information concerning some of the books and thinkers mentioned in passing by Murray. The notes provided by Murray as part of the original pieces are lettered and presented at the end of each text.

As a final note on the materials included, Murray often quoted heavily from various thinkers, and so in some cases I have shortened the quotations when this did not alter her meaning. This was done very sparingly to enhance the material's "flow" and to better surface Murray's thoughts and opinions. Typographical errors are corrected, and in some cases clearly missing words have been added. Again, an effort was made to, in all cases, avoid changing Murray's intent. While this volume does not entail all there is to know about Murray's religious self, it does offer a sense of how she fit into the theological and religious crisis and creative moments that dotted her historical landscape. In this sense, it provides texture and tone to the nature of Pauli Murray's life—a glimpse into what about her thought and activism warranted her self-identification as "America's Problem Child."

The Gospel for a Fallen World

The Dilemma of the Minority Christian

Isaiah 53:3–6

He was despised and rejected by men, a man of sorrows, and acquainted with grief; and as one from whom men hide their faces, He was despised, and we esteemed him not. Surely, he has borne our griefs and carried our sorrows; yet we supposed him stricken, smitten by God, and afflicted. But he was wounded for our transgressions, He was bruised for our iniquities; upon him was the chastisement that made us whole, and with his stripes we are healed. All we like sheep have gone astray; we have turned everyone to his own way.

And the Lord has laid on him the iniquity of us all.

The Word of God comes to us and fastens upon our minds and hearts in many strange, wonderful, and unforeseen ways. The beginning lines of the passage just read first came to me not through reading the Bible but through music—a song written by an unknown Hebrew prophet living in exile in Babylon some 2,400 years ago, caught up in the music of the eighteenth-century German-born composer George Frideric Handel, who wrote the *Messiah* and brought to us through the voice of our own mid-twentieth-century American artist Marian Anderson.

I used to play the record *Great Songs of Faith* whenever I felt downcast and in despair, for immediately after the song "He was despised and rejected," Marian Anderson sang that consoling aria from Mendelssohn's *Elijah:*

O rest in the Lord; wait patiently for Him,
and He shall give thee thy heart's desires.

Commit thy way unto Him, and trust in Him,
    and fret not thyself because of evil doers.
Tortured, he endured it submissively,
    and opened not his mouth.
Like sheep that is led to the slaughter,
    like a lamb before its shearers,
    He was dumb and opened not his mouth.[1]

Here, then, in poetry, in music, in the gift of the human voice, we encounter the suffering servant, the Servant of the Lord. Behind this song was the longing of the people of Israel for a savior, a redeemer, who would deliver them from their enemies and restore them to their status as a nation. They looked for a Messiah, a royal king, a powerful political leader, who would restore the throne of David and vindicate them as God's chosen people, God's elect before all nations.

But the poet-prophet who wrote the Servant Songs had something else in mind. He knew that what was needed before restoration could take place was conversion, someone who could call the people back from their sins, someone who could intervene on their behalf and bring about atonement for their alienation from God.

The savior he envisioned was not a royal, kingly, powerful leader but a man loathed and shunned by the community and looked upon with contempt. We are told earlier in the song:

He had no form or comeliness that should have made us give heed to him;
    there was no beauty that should have made us desire him;
His appearance was so marred, beyond human semblance,
    and his form beyond that of the sons of men.

Yet this was the man chosen by God for a special task—to lead the people of Israel to true penitence and godliness, and thus make possible true restoration and bring back to Jerusalem those who were scattered in exile. A man who was burdened by suffering—not for his own sins but for the sins of others. A man who must endure disease, misery, and pain in order to accomplish his mission—the salvation of others. He is subjected to opposition, ridicule, many blows, ill-treatment, and humiliation. For his suffering, healing and forgiveness are brought to others.

How is he able to endure his miserable lot? He knows that he has been chosen by God for his task. He tells us:

God formed me from the womb to be his servant . . .

The Lord Yahweh says, "therefore I will make you a light to the nations,

that my salvation may reach to the ends of the earth . . ." (Isaiah 49:6)

The Servant is discouraged with his mission, but God tells him it is greater than the mere redemption of the people of Israel. It is for the salvation of all the peoples of the world.

Some five hundred years after these Servant Songs were written, they found their most perfect expression in the life and work of another prophet and teacher, Jesus Christ. He was in conflict with the Jews because he saw his mission not as the powerful political Messiah who would restore the kingdom of David but as the self-giving suffering servant of the Lord, obedient to God even unto death.

For me, as perhaps it is for many thoughtful Christians, this is one of the most difficult passages in the Holy Scripture—difficult because it is the model which Jesus Christ chose for his own life, the standard he has set for us to attempt to meet if we profess to be Christians—and therefore I must take it with the utmost seriousness. The suffering servant says of himself:

But I was not rebellious, I turned not backward;

I gave my back to the smiters;

My cheeks to those who pulled out the beard;

I hid not my face from shame and spitting. (Isaiah 50:6)

But I *am* rebellious; I *am* impatient. I do not want to suffer for others; I do not want to suffer silently. When someone is unjust to me, I want to scream and yell and tell them off. I do not want to be despised and rejected. I do not want to be humiliated. When things get too tough, I want to run and hide. The Servant of the Lord answers:

But the Lord Yahweh helps me, therefore I shall not be put to shame.

Therefore I set my face like a flint, and know that I shall not be made ashamed.

He that vindicates me is near;

who will contend with me? (Isaiah 50:7–8)

Here, then, is the challenge and the promise of the Christian message—but am I willing to accept it?

Am I willing to relinquish my self-interest, my self-centeredness, my dependence upon my own resources or upon others, and surrender my entire will, my entire life to God? Am I willing to trust in God absolutely and without any reservations? Am I prepared to acknowledge that all I am and all I have belongs to my Creator, that I am not here for my own purposes, my own glory, but for the purposes and glory of God? Am I ready to confess that the only way to salvation and redemption is my utter surrender to God's will?

And if I cannot do this, am I prepared to face God's judgment? What does salvation mean to me, anyhow? Too often we have thought of salvation as something to be hoped for when we die—an insurance against the consequences of death and judgment. But salvation is here and now we are beginning to learn. Eternal life is here and now, as Jesus Christ taught us when he said, "the Kingdom of God is at hand."

Put in its simplest terms, salvation is feeling safe, living without fear, living with serenity in confidence that we are the objects of God's unfailing love, and that we will always be safe whatever happens, in life or in death, if we have a complete and childlike trust in God's love and tender mercy.

This is the great leap of faith which does not come easy, which deserts us continually, and which we achieve only by the greatest pain and effort—every day a trial, every breath a prayer. Salvation does not mean that we will avoid suffering, shame, humiliation, or defeat. It does not mean that we are not alone—that God's love which was poured out for us in Jesus Christ is always with us, to strengthen and save us in every situation if we have trust in his love.

To be a Christian, to follow Jesus Christ, means to be self-giving, pouring out love upon others even when they are unlovely and unlovable. And this is the hardest part of our faith. We were not made to live alone. We were made to live in community. And it is in community that we come in conflict with others. It is easy to respond to those who love and cherish us. It is much harder to see Jesus Christ in those who dislike us, who even hate and despise us, or who try to hurt us. It is difficult to be gentle with those who are unkind, who say and do harmful things about us and to us. Yet the hard truth is that this is the only way. For when we respond with resentment and retaliation, the greatest damage is not what we do to others but what we do to ourselves—by cutting ourselves off from God's love, by alienating ourselves from a sense of community, and winding up feeling lost and alone.

For those of us who have been born into a group which has been the object of contempt, injustice, and oppression, the figure of the suffering servant, the example of Jesus Christ, presents us with a most difficult dilemma. On the one hand we strive for self-respect and pride in ourselves and our achievements against those who would deny our humanity and our personhood. On the other hand, we are told that self-pride is a stumbling block to salvation. Are we expected to endure injustice submissively? To give our backs to the smiters?

Not to be rebellious when all around us we see evil and injustice?

I would be dishonest if I told you that I have answers to these questions. I wrestle with them daily. For in them lies the ultimate test of our faith in God—a faith that God is in control of the universe and of our own destiny, that God moves in history, that God is continually working to reconcile human-kind to himself and his love, that whatever we suffer is a part of God's ultimate plan, that we are in fact God's suffering servants in the salvation history of the world.

Somehow, I feel that we have a destiny which is beyond our struggle for civil rights and human rights or social justice, and that our consciousness of this destiny must permeate all that we do here and now, in this time and this place, and in this country.

In the words of a great prophet of our own time, the late Dr. Martin Luther King, who, when faced with the massive violence of the segregation system, told his followers:

> Our most fruitful course is to stand firm, move forward nonviolently, accept disappointments, and cling to hope. Our determined refusal not to be stopped will eventually open the door to fulfillment. By recognizing the necessity of suffering in a righteous cause, we may achieve our humanity's stature. To guard ourselves from bitterness, we need the vision to see in this generation's ordeals the opportunity to transfigure both ourselves and American society.[2]

Critics of Dr. King charged him with not dealing squarely with the issue of *immoral power* in collision with *powerless morality,* but in retrospect it becomes crystal clear to us that Jesus Christ uttered an incontestable truth when he said, "Those who take to the sword shall be slain by the sword." And one wonders if Dr. King did not glimpse the true problem when he said, "The struggle is not between black and white, but between good and evil."[3]

And since Dr. King's death, another prophet has arisen to tell us that "the apparent chaos, the deadly atmosphere which pervades America"—of which racism, sexism, or the accumulated social injustices and corruptions are symptoms—

"is a condition which the Bible designates as the Fall." In his provocative book, *An Ethic for Christians and Other Aliens in a Strange Land,* William Stringfellow writes,

> The nation is fallen. America is a demonic principality, or a complex or constellation, or conglomeration of principalities and powers in which death furnishes the meaning, in which death is the reigning idol, enshrined in multifarious forms and guises, enslaving human beings, exacting human sacrifices, capturing and captivating Presidents as well as intimidating and dehumanizing ordinary citizens.[a]

Stringfellow sees the death of a nation as the great Old Testament prophets—Amos, Hosea, Micah, Isaiah, and Jeremiah—saw the destruction of the people of Israel. He asks, "Is there no promise for America? Is there no American hope? The categorical answer is no." He goes on, "The answer for those who are Christians is no, and therefore, the answer which Christians commend to other human beings is no."[b]

If Stringfellow is right—and we cannot afford to take lightly his prophecy of doom, for we too have seen the signs of moral corruption and decay—then we are aliens as Christians in a profound sense which transcends our racial or social status. Although in our daily lives we must continue to carry on our struggles for social justice and human dignity, for honesty and integrity, we as Christians find ourselves called to a higher purpose than a social ethic—a call which we can no longer evade—a call to righteousness, to repentance and salvation. Jesus Christ has shown us the way—faith which transcends death and gives us hope.

And if we make the effort to enter upon this path, we can say with the suffering servant of the Lord: "But the Lord Yahweh helps me, therefore I shall not be put to shame."[c]

And we can join that magnificent chorus in Handel's *Messiah,* singing,

> But Thou didst not leave his soul in hell; nor didst Thou suffer Thy
> Holy One to see corruption.

Notes

[a] William Stringfellow, *An Ethic for Christians and Other Aliens in a Strange Land* (Waco, TX: Word Books, 1973).

[b] Ibid.

[c] Isaiah 50:7.

Father's Day Sermon

Isaiah 30:20–22

And though the Lord give you the bread of adversity and the water of affliction, yet your teachers will not hide themselves anymore, but your eyes shall
see your teachers. And your ears shall hear a word behind you saying, "This
is the way, walk in it," when you turn to the right or when you turn to the
left. Then you will defile your silver-covered graven images. You will scatter
them as unclean things; you will say to them, "Begone!" ("Good riddance!")

My return to St. Philip's this morning as a candidate for Holy Orders in Christ's
Holy Catholic Church, after an absence of many years, is somewhat like the
homecoming of a prodigal. For it was here at St. Philip's that I had my first spiritual crisis. When I came to live in Harlem as a teenaged freshman at Hunter
College, I roomed at the West 137th Street YWCA, Emma Ransom House,
worked part-time jobs as [a] waitress, switchboard and elevator operator, cafeteria dishwasher, or secretary-typist—whatever I could get to help me finish
school. And as a child of our church whose uncle was a priest, I immediately
affiliated with St. Philip's.

My first assignment as an active church member was to teach a Sunday
School class of twelve-year-old boys, and the theme for the church year was the
life of Jesus Christ. This seemed easy enough at first. I had grown up in the
church. It was my second home. And living in a family of public-school teachers,
teaching was as natural as breathing to me.

After about two lessons with those squirming youngsters, I experienced
perhaps my first defeat in performance. I could not hold their interest. Coming

27

from a teacher's family, I had lived under the injunction, "Show me a child who cannot learn and I will show you a teacher who cannot teach!" The realization that what I had taken for granted all of my life could not be communicated to others was a traumatic experience. How could I grasp the minds and hearts of twelve-year-old boys and help them to understand a life which was both human and divine—a life about which nothing is known from the age of twelve to thirty?[1] Biblical scholarship had not developed ways of interpreting the scriptures to twentieth-century Christians, and if it had, these insights had not filtered down to the local churches. There were no educational materials to help me out of my dilemma.

And so, a crisis in teaching became a crisis of faith. Until I could know and understand the human Jesus, I would never be able to interpret the Christ of faith. It would be many years before I learned that faith cannot be proved by evidence, or else it is not faith. As my namesake, St. Paul (a name I take with utmost seriousness), has said, "Faith is the substance of things hoped for, the evidence of things unseen."[a]

I resigned from teaching the Sunday School class, eventually dropped out of church for several years, and began a lifelong quest for the meaning of Jesus Christ in my life. I had to learn the hard way the meaning of this morning's text, "And though the Lord give you the bread of adversity and the water of affliction, yet your Teachers will not hide themselves any more, but your eyes shall see your Teachers." We are told that the prophet Isaiah in this passage was referring to the prophets of the Word of God.

It is this quest which brings me here this morning, as one who has wandered about the world and who in later years, after many failures and some successes, feels called to prepare for priesthood in our church, a step I could not take until after the General Convention of the Episcopal Church in 1970, and which I cannot complete until the General Convention has acted in the fall of 1976. It is fitting that I make this confession at St. Philip's on Father's Day, for this congregation belongs to the priesthood of all believers.

When we reflect upon the connection between this morning's lesson and Father's Day, we are reminded of the great legacy which Jesus Christ left to all believers—the Lord's Prayer—"Our Father, who art in heaven." It is the first prayer we learn as children and say at every service of worship. It is addressed to God, the Father and Creator, and through it we experience the meaning of Isaiah's prophecy: "And your ears shall hear a word behind you, saying, 'This is the way, walk in it,' when you turn to the right or when you turn to the left."

You will recall that in the Gospel narrative of St. Luke, when Jesus was praying in a certain place, one of his disciples came up to him when he had finished and said, "Lord, teach us to pray, as John (the Baptist) has taught his disciples." And Jesus answered him and said, "When you pray, say, 'Father, hallowed be thy name.'"[b]

We address ourselves to God as children of God. As Paul of the first century of the Christian era wrote to the Galatians, "Because ye are sons, God sent forth the spirit of his Son into our hearts, crying, 'Abba, Father.'"[c] Jesus spoke Aramaic, one of the Hebraic languages of his time, and the word for "Father" in Aramaic is *Abba*. Jesus and Paul, the apostle, both lived in a patriarchal society in which the human father was the head of the household and responsible for all those under his roof—wife, wives, children, manservants, maidservants, or slaves. They therefore spoke in images which people of their era could understand.

In the late twentieth century, the theologian must also speak to his or her own era, and it is my understanding as a student of theology that God is not limited by any man's notion of sex, or gender, or race, or ethnic origin, or status— God is all inclusive. Therefore, I would modify my namesake's text to read, "Because you are sons and daughters, God sent forth the spirit of his Son into our hearts, crying, 'Father-Mother God,'" in recognition that the love and acceptance poured upon us despite our unworthiness by the Divine Being is the love we associate with both parents. And perhaps the time will come when we celebrate one Sunday, as Father's and Mother's Day, instead of two. For those of us whose parents died when we were very young, as in my case, or who have reached that age in life when their parents are no longer living, we can celebrate Sister's and Brother's Day.

One of the greatest books I have ever experienced is a meditation on the Lord's Prayer, entitled *Abba,* written by the English scholar and mystic Evelyn Underhill (1875–1941), daughter of a barrister.[2] She was appointed a fellow of King's College, London, in 1927—quite a precedent for a woman of her time.

Underhill tells us that this is "the prayer of those 'sent forth' to declare the Kingdom, whom the world will hate, whose unpopularity with man will be in proportion to their loyalty to God. . . . The disciples sent out to do Christ's work were to depend on prayer, an unbroken communion with the Eternal, and this is the sort of prayer on which they were to depend. We therefore, when we dare to use it, offer ourselves by implication as the fellow workers for the Kingdom; for it requires an unconditional and filial devotion to the interests of God. Those who use prayer must pray from the Cross."[3]

To think of oneself as a child of God is a liberating experience—it is to free oneself from all feelings of inferiority—whether of race, or color, or sex, or age, or economic status, or position in life. When I say that I am a child of God—made in his image—(the theologians like to use the term *imago dei*)—I imply that "Black is beautiful," that White is beautiful, that Red is beautiful, or Yellow is beautiful. I do not need to make special pleading for my sex—male or female or in-between—to bolster self-esteem. When I truly believe that God is my Father and Mother, in short, my Creator, I am bound also to believe that all men, women, and children of whatever race, color, creed, or ethnic origin are my sisters- and brothers-in-Christ—whether they are Anglicans, Roman Catholics, Methodists, Black Muslims, members of the Judaic faith, Russian Orthodox, Buddhists, or atheists. I am grasped by the words of the Fourth Gospel (St. John): "For God so loved the world that he gave his only Son, that whoever believes in him should not perish but have eternal life. For God sent the Son into the world, not to condemn the world, but that the world might be saved through him."[d] If I am a child of God, a sister-in-Christ, and belong with all of you to the priesthood of all believers, then my job is to love, not hate, to be creative, not destructive, to follow Christ's cross. This is the lesson of the great prophets down through the ages, and many of us were privileged to see it reflected in the life and death of our own great prophet of the twentieth century—the late Dr. Martin Luther King Jr.

If I am a child of God and follow Jesus's example of utter dependence upon and radical obedience to God, I find as Underhill says, that "there is ever the sense of that strong and tranquil presence, ordering all things and bringing them to their appointed end; not with a rigid and mechanical precision, but with the freedom of a living, creative, cherishing thought and love. Throughout his life, the secret, utterly obedient conversation of Jesus with his Father goes on. He always snatches opportunities for it, and at every crisis he returns to it as the unique source of confidence and strength; the right and reasonable relation between the soul and its source."[4]

But if I am a child of God, made in his image, I am also human—self-willed, wayward, rebellious, defiant, spiteful, mean, petty, vindictive, gossipy, hurtful of others—in short, sinful—"kept in perpetual tension between the pull of heaven and the pull of earth."[5] My soul is a battleground between what God *wants* me to be and what I *will* to be.

I say with my lips, "Thy will be done," and then I turn around and argue with God to get my own will. This is the ambiguity of human existence. We our-

selves try to be God. We make for ourselves "silver-covered images"; we seek security in the tyranny of possessions; we tend to worship power and prestige and
money; and whether we are white or Black, male or female, rich or poor, strong
or weak, we find in the end that they do not give us peace of mind or permanent
joy. In the hour of dark bereavement, when we have lost those we love best; in
that moment of utter failure of all our dreams and plans; when we barricade
our homes like fortresses to protect our lives and our possessions, and find that
nothing is safe or secure, we learn at last the truth of Isaiah:

> And though the Lord give you the bread of adversity and the water of afflic-
> tion, yet your Teachers will not hide themselves anymore, but your eyes shall
> see your Teachers. And your ears shall hear a word behind you saying, "This
> is the way, walk in it," when you turn to the right or when you turn to the
> left. Then you will defile your silver-covered graven images. You will scatter
> them as unclean things; you will say to them "Begone!" ("Good riddance!")

Amen.

Notes

[a] Hebrews 11:1.
[b] Luke 11:1.
[c] Galatians 4:6.
[d] John 3:16.

Sermon Given on January 4, 1976

Isaiah 61:1–4

The Spirit of the Lord God is upon me; because the Lord hath anointed me to preach good tidings unto the meek; he hath sent me to bind up the brokenhearted; to proclaim liberty to the captives, and the opening of the prison to them that are bound; to proclaim the acceptable year of the Lord, and the day of vengeance of our God; to comfort all that mourn; to appoint unto them that mourn in Zion, to give unto them beauty for ashes, the oil of joy for mourning, the garment of praise for the spirit of heaviness; that they might be called trees of righteousness, the planting of the Lord, that he might be glorified. And they shall build the old wastes, they shall raise up the former desolations, and they shall repair the waste cities, the desolations of many generations.

Our lesson from the prophet Isaiah this morning which begins, "the Spirit of the Lord is upon me," is a fitting reminder of our Christian calling as we face the New Year and enter into the Epiphany season which begins on Tuesday. Epiphany means "manifestation" or "appearance," and it is the celebration of the manifestation of Christ to the Gentiles when the wise men from the east came to Jerusalem saying, "Where is he that is born king of the Jews? For we have seen his star in the east and are come to worship him."[a]

The lesson also recalls to us the beginnings of Jesus's ministry according to the Gospel of Luke. Following his baptism and forty days of temptation in the wilderness, Jesus returned in the power of the Spirit to Galilee and came to Nazareth, where he had grown up. As was his custom, he went to the synagogue on the Sabbath Day. He stood up to read and there was given to him the book of the prophet Isaiah. He turned to the passage where it was written, "The Spirit of the Lord is upon me, because he has anointed me to preach good news to the poor, He has sent me to proclaim release to the captives and recovering of sight to the blind, to set at liberty those who are oppressed, to proclaim the acceptable year of the Lord."

Ministry means service to others. Too often we think of ministry in a narrow sense, as if it were the special province of the ordained clergy. It is true that some of us feel a special call to seek Holy Orders, not because we are better Christians or more able than our brothers and sisters, but because something has happened to us and there has taken place a radical shift of God's moving from periphery to the very center of our lives. And we feel compelled to seek full-time service to God as our vocation.

But we must continually remind ourselves that every Christian who is baptized into the church is admitted to the royal priesthood of all believers in Christ, and that each of us has a ministry, whether we are young or old, male or female, lay member or clergy. To be a Christian is to follow Jesus Christ's example of ministry, to be God's representative on earth. Each of us has been called by God to love and serve him and our fellow human beings. However sinful, rebellious, or inadequate we may feel, we cannot escape God's claim on us. If we respond to God's call, we are given the power of the Holy Spirit and God uses us as instruments of his divine will in working out his plan for the redemption of the world.

We minister when we pray for others, when we stand before God holding them in our thoughts. We minister by our presence with another in time of trouble, giving reassurance that the other is not alone in adversity. We minister when we simply listen with a sympathetic ear to one who is full of sorrow and grief, or when we telephone a shut-in just to let someone know that he or she is not forgotten, or when we offer a warm smile and a welcoming handclasp to a stranger in our midst. We minister to one another when we act upon the conviction that our worship service is a corporate undertaking and that it makes a difference in the quality of that worship whether we ourselves are present or absent.

We encounter God in our ministry to others, for only as we love and serve others do we love and serve God. St. John's letter to the early church stresses this aspect of the Christian's response to God's love. He wrote,

> Little children, let us not love in word or speech but in deed and in truth....
> Beloved, let us love one another; for love is of God and knows God. He who

does not love does not know God; for God is love. In this the love of God
was made manifest to us, that God sent his only Son into the world, so that
we might live through him. In this is love, not that we loved God but that
he loved us and sent his Son to be the expiation for our sins. Beloved, if
God so loved us, we also ought to love one another. No man has seen God;
if we love one another, God abides in us and his love is perfected in us.[b]

God is as close to us as our neighbor's hand. We see Jesus Christ in our neighbor's face. And our Lord Jesus Christ, through his ministry on earth, his death and resurrection, has shown us the way to a higher destiny than our transitory life in this world.

Prayer for Christian Service

Lord, our heavenly Father, whose Son came not to be served but to serve; bless all who, following in his steps, give themselves to the service of their fellows. Give them wisdom, patience, and courage to strengthen the weak and raise up those who fall; that, being inspired by your love, they may minister in your Name to the suffering, the friendless, and the needy; for the sake of your Son, who laid down his life for us, Jesus Christ our savior.[1]

Amen.

Notes

[a] Matthew 2:2.

[b] 1 John 3:18.

The Gift of the Holy Spirit

John 14:16–17

And I will pray to the Father, and he will give you another Counselor, to be
with you forever, even the Spirit of truth, whom the world cannot receive,
because it neither sees him nor knows him; you know him, for he dwells
with you, and will be in you.

This was the promise Jesus gave to his disciples during his farewell meal with
them in the Upper Room before he went out to meet his death by crucifixion.
And, according to the book of Acts, this promise was fulfilled on the day of
Pentecost, the "fiftieth day" after Passover, commemorated in Jewish tradition
as the day on which the Law of Moses was given. In Christian tradition, Pentecost or Whitsunday is the day on which the apostles received the gift of the
Holy Spirit and has become the climax of the Easter season.[1]

Acts gives us a dramatic account of this event. The apostles had come
together in Jerusalem to observe Pentecost, when suddenly the Holy Spirit filled
the heavens with sound like the rush of a mighty wind, and the apostles were so
filled with it that they seemed to be on fire. They could not contain themselves
and each broke into ecstatic utterance praising the mighty works of God. Their
enthusiasm communicated itself to the people in the vicinity, and a great multitude assembled to find out what had caused all the excitement. The apostles'
speech transcended barriers of language and nationality so that many people
from different countries living in Jerusalem were able to understand what they
were saying. We learn that after Peter stood up and preached that day, three

thousand souls were baptized into the Christian faith and devoted themselves to the apostles' teaching and fellowship, to the breaking of bread and prayers.

As in the apostles' time, the Holy Spirit comes to us in moments when we least expect it—it may be a great church festival when thousands of people are united in prayer and hymns of praise, or it may even manifest itself in a political event. In retrospect, I think the Holy Spirit was very much in evidence on that day in August 1963 when 240,000 people of all colors, ages, and religions came together in Washington for a common ennobling purpose, marched to the Lincoln Memorial, and heard the late Dr. Martin Luther King Jr., among others, burst into what was essentially a Spirit-filled utterance—"I have a Dream that one day every valley shall be exalted, every hill and mountain shall be made low, the rough places will be made plain and the crooked places will be made straight, and the glory of the Lord shall be revealed, and all flesh shall see it together."[2]

We pray for the gift of the Holy Spirit on very special sacramental occasions in our church life—at baptism, at confirmation, and during ordination. We may consciously *feel* the Spirit in such deeply devotional moments. We need to remind ourselves, however, that the Holy Spirit is God's abiding presence with us at all times and in all places, in every possible situation—at home, at work, in school, in the marketplace, in social life, in politics, in joy, in the depth of sorrow, sin, sickness, and despair—the ever-faithful companion, friend, and Counselor, the Eternal One working in and through every moment of history in the affairs of mankind.

I think sometimes we shrink from the thought of this ever-present Spirit because our awareness of being in God's presence at all times is a fearful and awesome thing. We *are* afraid when we contemplate the Holy, the fear which a priest or a lay minister experiences standing at the altar or attempting to preach the Word of God. Our realization of how small we are and how infinitely great is the Creator and Preserver of our universe inspires our awe. Our consciousness of how far we fall short of our true selves, and that God's judgment is upon us every moment of our lives, makes us afraid.

But God is not alien or distant from us, and his Spirit is as close as the touch of a loved one's hand. We were created for community with God, and we are linked with the eternal in the midst of our transitory life. We become alienated from God when we forget our link to eternity and elevate the things of this world to supreme importance. When, however, we rest ourselves in God and are open to the Holy Spirit, we feel a certain serenity in the midst of all the conflict and confusion of life. God's power is working in us and through us, to guide us in our critical decisions, to strengthen us when we are disheartened, to comfort us when we are bereaved. In the words of a Christian writer, "There is a wonderful, loved, protected feeling that embraces one who realizes that God is always near."

Yet it would be wrong to think that the Holy Spirit comes to us merely to give us comfort or ease. The work of the Holy Spirit is to transform our lives and to conform us to Christ, to perfect us. We are told in the Outline of Faith of our proposed Book of Common Prayer that "we recognize the presence of the Holy Spirit when we confess Jesus Christ as Lord and are brought into harmony with God, with ourselves, with our neighbors, and with all creation."

This transformation is an ongoing process requiring struggle and sacrifice of our own selfish desires, slowly and often painfully learning obedience to God's will. It involves a discipline made possible only by the Holy Spirit, pressing upon us to bring our disordered lives into an integrated pattern of spiritual harmony.

The Holy Spirit works through humanity individually and socially. In a little book, *The Faith of the Church,* we are told that the Spirit brings men and women together for great purposes, "drives the people of the earth into closer community with one another . . . insists that the order of human society be conformed more closely to the will of God, and shatters our complacent self-interest until we are prepared to cooperate toward that end."[3]

We may often doubt that this is the case when we read the daily headlines or listen to the news media of all the violence, hunger, poverty, crime, corruption, disorder, and injustice in the world. In moments of spiritual crisis, we ask ourselves, "If God is all-good and all-powerful, what about the evil in the world? How can God's Holy Spirit be at work if these terrible things happen?"

This question has probably come to each of us at some time or other in our lives. It is at the heart of our Christian faith. But our faith teaches us that God has created us with the freedom to do evil as well as good. God is a loving God who does not coerce his creatures to do his will but seeks through love to draw them to himself. Evil is the fruit of sin, and sin means separation from God, from ourselves, and from our fellow human beings. We become separated from God when we forget the true source of our strength, intelligence, or well-being and feel ourselves self-sufficient, or on the other hand, when we become so preoccupied with our own concerns that we are consumed with self-pity when things go wrong and feel ourselves alone and desolate.

Faith teaches us that God has not abandoned us to evil and suffering, that his spirit is with us continually in our pain and brokenness, reconciling us and the world to himself. We believe that God came to us in Jesus of Nazareth, human as we are human yet so possessed by God that we can only say, "This is God with us as man." God in Jesus Christ met us where we are and suffered all that man can suffer in defeat and death. It was Christ's victory over the cross and the grave which gives us the hope that with God-in-Christ we, too, may conquer sin and death. This is the meaning of the words, "God so loved the world that he gave his only-begotten Son, to the end that all who believe in him shall not perish, but have everlasting life."

It was the disciples' conviction that they had seen the Risen Lord which set their hearts on fire and drove them to proclaim the Good News with such passion that thousands of people felt the overpowering experience of being in touch with the Living Christ.

On this belief stands the Christian Church, "the Body of Christ," "the blessed company of all faithful people," the place where we come together in community to worship and to receive the strengthening gift of the Holy Spirit, so that we may be empowered to witness God's redeeming love in Christ in all that we do. As baptized Christians, whether lay or ordained, we are all ministers of the church and have the same fundamental ministry—to represent Christ and his church, to bear witness to him wherever we may be, and according to the gifts given to us, to carry on Christ's work of reconciliation in the world.

The Holy Spirit replaces the visible presence of Jesus, and the church is the Spirit-filled community in which we are bound to one another in Christ. For it is only when we are one in Christ that we can rise above those things which separate us from one another—differences of race, sex, age, class, economic or social position—and share that supreme gift of communion expressed in the benediction, "The grace of our Lord Jesus Christ, the love of God, and the fellowship of the Holy Spirit be with us all evermore."

Amen.

Sermon Given on December 25, 1977

Luke 2:8–9

And in that region there were shepherds out in the field, keeping watch over their flocks by night. . . . And [the] glory of the Lord shone around them.

One of the most precious gifts of life is a sense of wonderment, a sense of awe, a sense of the holy. Yet often we are so consumed by our own troubles or we become so conditioned to extravagance in modern living that we are in danger of losing this gift. We are assaulted by constant images, instant coverage by on-the-spot television of today's significant events, which are soon crowded out of memory by the next day's news. We expect elaborate ceremonies to attend any important happenings in the world. As the historian Arthur Schlesinger Jr. commented a few days ago: "President Sadat's visit to Jerusalem has already passed into the realm of the commonplace, rather like the first landing of men on the moon. The insatiable consumption of novelty by our high-velocity age has enfeebled our capacity for wonder." The wonder of Christmas is often overshadowed by the bustling preparations for the holiday season—the dazzling lights and decorations; the frantic shopping for gifts; the record sales of jewelry, furs, accessories, and gourmet items; the feasts and parties.

But if we really take the time to listen to Luke's beautiful Gospel narrative of the birth of Christ, we cannot help but be filled with wonderment—not so much because of an angelic host singing "Glory to God in the Highest" but because of the utter simplicity and unpretentiousness of that heavenly event in Bethlehem. As one biblical scholar has said, "God, who is the source and meaning of all life, reveals himself in a little child coming unnoticed in the stable of an unregarded town," as if to say to us, "here in this lowly place in the most ordinary circumstances, I have come to dwell with you."[1]

For what could have been more ordinary—and yet more amazing—than the Prince of Peace being born among animals? What could be more astonishing by today's standards than the fact that the universal Savior who came to demonstrate God's great love for all human beings appeared among the poor and needy, his coming first announced to lowly shepherds out in the field?

And what is more remarkable in a commercialized society than the simple truth that the greatest gift of Christmas is the gift of oneself? When those shepherds heard the glorious message, "for to you is born this day in the city of David a Savior who is Christ the Lord," they did not stop to consider how they looked or hesitate because they had nothing of material value to present to the Christ child. They hastened to the manger in their rough working clothes, bringing only *themselves* and their simple faith. But that was enough. What they found was the miracle of God's presence in a humble human family and a little human child. "And the shepherds returned, glorifying and praising God for all they had heard and seen, as it had been told to them."

The wonder of Christmas is that the greatest event in the history of humanity came silently in the night; that the salvation of the world should hang on the slender thread of a helpless baby with no special care provided for its safety or health, no shelter except an open stable, no cradle except a manger of straw.

The wonder of Christmas is that in the darkest hour of loneliness and despair, new hope is born if we have faith. In the gloom and anguish of the eighth century B.C., when Isaiah saw the kingdoms of Israel and Judah being swept away, he nevertheless saw the vision of a new kingdom, and he proclaimed, "The people who have walked in darkness have seen a great light. . . . For unto us a child is born; unto us a son is given; and the government will be upon his shoulder, and his name will be called 'Wonderful Counselor, Mighty God, Everlasting Father, Prince of Peace.'" St. John takes up the theme in the New Testament: "The light shines in the darkness and the darkness has not overcome it. . . . And the Word became flesh and dwelt among us, full of grace and truth."[a] Finally, an anonymous writer of our own time is moved to say:

> He was born in an obscure village, never visited a big city. He never traveled two hundred miles from the place where He was born. He did none of the things that usually accompany greatness. He had no credentials but Himself.

He was only thirty-three when the tide of public opinion turned against Him. His friends ran away. One of them denied Him. He was turned over to His enemies and went through the mockery of a trial. He was nailed to a cross between two thieves.

While He was dying His executioners gambled for His garments, the only property He had on Earth. When He was dead, He was laid in a borrowed grave through the pity of a friend. Nineteen centuries have come and gone, and today He is the central figure of the human race.

All the armies that ever marched, all the navies that ever sailed, all the parliaments that ever sat, all the kings that ever reigned, have not affected the life of man[kind] on this Earth as much as that One Solitary Life.[2]

The wonder of Christmas is that suffering and death are not the last word. Emmanuel—God—is with us in every human situation. The little unprotected baby in the manger and the desolate man on the cross revealed that where God is least expected, in the most unlikely times and places—whether at the beginning of life or in the emptiness of death—God is at hand! In every agony, every crisis we are not alone. The light of God's eternal love shines in the darkness, and we shall be safe.

Amen.

Notes

[a] John 1:5.

The Last Judgment

Matthew 25:40
And the King will answer them, "Truly, I say to you, as you did it to one of
the least of these my brethren, you did it unto me."[1]

The parable of the Last Judgment in Matthew's Gospel text this morning points to
the climax of the Christian faith, the consummation of history, the final triumph of
God's love over the forces of dissolution which frustrate the harmony of God's creation of a "new heaven and new earth." Christians affirm this in the Nicene Creed
when we say, "And he shall come again in glory to judge the living and the dead."[2]

In this story, we are confronted with the ultimate meaning of our own
lives as we encounter the universal human condition. Jesus sets before us a vision of the destiny of humankind, the full realization of our human potential.
He speaks of this destiny in terms of judgment, which theologian Langdon
Gilkey has called "the ultimate norm embodied in Jesus by which our lives are
to be evaluated."[3] Since Jesus was fully human, he was one of us. He understood
our possibilities as well as our human frailties and limitations, and he was di-
recting us toward our highest potential. The standard he used was not our intellectual and social achievements but the depth of his own self-giving love and
compassion, his total identification with suffering humanity. His words here are
among the most beloved in scripture because they speak so directly to the
human situation throughout the ages:

> I was hungry and you gave me food,
> I was thirsty and you gave me drink,

> I was a stranger and you welcomed me,
> I was naked and you clothed me,
> I was sick and you visited me,
> I was in prison and you came to me. . . .

And then he says,

> as you did it to one of the least of these my brethren,
> you did it to me.

He made our actions toward strangers and outcasts the test of our love of God. By referring to the "least of these" as his brothers and sisters, he emphasized the divine potential in every human being[a] and our responsibility before God for the well-being of the weak and powerless, the despised of the earth. He was saying that we are all bound together in our relationship to one another and to God. As Bishop John Coburn once said, "There is no separation between what we do, on the one hand, in response to men [and women], and on the other, in response to God. Our response is to man in society and to God at the same time." In other words, there can be no individual salvation for us apart from our commitment to "the least of these" in whatever circumstance we find them, for when we ignore or reject them we reject God-in-Christ.

Christ then is present in every aspect of the human situation, and we are enjoined from picking and choosing those whom we would accept or reject based upon our own notions of approval, desirability, or affection. We are commanded to identify at all times and in all places with the common humanity of others, to enter into their pain, sorrow, and need as if it were our own, and to do so without any thought of reward. In the Gospel story, many of those adjudged righteous were not even aware that they were serving Christ when they ministered to others. They asked in surprise, "Lord, when did we see you hungry and feed you, or thirsty and give you drink?" Equally surprised were those who had not recognized Christ in their fellow beings and had gone their way without responding to human need.

Our human dilemma is that however much we may desire to obey Jesus's imperative, our proneness to inject our own likes and dislikes into our dealings with others, our self-centeredness is so pervasive that, like St. Paul, we must confess, "I can will what is right, but I cannot do it. For I do not do the good I want, but the evil I do not want I do." Reinhold Niebuhr, writing of human sinfulness, referred to Christ's law of love as "impossible possibility."

To follow Christ is costly; it involves suffering, rejection, unpopularity, sometimes violence and death. Most of us shrink from decisions which require great personal sacrifices on behalf of strangers whom we do not know and with whom we have no cultural, racial, or political affinities.

The words "I was in prison and you came to see me" recall to us a news report several weeks ago of the marriage in prison of James Earl Ray, serving a life sentence for the confessed assassination of Dr. Martin Luther King Jr. The marriage was performed by the Reverend James M. Lawson Jr., who was Dr. King's close associate and representative in Memphis in 1968, and the man responsible for Dr. King's decision to come to Memphis on this fatal mission, which ended in his death.

Reverend Lawson, who now lives in Los Angeles, had traveled to Tennessee some months earlier after receiving a letter from Ray asserting that he did not kill Dr. King. Lawson wanted to question Ray in person, and during his visit he met Ray's future wife. When the couple decided to get married, they turned to Reverend Lawson as the only person they knew well enough to ask to perform the ceremony.

Given his close friendship with Dr. King, the terrible impact of this disaster on Negro communities throughout the nation, and the painful memories revived by the current congressional investigation into Dr. King's death, Reverend Lawson's decision required considerable moral courage. He was acutely aware that his action might cause notoriety and alienate a number of the 2,300 members of his predominately Black congregation at Holman United Methodist Church in the Los Angeles area. He told the press, "I asked myself what Jesus would do. He was condemned by upstanding church people for associating with undesirables. Obviously, James Earl Ray is one of the undesirable people. . . . I have a few severe critics who will walk out of my church as a result. But there's no way I know of to do anything of significance without having those critics."

During the past week we have been made painfully aware of the ultimate cost of compassionate action by the horrifying news of the tragedy in Guyana which has dominated public attention and which defies our comprehension. Shock upon shock has reverberated around the world as the gruesome story has unfolded—first the murder of California congressman Leo J. Ryan and four other Americans, followed by the grisly mass murder-suicide deaths of more than nine hundred members of the Peoples Temple cult at an American settlement in a remote jungle in Jonestown, Guyana. Although the massive horror of what happened at Jonestown has almost overshadowed Ryan's death, he will be remembered as "a brave and compassionate man" whose deep concern for others led him to sacrifice his life in an effort to make a firsthand investigation of complaints from California constituents that their relatives were being severely mistreated at the camp.

One of the most poignant disclosures of this macabre event is that many of the American victims of a demonic, self-destructive force which had brought about this disaster were lowly and confused people searching for some meaning to their lives. They were led to remove themselves from the United States to this isolated spot in the belief that they were creating a society in which human dignity was paramount and racial and economic barriers were overcome. They were also taught that if they could not live as they intended it would be better to be dead.

This terrifying incident is one more tragic reminder that we live in a shrunken and interdependent world and that what we do individually and collectively profoundly affects whole communities and nations. The great majority of the human race are among the "least of these." Christ's call transcends individual charity and summons us to contend against the social structures of evil which breed hunger, alienations, poverty, injustice, war, and all conditions of life which diminish human dignity.

We have just celebrated Thanksgiving against a background of world hunger. As President Carter pointed out in his Thanksgiving Proclamation, "While Providence has provided America with fertile lands and bountiful harvests and each year growing food supplies give us greater cause for thanks, yet one person in six worldwide still suffers from chronic hunger and malnutrition." One recent study estimates the world's hungry at close to 1 billion people, of whom 15 to 20 million die each year from starvation, most of them children under five.

How do we as Christians respond to the manifold human suffering all around us? Do we feel an imperative to become personally involved in the struggle for human dignity? Or do we shrink from conflict and seek in our religion a refuge from turmoil, like the priest who told Henri J. M. Nouwen he had canceled his subscription to the *New York Times* "because he felt the endless stories of war, crime, power games and political manipulations only disturbed his heart and mind and prevented him from meditation and prayer"?

When confronted with controversial issues, such as desegregation, affirmative action, ERA, capital punishment, homosexual rights, abortion, and so on, do we ask ourselves, "What would Jesus do?" Or are our decisions determined by our own self-interests, group loyalties, and the notion of "we" and "they"?

In his deep humanity, Jesus was transparent to God's love and compassion for us. I believe that compassion is a gift of God's grace, our response to God's love. It is the capacity for placing ourselves in another's predicament, feeling "from the inside" what it means to be another person, "feeling with," "suffering with," so that another's pain becomes our pain, another's struggle our struggle. Without compassion all our good works are meaningless. With it, we become more like Christ.

Jesus's parable of the Last Judgment affirms that our actions have a lasting significance and consequences which are felt throughout eternity. Therefore, we need not despair because we seem to fail or cannot see the fruition of our efforts on behalf of others. If we build with love and compassion we can build with hope. Our Christian hope is that God will "finally complete our incompleteness," redeem the work which we have done on earth. And while we cannot know the specific details of our ultimate destiny, we believe that the God of judgment is the God of love and mercy and that our work and ourselves will find a proper place in God's kingdom.

Amen.

Notes

ᵃ Matthew 25:35–40.

Ministry

Mark 6:7
Jesus called to him the twelve, and began to send them out two by two.

The first thing we note about the Gospel story of Jesus sending the twelve forth on their first mission of service is that the disciples were not professional ministers or clergy. They were rough men of the world—fishermen, a tax collector— a diverse lot who earned their living in various ways. In fact, as Dr. Hans Kung has pointed out, Jesus himself was neither a priest nor a theologian but [an] "ordinary layman."[1] From the very beginning of his public ministry he chose simple everyday folk to join him in building the kingdom of God. His own ministry was very practical; he drew upon his own experiences and the common experiences of life in his community both in teaching and in helping people.

The word "minister" has come to be associated with the idea of professional clergy, and so we tend to overlook the fact that all baptized Christians belong to a universal ministry given to them in baptism, and all share in Christ's mission service. The fundamental ministry of the church is the same for all— whether they be laypersons, elders, pastors, bishops, priests, or deacons, namely, "to represent Christ and his Church to bear witness to him wherever they may be; and according to the gifts given to them, to carry on Christ's work of reconciliation in the world."[2] In every situation of life, then, we are ministers of Christ, whether as the gathered church when we join in common prayer and worship as we are doing now, or whether as the scattered church when we leave here and individually go about our daily pursuits. The ordained minister adds a special ministry to his/her lay ministry but does not cease to belong to the universal ministry given in baptism which [is] entrusted to all members of the Christian Church of whatever denomination.

A second thing to note about the Gospel story is that Jesus sent out his disciples with nothing except the clothing they wore, sandals, and a staff to help them walk over rough countryside. It would be a mistake to assume by this that Jesus had no regard for the value of material resources in serving the needs of others. Here, the disciples were making a short journey in Galilee and could rely on the custom of hospitality of their time for food and lodgings. What Jesus seemed to be emphasizing is that the essence of the ministry he sought to bring to the people is the power of faith and the giving of ourselves. Without faith and self-giving, financial resources, special training, and elaborate preparations are meaningless. In our materialistic age, we tend to underrate the importance of giving ourselves in ministry to others, yet this was exactly what Jesus did. As one Christian writer has said, "His ministry was his presence" (Bishop John Coburn).[3]

It has been suggested that our ministry is nothing more or less than just going about our day-to-day activities, "just going about our lives, doing what we have to do . . . and sometimes just hanging on through the day" and trying to be decent members of our family and our society and "being loyal to our best selves" in whatever circumstances of life we are placed in. Bringing ourselves may be all that we can do in situations where we can only wait and pray. Inadequate as we may feel at such times, our prayerful presence witnesses to the loving presence of God-in-Christ with us at all times and in all situations. God enters into our pain and suffering and completes the work of our own faltering efforts.

There are times in our attempts to minister to others who are undergoing great pain, sorrow, or grief that we forget we do not bear these burdens alone, and we feel an acute sense of powerlessness in crisis where we are not part of the physical action. I recall my seminary days of training as an assistant chaplain in a large metropolitan hospital. Often, we seminarians felt that the chaplain's presence on the ward was treated as an appendage, merely tolerated. In an emergency the action is with the medical team; the chaplain is ignored and must stand aside well out of the way, seeming to have no part in the struggle between life and death. Watching the skilled professionals surround the bedside of a patient in critical condition, working efficiently with an arsenal of machines and instruments, it was exceedingly difficult for one holding only a prayer book at a distance not to feel utterly useless.

Then one day I was called down to the Emergency Room to minister to an elderly woman brought in by ambulance suffering from cardiac seizure. The doctors and nurses hooked her up to various machines, slashed her windpipe to get air into lungs, and tried artificial respiration. After quite some time of this frantic activity, they suddenly withdrew, leaving her entirely alone. When I asked the chief physician what had happened, he told me they had done all they could do and that the woman was dying.

I went to the patient's bedside; her eyes were covered, her nose and mouth were full of tubes, her hands were strapped to the bed, and she appeared to be unconscious. All I could do was to read the 23rd Psalm aloud but very softly, not knowing whether she could hear or understand me at all. After the medical prognosis, the little I could do seemed horribly inadequate in my eyes. When I left her, I was firmly convinced that she would not live through the night.

Nevertheless, I went straight to the Emergency Room when I came on duty early next morning. I was surprised to find her still alive although her condition was unchanged. This time I addressed her by her name, told her I had read and prayed for her the day before, and asked if she wanted me to read a Psalm. She could not see me and there had been no sign of consciousness until I spoke, then there was a slight movement of her head. As I began to read the 23rd Psalm again her lips tried to say the words with me. For me this was an astounding experience. The woman survived, and before my training period ended a few weeks later, I was privileged to see her walking about her ward and complaining—a sure sign she was recovering! This woman's faith taught me that when medical science has gone as far as it can go, the battle is not finished. God's power is still present, and she was aware of God's presence.

Finally, the Gospel story tells us something about failure. Jesus recognized that his disciples might be rejected. He told them, "if any place does not welcome you and people refuse to listen to you, as you walk away shake off the dust from under your feet as a sign to them."[a] In Jesus's time this was a symbolic act of disclaiming responsibility for consequences when the town's people stubbornly refused to hear the message, but it also suggested ongoing-ness. We cannot let our failures overwhelm us or quit when the going is rough. We close that chapter in our lives and move on to something else.

Often close friendships end in disappointment; we lose people we love through misunderstandings; marriages break up; parents and children become estranged; people in our immediate environment become enemies. Jesus understood this suffering; he experienced alienation within his own family circle. When he began his dangerous public ministry, "his relatives . . . set out to take charge of him, convinced that he was out of his mind."[b] His mother and brothers came to speak to him. Jesus had to make a choice between following his own convictions and living up to his family's expectations. It was a painful choice, but he said, "here are my mother and brothers," pointing to those around him, "Anyone who does the will of God, that person is my brother and sister and mother."[c] When we meet with defeat in our own close relationships and we have done all we can do toward reconciliation, we have to leave our loved ones to God's care and move on.

The fundamental ministry of reconciliation, says noted theologian John Macquarrie, "is our cooperation in God's great work of letting-be," or helping others to reach their full potentialities. "Love is letting-be even where this may demand the loosening of the bonds that bind the beloved person to oneself; this might well be the costliest of demands. For it may well be that to really love someone we must renounce our claims upon that person and forego the treasured contact and association with that person, if only so that person we love is free to grow and realize what there is in him or her to be."[4]

All of us, then, have a ministry to witness to the presence of Christ in our own lives wherever we are, to be steadfast in our faith and trust in God whatever the circumstances, and to conform our lives to Christ so that in all that we do we manifest "the letting-be of love."

Amen.

Notes

[a] Matthew 10:14.

[b] Mark 3:21.

[c] Matthew 20:50.

Sermon Given on December 23, 1979

Matthew 11:2–3

Now when John heard in prison about the deed of the Christ, he sent word by his disciples and said to him, "Are you he who is to come, or shall we look for another?" And Jesus answered them, "Go and tell John what you hear and see: the blind receive their sight and the lame walk, lepers are cleansed and the deaf hear, and the dead are raised up, and the poor have good news preached to them. And blessed is he who takes no offense at me."

John's question, directed to Jesus whom he had baptized and whom he believed to be the Messiah, reflects the hopes, the fears, the doubts of men and women in every age, as humanity struggles with the ambiguities, contradictions, and sorrows of the human condition and longs for certainty and security in a world which seems the antithesis of peace and happiness. Despite humankind's brilliant achievements in science and technology, humanity has been unable to control evil and suffering. Like John the Baptist, do we not ask ourselves the same question today in moments of doubt as we experience feelings of impotence and helplessness over the upheavals of our own time? We search for [the] meaning of existence as each day television brings the dramatic details of our desperate state: hundreds of "small" wars, massacres, assassinations, persecutions, escalating terrorism, the starvation of whole populations, violence in the streets, and the ever-present threat of mankind's self-destruction through nuclear war.

John's question, "Are you the one who is to come, or shall we look for another?"ᵃ has particular urgency for Christians as once again we prepare to cele-

brate the incarnation, the coming of Christ into the world. In the midst of uncertainties about the future, as we approach this Christmastide, John's question
becomes, "Who is Jesus Christ for us?" Who is this Prince of Peace, King of
Kings, and Lord of Lords of whom we sing in the majestic music of Handel's
Messiah"?

And here we are faced with a paradox. By worldly standards, Jesus's life
was a failure. He was not a member of the religious or political establishment
or of any group who wielded power. He was a wandering lay preacher without
visible means of support. He associated with sinners and outcasts and the despised and rejected of the earth. While he called into question the existing social order, he left no blueprint for social change, he resisted the temptation to
use his popularity among the masses to gain political power, and he renounced
violence as a means of bringing about change. His entire cause was God's cause,
and he insisted that the kingdom of God must be sought first above all else,
after which those things for which humanity hungered would be added. From
beginning to end he was a controversial figure, and while he avoided all claim
to be a political Messiah, he was condemned for sedition and sentenced to
crucifixion—a horrible death reserved for the worst of criminals. He faced his
death with fear, sorrow, and doubt, with loud cries and tears we are told in Hebrews, and at the end his ultimate defeat was that he felt abandoned by God.

This final failure was all the more devastating just because, as one biblical
scholar puts it, Jesus's "life had been lived in extraordinary immediacy to God.
He had proclaimed the saving nearness of God's kingdom and often spoke of
God in familiar terms as 'my Father.' To be abandoned by God in the full awareness of the gracious nearness of God, and to be delivered up to the death of a
criminal, is the torture of hell; indeed (Martin) Luther interpreted the tradition
of Christ's descent into hell as referring to his death in God-forsakenness."[b]

If this were the end of the story, the feelings of helplessness and hopeless-
ness which attack us from time to time would be justified. But the uniqueness
of the Christian faith is that it was born "in the experience that Jesus, having
died, was *not* abandoned by God, but was raised from the dead, thereby gaining
victory over death. . . . The resurrection was both the vindication of Jesus by
God—the vindication of Jesus' claim that God was near and gracious—and the
empowerment of Jesus as the agent of God's liberating power in the world." God
is our future and this coming kingdom of love, "the kingdom of freedom, and
liberation from sin and death . . . are the work of the risen Jesus, who is now the
agent of what he once proclaimed."[c]

Who Is Jesus Christ for Us?

The Christian faith proclaims that he is the perfection and fulfillment of all human history. In our co-humanity with Jesus, we share the promise of participating with him in the new creation, the new humanity, the consummation of God's kingdom of love. Death does not have the last word but is the gateway to new beginnings.

As we celebrate the incarnation on Christmas Day once again, we reaffirm our faith that through the man Jesus, God revealed what humanity can become. John Macquarrie, a contemporary theologian, points to the human potential for Christhood when he speaks of incarnation and Christhood, not as an instantaneous happening at Jesus's birth but as an "emerging," a process of growth and coming together of divinity and humanity. He suggests that Jesus progressively realized his Christhood through the submission of his life to God—in his baptism, his temptations, ministry, passion, and death. He says, "Christ's self-giving, his love and letting-be, becomes complete and absolute in accepting the cross. Selfhood passes into Christhood, the human Jesus becomes the Christ of faith, there is a convergence of the human and divine 'natures' in one person. . . . Christ breaks out of the sin-bound human situation, and opens up a new life, symbolized by the resurrection. . . . And what we see in Christ is the destiny that God has set before humanity; Christ is the first fruits, but the Christian hope is that 'in Christ' God will bring all men (and women) to God-manhood (and God-womanhood). . . . Although the incarnation is from first to last the work of God, it implies also the cooperation of this truly human person, Jesus of Nazareth, tempted like other men, yet 'obedient unto death, even death on a cross.'"[1]

This is the hope which permits us to live by faith with the paradoxes of our time. Because of what God wrought in the man Jesus Christ, we are called to participate in the human struggle against suffering, injustice, and evil, confidently entrusting ourselves and the future of the world to God's all-embracing and saving love.

The essence of the Christmas message is that the Word of God which was with God from the beginning "became flesh and dwelt among us, full of grace and truth," that in Jesus Christ we have a vision of our higher destiny beyond our finite existence, and that Christ goes before us pointing the way. In this faith we can be hopeful amid the uncertainties of the world about us, and we can be joyful even in the midst of sorrow and pain.

Amen.

Notes

[a] Matthew 11:3.

[b] Peter Hodgson, *New Birth of Freedom: A Theology of Bondage and Liberation* (Philadelphia: Fortress Press, 1976), 251.

[c] Hodgson, *New Birth of Freedom,* 266.

Sermon Given on June 24, 1979

Galatians 3:25–26

But now that faith has come, we are no longer under a custodian; for in Christ Jesus you are all sons (and daughters) of God, through faith.

In his letter to the Galatians, St. Paul was trying to convey to his congregation the full meaning of the coming of Christ. Before Christ, the law had been the guide to right conduct. But over the centuries the Jewish law had developed into such elaborate and complicated regulations and interpretations, no one could possibly fulfill its requirements. The inability to keep the law completely revealed to men and women their impotence and sinfulness and made them feel hopelessly distant from God. Paul was saying that in Christ, through faith, all humanity is brought into fellowship with God. In Christ, we are the sons and daughters of God.

Faith is not the mechanical following of rules and regulations. It is hope and trust and commitment. The Christian faith, says Avery Dulles, "affirms that man in the discipline of his being, is in contact with God, that God, to whom the human spirit reaches out in darkness, has lovingly chosen to make himself immediately accessible to every human person."[1]

When we feel this faith surging up in our own lives and are aware of God's nearness, our hearts are filled with praise and thanksgiving like the Psalmist who said, "Bless the Lord, O my soul; and all that is within me, bless His Holy Name." Or, "shout with joy to the Lord all ye lands; lift up your voice, rejoice and sing."[a]

But all too often our faith is challenged by the confusions and cross-currents in our modern society. Who among us does not experience uncertainties and doubts, moments of discouragement and despair? Who has not felt helpless in the face of the cruelties of existence? Who has not—at some time or another—felt desolate, abandoned, alienated from God, broken in body and spirit, overcome by a sense of uselessness which calls into question the whole meaning of our lives? Who has not felt the unfairness of circumstances and cried out in anger to God, "Why did it happen to me?"

The crisis of doubt is inseparable from our human condition. Faith is not certainty, for if all things could be proved by scientific evidence, it would not be faith. "Faith is the substance of things hoped for, the evidence of things not seen," said the author of Hebrews. Faith is subject to constant questioning. As Dr. Hans Kung has said, "Faith is not a once-and-for-all decision. . . . The sustaining reality of God is never granted to us free of doubt. . . . Throughout life there will always be temptations to give up the faith, [and] at the same time the challenge to maintain and deepen it . . . despite all doubts, insecurities, and obscurities."[2] Like the father whose epileptic son was healed by Jesus of Nazareth, we find ourselves saying, "Lord, I believe, help my unbelief."[b]

Faith is trust in spite of the apparent evidence. God is never closer to us than when all our human efforts have failed, and we acknowledge our helplessness and defeat; when our lives are wrenched apart by devastating loss, and we are numb with grief; when our bodies are filled with pain and weakness, and we are compelled to face the inevitability of death. In our inability to solve the problems of evil and suffering, in our deep despair, we learn that our ultimate support and strength come from God who loves us, accepts us with all our weaknesses, and enters into our suffering with us. In the major crises of our lives we abandon all illusions of self-sufficiency and find refuge in God's infinite mercy and grace.

Faith is commitment to the belief that humanity has a higher destiny than the things of this world, that we belong to God. We are confronted by the eternal in the midst of the temporal, and God is constantly calling us to our true greatness which transcends the struggles of our finite lives. The Christian faith proclaims that Jesus Christ is the fulfillment of the highest human potential. He was fully human as we are human, with all of the human "capacity of suffering, fear, loneliness, insecurity, doubts, possibility of error. As true man, by his proclamation, behavior and fate, he was a model of what it is to be human, enabling each and every one who commits himself (or herself) to discover and realize the meaning of being human and of his/her freedom to exist for his/her fellowman. As confirmed by God, he therefore represents the permanently reliable standard of human existence" (Hans Kung).[3]

In the full humanity of Jesus Christ, God revealed to us our true identity. He is our friend and brother as well as the Risen Lord, and we are called to have faith in him and to be like him. The central fact of his life was his consciousness of God, his childlike trustfulness in God, his recognition that he had no power apart from God, and his steadfast obedience to God's will even unto humiliation and death. As a Christian priest once said, "This was a man God found he could use, and he used him to the hilt."

The climax of Jesus's life of service to God and his self-giving was total defeat and disgrace, a shameful death upon the cross reserved for the worst of criminals, abandoned by his closest companions, and so utterly desolate that he cried out in an agony of doubt, "My God, my God, why hast thou forsaken me?"[c]

Yet it is precisely at the moment of ultimate human defeat that God's action in Jesus becomes most manifest. When the cruel forces of evil had done all they could to him, God raised him from the dead—an event which has no parallel in history, a mystery which defies human comprehension—and so we speak of it as a new creation, a new human being, the first-born of the dead. God demonstrated through Jesus's death and resurrection the triumph of love over the forces of hatred and death.

Faith through Jesus Christ affirms that suffering and death are not the last word. He points the way to a new existence, the nature of which we cannot conceive fully but which we call "eternal life." If we follow him, trusting as he trusted in God's power working in us and through us, giving ourselves in loving service to God and to our fellow human beings, we become like him. It is the faith of which St. John spoke when he said, "Beloved, we are God's children now; it does not yet appear what we shall be, but we know that when he appears we shall be like him, for we shall see him as he is."[d]

In this faith our lives are transformed. This does not mean that we will be free from doubt, for as Paul Tillich says, doubt "should not be considered as the negation of faith, but as an element which *was* always and *will* always be present in the act of faith."[e] Faith is an act of courage which carries us beyond the defeats, failures, conflicts, suffering, and death inherent in our finite condition, which enables us to believe in spite of our doubts, and to say with St. Paul that "I am sure that neither death, nor life, nor angels, nor principalities, nor things present, nor things to come, nor powers, nor height, nor depth, nor anything else in all creation, will be able to separate us from the love of God in Christ Jesus our Lord" (Romans 8:38–39).

Let Us Pray.

Lord increase our faith. Grant us to know in life the faith that removes mountains; the faith that overcomes the world; the faith that works through love; the faith that makes all things possible. Grant that relying on thee as thy children, we may trust where we cannot see, and hope when all seems doubtful, that we may go out with good courage, not knowing whither we go, but only that thy hand is leading us, and thy love supporting us; to the glory of thy name.

Amen.

Notes

[a] Psalms 103:1; 47:1.

[b] Mark 9:24.

[c] Matthew 27:46.

[d] 1 John 3:2.

[e] Paul Tillich, *Dynamics of Faith* (1957; reprint New York: HarperOne, 2009), 21–22.

The Light of the World

Matthew 5:14, 16

You are the light of the world.... A city set on a hill cannot be hid.... Let your light so shine before men, that they may see your good works and give glory to your father who is in heaven.

Jesus of Nazareth recognized the "infinite moral possibilities" of all human beings, their capacity for goodness and grandeur. In his Sermon on the Mount when he told his disciples they were the light of the world, he was pointing to this human potential, which was perfected in his own being, expressed in the words of John's Gospel, "In him was life, and the life was the light of men. The light shines in the darkness, and the darkness has not overcome it."[a]

All too often we live in darkness, mired in pettiness and self-centeredness, blind to these glorious possibilities in ourselves and others. Then, suddenly, out of the gloom comes a shaft of eternal light and we glimpse Jesus's vision of human capability—the beauty and grandeur of ordinary human beings reflecting the light of God's love.

We have just experienced one of those rare moments in human history, an entire nation caught up in a vast outpouring of joy and thankfulness as its people responded to the light of freedom and celebrated the triumph of the human spirit over darkness and despair. For a brief moment we rose above our differences of race, religion, gender, and politics; we put aside our worries over debts and taxes, rising prices and crime in the streets. During that moment even political muscle flexing was subdued as we rediscovered the power of faith and prayer, of steadfastness, patience, and restraint in the resolution of a fourteen-month-long crisis of incalculably dangerous implications to our own and other nations.

We gained new insight into our national character as we watched split-screen simultaneous television coverage of a presidential inauguration signaling the transfer of political power in our nation and the release of the American hostages in Iran. Our eyes took in the pageantry of the Reagan inauguration, but our hearts were bound up in the fate of fifty-two individuals thousands of miles away. And when those fifty-two men and women, dressed in nondescript clothing, looking haggard and a little bewildered but walking upright, filed down the steps from the plane which touched down in Algeria on the night of January 20, a great sob of relief went up from millions of throats. In that moment we realized that not only were the former hostages released from their individual ordeals but also that the American people as a whole, in every walk of life, were delivered from long, weary months of anxious waiting and uncertainty, from repeated disappointments, from frustration and a sense of national impotence.

In the mood of euphoria which swept over the land, millions upon millions of us were suddenly transported out of our humdrum existence into an unrehearsed, spontaneous festival of "new beginnings," celebrating a new appreciation of our heritage as a free people and our commitment to individual worth, however flawed our devotion to this heritage may appear in normal times. What we experienced was a communal spiritual reawakening, akin to a sudden conversion or metanoia, a turning away from our narrow concerns and apprehensions and a reaching out toward new hope. Rejoicing rang out from church bells in countless cities, towns, villages, and hamlets across the country; exultation burst forth in flags and yellow ribbons everywhere, in the flowers, banners, and bands of schoolchildren, in displays on dump trucks and fire engines, in the faces of the crowds who lined the country roads and city streets in a spiritual embrace of the returning Americans—waving handmade signs, "WE LOVE YOU! WELCOME HOME!"—and in the silent tributes of unseen millions of us who hugged our radios and television sets throughout the nation.

Not in the lifetime of most of us here have we experienced such a ritual of universal thanksgiving and national pride, such an explosion of compassion and human warmth, which transcended our parochial liturgies and gave us a foretaste of what Christians call the Kingdom of God. By some quirk of circumstances or selection, the returning Americans were a microcosm of the rich diversity of our nation (which in turn reflects the diversity of human races and cultures around the world). The former hostages came from north, south, east, and west; they were men and women, Black and white and brown, military and civilian, old and young, Roman Catholic, Protestant, and Jew, and springing from many ethnic origins and strains. In them we saw ourselves, our hopes and fears, our strengths and weaknesses—we were all there—vicarious participants in an international drama which rivaled the genius of a Shakespeare and eclipsed the spectacular productions of a Hollywood.

As this drama unfolded before our eyes, made personal and compelling to us through the media of the electronics age, we are forcefully reminded once again that the God of the Judeo-Christian faith is the God of history, working through history to perform mighty works. The compression of fourteen months of dramatic events into a few hours of television review vividly recalls the scriptures:

> The God of Abraham and Sarah, Isaac and Rebekah, Jacob and Rachel, The God of Moses, Aaron and Miriam, Leading the Israelites through the Red Sea, Through their wanderings in the Wilderness and into the Promised Land; The God who chastened Israel in Exile; The God of Prophets, The God of Jesus of Nazareth in his ministry, death and resurrection.

Is the God of Jimmy Carter and Ronald Reagan still moving in history, still calling upon us and all the peoples of the world to abandon our false gods, instruments of war, violence, and terrorism, and to learn the ways of love, peace, and neighborliness?

For it was not military might but prayer and trusting faith which brought our compatriots home. Our own experience here as well as the testimony of many of the returnees is an affirmation that in God's mercy millions of prayers were answered and they were restored to their families and loved ones alive and in comparatively good shape. These witnesses told how, when everything was taken from them—their intimate possessions, their Bibles, human contact, even the light of day—their religious faith and prayers supported them in captivity.

Moorhead Kennedy, speaking at the service of thanksgiving in Washington's National Cathedral, recalled that he remembered the plight of the apostles Paul and Peter in prison and the biblical passage:

> So Peter was kept in prison, but earnest prayer was made to God by the Church. . . . Peter was sleeping between two soldiers, bound with two chains, and sentries before the door were guarding the prison; and behold, an angel of the Lord appeared . . . and rescued him.[1]

Colonel Thomas A. Schaefer, who was military attaché of the American Embassy in Teheran, delivered a powerful sermon in two words: "Thank God! Thank God it is over." Richard Queen, the fifty-third hostage released earlier, told of facing the wall expecting to be shot and in that moment of ultimate terror he tried to give himself last rites, saying the Lord's Prayer. Kathryn L. Koob rejoiced in her Lutheran upbringing, testifying that her imprisonment confirmed the faith she had received through her parents' training and her church back home in Iowa. She said she "grew very much in captivity," and that "I always knew I was going to walk away from there, whether it was five days, five months, or fifteen years." She didn't know why it had been her fate to be a hostage but believed that God had some purpose in her being there.

As I listened to her testimony, felt her spiritual resiliency, and saw the radiance of her face, it seemed to me that the divine purpose of her imprisonment might well be that she and her fellow prisoners become living demonstrations of the power of prayer over the threat of force. On a personal level, as she said, "they didn't break us; we walked away." In a broader sense, it was God's mercy that the freedom of these Americans—bound up as it was with national honor and integrity—was accomplished without plunging the United States into an international war in the process. I cannot help thinking that the chastening, tragic episode of the ill-fated rescue mission in the Iranian desert—a self-inflicted wound—was the judgment of God upon a powerful nation, a warning that this crisis was not to be resolved by reliance upon military force but must be unraveled by the agonizingly slow, painstaking use of instruments of peaceful negotiation, in spite of insult and provocation, relying upon the cooperation and help of nationals of many smaller countries acting as intermediaries, and working through political and financial institutions on four continents. For once the value of human life took precedence over false notions of national pride.

And since this week marks the beginning of Black History Month, it is well to remember that the public official upon whom rested the ultimate responsibility for bringing this crisis to a peaceful conclusion, Jimmy Carter, is a man who came under the influence of the late Dr. Martin Luther King Jr., the apostle of nonviolence in the United States. In his final book—*Where Do We Go from Here: Chaos or Community?*—Dr. King threw out a challenge to all Americans. He wrote, "Therefore I suggest that the philosophy and strategy of nonviolence become immediately a subject for study and for serious experimentation in every field of human conflict, by no means excluding the relations between nations. It is, after all, nation-states which make war, which have produced the weapons that threaten the survival of mankind and which are both genocidal and sui-cidal in character."[2]

The successful outcome of former President Carter's groping, sometimes awkward efforts to effect the release of the American diplomats without military retaliation against Iran is a vindication of Martin Luther King Jr.'s prophetic leadership, and in time I believe it will be seen as Mr. Carter's distinctive con-tribution to the future peace of the world. It points the way once more to the renunciation of violence in the settlement of complex international conflicts.

Those who quibble over whether the former hostages are "heroes" or "vic-tims," or look upon the recent outpouring as "national hysteria" or an "emotional quick fix," fail to recognize that Jimmy Carter, Cyrus Vance, Senator Muskie, Warren Christopher, and the countless prominent and anonymous individuals in this and other countries who worked assiduously to bring about a peaceful result were being directed consciously or unconsciously by a cosmic force greater than all the nuclear power in the world.[3] And the multitudes in our country in-stinctively responded to this moral force. In the words of the prophet Isaiah, "The people who walked in darkness have seen a great light, those who dwelt in a land of deep darkness, on them has light shined."[b]

Finally, as Christians, we are reminded again of the cost of Christian dis-cipleship. To be "a light to the world" involves sacrifice, the renunciation of per-sonal glory, and, if necessary, the acceptance of humiliation and defeat without relinquishing either faith or steadfastness. In the case of Mr. Carter, a visibly devout Christian, his finest hour came not in the exuberance of his walk down Pennsylvania Avenue on Inauguration Day 1977, nor in his brilliant execution of the Camp David Accords, but rather in the final hours of his repudiated presidency, as he labored through sleepless nights in the twilight of his power to complete the process of freeing the American hostages, to lift the burden of anxiety from the shoulders of his successor and his fellow citizens, and to hand over the levers of government with dignity and grace.

And while Mr. Carter was not permitted to savor the success of his mis-sion before his presidency expired, neither he nor anyone else could conceive of the magnitude of the result and its impact upon the spirit of the American people. At the moment of greatest uncertainty, after he and his aides had done everything they could and left office bewildered by the delay, the prison doors "burst open," so to speak, the former hostages were in the air. And with their freedom came a resurrection of faith in millions of hearts, symbolized by the jubilance which greeted them at every stop on their long journey home.

The eternal God is timeless and is no respecter of human timetables and deadlines—"with the Lord one day is as a thousand years, and a thousand years as one day."[c] In the long sweep of history it makes little difference whether the official announcement of the hostages' release came from outgoing President Carter or incoming President Reagan: both were instruments of God's mighty works and the glory of that moment belonged to God. As George A. Buttrick has written, "The light coming from God, belongs to God and should shine for his glory. If it should shine for man it might be a pride-filled exhibitionism; shining for God it is true piety. God's glory is man's joy."[d]

In sum, the gift which the American former hostages brought back with them from Iran is the gift of God's saving grace—the gospel, the "Good News" made visible. It was almost as if they had returned from the dead. As one of them, Malcolm Kalp, said, looking at the throng of friends, neighbors, and well-wishers who greeted him in his home community, "I could never have believed it possible. If this is what it has done, brought us together like this, I'd go through it all over again."

In our time we have witnessed a moment of grandeur of the human race. God's love has suddenly burst upon us and, like the disciples on the road to Emmaus, we have felt the presence of the living Christ. Will we follow the light of this love? Or will we continue in bondage to the false god of nuclear military power?

Notes

[a] John 1:4–5.

[b] Isaiah 9:2.

[c] 2 Peter 3:8.

[d] 2 Corinthians 4:6. [This is the biblical passage being paraphrased by Buttrick.]

The Prodigal Son

Luke 15:11–32

Then He said: "A certain man had two sons. And the younger of them said to *his* father, 'Father, give me the portion of goods that falls *to me.*' So he divided to them *his* livelihood. And not many days after, the younger son gathered all together, journeyed to a far country, and there wasted his possessions with prodigal living. But when he had spent all, there arose a severe famine in that land, and he began to be in want. Then he went and joined himself to a citizen of that country, and he sent him into his fields to feed swine. And he would gladly have filled his stomach with the pods that the swine ate, and no one gave him *anything.* But when he came to himself, he said, 'How many of my father's hired servants have bread enough and to spare, and I perish with hunger! I will arise and go to my father, and will say to him, "Father, I have sinned against heaven and before you, and I am no longer worthy to be called your son. Make me like one of your hired servants."' And he arose and came to his father. But when he was still a great way off, his father saw him and had compassion, and ran and fell on his neck and kissed him. And the son said to him, 'Father, I have sinned against heaven and in your sight, and am no longer worthy to be called your son.' But the father said to his servants, 'Bring out the best robe and put *it* on him, and put a ring on his hand and sandals on *his* feet. And bring the fatted calf here and kill *it,* and let us eat and be merry; for this my son was dead and is alive again; he was lost and is found.' And they began to be merry. Now his older son was in the field. And as he came and drew near to the house, he heard music and dancing. So he called one of the servants and asked what these things meant. And he said to him, 'Your brother has come, and because he has received him safe and sound, your father has killed the fatted calf.' But he was angry and would not go in. Therefore his father came out and pleaded with him. So he answered and said to *his* father, 'Lo, these many years I have been serving you; I never transgressed your commandment at any time; and yet you never gave me a young goat, that I might make merry with my friends. But as soon as this son of yours came, who has devoured your livelihood with harlots, you killed the fatted calf for him.' And he said to him, 'Son, you are always with me, and all that I have is yours. It was right that we should make merry and be glad, for your brother was dead and is alive again, and was lost and is found.'"

The Gospel story of the Prodigal Son, which Jesus told as a parable in answer to the criticism of the scribes and Pharisees that he ate with publicans and sinners, brings to mind the recent newspaper account of the refusal of the Roman Catholic hierarchy to allow a requiem mass for the slain New York gangster Carmine Galente, a baptized Catholic. The refusal was based upon a church law—written in the Middle Ages—which permits the hierarchy to deny a funeral mass to public sinners. Coleman McCarthy, *Washington Post* columnist, commented on the church's action as follows:

> Little doubt exits that Galente had fallen into the ways of public sin. High in the ranks of the New York mob, this godfather had long been prospering in low-life rackets and violence. But some question does remain—protruding like the horns of Satan, perhaps, but still there to be faced—that, however mean a fellow Galente may have been, he was still worthy of a requiem mass. The hierarchy, understandably, didn't want to give scandal. Funeral masses for all seedy thugs of organized crime are an affront to all decent church-goers. But the affront was built into the religion long ago, in the scandal of Christianity's teaching that the Lord came to save sinners. The decent will do fine on their own.

We wonder, however, if the point of Jesus's parable is that the decent may sin in their very lack of compassion for and their condemnation of the obviously sinful? Is not the parable the story of *two* sons, and are we not left with the question as to which of these two brothers was in fact the prodigal son?

Here were two sons very different in makeup but both having potential for full, rich lives. They were not poor and they had all the advantages of loving parental care. The younger son was not dissolute at the outset. He was apparently imaginative, ambitious, and adventuresome. He wanted to see the world and to enjoy his life while he was young. It was not unusual for a younger son to ask for his legal share of an inheritance and to emigrate to a far country. Under Jewish law a father was bound to give his elder son two-thirds of his estate and the remaining one-third to his younger son. Palestine was a land beset by frequent famines and could not support all the people of Israel. Only a half million Jews lived there; 4 million Jews lived in the diaspora, scattered in Egypt, Syria, Mesopotamia, Babylonia, Greece, Italy, and other areas of the Mediterranean world. Migration to the great trade centers outside Palestine was the thing to do for a young Jew who wanted to get ahead.

The inheritance was given without hesitation. Jesus was teaching that God gives us freedom of choice and that this freedom is that of choosing a downward path; we seek worldly experience but in doing so we may pay the price of recklessness. The younger son converted his inheritance into cash and set off on his journey full of self-confidence, feeling he had no further need of parental guidance.

The elder son who stayed at home was a respectable, law-abiding citizen, stable and dependable, the backbone of his society. He was hardworking and faithful, morally upright with a strong sense of right and wrong. He was obviously successful and considered a good man. He was always there when his father needed him, and doubtless his father relied heavily upon him as the years passed. But one suspects that he was also a joyless person, lacking in imagination and the courage to live life fully. His loyalty to his father seemed more an expression of duty than of love. If the younger son risked the dangers of recklessness, the elder son risked stunted growth, becoming narrow-minded, bigoted, and unforgiving.

We see our own strengths and weaknesses reflected in *both* of these brothers because they are two sides of a single coin, pointing up the contradictions in human personality. Reflecting on this parable, R. H. Ward (*The Prodigal Son*, 1968) has said, "Each of us believes himself to be a single person; but we are many sided, and our consciousness is diverse. . . . Indeed much of our time is spent passing from one 'I' to another in contradictions of mood, desire, opinion. . . . To be human is to be inconsistent. . . . (In reality) the two sons are one son . . . in all individual men (and women) the two sons co-exist." As the story continues, the younger son left to his own devices quickly runs through his inheritance in riotous living. The consequences of his folly are inevitable. He becomes destitute and, to make matters worse, a famine comes upon the country in which he is living. His fair-weather friends desert him and he is all alone. He sinks so low that he is compelled to hire himself out to a pig-farmer, the worst possible fate for a Jew because the Jewish law said, "Cursed be he who feeds swine." He is not even permitted to relieve his hunger by eating the husks of fodder fed to the pigs because these husks are the property of his employer.

Degraded as this man has become, however, he is not beyond redemption. He comes to his senses and remembers who he really is. He is ruthlessly honest with himself and does not blame his condition on circumstances beyond his control. He knows that he is responsible for his dire straits because he has forgotten his birthright and alienated himself from God and from his loved ones. In this recognition there is penitence, *metanoia,* a "turning around." He says, "I will arise and go to my father, and will say unto him, 'Father, I have sinned against heaven, and before thee, and am no more worthy to be called thy son; make me one of your hired servants.'" In his humility the young man identifies himself with the lowest rank of servant, lower even than a slave who to some extent is a member of the family. A hired hand is no part of the family and can be dismissed at any time.

So the younger son sets his face toward home. Meanwhile, his loving father has been watching and waiting for his lost son through the years. I remember as a small child seeing my grandmother wait for news of her only son who had left home at the age of nineteen and had not been heard from since. Although twenty-five years had passed, any rumor, however far-fetched, that he might still be alive was enough to revive her hopes and renew her search. Until her death she clung to the possibility that some day he might return or she might get some word of him.

The father in the parable does not wait to have his son come to him in abject humility but sees him afar off, runs to meet him, and welcomes him with embraces and kisses. He interrupts his son's confession and directs that he be invested with all the symbols of complete sonship—the best robe; the ring; shoes, which distinguish children of the household from slaves; and a feast of fatted calf in celebration of his homecoming.

Here Jesus emphasized God's compassion for the sinful, God's readiness to forgive us, even before we ask. God's forgiveness is unconditional; it is not based upon our achieving greater maturity but solely upon the miracle of God's love. This does not mean that we can take God's love for granted. It was necessary for the son to repent and to return home before the father could forgive. Nor does forgiveness mean that we escape judgment—the inevitable consequences of our acts. Judgment was present in the case of the Prodigal Son. He suffered poverty, hunger, humiliation, and shame. He had to return home and face his father in rags.

The scene shifts to the elder brother whom we glimpse as stiff-necked, self-righteous, self-pitying, and furious when he learns of his brother's return and all the fuss being made over him. He can only see the unfairness of it all and feels that he has been wronged. His jealousy knows no bounds. He refused to welcome his brother or to join in the merry-making. We must remember that he has not been harmed in any way. His inheritance is intact; he is secure in his father's home. Nothing has been taken from him. What he objects to is a fancied preferential treatment to his brother, when all that is being done is restoring the younger brother to his rightful place as a son of the household. His attitude is strikingly similar to the attitudes of those today who oppose affirmative action and other social programs designed to restore disadvantaged citizens to their rightful heritage of human dignity. He is so self-centered that he thinks his meritorious work has gone unrewarded while the wastrel brother is getting all the attention and a glory he does not deserve.

The father, however, does not reject the older son or rebuke him when he complains, "You know I have slaved for you all these years; I have never once disobeyed your orders; and you never gave me so much as a kid for a feast with *my* friends. But now that *this son of yours* turns up after running through your money with his women, you will kill the fatted calf for him." The older son does not even acknowledge his relationship to his brother but refers to him as *"this son of yours."* The father assures him that he too is loved and valued: "Son, you are always with me, and everything I have is yours. It was meet that we should make merry and be glad; for this thy brother was dead, and is alive again; and was lost, and is found."

Jesus does not tell us how the older son responded to his father's reassurances. He leaves the impression that each son sinned in his own way. The major difference between them was that one recognized his faults and was penitent; the other was blind to his faults, perceiving them as virtues, and remained both unrepenting and unforgiving. In the end, although he physically stayed in his father's house, he had become more alienated than the brother who went away.

In the words of New Testament scholar William Barclay, "Once again we have the amazing truth that is easier to confess to God than it is to many a man; that the love of God is more merciful in his judgments than many an orthodox man; that the love of God is broader than the love of man; and that God can forgive when men refuse to forgive. In the face of a love like that we cannot be other than lost in wonder, love and praise."[a]

Amen.

Notes

[a] William Barclay, *Gospel of Luke* (Philadelphia: Westminster Press, 1971).

On the Strength of Women

Out of the Wilderness

Genesis 21:17–18

And God heard the voice of the lad; and the angel of God called to Hagar from Heaven, and said to her, "What troubles you Hagar? Fear not, for God has heard the voice of the lad where he is. Arise, lift up the lad, and hold him fast with your hand; for I will make him a great nation."

Most of us are familiar with the story of Hagar and Ishmael. It is so akin to our own historical experience that sometimes we have been referred to as "Aunt Hagar's Children."[1] In biblical tradition, it is one of a cycle of stories about the Hebrew patriarch Abraham, who lived nearly two thousand years before the birth of Christ. Hagar's story acknowledges the common ancestry of the Israelites and a kindred but hostile people, the fiercely independent Bedouin tribes who ranged over the desert, from Ishmael.

We must keep in mind that the authors of these Old Testament stories were recounting the traditions of their religious faith and how the people of Israel were chosen by God to be a light to all nations. In Abraham's time the Jews were not a distinct people but part of the wandering Semitic tribesmen in the great population movements of the ancient Near East. The nation of Israel was born of many diverse nationalities and cultures over many centuries. The traditions of this unique people who worshipped one God instead of many gods were passed down orally from generation to generation for hundreds of years before they were gathered up by different writers in different periods and finally brought together in Genesis and other books of the Old Testament. Accordingly, we often have two versions of the same story varying in details, as in the two accounts of Hagar in Genesis 16 and Genesis 21. Our concern is not with the historical accuracy of the details but with the religious truth these stories represent. Through Hagar's ordeal we experience the power of faith.

According to traditions, Abraham, the ancestor of the future nation, has answered God's call to leave his country in the North Arabian desert and journey to the land of Canaan. God has promised to make him a great nation, but after ten frustrating years in Canaan he and his wife, Sarah, still have no children. They are now old and Sarah is barren, and they begin to doubt God's promise.

In the ancient society, it was considered a disgrace for a woman to be sterile and was customary for a barren wife to offer her handmaiden to her husband in the hope of providing an heir. A child born of such a union was treated as the child of the wife by adoption and shared in the inheritance. Sarah followed this custom and gave her Egyptian handmaiden, Hagar, to Abraham for a wife. Hagar conceived and Ishmael was born.

Hagar is variously depicted as a strong, proud, independent woman of the desert, conscious of her own worth who feels herself the equal of her mistress, and as the innocent victim of Sarah's jealousy. When Sarah herself conceives and Isaac is born, the thought that Ishmael will share with her own son in the inheritance becomes intolerable. Hagar and her child are driven out into the wilderness of Beer-sheba.

We can understand the loneliness, the despair, the anguish of this mother in the wilderness—cast out from all that is familiar to face the unknown, her child stripped of all rights, her food and water exhausted, and her child dying of hunger and thirst. Unable to bear his pitiful cries and to watch him die, she lays him under a bush and goes some distance away.

But the God of the wealthy patriarch Abraham is also the God who hears the cry of the afflicted and oppressed. As the long hours of her vigil pass, Hagar begins to realize that she is not alone in her great need. She hears in her own heart the message of God, "Fear not, for God has heard the voice of the lad where he is. Arise, lift up the lad, and hold him fast with your hand; for I will make him a great nation."[a] As her faith deepens, her eyes are opened. She sees a well of water in the wilderness. She fills her water skin and gives it to her son to drink. The story concludes, "And God was with the lad, and he grew up; he lived in the wilderness, and became an expert with a bow ... and his mother took a wife for him from the land of Egypt."[b] Through her faith and determination, this heroic woman found her way out of the wilderness and led her son to freedom and dignity.

Several thousand years later, Hagar's ordeal is reenacted in the experience of many Black slave women in America who were forced to become the concubines of white masters. The sexual exploitation of Black women by white men was so widespread that it was practiced by leading statesmen who proclaimed inalienable human rights, as a recent biography of Thomas Jefferson vividly illustrates. . . . A white woman of the antebellum South, Mary Boykin Chesnut, confided to her dairy: "God help us, but ours is a monstrous system. . . . Like the patriarchs of old, our men live all in one house with their wives; and concubines; and the mulattoes one sees in every family partly resemble the white children."[2] But over against the debasement of Black women by a barbarous system must be set the history of courage, strength, and determination in which Black women, by example, have constantly reaffirmed their faith in God's promise to the oppressed. One reads the documentary history *Black Women in White America*, compiled by Gerda Lerner in 1972, with a growing sense of the richness of our heritage and the bright thread of hope which these women, many of whom are anonymous, have woven into the fabric of our experience.[3]

Consider the example of Harriet Tubman, born a slave in Maryland in 1823, who escaped to freedom in her early twenties, going on alone when her husband refused to join her and her brothers lost heart and turned back. Not content with deliverance for herself alone, she made nineteen trips back South and brought three hundred or more slaves on the Underground Railroad. It was her pride that she "never lost a single passenger," notwithstanding the fact that a $40,000 reward for her capture hung over her head. During the Civil War she worked as a nurse, spy, and scout for the Union forces. Several times she commanded troops, both Black and white, on scouting raids, and on one of these raids rescued 756 slaves.

One remembers the magnificent Sojourner Truth, a slave in New York for forty years before gaining her freedom, who spent the next forty or more years of her life traveling the countryside speaking out on behalf of those doubly oppressed by race and sex. She saw clearly the connection between the abolition of slavery and the rights of women.

There are others whose names are less well known or have been lost to us but whose deeds reflect the same remarkable courage and determination. There is the story of the young expectant slave mother, so determined that her child should be born free that, during the winter of 1857, she had herself boxed and shipped as freight from Baltimore to Philadelphia, breathing only through a tiny hole she had cut in the box with her scissors, and enduring the agony of being turned upside down more than once while she lay in the cold and darkness of the freight depot.[4]

There is the example of Milla Granson, a slave woman in Natchez, Louisiana, who had learned to read and write from her master's children back in Kentucky where she grew up. She secretly opened a midnight school in the teeth of laws which imposed severe punishment or even death upon those who dared to educate slaves. The school opened around midnight and closed around 2 a.m. She would take twelve students at a time, and when she had taught them all she had learned, she would dismiss them and take on another twelve. In this way she had educated hundreds before she was found out. Many of her students wrote their own passes to get through the slave patrols and started for Canada and freedom.

Our history abounds with instances of women as well as men who labored for years at extra jobs to purchase freedom, and then continued to work to buy the freedom of husbands, mothers, sisters, brothers, or children. One of these women named Jackson, in Marseilles, Kentucky, worked seven years at washing and ironing nights after she had finished her mistress's work, not allowing herself to sleep except for little naps over her ironing board and undressing only to change her clothes.[5] After she bought her own freedom and began saving to purchase her daughter's freedom, her master offered the daughter for sale to pay off a debt. The mother went from door to door until she could find a buyer to advance the balance of the purchase price and take a mortgage on herself until she could pay it back.

These and countless other brave women resisted slavery, risked their lives in the struggle for freedom, and after Emancipation established schools and carried on crusades against lynching. So strong has been this tradition of courage that the late gospel singer Mahalia Jackson wrote in her memoirs, "Ever since slavery times it's been the Negro woman in the South who has had to shoulder the burden of strength and dignity in the colored family. . . . When I hear people talking about Communists being behind [those brave colored children and college students down South], I have to laugh. It's not Communists[,] it's Negro mothers who believe it is time for their children to fight for their rights and a good education."[c]

On July 10, the late Dr. Mary McLeod Bethune, one of the foremost Black leaders of the Roosevelt era, became the first Black American to be honored by the monument in the nation's capital. Mrs. Bethune established a college in Florida on a garbage dump and founded the National Council of Negro Women.[6] In her last will and testament, she wrote, "I leave you racial dignity; I have risen from the cotton fields of South Carolina to become a public servant and a leader of women. I would not change my color for all the wealth in the world."[7] On the base of her monument in Washington are inscribed the words of her legacy to Negro children: "I leave you love. I leave you hope. I leave you faith. I leave you a desire to live harmoniously with your fellow man. I leave you a responsibility to our young people."

As we continue to move through the wilderness, let us renew our faith and remember with thankfulness those Black foremothers who, like Hagar, acted upon God's promise: "Fear not, arise and lift up the lad and hold him fast with your hand, for I will make him a great nation."

Let Us Pray.

Notes

[a] Genesis 21:16–18.

[b] Genesis 21:20.

[c] Mahalia Jackson, *Movin' on Up* (New York: Avon Books, 1969).

Sermon Given on June 12, 1977

2 Samuel 11:27b

But the thing David had done displeased the Lord.

Luke 7:47–50

Therefore I tell you, her sins, which are many, are forgiven, for she loved much; but he who is forgiven little, loves little. And he said to the woman, "Your faith has saved you; go in peace."

Today's lessons give us two contrasting stories about women who are the objects of age-old sexual exploitation. In the first narrative, the woman is a pawn manipulated in a man's world. In the second story, the woman scorned by society as a sinner finds liberation and wholeness in Jesus's acceptance of her as a human being of intrinsic worth.

In the Old Testament narrative, the writer is primarily concerned with David's great sin and the woman seems almost incidental. David, the Lord's anointed and a powerful king, is nevertheless not above acts of adultery, deception, and murder to satisfy his selfish desires. From his roof he sees Bathsheba, [a] beautiful woman of low estate, bathing herself. The fact that she is a married woman, wife of one of his professional soldiers, Uriah, who is away on an expedition, does not deter David from his lustful objective. He sends for her, and Bathsheba, completely subject to the king's will, has little choice but to submit to his sexual advances. To protest would be futile.

As a result of this episode, Bathsheba becomes pregnant. When she sends word of her condition to the king, David finds himself in an embarrassing situation. Obviously, she was a mere passing fancy; he did not love her and had no desire to marry her at this point. He attempts to cover up his indiscretion by having it appear that her husband, Uriah, is actually the father of her unborn child. So he recalls Uriah from his army assignment and uses various pretexts to persuade Uriah to go home and spend a night with his wife. Uriah, however, clings to the soldier's code of avoiding any sexual contact when he is in battle, and none of David's ruses succeeds in getting him to break the taboo. Finally, David has him assigned to the most dangerous position on the battlefield and, predictably, Uriah is killed. David now takes Bathsheba as his wife and she bears him a son. We do not know her feelings about all this; the writer focuses only upon David's [sin] against the Lord. Nothing is said about his wrong of the woman, the destruction of her home and the loss of her husband. The story is concerned about David's relationship to God, not to the woman.

In the New Testament story, however, Jesus of Nazareth reverses the tradition, lifts an unknown woman, an outcast, out of her obscurity, and makes her a symbol of love and penitence who knows the meaning of forgiveness. We do not know where she came from or how she knew Jesus. She may have been one of those in the crowd who heard him say, "I have not come to call the righteous but sinners to repentance," and she believed him.[a] Her response is central to the narrative.

Jesus has been invited to a meal at the home of Simon the Pharisee. The food is apparently served in the open courtyard where people may come in and listen to the wisdom of this remarkable teacher as he converses with Simon. The woman has learned that he is there, and she slips in and stands behind him. She observed that Simon has extended to his guest none of the common courtesies expected of every host in those days. He has not given Jesus the customary kiss of peace. Although Jesus's feet are tired and dusty from the road, Simon has not bothered to pour cool water over them to make them clean and comfortable, nor has he anointed Jesus's head with a drop of perfume as good manners required.

Having nothing but a small alabaster flask of ointment, the woman wets Jesus's feet with her tears, wipes them with her flowing hair, kisses them, and pours her ointment over them. She is overwhelmed with love and gratitude that Jesus does not reject her ministrations.

Simon, arrogant and self-satisfied, watches all this with disdain. As far as he is concerned, the woman is a known sinner, probably a prostitute, and under Jewish custom no man of Jesus's reputation would permit her to come anywhere

near him. He mutters to himself that Jesus cannot be the prophet he is supposed to be or else he would know the sort of woman she is and not allow her
to touch him.

Here Jesus reveals his radical departure from traditional treatment of the
lowly and particularly women. He looks beneath the external condition and sees
the true human being within, a person of great longing, reaching out for acceptance. Her tears tell him the depth of her need of forgiveness. *Simon* thinks of
himself as a righteous man and does not feel the need of love and forgiveness.

Jesus demolishes Simon's self-complacency. He tells the parable of the Two
Debtors, and Simon agrees that the one who is forgiven the more loves more.
Then Jesus confronts Simon with the contrast between his own behavior and
that of the woman. He apparently was interested only in exploiting Jesus's fame
for his own social prestige, and he had no compassion for the weary traveler.
The woman wanted only to love and serve the Rabbi in the only way that she
could. "Therefore I tell you, her sins, which are many, are forgiven, for she loved
much; but he who is forgiven little, loves little." And to the woman he said, "Your
faith has saved you; go in peace."[b]

Although these two stories deal ostensibly with sin in the form of adultery
and prostitution, underlying both is the fact of cultural oppression of women
which runs throughout the Judeo-Christian tradition. In the Old Testament
world women were regarded of low value. The Law of Moses in the 27th chapter
of Leviticus makes this very clear in its provision for the monetary redemption
of special vows. A male twenty to sixty years of age was worth fifty silver shekels;
a female in the same age group was worth thirty. (This kind of devaluation of
human worth is familiar to us. We recall in our own recent history how a human
being in slavery was counted as three-fifths of a person.) In ancient Hebrew
tradition, sons were desirable and daughters were undesirable. Women were not
permitted to study the Torah or to enter into discussions with men, particularly
in public. Only if ten males were present could a prayer meeting be held. We are
so conditioned by Old Testament exclusively male tradition that even in the
language of our modernized literature we speak of the "God of Abraham, Isaac,
and Jacob." Why not "God of Abraham and Sarah, Isaac and Rebecca, Jacob and
Rachel?"

Jesus of Nazareth ignored these traditions and treated women as persons
of equal dignity and worth with men. His long conversation with the woman of
Samaria at the well in Sychar was unheard of in his time. When his disciples

returned from their errand to buy food, "they marveled that he was talking with a woman" (John 4:27). When he visited the home of Mary and Martha in Bethany, he approved of Mary's rejection of the kitchen role and permitted her to sit at his feet and listen to his teaching as if she were a male rabbinical student. And when he was teaching in the Temple, he refused to condemn the woman charged with being caught in the act of adultery, saying to the men who had brought her in, "Let him who is without sin among you cast the first stone."[c] We can agree with Alice Craig Saxon who wrote, "In all four Gospels, Jesus is never reported as acting or speaking to women in derogatory fashion. He always treated them as equals, individuals and persons. He testified in his practice and in his doctrine that he saw woman, as created by God, equal to man."[d]

And women responded as disciples of Jesus, following him as he went about preaching the good news of the Kingdom of God and using their own means to provide for him and his company. They followed him to the cross and stood by him during those agonizing hours of crucifixion when the other disciples had run away in fear. Women discovered the Resurrection on Easter morning and went to tell the eleven, and, according to John's Gospel, Mary of Magdala was the first person to whom the Risen Lord appeared.

We also learn from the book of Acts and Paul's letters that women were prominent in building the early Christian Church, serving as missionaries, prophets, and deacons. They were educated in the scriptures and assumed roles of leadership, working with Paul and the other apostles to spread the Christian message. Jesus's example provided a radically new basis for relationships between men and women—a basis for equality and wholeness in the church as the Body of Christ.

As the church expanded in influence and power, however, the example of Christ was forgotten and the Christian community drifted back into the old patriarchal cultural patterns. Women were gradually eliminated from organizational structures of the church and had no voice in the great councils which determined the course of Christianity in the centuries ahead. While the church adhered to a *theology* that all souls were equal in Christ, it followed in *practice* the view that women were inferior to men, with the consequence that throughout the history of the church women have been excluded from "responsible and equal roles" in shaping the church's theology and its spiritual and institutional life. By and large they have served under the supervision of men.

We might ask ourselves what has been the social cost of a theology which has been exclusively masculine? Theologian Anne McGrew Bennett raises crucial questions when she writes,

> Over and over during the long centuries Western nations, Christian peoples, have glorified war and sanctioned torture. Could it be that the separation of the so-called "masculine" from "feminine" qualities leading to the emphasis on aggressive physical force, military power, pride of place, and domination has led to a failure of Christians to stop the killing of the neighbor? Could it be that the ecological crisis—the wanton destruction and pollution of land, sea, air, plants and animals—is related to a drive to *dominate* without the corresponding drive to *nurture?* Could it be that when religious sanction is given for a man to hold the woman he loves and who loves him in an inferior, submissive place, there are no limits to rationalizing violence toward, and exploitation of others?[e]

Can it also be that an exclusively male hierarchy has obscured the important truth that *all* baptized Christians are ministers of Christ and his church? Writing out of her experience as an ordained Lutheran minister, Karen L. Bloomquist has said, "Potentially, ordination of women can serve as a symbol and motivating power for other *women and men* to claim their own ministries rather than unquestioningly accepting a derivate status in the church. The lay ministry of the church needs to be affirmed in its own right, rather than treated as secondary to that of the ordained."[1]

The message of Jesus of Nazareth was that wholeness of being lies, not in superior status or exclusiveness like that of Simon the Pharisee but in the ministry of love and service which recognizes human worth. And many women today, responding to that message, are seeking a "theology which in symbol and language will help people to understand the wholeness of God and the one-ness of humankind."[2]

Amen.

Notes

[a] Luke 5:32.

[b] Luke 4:47.

[c] John 8:7.

[d] Alicia Craig Faxon, *Women and Jesus* (New York: HarperCollins, 1973).

[e] Anne McGrew Bennett, *Overcoming the Biblical and Traditional Subordination of Women* (New York: American Community for Religious Research and Education, 1974).

Sermon on the Ordination of Women

1 Kings 19:9–12

And there he came to a cave, and lodged there; and behold, the word of the Lord came to him, "What are you doing here, Elijah?" He said, "I have been very jealous for the Lord, the God of hosts; for the people of Israel have forsaken thy covenant, thrown down thy altars, and slain thy prophets with the sword; and I, even I only, am left; and they seek my life to take it away." And he said, "Go forth, and stand upon the mount before the Lord." And behold, the Lord passed by, and a great and strong wind rent the mountains, and broke in pieces the rocks before the Lord, but the Lord was not in the wind; and after the wind an earthquake, but the Lord was not in the earthquake; and after the earthquake a fire, but the Lord was not in the fire; and after the fire a still small voice. And when Elijah heard it, he wrapped his face in his mantle and went out and stood at the entrance of the cave.

Elijah's encounter with the Lord on the desolate, storm-swept slopes of Mount Horeb seems too awesome an experience to compare with the present controversy over the ordination of women to the priesthood in the Episcopal Church. But Elijah's story tells us more than the image of [a] majestic God passing by the mountain in tempest, earthquake, and fire. It tells us that we often seek God in the wrong places.

No other issue in our time has so divided our church as to have it almost torn apart. Ecclesiastical trials and convictions, censured bishops, a contempt citation against the presiding bishop, actual or contemplated legal actions, violent gestures against women deacons in the midst of the Holy Eucharist at the communion rail, and threats of schisms are merely the visible signs of conflict.[1] The inward suffering is much deeper and more widespread. Members of the clergy who are divided over the issue express almost identical pain.

An opponent of women's ordination writes, "The conflict between bishops and bishops, between bishops and clergy and between clergy and laity and amongst laity themselves, between man and woman, between parent and child, what confusions and bitterness has come upon us! Charges, trials, illegal celebrations, angry recriminations—is this chaos to be understood as God and the Holy Spirit working his good will among us?"[2]

In the same publication, Bishop Ned Cole, who supports the principle but will not act before the General Convention of 1976, says, "The divisions, hurts and pains caused by this issue have wounded deeply this part of the body of Christ. In no way can I see our actions as pleasing in God's sight."[a]

Everyone seems to agree that the issue of ordination of women to the priesthood and episcopacy is perhaps the strongest issue to tax the strong unity of the Episcopal Church in many years. But as the late Stephen Bayne, reporting on the issue to the House of Bishops, said in 1972, "I don't like the pain and division it will cause. I wish it would go away. But the question is here now. It is an issue we've got to face."

Our presiding bishop has said that the main questions to be faced are:

How do we agree?

How do we sustain our agreements?

How do we agree to disagree or to change our agreements?

How do we proceed?

These questions must be faced and answered not only by the General Convention of 1976 but also by every local church and parish and in the hearts of each one of us.

Bishop Allen [the presiding bishop] is referring to the orderly procedure by which the church in its political form arrives at a decision. Perhaps the deeper question is what decision we arrive at as members of the Body of Christ. Where does the answer lie?

Do we find the answer in theological arguments? The theologians are as sharply divided on the issue as everyone else. The question boils down to whether the doctrine of creation found in Genesis 1 ("So God created man—in a generic sense—in his own image, in the image of God he created him; male and female he created them.") supports the view that both men and women are capable of representing humanity, or whether the image of God is a male principle and only a male can represent Jesus Christ in the priesthood. The debate rages—"and a great and strong wind rent the mountains, and broke in pieces the rocks before the Lord, but the Lord was not in the wind."[b]

We know, of course, that the House of Bishops has found no theological impediment to women's ordination to the priesthood and has twice voted by increasing majorities to approve the principle.

What of historical and cultural arguments? What of the tradition of the church? We learn that "the role of women in the church is shrouded in silence" and that biblical references to the ministry of women offer little guidance. We also know that traditions change, that human slavery, which was taken for granted in biblical times and existed in our own country until a little more than a century ago, is unacceptable to modern society. It took a bloody civil war which tore our country apart to teach us this lesson.

"And after the wind an earthquake, but the Lord was not in the earthquake."[c]

What of the politics of church unity, the argument that ordination of women to the priesthood now will endanger the possible reunion of Anglicans with Roman Catholics and [the] Orthodox Church? Is unity to be preferred above justice? And is not justice delayed justice denied? "And after the earthquake a fire, but the Lord was not in the fire."[d]

After pondering all the arguments pro and con, we need to ask ourselves *why* it is that this particular issue at this particular time threatens to tear our church apart?

The more violent issue of human slavery in the nineteenth century did not create such dissension within the Episcopal Church. And here we may very well come to the heart of the matter. The women's ordination issue may be the tip of an iceberg which, as Bishop Ned Cole has pointed out, involves more issues than just ordination of women, issues such as authority, obedience, disobedience, diocesan versus national authority, sexuality, [and] priesthood, to name a few.

What is God saying to us through the uproar this issue has created? I suggest that underlying this conflict may be the historic tension between the spirit of prophecy and the spirit of order which has been present in the church since the early medieval period when Christianity was no longer a persecuted minority religion but became the established religion of the Roman Empire.

Prophecy, in the tradition [of] Isaiah and Jeremiah and our own William String-fellow, sees the world as under judgment and seeks a radical transformation of the social order to bring it back to God. Order is content to seek more moderate reform, working more slowly within the existing social structures. Both strains are inherent in the church and necessary to its life and well-being, but when the balance of tension is upset the uneasy union begins to disintegrate and polar-ization may follow. When the church in its search for order becomes too closely identified with the established secular order, too inflexible in its orthodoxy and social structures, too static to achieve self-reform and self-renewal, prophetic movements arise to call the church back to its prophetic mission. Judgment on the church may take the forms of withdrawal, schism, or heresy. Monasticism was the instrument of prophecy from the fourth century on. In the Middle Ages the rebellion against the spirit of order was reflected in the increase of monas-tic orders, in movements of personal piety, in mysticism, and in new movements of heresy. Charismatic movements in our own time are seen as a similar revolt against the church's loss of its prophetic mission.

Is the movement for women's ordination a prophetic movement? Why is it that at this particular moment in the history of our church and of other faiths women are beginning to rise up and seek the ordained priesthood with such determined insistence? Is it a product of women's liberation, as some suggest, or are these women driven by a prophetic *call* which makes them refuse to be silenced and to proclaim the Word of God at all costs?

One is reminded of Amos, when he was driven out of the royal sanctuary at Bethel by the official priest Amaziah, [who] said,

> I am no prophet, nor a prophet's son, but I am a herdsman, and a dresser of sycamore trees, and the Lord took me from following the flock, and the Lord said to me, "Go prophesy to my people Israel!"[e]

The God of Christian faith and of the prophets of Israel moves, acts, and speaks in history through events and through individuals. The United States today is frighteningly like the people of Israel with their divided kingdoms in the eighth and seventh centuries B.C. In both periods of history we see common features: a comparatively advanced civilization; militarized power; governmen-tal intrigues; political assassinations; exploitation of the poor by the rich; dis-honesty and deceit in marketplace; bribery and corruption in the administra-tion of justice; the drive for lavish living; the jockeying for supremacy by the international great powers—and above all, the apostasy of the chosen people, the falling away from God.

In such periods marked by deep and pervasive national crisis, God has called forth prophets who will not be silenced or coopted by the established hierarchies. The role of these prophets is to call the people to repentance. They bring the two-folded message of God's judgment and salvation. We are reminded that Jesus Christ himself was prophet as well as priest and king.

God chooses his messengers from those who have listened to his word and are open to feel deeply human sorrow and need. He often chooses them from the most unlikely persons, as we saw in the [story] of Amos the shepherd, or Isaiah who when he first heard the call of the Lord said, "Woe is me! For I am a man of unclean lips," or reluctant Jeremiah who said, "Ah, Lord God! Behold, I do not know how to speak, for I am only a youth." But the Lord answered Jeremiah, "Behold, I have put my words in your mouth."[f]

Talking with some of these women, or listening to them preach, or reading their accounts of their own call, one is increasingly struck with the idea that nothing less than the urgency of their mission, born of their responses to the depths of our moral and spiritual crisis, could impel them to face the incredible barriers which have existed for thousands of years, to endure the ridicule and even violence of their detractors, and to persist in the face of the continual heartache of rejection which blocks their path and denies the authenticity of their call. Dare we say that they and their supporters are not answering to a higher authority than that of the political structures of our church? Is God using this movement to call our church and ourselves to judgment? How do we answer?

> And after the fire a still small voice. And when Elijah heard it, he wrapped his face in his mantle and went out and stood at the entrance to the cave.

Notes

[a] Ned Cole, "Why I Will Not Ordain a Woman Until General Convention Authorizes Me," in *The Ordination of Women: Pro and Con,* ed. Michael P. Hamilton and Nancy S. Montgomery (New York: Morehouse Barlow, 1975), 70–81.

[b] 1 Kings 19:11.

[c] Ibid.

[d] 1 Kings 19:12.

[e] Amos 7:14.

[f] Isaiah 6:5; Jeremiah 1:6; Jeremiah 1:9.

Has the Lord Spoken to Moses Only?

Exodus 15:20–21

Then Miriam, the prophetess, the sister of Aaron, took a timbrel in her hand; and all the women went out after her with timbrels and dancing. And Miriam sang to them, "Sing to the Lord, for he has triumphed gloriously; the horse and his rider he has thrown into the sea."

Numbers 12:1–2a

Miriam, and Aaron too, spoke against Moses in connection with the Cushite woman he had taken. . . . They said, "Has Yahweh (the Lord) spoken to Moses only? Has he not spoken to us too?"

Today combines several celebrations—Mother's Day in our secular society; the Feast of Dame Julian of Norwich in our church year, honoring an English mystic who died around 1417; and in many churches the annual Women's Day service, which underscores the role of women in the religious life. The enthusiasm with which women in a number of local churches have sought to have a woman priest as preacher and celebrant in these Women's Day services suggests a deep-felt desire on the part of these women to reclaim a heritage in prophetic leadership and ministry which has been lost in the midst of early human history.

Miriam was the first recorded woman prophet of the Judeo-Christian tradition, apparently the sister of Moses and Aaron, and member of a family blessed with the gift of prophecy. The "Song of Miriam" is said to be one of the oldest poetic couplets in the Old Testament and the fact that it survives bearing her name is testimony to her importance. She emerges as a religious leader along

88

with her brothers, just as the people of Israel escaped from bondage in Egypt, and she is called a prophet because of her power to rouse the people to praise the Lord in song and dance. Her ministry is a joyous one. When she challenged *Moses's* authority, however, according to the tradition she was stricken with leprosy, or more likely a minor skin affliction since it took only a few days to heal. But the power of her leadership was such that while she was shut up outside the camp for seven days, the people waited for her and did not set out on the march again until she was brought back to camp.

The fragmentary story of Miriam in the Old Testament is symbolic of what happened to women in the field of religion. As Dr. Margaret Brackenbury Crook, Smith College professor and biblical scholar, wrote in 1964 (*Women and Religion*): "A masculine monopoly in religion begins when Miriam raises her indignant question, '*Does the Lord speak only to Moses?*' Since then, in all three of the great religious groups stemming from the land and books of Israel—Judaism, Christianity, and Islam—men have formulated doctrine and established elaborate systems of worship offering only meager opportunity for expression of the religious genius of womankind."[a]

"We need as women in the interests of humanity as a whole," Dr. Crook continues, "a reconnaissance of some of the mighty principles operative in these religions before we can estimate our position in the present time or mark out our direction. We are being thrust into a wider partnership between men and women in numberless fields without a sufficient sense of motivation to sustain it or theory to guide it."[b] She points out that "from time immemorial woman, as the life-producer, had a leading place in religious thought and practice, until the day came, with changing forms in the life of communities, for self-realization of the male. Under his aegis we have lived and worshipped for the entire period that has seen the rise of Judaism, Christianity, and Islam. We now face an era filled with both promise and danger, in which a better understanding of women by men and men by women is urgently called for."[c]

Dr. Crook goes on to say that

> any woman born and bred in Judaism, Roman Catholicism, Eastern Orthodoxy, or Protestantism who takes a good look at the form of theology best known to her discovers that it is masculine in administration, in the phrasing of its doctrines, its liturgies and hymns. It is man-formulated, man-argued, man-directed. To bring this charge against the religious leaders is not to display animosity, it is to recognize the actual state of affairs. In the

Christian field, for instance, it is taken for granted that all the leading seminaries are man-staffed, all the leading pulpits man-filled, that no woman
can ever expect to become Archbishop of Canterbury or fill the papal
chair. . . . The time is ripe for a bold incursion into the field of theory. Theology is man-constructed; but women have to live with it and must aspire
to share it.[d]

We know now that a better understanding between men and women cannot come without great pain and conflict. The recent controversy over admission of women to the priesthood in the Episcopal Church USA was only the
visible tip of a deeper and continuing struggle to reform religious life to reflect
the full dignity, equality, and partnership of men and women. Patricia Martin
Doyle, who teaches at the School of Theology at Claremont, California, has not
overstated the case when she writes, "The debate on women and religion is the
single most important and radical question of our time and the foreseeable
future *precisely* because it concerns religion and because it affects all possible
people or peoples."[1] Since "religion concerns the deepest and most ultimate
aspects of life . . . we should not be surprised if the dispute thus results in radical resistance within the churches and individual men and women, as well as in
the possibility of radial cultural, psychological and religious transformation for
others."[2]

I recall the transformation I went through when I attended the ordination of the Philadelphia Eleven women priests in July 1974. Starting out, I was
torn with fear and uncertainty—like one breaking a sacred tribal taboo—a
lifetime of deference to traditional religious authority pulling me in backward,
an urgency to witness to what I believed to be God's inclusive plan pulling me
forward. Many of us who attended that event shared ambivalence at the outset
and were completely unprepared for the resultant joy and the sense of presence
of the Holy Spirit on that remarkable occasion. We could not know then that
because of that courageous witness on the part of those eleven women, their
bishops, and two thousand people who joined them, I can be with you today, a
regularly ordained priest in our church. Each step forward that we take to make
our church more inclusive and thus more capable of fulfilling Christ's mission
is an act of faith in the face of entrenched opposition, and a risk of God's judgment that we are wrong in our choices. We cannot know the outcome in advance; we can only pray that we are acting in accordance with God's will and
then leave the outcome to God. If we truly believe that we are called by God to

witness for a given principle—and sometimes that is a *big IF*—we have the difficult task of standing firm while simultaneously sharing the pain to our brothers and sisters which our acts may bring about.

The recurring phenomenon of religious wars tells us how volatile are the feelings attached to deeply held beliefs, and women cannot expect to challenge or transform traditions built up over thousands of years without inner turmoil, sacrifice, often bearing the brunt of ridicule and possible violence.

I am reminded of a current controversy at a local Episcopal seminary, which shall be nameless, of some two-hundred-odd students, about one-fourth of whom are women. These women are exposed daily to imagery which emphasizes masculine exclusiveness. Language, of course, is one of the most powerful instruments of communication of religious belief. As ordained ministers we are required to read and preach the Word of God as well as to administer the Holy Sacraments. Recently, in response to an innocuous request to avoid the use of sexist language in worship wherever possible, male seminarians drafted and circulated a petition which declared in part: "We, the undersigned members of the Seminary community, believe that the words *mankind, man, men, son, sons, brother, brothers, brethren, he, his, and him,* when they occur in translations of the Holy Scripture, the liturgy of our Church, or hymns, are to be applied generically, applying equally to both sexes, unless the context clearly demands another interpretation." As I reflected upon this petition, which threw the entire seminary community into turmoil and disrupted its normally placid routine, I wonder how my brethren might react if we women insisted upon the generic application of *Motherhood of God, sisterhood of woman, sisters, she, and hers,* and argued that we intended these words to include men as well as women. I suspect the response would be NO WAY!

On this Mother's Day, when we pay tribute to the essential qualities of motherhood, is it so unthinkable to enlarge our admittedly inadequate human symbolism of the infinite to include the concept of the *Motherhood of God?* Test yourselves. Does it bring you closer to Divine Love when you think of God as both Mother and Father? Does it surprise you to know that Julian of Norwich, whose life and work our church officially recognizes on May 8 and who believed that Divine Love holds the clue to all problems of existence, particularly the problem of evil, often pictured God and Jesus in female imagery? She wrote, for example, "The human mother will suckle her child with her own milk, but our beloved Mother, Jesus, feeds us with himself and with most tender courtesy does it by means of the Blessed Sacrament."[3] Are we women to be told that we are made in God's image and yet forbidden to express our own identity when we address the Almighty?

This is no feminist ego-trip with which we are dealing. To Paul Tillich, the great twentieth-century theologian, and to Erik Erikson, eminent contemporary psychiatrist, the motherhood of God might be the first important statement to be made about divinity. Both have expressed concern about the giant one-sidedness of the male cultural patterns and beliefs which dominate our present society and even invoke the concept of God "to substantiate a destructively masculine world."

Both have suggested that these values have just about reached their limit of usefulness and rationality unless they are greatly modified by the "tradition-ally feminine values of realism in house holding, responsibility in upbringing, resourcefulness in keeping and making the peace, devotion to healing, creativ-ity in fostering life"—all of which have hitherto been ignored in an increasingly threatening nuclear age which expresses itself not only in total war but also in individual terrorism.[4] Does the future of humanity depend upon how quickly these feminine principles can be incorporated into our religious life and thought? Is God calling women to reassert prophetic leadership and ministry before it is too late? And Miriam said, "Does the Lord speak only through Moses?"

Let Us Pray.

O God, you have bound us together in a common life—male and female. In our struggles for justice and inclusiveness to proclaim your word and do your will, so that all humanity may be brought into the merciful embrace of Divine Love, help us to discern the truth, to confront one another without hatred or bitterness, and to work together with mutual forbearance and respect; through Jesus Christ our Lord.

Amen.

Notes

[a] Margaret Brackenbury Crook, *Women and Religion* (Boston: Beacon Press, 1964), 1.

[b] Ibid.

[c] Ibid.

[d] Ibid.

Mary Has Chosen the Best Part

Luke 10:42b

The part that Mary has chosen is best; and it shall not be taken away from her.

Our Gospel reading today is also the Gospel text for July 29, set aside in the church calendar as a day of special devotion for Mary and Martha of Bethany. This little story of Mary and Martha is found only in Luke. One New Testament scholar has noted that we find many more stories that include women in Luke than in Matthew and Mark. She believes that Luke appears to be addressing his Gospel to a setting in which there were a substantial number of women present, either as students of the primitive catechism or potential converts to the early missionary churches. Quite often he puts together the parables in "pairs"—for example, he couples the parable of the Man and the Lost Sheep with that of the Woman and the Lost Coin. Just before the passage we read today, Luke records the parable of the Good Samaritan, which is directed toward men; the Mary and Martha story is directed toward women. And so, we will talk about women today.

Luke gives us an intimate glimpse of two women who were disciples of Jesus of Nazareth. Martha, the mistress of the house, seems to be a fussbudget who wants to make elaborate preparations for their guest. She is "distracted with much serving." She is concerned with material things, and in her anxiety to make Jesus welcome, she takes on too much. She bustles about, tiring herself out, and getting more and more frustrated because she is missing all the joy of Jesus's conversation. She becomes irritated because her sister Mary is not lending a hand.

For Mary, however, it is more important to give her undivided attention to the Lord and listen to his words than to overwhelm him with food and entertainment. Jesus, who has been watching this little human drama, perhaps in fond amusement, is probably not at all surprised when Martha complains to him about Mary's behavior. He gently chides her, "Martha, Martha, you are fretting and fussing about so many things; but one thing is necessary." Martha's failing was not one of intent. She loved the Lord and wanted to serve him, but she was so entangled in her own plans and preparations that her encounter with the Lord became an onerous duty instead of an occasion for joy.

Martha's dilemma is, of course, our own today. All too often we are caught up in the frantic search for security, for material comforts, for worldly success, for new experiences and more and more *things;* in fact, we may become so enslaved to the tyranny of possessions that we lose the ultimate meaning of our lives. One is reminded of those lines from Wordsworth:

> The world is too much with us; late and soon;
> getting and spending, we lay waste to our powers.[1]

When we are younger, we may be too involved in the competitive rat race to consider this possibility. When we become older and acutely aware of eternity, we are more apt to reflect upon our past and wonder what we have done with our lives that has any significance beyond our own struggle for existence.

Perhaps it is here that we can see another level of meaning in the story of Mary and Martha. Martha followed traditional custom in conformity with the position of women in her time. Women in Jewish culture were not permitted to study the Torah or to engage in theological conversation with a rabbi. In society they were invisible; a husband was not even to speak to his wife in public. In this perspective, we can see Mary as an unusual woman, one who was unwilling to accept the role defined for her and was drawn to Jesus of Nazareth because he treated her as a *person* with an intellect and a quest for knowledge of God. Jesus recognized her thirst and encouraged it. He permitted her the privilege of sitting at his feet as if she were a young male divinity student and he defended her decision: "The part that Mary has chosen is best; and it shall not be taken from her."

We do not know how Mary translated this experience into action; we are permitted to see only her impulse to enlarge her vision beyond the ordinary—

in her case an intense concentration upon the Word of God. But we do know what Jesus expected of all disciples and all Christians. In the very next passage of Luke, he teaches his disciples to pray "Thy kingdom come," and according to one witness, "Thy will be done, on *earth* as in heaven."

The central purpose of our existence, then, is that God's will be done on earth. Salvation is not some otherworldly experience; it is a process which begins here and now. I do not believe that we can hope for individual salvation without reference to the world in which we live. I believe that the heart of the gospel message in the two Great Commandments means that Christians are called upon by God to transform the world, to work for a more just and humane history to the end that God's will *is* done on earth.

None of us can escape the deeper implications of a society which breeds the kind of lawlessness and looting which happened in New York City last week on the night the lights went out. Without for one moment defending the looters, we have to ask ourselves, "What does it mean to live in a world in which one's appetite is constantly whetted for *things* through advertising, and yet one lives in a crowded ghetto where unemployment among Black and Hispanic teenagers soars from 40 percent in some areas, to 80 percent, where people are hungry and angry, and where they live without hope, without goals?"

Obviously, no simplistic diagnosis can explain this human tragedy, but I think it may be a symptom of the moral disintegration within society which neglects the deep-seated causes of poverty and powerlessness within its own population in its preoccupation with world power relationships. For example, the United States since 1945 has stockpiled enough nuclear weapons *to have a potential kill-power of twelve times the present world population.* What does this say for our moral values? What does it say about the millions of people in this country who call themselves Christians?

To say that the Christian mission is to transform the world is frightening to most of us. We feel that the problems of our time are too complex, that we are only one person, and that we, individually, can make very little impact upon society. Jesus himself was aware of this human frailty when he said to his disciple, "O Ye of little faith!" Yet all around us are examples of individuals who felt themselves called to a mission and who helped to change the face of society.

It seems appropriate here to point to the life of Alice Paul, founder of the National Woman's Party, who died last Saturday, July 9 [1977], at the age of ninety-two. Her life, spanning almost a century, bridged the two movements for women's rights in the United States. Born of Quaker parents, she was educated to become a social worker. At the age of twenty-two, after two years of settlement house work in New York, she went to England to study social work, and while there she met the leaders of the British women's suffrage movement and began her lifelong advocacy of women's rights.

When she returned to this country around 1912, she joined the suffrage movement, which had reached an all-time low, and infused it with new energy. She made her headquarters in Washington and for the next eight years led marches, demonstrations, and parades with banners and costumes. In 1917 Dr. Paul, who had earned her PhD, and several of her followers were jailed for their activities and went on a hunger strike, which lasted three weeks and as a result of which she was force-fed. Such harsh treatment of these imprisoned women aroused angry public response and brought about national recognition of the suffrage issue. In 1920, as you know, the Nineteenth Amendment to the Constitution was adopted and women had the vote after seventy-two years of continuous agitation.

Alice Paul quickly realized that the struggle for equality was not over, and in 1923 she wrote and had introduced into Congress the first Equal Rights Amendment ever proposed for women. For forty-nine years Dr. Paul and her valiant little band of women in the National Woman's Party introduced the Equal Rights Amendment into every session of Congress until its final passage in 1972. She lived to see thirty-five states ratify the amendment and only three more are required to make it become part of [the] Constitution.

Alice Paul possessed a single-mindedness bordering on fanaticism, but only such singleness of purpose and total dedication could have kept this issue alive during the intervening years. She was well equipped to supply the leadership and vision necessary for this task. Ten years after earning her PhD at the University of Pennsylvania, she took a law degree, and by 1928 had earned both a master's and a doctorate in law at American University. She had the courage to outface the criticism and ridicule heaped upon her and the dwindling membership of her organization as the members of the suffrage movement passed off the scene. She held to her course until [the] ERA caught the imagination of a new generation of young feminists in the late 1960s and blossomed into a national movement. Miss Paul remained in Washington until Congress passed [the] ERA and then continued active work on behalf of the various states' campaigns in Connecticut until about three years ago, when she became incapacitated by ill health.

Here, then, was a life pervaded by a sense of purpose and wholly dedicated to the fulfillment of her mission. We are reminded of another great contemporary of Alice Paul—Mrs. Eleanor Roosevelt. Miss Paul was one year younger than Mrs. Roosevelt, and her life continued for fifteen years after Mrs. Roosevelt's death. And while their lifestyles were different and they operated in different arenas, each of these two women in her own way, standing in the Christian tradition, made a lasting impact upon the world in which they lived by their unswerving devotion to the cause of human rights. Of Alice Paul, as of Eleanor Roosevelt, I think it can be said, "She has chosen the best part; and it shall not be taken away from her." What have *we* chosen?

Amen.

Notes

ᵃ Luke 10:41.

Healing and Reconciliation

Luke 6:17–18

And he came down with them, and stood in the plain, and the company of his disciples, and a great multitude of people out of Judea and Jerusalem, and from the sea coast of Tyre and Sidon, which came to hear him, and to be healed of their diseases. And they that were vexed with unclean spirits, and they were healed.

"A great multitude of people" always, it seems to me, is a signal of a deeply religious experience—joyous, friendly, full of song and praise, inclusive—embracing all sorts and conditions of humankind—men, women, and children; old and young; the lame, the halt, the blind; the Jew and Greek; the Black, White, Red, Yellow; Republicans and Democrats; rich and poor.

In our own time we have seen these great multitudes. One of the most spectacular multitudes of the twentieth century was the March on Washington in August 1963, when an estimated 240,000 people thronged from the Washington Monument to the Lincoln Memorial and heard, among others, the late Dr. Martin Luther King Jr., a son of the American South, give his famous "I Have a Dream" oration ending with the glorious shout, "Free at last, free at last, Thank God Almighty, free at last!"[1]

On that day, the crime rate in many American ghettoes dropped to near zero, and as I recall, there was not a single instance of violence connected with the march itself. Typical of human life, which combines the sacred and the profane, I marched twice that day—first, under the banner of the American Civil Liberties Union with my niece and my Howard University schoolmate, whom you know as the Honorable Patricia Roberts Harris, President Jimmy Carter's secretary of housing and urban affairs. Then my niece and I reversed our field and walked backward to meet the oncoming thousands, until I found and fell in line with my own parish church contingent from St. Mark's-in-the-Bowery, New York City. Those who experienced that witness for jobs and freedom said it was more like a great religious festival of the people of Israel at the time of Jesus of Nazareth than a political crusade. All I could think of that day was the old familiar song, "Oh when the Saints come marching in, oh when the Saints come marching in, Lord I want to be in that number, when the Saints come marching in." I see the events of the past nearly two centuries roughly from 1789 through 1976 as efforts to complete the first American Revolution. I like to think of January 1, 1977, as a signal for the visible beginning of the Second American Revolution—a revolution marked by the healing of vexatious unclean spirits, the reconciliation of groups of Americans now alienated from one another by reason of race, color, religion, sex (gender), age, sex preference, political and theological differences, economic and social status, and other manmade barriers. This is not to suggest the coming of the millennium. It is to suggest that I take with utmost seriousness the words of Jesus as the Christ—to use Paul Tillich's phrase—when Jesus said, "The Kingdom of Heaven is within you."[a]

Why January 1, 1977? On that day, an important segment of the Anglican Communion, which exists as a hybrid—a bridge between the Roman Catholic and Eastern Orthodox faiths on the one hand and the more Protestant faiths on the other hand—broke a two-thousand-year tradition and admitted women to the priesthood in the Episcopal Church USA. (And lest we appear to be too exclusive, let us remind ourselves that our communion is merely the grandchild of Judaism and that we resemble our grandparent in more ways than we are sometimes willing to admit.)

This event will take its place in significance with the great changes in the history of religion and more particularly in the history of the Christian Church. God moves and works the divine purposes out, in, and through history, and in historical perspective the ordination of women to the priesthood may rank with the admission of the Gentiles to the faith of the followers of Jesus Christ in the first century, the Protestant Reformation of the sixteenth century, and the liberation theology of the late twentieth century, which is reflected in the revolt of Roman Catholics against authoritarian oppression and apartheid in Latin America and South Africa, respectively.

These ordinations evoked an outpouring of spirit and excitement which confirmed the fact that the struggle of Episcopal women to fulfill God's call to the priestly vocation was the number one religious news story of 1976! The mass media reflected the upsurge of religious witness. For the first two weeks of January 1977, they were front page news in the national and international press and prominent features on the radio and television networks. Regions and local communities vied with one another to be included in the ceremonies, and to publicize their "firsts": the first regularly ordained woman in the entire United States on January 1—Jacqueline Means in Indiana; the first woman in New York—Carol Anderson on January 2; the first woman in Virginia, Pat Park; on January 3, the first woman in New England, Janet Kelly Brown in Vermont; the first woman from Massachusetts, January 8; the first woman in Alaska, Jean Diminti, January 7; and Page Smith Bigelow, a grandmother in New Jersey; the first woman in Los Angeles, California, on January 15, Victoria Hatch, and so on.

And if I may sanitize an old familiar expression, when a "woman of color" popped up out of the woodpile, moving along in the ordinary course of procedures, was ordained at the National Cathedral in Washington, as one of three women and three men, the national media really outdid themselves. To the national wire services and television networks, she was the Episcopal Church's ["]first Black woman priest." To the Boston newspapers, she was "Massachusetts's first." To the local *Morning Herald* in your rival twin city, she was a "woman priest from Durham"; to the *Washington and Baltimore Afro-American,* she was headlined, "Baltimorean Is an Episcopal Priest."[2] A friend of mine, taking her first venture into marriage in her sixties and honeymooning in Australia, sent me a clipping from *The West Australian,* Perth, Australia, dated Monday, January 10, and headlined, "History as Black Woman Ordained." And here we have the clue to all of the hubbub. When the Episcopal Church dropped the barriers to one-half of the human race, it not only leaped from the fifteenth to the twentieth centuries, but it witnessed to inclusiveness—"the least of these," as part of the Anglican Communion. In secular terms, it moved from 1789, the year in which both the Constitution of the United States was ratified and the Protestant Episcopal Church USA broke away from the mother Church of England and became its sister church, to the year 1977 in which we hope and pray the Equal Rights Amendment will be ratified.

I attended three of these ordinations and have seldom seen such joy unconfined. At the passing of the peace, the congregations could hardly contain themselves—people embraced one another and wept unashamedly. The National Cathedral, jammed with two thousand people, many crowding the balconies, "erupted in happy chaos" as one reporter put it. As the ordination of the last of the six priests took place, I'm told, the sun burst through the clouds and sent rainbow-colored shafts of light down through the stained-glass windows. And to me the most moving symbol of what was taking place in history was the sight of the new priest, Pat Park, mother of two small children and wife of an Episcopal priest, processing out during the recessional in her gorgeous Eucharistic vestments, her tiny daughter skipping along beside her, clinging to her hand.

This joy unconfined is part of the process of reconciliation after a long and painful struggle which almost tore the Episcopal Church apart—censured bishops, ecclesiastical trials, violent gestures against women deacons at the altar rail during the Holy Eucharist, close friends and members of families alienated from one another. And the victory for women's ordination in 1976 has come at the cost of great pain to those members of the clergy who hold it as an article of faith that only a male can represent the sacramental sign of Christ. They do not dare go further and say that only a "white Jewish male" is eligible for the priesthood, for that would make Paul VI ineligible to be pope; all Caucasian Gentile males would be excluded, to say nothing of the two-thirds of the world's population which are not white. Despite their selective theology, I take very seriously the pain of those who cling to an article of faith which appears to be overtaken by history. Having been on the losing side for so much of my life, I find it significant that I come out on the winning side in the one decision I made to put God in the center rather than on the periphery of my existence.

And so as we rejoice, as we feel healed of the sickness that came upon our communion during the course of this struggle, let us not forget that, along with our brethren who hold with the Vatican that the church is not authorized by God to admit women to the priesthood, we all stand in judgment before God for our choices.

Every break with longstanding tradition is both a moral victory and a risk. In the first century it was a risk to accept the uncircumcised Gentiles into the primitive church. There was a risk in parting company from the Roman Catholic Church and establishing the Church of England. There was a risk in emancipating 4 million Negro slaves without compensation to their masters to whom they represented a heavy capital investment, or compensation to the slaves for two centuries of forced labor. There was a risk in declaring unconstitutional state-enforced segregation. The race of that last victory was the blood of the martyrs, Black and white—in Mississippi, in Alabama, in Tennessee, in Texas, in California, and elsewhere. All of us who are adults and who have lived in the South have suffered in various ways in the course of this struggle. Yet one of the veterans of the struggle, victim of the University of North Carolina's rejection thirty-nine years ago (1938), stands before you today in Chapel Hill, the site of that rejection, proclaiming the healing power of Christ's love, who paid the ultimate price of crucifixion for our redemption. As followers of Christ, we are called upon to take risks; to work for the liberation of the body, mind, and spirit; to exorcise the unclean spirits which vex us and prevent us from being our true selves created in the image of God and inheritors of the Kingdom of Heaven.

The late Dr. Frank P. Graham, who was president of the University of North Carolina in 1938 when I applied unsuccessfully for admission to the graduate school, and with whom I was later privileged to serve on the Board of the National Sharecroppers' Fund, used to speak of our country as "this little island of Christianity." By this, he did not mean to put down other religions but to express the fact that Christianity is a minority religion often suppressed in other parts of the world, and that here in the United States we are free to practice it.

As baptized Christians, we are all ministers of Christ. In the Outline of Faith in the new Book of Common Prayer, we learn that the ministers of the Church "are laypersons, bishops, priests, and deacons." All of us, without exception, belong to the royal priesthood of all believers. Today, at this time and in this place, we are the gathered church . . . whether lay ministers or ordained clergy, we all have the same fundamental calling, to represent Christ and his church, to bear witness to him wherever we may be, and according to the gifts given to us, to carry on Christ's work of reconciliation in the world.

Each of us, therefore, is called upon to proclaim the Good News of God-in-Christ's redeeming love. And the Good News today, in our small corner of the planet, in the American South, is that the South is rising out of its own ashes; out of its redemptive suffering it is becoming purified; it is being healed of its unclean spirits, and its representatives—notably Jimmy (and Rosalynn) Carter in the White House—are beginning to fulfill that beloved song now sung around the world wherever people are striving for freedom from oppression—"We Shall Overcome . . . Black and White Together, We Shall Overcome."

"Deep in my heart, I do believe" that the American South will lead the way toward the renewal of our moral and spiritual strength and our sense of mission. The initiative has passed from New England where those first Pilgrims back in the seventeenth century saw the new country as the "new Jerusalem," "a

city set on a hill," "a light to the world," to places like Chapel Hill, North Carolina, where we are today witnessing to the reconciling of Isaac and Ishmael in
the House of Abraham.

I owe much of my religious devotion and my Episcopalian heritage to my
grandmother Cornelia Smith Fitzgerald, born February 10, 1844, baptized in
this parish next door in the old Chapel of the Cross on December 20, 1854, at
the age of ten, as one of "five servant children of Miss Mary Ruffin Smith," according to this church's registry. The registry added, "the mother of these Children is Harriett." And here the Old Testament story of Abraham, Sarah, Hagar
the bondswoman, Isaac the legitimate heir, and Ishmael the outcast comes alive
in our own time. The promise of the angel of the Lord to Hagar in the desert to
make Ishmael and his descendants "a great nation" is being fulfilled. And this
great nation is the American nation—neither Black nor white but all colors.

It was my destiny to be the descendant of slave owners as well as slaves,
to be of mixed ancestry, to be biologically and psychologically integrated in a
world where the separation of the races was upheld by the Supreme Court of the
United States as the fundamental law of our Southland. My entire life's quest
has been for spiritual integration, and this quest has led me ultimately to Christ
in whom there is no East or West, no North or South; no Black or white, no Red
or Yellow; no Jew or Gentile, no Islam or Buddha; no Baptist, Methodist, Episcopalian, or Roman Catholic; no Male or Female. There is no Black Christ nor
white Christ nor Red Christ—although these images many have transitory cultural value. There is only Christ, the spirit of love and reconciliation, the healer
of deep psychic wounds, drawing us all closer to that goal of perfection which
links us to God our Creator and to eternity.

Let Us Pray.

O God, who created all peoples in your image, we thank you for the wonderful diversity of races and cultures in this world. Enrich our lives by ever-
widening circles of fellowship, and show us your presence in those who differ
most from us, until our knowledge of your love is made perfect in our love for
all your children; through Jesus Christ our Lord.

Amen.

Notes

ª Luke 17:21.

Gifts of the Holy Spirit
to Women I Have Known

Acts 2:1–11

And suddenly a sound came from heaven like the rush of a mighty wind, and it filled all the house where they were sitting. . . . And they were filled with the Holy Spirit and began to speak in other tongues. . . . And at this sound the multitude came together, and they were bewildered, because each one heard them speaking in his own language. And they were amazed and wondered saying, "Are not all these who are speaking Galileans? And how is it that we hear, each of us in his own native language?"

It is entirely appropriate that my first sermon and celebration as a priest in Christ's one, Holy, Catholic, and Apostolic church in my "hometown" where I grew up be performed on Mother's Day in this Church of St. Philip's. For it was this church that my grandmother, my aunts, and my mother attended before I was born, and it is about grandmothers, mothers, and sisters that I wish to speak.

Because today is the day of Pentecost, when the Holy Spirit descended upon the disciples of Christ and set their hearts on fire, and because Pentecost, or Whitsunday, this year coincides with Mother's Day, I feel moved to share with you some reflections upon women I have known who had the gift of the Holy Spirit and whose impact on my life brings me to you today in a unique homecoming. The first was my grandmother Cornelia Smith Fitzgerald, a citizen of Durham until her death in 1923. A devout Episcopalian, she sent three of her daughters, one of whom was my mother, to St. Augustine's School in Raleigh, and they in turn were confirmed [in] and attended St. Philip's. An article in the *North Carolina Historical Magazine,* January 1977, will tell those of you who are interested why people like my forebears began to establish missions like St. Titus around 1908 and why I was confirmed in St. Titus rather than in St. Philip's.

Cornelia Smith Fitzgerald was a firebrand with a gift of prophecy and a candid tongue. She feared nobody and spoke her mind, letting the chips fall where they may. Her favorite literature came from the poetic passages of the Old Testament—the Psalms and especially the Prophets. And she had a gift of language, coining her own words to express her thoughts. She had a fine intelligence imprisoned within a restricted education, but she absorbed much knowledge from observation and listening, and she had a wisdom which comes only from facing life courageously whatever the cost. If I have been a firebrand in my time and singed the feathers of the good brothers and sisters of the establishment— and heaven knows we are an Establishment Church—I owe it to my grand-mother, with whom I had an affinity which bridged the sixty-six years she had lived in North Carolina and I had not. Her language was salty and her fuses short—but in a curious way which I am only beginning to understand as I grow older, she was more free than most people—in spite of poverty, racial segrega-tion, and the growing alienation between the races. And this was so because she had no pretenses, no hypocrisies. And she spoke in short Anglo-Saxon words that anybody around her could understand. There was no double-talk in my grand-mother. She taught me by example certain approaches to life without which all my university and professional training would have been comparatively useless. My grandmother was born in slavery, but she recognized no master or mistress save the living God.

My Aunt Pauline Fitzgerald Dame, who was responsible for my upbring-ing here in Durham, had the gift of teaching. Some of you may be old enough to have remembered the delightful short story "Good Morning, Miss Dove," written by a woman who lived in Durham. I have often wondered who the model of that story might have been because "Miss Dove" was a dead ringer for my Aunt Pau-line. *What am I saying here?* I am saying that without the gift of the Holy Spirit we can live in a town as small as Durham was when I was a child and never know one another; we in fact speak in alien tongues.

Let me illustrate with a modern example: One of the saddest stories I have read recently appeared in the *Greensboro Daily News,* Sunday, March 12, 1978, entitled "Racial Peace: It's Separate and Strained," by Warren Brown, a reporter for the *Los Angeles Times–Washington Post* News Service. It began,

> Both the black and white students could tell he [the reporter] was a visitor because he sat at the wrong table. Blacks seldom ate in that part of the cafeteria. They usually carried their trays to the "black section," in an adjacent room. . . . That is the way things are done at Duke University in Durham, N.C., at Cornell University in Ithaca, New York, and at many other predominately white campuses across the country, where 72 per cent of the nation's 948,000 black college students attend school.

I am tempted to say, "What nonsense!" My grandmother would have used more graphic syllables. If those same "black and white" students were dropped in the heart of Russia today, or in Amin's Uganda in Africa, they would find that their "separatism" would disappear like the rush of a mighty wind and they would become instant brothers and sisters of their native land—America.

Even as I lash out against this wrongheadedness, I should know better. If it has taken me the better part of six decades—two-thirds of a century—to arrive at my present stance, how can I expect the young who have lived less than a third of that time—the most tumultuous third—to have the answers for racial alienation? It is true that although Blacks/Negroes and whites have occupied the same geographical space, they *have* had a different historical experience. And while men and women have also occupied the same more intimate space, in the home for example, they too have had a different historical experience. And much of our social turmoil today stems from our inability to share these different experiences, to help others enter into our own joys and sorrows and to feel as we feel, suffer as we suffer, and rejoice—to hear one another speaking in our own language. "I hear you"—meaning I *understand* you—has become part of our contemporary vocabulary.

This hearing one another cannot be done through racial pride, although it helps to have a strong sense of identity and self-esteem. It can only be done by joining up with the *human* race and seeing ourselves and others as children of God. In theology we call it *imago dei*—made in the image of God. When we surrender our false pride and our false idols—money, "white tradition," "Black solidarity," position, prestige, and power—and see ourselves as I have seen people in the recovery room of a surgical ward—utterly stripped of every pretension and wholly dependent upon God's grace and the skill of others—then we begin to realize, if even dimly, that every man, woman, or child is our brother or sister, and we become eager to share their experience because we grow richer in our own personalities through sharing.

The great contribution which Alex Haley has made to America is to open up the experience of slavery in such a way that millions of people to whom *slavery* was a remote concept could live it imaginatively in *Roots.* The contribution I hope to make as one of the successors to Martin Luther King Jr. is to address myself to the possibility of reconciliation. But reconciliation cannot come without a simultaneous transformation of our society into a *caring, humane society*—where people are not just numbers in a computer; where human services are not tainted with the idolatrous notion of profit, power, and privilege; where the elderly are seen as repositories of our collective wisdom and not inconveniences to be endured; where children are given responsibility and expected to pull their weight in family and social undertakings; where waste becomes as socially undesirable as theft; and where it is the national ethos that *human beings* are our most important resource, that spiritual and physical energy is as important as energy from coal and oil.

Reconciliation cannot come without pain and suffering—the suffering of a well-intentioned white person when a Negro/Black rejects his/her kindly gesture because it is seen as arrogant and paternalistic; the suffering of an inadequately trained white male when he suddenly finds the jobs or positions he has been accustomed to get are taken by better trained Blacks, other minorities, or white females pursuant to a national policy of affirmative action; the anger and suffering of a young Black when he or she finally realizes the extent to which he or she has been robbed of a heritage and then penalized for "inferior" performance. Yes, we must suffer with and for one another before we will be healed of the sickness of our common history, before we will be free to face one another and walk together toward a brighter future.

But we are not without resources if we will only take seriously our Christian faith. Paul of the first century (whom I think of as my first Christian namesake) pointed them out to us when he wrote, "To one is given through the manifestation of the Spirit for the common good. To one is given through the Spirit the utterance of wisdom, and to another the utterance of knowledge, according to the same Spirit, to another gifts of healing, to another the working of miracles, etc. . . . All of these are inspired by one and the same Spirit, who apportions to each one individually as he wills."[a]

When I think of the gift of healing, I think of my own mother, Agnes, whom I never knew and who died at the age of thirty-five with a cerebral hemorrhage when I was three. She broke the family tradition of teaching and became a nurse, and the name Agnes in our family has become associated with the healing professions. If my mother had lived until today, she would be ninety-nine years old. Last Saturday, May 6, I attended the 45th reunion of my class and the 108th birthday luncheon of Hunter College. It was a profoundly moving experience when one of the distinguished guests on the dais addressed us in the clearest, most precise English: she was Jessica R. Engleson, member of the Class of 1899, and she was ninety-nine years old!

Eleanor Roosevelt had many gifts of the Holy Spirit, but those which made the greatest impression upon me were her generosity of being, her compassion, her rigorous honesty about herself and those she loved, and her sense of mission, which permitted her to waste no time which could be used productively. One of my unforgettable memories of her was a lively political discussion we were having one weekend at her cottage in Hyde Park. And while she talked, I watched her filling in her name and putting money into her weekly pledge envelope for her church, St. James in Hyde Park. My Aunt Sallie, Mrs. Sarah A. Fitzgerald Small, wife of the vicar of St. Titus for several years, had the gift of laughter, of seeing the absurdities of the human condition even in the midst of woe.

Finally, I come to the woman whose name means nothing to younger Durhamites but of whom Durham can be proud. Her name is Susie A. Elliott and on Sunday, May 7, she reached her ninetieth birthday. Many years ago, when North Carolina Central University was called the National Training School and Dr. James E. Shepherd was its president, Miss Elliott taught home economics there. From there she went on to do graduate work at Pratt Institute in New York and was house director of Emma Ransom House, YWCA, in Harlem when I was a teenage college freshman. From there she became head of the Home Economics Department at Tuskegee Institute, and finally dean of women at Howard University when I was a law student there, from which position she retired in the late 1950s. One of the young women whom she nurtured during her deanship is Patricia Roberts Harris, our secretary of housing and urban development. Hundreds of her "daughters" are outstanding women at the top of their professions today—a "credit to their space."

Dean Elliott is the essence of graciousness, having the gift of living creatively with the advancing years—giving herself to her church work, to the YWCA, to community endeavors, and to entertaining small groups in her home. On April 21, she was the guest of honor at the twenty-fifth Anniversary Dinner of the Howard University Chapter of Phi Beta Kappa. She prepared her own brief remarks for her response. About ten days before the dinner she suffered a slight stroke. A brain scan revealed a blockage in the left carotid artery, which carries blood to the head. Immediate surgery was indicated but held up for further consultation because of her great age. Knowing that she might have a massive stroke at any minute she calmly appointed me as her "stand-in," in case she was unable to perform her speaking obligation. When the time came, however, she walked unassisted to the platform and delivered her speech. Three days later she entered the hospital for the planned surgery, only to have another slight but warning stroke. Surgery was put off—it was too risky. But the doctors felt that she was such a young ninety they wanted her to have a chance to live. They explained the risks to her and she decided to gamble on surgery, signing her own papers. Three days ago, on Thursday, she underwent surgery—while several of us—her "daughters"—walked the hospital corridor praying. They had a difficult time of it because at one point she suffered a heart blockage. I had the signal honor of being admitted to the recovery room a few minutes after she began to wake up, to see her respond to all commands, to feel her squeeze my hand, and finally to accompany her as she was wheeled down the long corridor to the Surgery Intensive Care Ward. As we left the ward, her other surrogate daughter and niece-in-law said, "Thank you Jesus!"

These are the women of whom it can be said, "We hear them telling us in our own tongues the mighty works of God."

Amen.

Notes

[a] 1 Corinthians 12:8.

Sermon Given on April 22, 1979

John 20:18

Mary Magdalene went and said to the disciple, "I have seen the Lord"; and she told them he had said these things to her.

In John's Gospel, Mary of Magdala gives the first personal testimony of the Easter faith—"I have seen the Lord!"—a spontaneous proclamation, so powerful, so urgent, so convincing that it echoes across three centuries from that first Easter morning. John's story of the appearance of Jesus Christ to Mary in the garden is one of the most movingly human of all the accounts of the Risen Christ. It speaks to us with special force because in Mary we see ourselves in those moments when we have been stricken with inconsolable grief over the loss of a loved one whose presence was the greatest blessing of our lives. Through her encounter with the Risen Lord, we can enter the mystery of the Resurrection.

There has come down through Christian tradition a popular notion that Mary of Magdala was a reformed prostitute whose sins were forgiven by Jesus of Nazareth. This conception was due to earlier scholars who identified her with an unnamed woman described as a sinner in Luke's Gospel, who watered Jesus's feet with her tears, wiped them with her hair, and anointed them with precious ointment. Contemporary scholars agree that there is no evidence to support this idea. It is true, however, that Mary was a woman with a sorrowful past. She came from a small fishing village called Magdala on the southwest coast of the Sea of Galilee not far from Capernaum, where Jesus had often preached and healed the sick during his ministry in Galilee. She had apparently suffered a serious mental disorder, which might be described today as multiple schizophrenia. Mark and Luke tell us that she was possessed by "seven demons." Jesus had healed her early in his ministry. Apparently, a woman of some means and influence in Magdala, she was one of several women who became followers of Jesus. They supported Jesus and his disciples out of their worldly goods in Galilee and had come up with him to Jerusalem.

These devoted women had not run away in the crisis of Jesus's arrest and execution as his disciples had done. They followed him to the cross and stood there through those agonizing hours of the Crucifixion. They endured the horror of his death and looked on while his lifeless body was wrapped in linens and buried in the tomb. They had known the ultimate sorrow.

We can understand the agony of Mary, the mother of Jesus, of Mary of Magdala and the other women as they watched the slow torture of Jesus's last hours, if we have ever had to stand by the bedside of a loved one who is dying, helpless to relieve the suffering. They were powerless, numb with misery and disbelief that this could be happening before their very eyes, filled with suppressed rage. When have we not cried out in anger at God when we have seen someone we love slipping away from us?

Little is known about the day which followed Jesus's burial. His followers, we must remember, were not looking forward to Easter morning. All their hopes had perished with the Crucifixion. They may have felt that God had deserted them, and that Jewish Sabbath day must have been an eternity of mental and spiritual darkness, utter despair, of being cast adrift with no future. Their beloved teacher whose very presence was the light of their existence, on whom all their dreams and plans depended—so vital, so responsive, so strength-giving—was suddenly cut off from time—gone—irrevocably beyond communication—never again to speak to them, to touch them, to renew their spirits, to heal them.

For Mary of Magdala, the disaster went beyond the loss of a friend and teacher. Jesus had destroyed the darkness of her being, the demons who filled her with nameless terrors. He had helped her to find purpose in her life: he had rescued her from a feeling of worthlessness. Jesus's remarkable sensitivity to women and his inclusion of them in his ministry had made her feel like a *person*. His treatment of women was unusual in his day. The prevailing attitude toward them was expressed in the words of Ecclesiasticus: "Better is the wickedness of a man than a woman who does good; it is a woman who brings shame and disgrace."[a]

Jesus had ignored the customs; he treated women as equals, as individuals and persons. He accorded Mary of Bethany the right to sit at his feet and study scriptures in the same manner as a young rabbinical student. He entered into conversation with the Samaritan woman at the well in the face of the law which decreed, "A man should hold no conversation with a woman in the streets, not even his own wife, lest men should gossip."[b] He encouraged women to become his disciples and to follow him in a society in which not only were women not to read and study the scriptures but also in the more observant homes they were not even to leave their households. And, according to John's Gospel, he chose a woman to witness his first appearance after the Resurrection.

The security of being accepted for oneself in Jesus's reassuring presence had now been swept away. Fear of the return of the old mental chaos, dread of the "demons," and of complete disintegration may have revived in Mary of Magdala. There was no one she could turn to for help, no one with whom she could share this dread. We can envision her desolation as she paced restlessly through the hours, waiting for the Sabbath to end so that she can go to the tomb where Jesus was buried, as if nearness to his bodily remains could somehow continue the relationship. We know that feeling when we have lingered beside the casket of our newly dead, unable to accept the finality of death. Somehow they seem close to us even though they cannot speak to us or touch us.

In the other three Gospels, Mary visits the tomb with other women. In John's Gospel she is alone. She was dismayed to find the stone rolled away. She ran to Simon Peter and the Beloved Disciple and told them, "They have taken the Lord out of the tomb and we do not know where they have laid him."[c] Peter and the Beloved Disciple came to the tomb, investigated, satisfied themselves that it was empty, and went back to their homes.

But Mary of Magdala was not satisfied. She continued to search and came back to the tomb, unable to comprehend this new disaster. As she stood there looking at the tomb and weeping, two angels sitting where the body of Jesus had lain spoke to her. In the depth of her despair she felt the presence of Jesus, turned and saw him, and he spoke to her. Even then, in her preoccupation with death she mistook him for the gardener and did not recognize him until he called her by her familiar name—"Mary."

In that moment when Mary could see and know Jesus with the eyes of faith, she was transformed; her suffering vanished. She saw him imperfectly at first, not yet fully aware that the earthly Jesus was the Risen Christ, but she had found her mission—to carry the Good News that Jesus lives! In exaltation, she ran to the disciples bursting with her message, "I have seen the Lord." And she told them what he had said: "I am ascending to my Father and your Father, to my God and your God."[d]

The message which Mary brought to the disciples was the message of faith, of complete trust in a loving God whom we do not need to fear and who does not abandon us in death. And it is only through faith that we can enter into the mystery of the Resurrection, by "turning around" as Mary turned around. As long as she looked at the tomb, searching for the dead, clinging to the past, she could not recognize the Risen Lord. But the message of the Easter faith is that he is not of the past; he has overcome death and goes before us into the future. God's saving act in Jesus Christ, who was human as we are human, revealed the potential of humanity.[1]

Many of us, like the disciple Thomas, are torn by doubt, but doubt is part of being human. Faith is not certainty, provable by scientific evidence, or it would not be faith. Doubt is an element of faith. Remember how Jesus said to Thomas after he had shown him the marks of the nails in his hand and the spear in his side, "Have you believed because you have seen me? Blessed are those who have not seen and yet believe."[e]

Faith is an act of courage, of trust in spite of our doubts. To me, one of the most comforting expressions of this faith came from a theologian when he was dying. He called his wife to his bedside and told her: "These last nights I have been thinking over and testing everything that we know and everything that we have been told about what will happen to us when we die. And now I am certain of one thing. I shall be safe."

Notes

[a] Ecclesiasticus 42:14.

[b] [Biblical scholar Ernst] Haenchen (John 4:27).

[c] John 20:2.

[d] John 20:16–18.

[e] John 20:29.

Exodus

Exodus 15:20–21

Then Miriam, the prophetess, the sister of Aaron, took a timbrel in her hand; and all the women went out with her with trimbels and dancing. And Miriam sang to them:

> "Sing to the Lord, for he has triumphed gloriously, the horse and his rider he has thrown into the sea."

The song of Miriam, praising God for the deliverance of his people from the perils of the Red Sea, is one of the oldest fragments of Hebrew poetry. Taken from the biblical story of the Exodus, it expresses the jubilance of a people who have surmounted incredible difficulties and stand at the threshold of new beginnings. It is an appropriate theme for this ceremony of thanksgiving because a college commencement is also the celebration of a triumphant exodus. It memorializes the ever-widening struggle of humanity through the ages to liberate itself from bondage to ignorance and superstition and to fulfill the highest aspirations of human intellect. . . . The community of scholars assembles to reaffirm its commitment to this high calling and to witness the exodus of the outgoing class it has nurtured through years of rigorous preparation. It is a time for a special thanksgiving for those of you who graduate today. You have survived the exacting discipline of study and the ordeals of the testing process. This is a joyous rite of passage as you look toward your future careers.

In Judeo-Christian tradition, the story of the Exodus is part of salvation history, God's action to liberate his people from tyranny and oppression.

Throughout history this story has heartened groups struggling against oppression. Recall the great Negro spiritual, a protest against Black slavery in the United States: "Go down Moses—Way down in Egypt land—Tell ole Pharaoh—to let my people go."

It is said that the subjugation of women is the oldest form of human oppression and has been the model for the subjugation of other groups in society. For women struggling against sexism, Miriam has emerged as a symbol of courageous womanhood, asserting new freedom and sharing leadership with her brothers Moses and Aaron in a time of national crisis. In later tradition she was remembered as a spiritual leader of great power and influence. According to the prophet Micah, the Lord says to the people of Israel: "I brought you up from the land of Egypt, and redeemed you from the house of bondage; and I sent before you Moses, Aaron and Miriam."[a]

The Old Testament narrative reveals brief glimpses of a remarkably fearless, independent woman who played a significant role in the national liberation of her people. She is presented as the unnamed sister of the infant Moses who watched over the basket in which he lay hidden among the reeds near the banks of the Nile River. Young Miriam's fearlessness and quick-thinking helped to save Moses to become the great Hebrew law-giver and statesman. When Pharaoh's daughter found the baby and took pity on him, Miriam offered to get a Hebrew woman to nurse the child, then fetched [her] own mother as the nurse. Years later, Miriam displayed the same courage in leading the women of Israel across the bottom of the Red Sea.

Miriam also seems to have been an example of feminist rebellion against patriarchal dominance. She opposed Moses's marriage to a Cushite woman and, with Aaron, took her grievance to the people, saying, "Has the Lord spoken only through Moses? Has he not also spoken through us?"[b] She was punished for her rebellion and stricken with a mild form of leprosy. Moses interceded with God on her behalf, and she was healed after a quarantine of seven days. The remarkable part of the story is that her rebellion and punishment did not affect her high standing among the people. They were so devoted to her they discontinued their march while she was in quarantine and did not set out again until Miriam was restored to camp.

Cedar Crest College stands in the Exodus tradition. It has played a pioneering role in broadening the horizons of women and preparing them for careers outside of the home.[1] Today we take for granted college and professional education for both sexes, but we must remind ourselves that women have won this privilege only in comparatively recent history. More than two hundred years elapsed between the founding of the first men's college in this country and the awarding of the first women's bachelor degrees by Oberlin College in 1842. Indeed, your own institution, founded in 1867, was among the earliest women's colleges in the United States and was born in the midst of stubborn opposition to higher learning for women.

Dr. Phyllis Stock's informative history of women's education describes how the women who braved college in the latter part of the nineteenth century did so in the face of terrifying predictions by male educators.[c] A book published by a Harvard College professor argued that higher education would destroy the ability of women to have children, by overtaxing them at a critical stage of their adolescent development. It was said to be almost obscene for women to attend college, that it would unsex them and make them "pathological invalids." Martha Carey Thomas, who became president of Bryn Mawr, recalled that when she went to Germany to obtain her doctorate in 1879, ["]family friends did not ask after her, as she was considered to have disgraced her parents."

Although women persevered and proved these fears to be groundless, resistance to their professional training continued until well into the twentieth century. Harvard Law School, for example, did not admit women students until 1950. (I had the misfortune to apply six years too soon, but I like to think my application kept the issue alive.)

As we celebrate this day of liberating achievement, we hold in remembrance those valiant women who have gone before us, whose determination opened the way for women to have wider opportunities for education, professional careers, and access to public life.

Today, women college graduates are entering a new era of new ideas, new lifestyles, new challenges, and new experimentation. This journey toward self-realization is not without dangers and uncertainties. Many of the old securities are being shattered in a world of unprecedented change. The times demand people who are willing to take risks and travel new paths, but as we know, in every exodus there are many who shrink from the implications of freedom and its responsibilities. Remember how the people of Israel murmured against Moses as they encountered each new difficulty. They cried out, "What have you done to us, bringing us out of Egypt? . . . For it would have been better for us to serve the Egyptians than to die in the wilderness."[d]

We find the same confusion and doubt among many women today who

falter in the face of new and difficult undertakings. . . . These conflicting views,
I believe, also reflect differences in theological perspective. The modern Miriams
are driven by a prophetic urgency as well as by a vision of a freer, more humane
society. They are concerned with human survival and, as Rosemary Ruether puts
it, "a restoration of the world to its proper destiny as the place where God's will
is done on earth, as it is in heaven." This enlarged view of human destiny recognizes the interdependence of all peoples and the interrelatedness of all life. We
have been forcefully reminded of this by such recent events as the impact of the
revolution in Iran upon our vital oil supplies and the terrifying implications of
the nuclear accident at the Three Mile Island plant near Middletown, Pennsylvania. It is becoming increasingly clear that the security of the home is determined ultimately by the transactions in the marketplace. Women's concerns are
embedded in every political and social issue; their experience is essential to the
solutions of such planetary problems as the threat of nuclear war; the depletion
of the earth's nonrenewable resources; the pollution of our land, water, and air;
and world poverty and hunger. In fact, many of the burdens flowing from these
problems bear more heavily upon women than men and will continue to do so
as long [as] they are absent from the public arenas in which vital policy decisions are made.

Significantly, some of the most radical critiques of contemporary society
are coming from women theologians in the Judeo-Christian tradition. They recognize that religion involves "the deepest and most ultimate aspects of human
life" ([Patricia Martin] Doyle) and that it is "the single most important shaper
and enforcer of the image and role of women in culture and society" (Ruether).
These theologians are reexamining and reinterpreting biblical doctrines in the
light of the female experience and offering correctives to the patriarchal worldview which has reinforced the subordination of women. They call upon the
church to give up its "patriarchal nostalgia" and to "take an active part in the
process of bringing into full function the neglected feminine half of the human
potential."[2]

In various ways, these biblical scholars point to the fateful consequences
of continued male dominance. Patricia Martin Doyle observes that a male-
dominated culture has developed which has become dangerously one-sided and
which "even—or perhaps, especially—infects the perception of God, so that the
Ultimate is invoked to substantiate a destructively masculine world." She warns
that "male cultural patterns have just about reached their limit of value, utility and rationality unless society becomes considerably modified by feminine

input. . . . The continued exclusion and negation of women and their concerns in a totally masculine culture," she says, "may almost inevitably lead to the end of the human (and other) species in a nuclear holocaust or some other form of destruction. . . . The traditional female values of realism in householding, responsibility in upbringing, resourcefulness in keeping and making peace, devotion to healing, creativity in fostering life, hitherto ignored, must find new emphasis and input into our cultural life. . . . Cultivation of the feminine in religious symbolizations and consciousness, in future ideologies and identities," Doyle believes, "is urgently needed if humanity is to be saved from possible catastrophe and become more whole."[3]

This religious perspective gives renewed meaning to the story of creation in Genesis, chapter 1, which all too often has been overshadowed by the interpretation of the Adam and Eve story of creation written by a different author and found in Genesis, chapter 2. In Genesis 1, God created male and female as equals and gave them joint stewardship of the earth:

> So God created man in his own image; in the image of God he created him, male and female he created them. Be fruitful and multiply . . . and have dominion over every living thing that moves upon the earth. . . . And God saw everything that he had made, and behold it was very good.[e]

The call for a new Exodus sets before you a vision of the possibility that, as Octavio Paz has said, "from the interplay of masculine and feminine a new and hitherto undreamed-of culture and creativity might arise."[4] It invites your commitment to this vision and your participation in the great undertaking to transform society and restore God's creation. It demands the courage to venture into [un]charted areas in the years ahead. It also involves suffering, hardship, and sacrifice as well as exciting experimentation, but as the late Dr. Martin Luther King Jr. once said, we can have deep faith in the future because we know that in our struggles for justice we have "cosmic companionship." In bidding you Godspeed as you go out to meet this challenge, I pass along the words of the late Dr. Reinhold Niebuhr: "Nothing that is worth doing can be achieved in a lifetime; therefore we must be saved by hope. Nothing which is true or beautiful or good makes complete sense in any immediate context of history; therefore we must be saved by faith. Nothing we do, however virtuous, can be accomplished alone. Therefore we are saved by love."[5]

Amen.

Notes

[a] Micah 6:4.

[b] Numbers 12:2.

[c] Phyllis Stock, *Better Than Rubies: A History of Women's Education* (New York: Putnam, 1978).

[d] Exodus 14:11–12.

[e] Genesis 1:20–31.

Sermon Given on June 6, 1982

Wisdom of Solomon 7:25a,b
For she is the breath of the power of God; and a pure emanation of the glory of the Almighty.

Revelations of Divine Love, by Dame Julian of Norwich
(c. 1417, commemorated in the church calendar, May 8)
I beheld the working of the blessed Trinity in which beholding I saw and understood these three properties: the property of the Fatherhood, and the property of Motherhood, and the property of Lordship—in one God. . . . The human mother will suckle her child with her own milk, but our own beloved Mother, Jesus, feeds us with himself and with most tender courtesy does it by means of the Blessed Sacrament.

These two texts—one taken from the Wisdom literature written in the latter half of the first century before Christ and the other [a] Christian classic written in the late fourteenth or early fifteenth century—express the hunger of humankind for a feminine dimension of the divine absent from our formulation of the Holy Trinity as God the Father, Son, and Holy Spirit. If one were to go to the other extreme and speak of God the Mother, Daughter, and Holy Spirit, probably you would be shocked, yet this juxtaposition of language dramatizes the effect which sexual imagery has upon our concept of God. In continuing our reflections upon this theme today, my purpose is not to propose sudden and drastic changes in our liturgy, as some of you may have feared, but to bring to your attention the growing tension in Judeo-Christian tradition between a rhet-

oric which undeniably emphasizes the maleness of God and the results of biblical research within the past fifteen to twenty years which point to the rediscovery of a long neglected "feminine dimension of the divine" in scripture. Our
dilemma is: how shall this feminine symbolization of God be expressed? New
currents of thought within Christian tradition are better understood when there
is a dialogue between laity and seminary-trained clergy who have an obligation
to share what they have learned through intensive study of theology and biblical criticism. I therefore propose that next Sunday's sermon time be set aside
for members of our congregation to respond to this and last Sunday's sermon
with their own comments and reactions.

When Paul says, as in today's Epistle, "So then brethren . . . all who are led
by the Spirit are sons of God. . . . When we cry 'Abba! Father!' It is the Spirit
himself bearing witness with our Spirit that we are children of God" (Romans
8:14, 15b–16), he seems to be speaking of a community in which women have
no place and of an attribute of the divine which excludes all feminine experience. In the Old Testament lesson, when God says to Moses, "I am the God of
Abraham, the God of Isaac, and the God of Jacob," ignoring their counterparts
Sarah, Rebecca, and Rachel, it has the same effect upon many thoughtful women
as the words "I am [the] God of white people" would have upon the Black members of a congregation. Such passages led biblical scholar Phyllis Bird to comment, "The Old Testament is a man's 'book' where women appear for the most
part simply as adjuncts of men, significant only in the context of men's activities . . . a collection of writings by males from a society dominated by males.
These writings portray a man's world. They speak of events and activities engaged in primarily by males (war, cult and government) and of a jealously singular God, who is described and addressed in terms normally used for males."[1]

Consequently, we have inherited from a male-oriented tradition metaphors such as God our Father, Lord, King, and husband. However, recent biblical scholarship has uncovered female imagery in the Old Testament, long ignored, sometimes mistranslated, and generally repressed, but which provides
scriptural basis for symbolizing God as "Mother" as well as "Father" if we are to
describe God in the language of human experience. Consider the opening verses
of the book of Genesis (1:1–2):

> In the beginning God created the heavens and the earth. The earth was
> a formless void; there was darkness over the deep. And the Spirit of God
> hovered over the water.

This is the image of God's life-giving power associated with birth, including the birth of human beings. It can be seen as the image of a mother hovering over her child, an image captured by the twentieth-century poet and coauthor of the Negro National Anthem, "Lift Every Voice and Sing," James Weldon Johnson. In his sermon-poem "The Creation," Johnson writes,

> And there was the great God Almighty
> Who lit the sun and fixed it in the sky,
> Who hung the stars to the most far corners of the Earth. . . .
> This great God, like a mammy bending over her baby,
> kneeled down in the dust toiling over a lump of clay
> till he shaped it in his own image.[2]

Old Testament scholar Dr. Phyllis Trible has discovered that while the Bible overwhelmingly favors male symbols for deity, there are also expressions of God in female images "such as God the pregnant woman" (Isaiah 42:14), the mother (Isaiah 66:13), the midwife (Psalm 22:9), and the mistress (Psalm 123:2). Trible found that the theme of God as Mother, "who conceived, was pregnant, writhed with labor pains, brought forth a child and nursed it," was "not a minor theme on the fringes of faith. To the contrary, with persistence and power it saturates scripture." In the song of Moses found in Deuteronomy, recounting the history of Israel, Moses says of Israel, "You were unmindful of the Rock (Creator) who begat you and forgot the God who gave you birth" (32:18). Here God is depicted as both father and mother. For while the Jerusalem Bible translates the second part of the text as "the God who fathered you," Trible points out that the Hebrew word used in the second phrase "only designates a woman in labor, and this activity the poetry ascribes to the deity."[3]

The book of Isaiah frequently uses maternal symbols for God as the compassionate mother. When Zion/Jerusalem lamented, "The Lord has forsaken me; my God has forgotten me," God answers, "Can a mother forget the infant at her breast, or a loving mother the child of her womb? Even these may forget, yet I will not forget you" (49:14). Again, when the nation of Israel is defeated, Yahweh (God) cries out, "I have kept silence and held myself in check; now I will cry like a woman in labor, whimpering, gasping and panting" (42:14).

The most dramatic references to a female figure in Hebrew tradition who personifies attributes of God are found in the Wisdom literature of the Old Testament and the Apocrypha, written between about 250 B.C. and the early years of the Christian era. In a well-documented study entitled *The Feminine*

Dimension of the Divine, Dr. Joan Chamberlain Engelsman points to the recent upsurge of scholarly interest in the role of Wisdom in the Old Testament "as well as a widening discussion of the affinities between Wisdom and Christ as they were developed in the New Testament."[4] In Jewish religious tradition overlapping the early Christian era, Wisdom is not only associated with the Spirit, depicted as God's helper, and with God from the beginning, but there are also remarkable similarities and parallels between Wisdom (whose Greek name is Sophia) as the Wisdom of God and the attributes ascribed to Christ as the Word of God in the New Testament writings of Matthew, Paul, and John. We can give only a few hints of these parallels.

Servanthood—Eleanor Roosevelt

The sobering news of the assassination of Indira Gandhi, head of the Indian state of more than 700 million people, and its effect on the stability of relations between nations comes to us as we face a crucial national election in our own country on Tuesday. More and more we realize the interdependence of human life that happens in other parts of the world has a profound effect upon our own lives, and that what we do ourselves affects the destinies of peoples beyond our borders. We are reminded of this interdependence of humanity [by] the seventeenth-century Anglican clergyman and poet John Donne, who wrote,

> No man is an island, entire of itself.
> Any man's death diminishes me, because
> I am involved in Mankind; and therefore
> never send to know for whom the bell tolls;
> It tolls for thee.[1]

Jesus's teaching in Matthew's Gospel lesson today that the greatest among you is the one who serves others confronts us with the standard of Christian living in a world which often seems hopelessly engulfed by selfishness, greed, hatred, violence, and increasing terrorism. Against these evils he has set the power of love, and he used the concept of "servant" not to suggest subordination to superior power but a voluntary self-giving which flows from our response to God's self-giving and forgiving love. Because God cares and values the lives of others, we must also care.

In John's Gospel, Jesus said to his disciples, "No longer will I call you servants . . . but I have called you 'friends,'" and I think we can understand the true meaning of servanthood as Jesus conceived it if we think of the command-ment to be a friend to others.ª Friendliness is not an obligation and does not rest upon coercion or fear. It is a frame of mind, a spontaneous attitude toward our fellow human beings, which creates an atmosphere of trust, a willingness to share, and a caring which considers the needs of others as our own concern. Our calling as Christians in an interdependent but fragmented world is to bear witness to the gospel message that politics based upon violence and coercion can never solve the world's problems and that "the only true source of power is servant-hood rather than dominion."[2] "A truth which must use violence to se-cure its existence cannot be truth. . . . Rather it relies on the slow, hard, and seemingly unrewarding work of witness, a witness which it trusts to prevail even in a fragmented and violent world."[3]

From time to time there arise in human history those men and women whose faithfulness to Christ's standard of servanthood makes them beacons of light to us as we strive to follow the teachings of Jesus Christ. This fall season it is especially appropriate to observe the one hundredth anniversary of the birth of Eleanor Roosevelt, First Lady of the United States from 1933 to 1945, who came to be known as the First Lady of the World and who died at the age of seventy-eight on November 7, 1962. Many of us here are old enough to remem-ber Mrs. Roosevelt when she was alive and can appreciate the tremendous in-fluence she had in the political and social affairs of her time. Recently I returned from her centennial celebration held at Hyde Park, New York, and nearby Vas-sar College as well as at the Smithsonian Institution in Washington, DC. For several days historians and other scholars came together with survivors of the New Deal era who knew and worked with Mrs. Roosevelt to reflect upon her career and the meaning of her life for her own time as well as for today.

Although Mrs. Roosevelt died twenty-two years ago, her vibrant spirit came alive, as speaker after speaker whose lives she had touched told of the impact she had made upon them. What stood out sharply in these memories was that Mrs. Roosevelt was a moral and spiritual force, radiating the essence of good-ness and compassion. One felt this Christ-like force whenever one was in Mrs. Roosevelt's presence. Faces lighted up in joy when she entered a room, and the magic of her personality ran like an electric current through a crowd wherever she passed. Because she was a world-renowned public figure, people approached

Mrs. Roosevelt with awe, but her warmth and simplicity were so embracing that within a few minutes after meeting her one felt at ease as if chatting with an old friend or an affectionate aunt.

Mrs. Roosevelt was an Episcopalian devoted to her church and always kept her Book of Common Prayer on her night table beside her bed. And while she was deeply involved in national and international politics for most of her career, her friend and biographer Joseph P. Lash wrote of her: "Fundamentally, Eleanor was neither stateswoman, politician, nor feminist. She was a woman with a deep sense of Spiritual mission . . . a woman of extravagant tenderness and piety. There was always a prayer in her purse to recall her to her Christian mission."[4] One of my most vivid memories of Mrs. Roosevelt was during a visit to Val-Kill Cottage, and while we were deeply engaged in an animated political discussion Mrs. Roosevelt was unobtrusively filling out and stuffing her church envelope for her weekly offering. When I was at Hyde Park in mid-October, I visited the Eleanor Roosevelt Wing of the Roosevelt Library and saw a glass case containing items Mrs. Roosevelt carried in her purse. Along with her I.D. cards and other documents was a slip of paper on which was typed "A Negro Preacher's Prayer," which reads,

> Lord, we ain't what we oughta be;
> we ain't what we wanna be;
> we ain't what we gonna be;
> but, thank God, we ain't what we WUZ.

Lash wrote that Mrs. Roosevelt lived her faith "every hour of every day. She had disciplined herself never to evade an issue or an appeal for help, and in every situation she asked not only what was to be done but what she herself must do."[5] During her . . . years in the White House, and particularly during the Great Depression, the millions of poor unemployed workers, disinherited sharecroppers, oppressed racial minorities, and women in need all felt they had a friend at the seat of government who would go to bat on their behalf. During her first year in Washington alone, more than 300,000 letters asking for help poured across her desk. Appeals to her did not cease, even after she left the White House. She once told me that while she could not help directly every person who wrote her, she tried to do something about every letter. She would answer personally or forward the letter to a government agency or official or to the National Democratic Committeeperson in the locality where the writer lived, for investigation and possible assistance with the problem described. No appeal was ignored. The story is told by a Black mother who felt her son was a victim of racial discrimination and wrote to President Roosevelt.

Although Mrs. Roosevelt held no public office during her White House years, she acted as the "conscience of the New Deal" and used her prestige as First Lady on behalf of the forgotten, bringing together influential people to promote social reforms, prodding public officials and particularly President Roosevelt as she pleaded for those who had no voice in government and no power. High on her list of priorities was civil rights; she served on the national board of [the] NAACP during the turbulent years of initial desegregation in the South, and the then executive director of [the] NAACP, Walter White, said of her in 1955, "She gave many Americans, particularly Negroes, hope and faith which enabled them to continue the struggle for full citizenship." From the White House she moved on to the United Nations, chaired the Commission on Human Rights, and was the moving force in producing the Universal Declaration of Human Rights, which has become a world standard of the goal of human dignity. Her last public service was to chair President Kennedy's Commission on the Status of Women.

Mrs. Roosevelt's humility and simplicity were apparent to all who encountered her. A former Red Cap told of seeing her standing alone on the platform at Pennsylvania Station waiting for a train that was delayed and declining to make her presence known to the station officials who would have insisted upon giving her VIP treatment. And Dorothy Height recounts the story told to her by the woman who was with Mrs. Roosevelt during her last illness. Mrs. Gussie Taylor, who had worked in the Roosevelt household in the early years but had retired because of illness, was called back in the weeks before Mrs. Roosevelt's death. "The day before Mrs. Roosevelt died, Gussie, as a faithful servant, had reached to help Mrs. Roosevelt turn over to a more comfortable position, only to hear her say, 'Remember, Gussie, the doctor told you not to lift anything heavy.'" And Mrs. Taylor, who would have done anything to help Mrs. Roosevelt in her dying hours, told Dorothy Height, "Just think, there she was thinking of me!"

Mrs. Roosevelt tried to see human life as a whole and to teach by example. She lived by the creed, "The influence you exert is through your own life, and what you've become yourself." While she never ran for public office herself, she believed in the importance of individual participation in the political process. She worked unceasingly within the Democratic Party and forged new roles for women in politics and in government. It seems fitting that in the one hundredth year of her birth, the party to which she gave her allegiance should choose a woman as candidate for vice president of the United States. If she were alive today she would remind us that there is no higher privilege and responsibility of citizenship than exercising the right to vote, that the ballot box is the one area of our national life where the vote of the lowliest citizen carries the same weight as the vote of the president, and that it is the solemn duty of each of us to cast our vote prayerfully and thoughtfully on Tuesday. Nor would Mrs. Roosevelt despair in the face of gloomy political predictions. Whatever the outcome of the election she would continue to ask the questions she did when confronted with the problems of her own time: "Can't something be done?" and "What can I do to help?"—questions which each of us must answer in our own hearts, as we seek to conform our lives to Jesus Christ who said, "The greatest among you is the one who serves others."[b]

Notes

[a] John 15:15.

[b] Matthew 23:11.

Sermon on Isaiah 6:1–4

Isaiah 6:1–4

The Spirit of the Lord God is upon me; because the Lord hath anointed me to preach good tidings unto the meek; he hath sent me to bind up the broken-hearted, to proclaim liberty to the captives, and the opening of the prison to them that are bound; To proclaim the acceptable year of the Lord, and the day of vengeance of our God; to comfort all that mourn; To appoint unto them that mourn in Zion, to give unto them beauty for ashes, the oil of joy for mourning, the garment of praise for the spirit of heaviness; that they might be called trees of righteousness, the planting of the Lord, that he might be glorified. And they shall build the old wastes, they shall raise up the former desolations and they shall repair the waste cities, the desolation of many generations.

I have selected this passage for our reflections because it seems to describe more eloquently than anything I can say to you this morning where I am and where many women of our church are who are seeking admission to Holy Orders as their vocation. Six months ago, you sent me forth as a member of your congregation with your blessings and prayers to begin my training for the sacred ministry. This is my first opportunity to return to my home parish church and give an account of myself. I must confess I am torn between the joy of being back in my sponsoring parish and the nervousness of any first-year seminarian called upon to proclaim the Word of God from the pulpit.

One of the first lessons we learn at seminary is a profound sense of our own unworthiness and the awesomeness of the task we have set for ourselves in tension with a commitment which will not permit us to escape the pain, the doubts, the fears that assail every confessed Christian in moments of personal crisis.

Secondly, we learn that every Christian baptized into our church is admitted to membership in the royal priesthood of Christ and has a ministry, whether one is male or female, old or young, white or Black, lay member or clergy. Those of us who feel a special call to seek Holy Orders do so not because we are better Christians or more able than our brothers and sisters but because something has happened to us and there has taken place a radical shift of God's meaning from the periphery to the very center of our lives. We dare to answer this call because, in a very real sense, we have no choice in the matter. God has spoken to us through an event or through a series of events, which point us in one direction—toward full-time service of God. Like the prophet Isaiah and the other prophets of the Old Testament, we are compelled to believe that sinful, rebellious, broken as we are, God is using us as instruments of his will—not ours—to love and serve him and our fellow human beings to the greater glory of God our Creator and Redeemer.

This decision makes us vulnerable to hurt, to heartache, to sorrow and suffering—for our very striving to be open to God's will intensifies our sensitivity to the tragedies of the human condition and we soon learn that without the love of God we are all lost, rudderless, without direction—an aircraft out of control and without a pilot. We have made the choice to reject our human drive to be self-sufficient and self-dependent and to follow the example of Jesus Christ in utter dependence upon God and radical obedience to God's will, not our own. Each day as we try to follow this example, we are chastened and humbled by our own shortcomings, our own self-willed disobedience and sinfulness and excessive self-centeredness in which state of being we hurt others and fail to live up to our commitments. Each day we are made more acutely conscious of how difficult it is to be a Christian, even in a small intimate community of committed Christians headed by twenty-three or more ordained priests.

Our failures, our weaknesses would overwhelm us were it not for the fact that each day we gain a growing sense of God's infinitely tender love and mercy, and the gifts of grace bestowed upon us impel us to sing out spontaneously in hymns of joy, thanksgiving, and praise.

Because I am a woman, I must speak of this call through the experience of a woman—my own experiences and those of other women seminarians who have shared their hopes and dreams and tears of heartbreak with me.

Why is it that at this particular moment in the history of our church and of other faiths women are beginning to rise up and seek the ordained priesthood with such determined insistence? Is it a product of the women's liberation movement as others suggest? Cannot women be content to serve as members of the royal priesthood of Christ as they have served from the beginning of the Church? Why do they clamor to be admitted to all levels of the clergy—the diaconate, the priesthood, the episcopacy? Why, in the face of the devastating rejection at the Louisville General Convention of last October 1973—a rejection which Bishop Paul Moore of New York has called the violation of the very core of their personhood . . . increased . . . determination to enter the higher levels of the clergy? And why must their call no longer be denied?

As I have pondered these questions since I left you last August and searched for answers, I find myself reflecting upon human history and looking at comparable periods in the long pilgrimage of humankind toward God, our Creator, Redeemer, and Savior, from death and nothingness.

The God of the Christian faith and the God of the prophets of Israel moves, acts, and speaks in history through events and through individuals. Throughout all human history—today as well as 2,500 years or more ago—our God is active in the affairs of humankind to bring us to redemption, salvation, and reconciliation with him, the source of our being. We were created in his image and are the objects of an ineffable love, which passes or transcends all human understanding. But we were also created with the freedom of will—the choice to love God and obey him or not to love God. Being human, finite, and therefore imperfect, each of us, all of us, from the dawn of human history cannot resist the temptation to try to be God ourselves, to set our wills, our goals, our selfish interests above the will of God.

The more our cunning brains invent and the more dominion we achieve over the world we live in, the more our tendency is to rely upon ourselves, and even to shift the blame for our own sins and shortcomings upon God. How often have we heard skeptics say, "How could a loving God let such terrible things happen in the world?" In our drive for possessions, for dominion over nature, for power, status, and prestige, we too often forget that our relation to the earth is that of stewardship—not ownership; that our destiny is not limited to our finite life; that we continually stand in God's judgment and that we can escape the terrible consequences of our many failings only through God's grace; that we are engaged in a pilgrimage toward a higher and better life—toward union with God—and that this life we now live is a stage of our preparation for this higher destiny.

This radical departure from our God-ward destiny has been particularly evident in certain periods of human history and has produced crises, which have destroyed whole nations and peoples. The United States of 1974 is frighteningly like the people of Israel with their divided kingdoms in the eighth and seventh centuries B.C. In both periods of history we see certain common features: a comparatively advanced civilization, militarized dominion over weaker peoples, governmental intrigues, political assassinations, exploitations of the poor by the rich, neglect of the weak and defenseless, dishonesty and deceit in the marketplace, bribery and corruption of public officials and of the administration of justice, the drive for affluent living, carousing and lavishment as in food and drink, the jockeying for supremacy by the international great powers, and above all the apostasy of the chosen people—the falling away from God. In the eighth century B.C., the people gave lip service to Yahweh and took for granted that as the elect, God's chosen people, they would be saved. In the United States of the late twentieth century, we have relied upon our military strength, our bountiful natural resources, our "America First" mentality, and our historical ethos of "Manifest Destiny."

And we are now in a deep and pervasive national crisis not unlike the crisis the eighth-century prophets and their successors foresaw in their own era. In such periods of human crisis, God has called forth prophets who will not be silenced, who will not be coopted by the established hierarchies whether they be clerical or secular. The role of these prophets is to call the people to repentance, to a return to the God of salvation. Their message is twofold. They speak of the awful judgment of God's anger and the infinite tenderness and mercy of God's love. They proclaim that the gloom, which attends the devastation, will be followed by salvation and joy and the rebuilding on the part of those who remain faithful to God.

I believe that today God has chosen his messengers to warn of God's judgment upon a sinful and rebellious people and simultaneously to bring a gospel of hope and joy to those who will listen and have faith. I believe that God is choosing these messengers from the ranks of the dispossessed, the oppressed, and from those who have listened to his word and are open to feel deeply . . . human sorrow and need.

Nothing less than the urgency of their mission, born of the depths of our moral and social crisis, could impel them to face the incredible barriers which have existed for thousands of years, to endure the ridicule and even violence of their detractors, and the continual heartache of rejection which blocks their path and makes their burden almost intolerable. I believe that these women are in truth the suffering servants of Christ, "despised and rejected," women of sorrows and acquainted with grief. They are answering to a higher authority than that of the political structures of our church, and in the fullness of time God will sweep away those barriers and free the church to carry forward its mission of renewal as a living force and God's witness in our society.

As I have already said, the remarkable quality of the Old Testament prophets is their dual message of judgment and salvation. It is this hope of reconciliation with God and our sisters and brothers, which is the Christian joy—an ebullient, loving, giving, and forgiving joyousness which we experience in our beloved associate rectors, Al Kershaw and Jack Greeley. (I hope you will forgive my irreverence when I tell you that I call Al Kershaw an outsized Pixie and Jack Greeley the Jolly Green Giant!) We see it in those great spirits like the late Eleanor Roosevelt and others who have endured many agonies of loss or privation or even oppression, but who, sustained by an abiding faith that they are children of God and the objects of his love, grow through their trials and radiate a spirit of loving kindness to everyone.

I sense this joy on the women of our church who, supported by their own faith and by the open and sincere concern by many of their brother clergy, realize that tears sown in this night of temporary despair will bring joy in the morning. As I have watched my sisters in seminary serving as acolytes at the altar, as crucifers carrying the cross, as lay readers and intercessors, as senior seminarians leading the morning prayer and evensong, as they carry on their ministries to one another, to their male brethren, to the sick and the dying, I am brought back to the words of Isaiah and the prophecy which will be fulfilled when the church recognizes their full humanity:

> The Spirit of the Lord God is upon me; because the Lord hath appointed me to preach good tidings unto the meek; he hath sent me to bind up the broken-hearted, to proclaim liberty to the captives, and the opening of prisons to them that are bound; . . . to give unto them beauty for ashes, the oil of joy for mourning, the garment of praise for the spirit of heaviness; And they shall build the old wastes, they shall raise up the former desolateness, and they shall repair the waste cities, the desolations of many generations.

Let Us Pray.

On the Strivings of the Faithful

Let Not Your Heart Be Troubled

John 14:1, 8–10

Let not your heart be troubled; you believe in God, believe also in me. . . .
Philip said to him, "Lord, show us the Father, and we shall be satisfied."
Jesus said to him, "Have I been so long a time with you, without your really
knowing me, Philip? . . . Do you not believe that I am in the Father, and
the Father in me? The words that I speak to you I speak not of myself; but
the Father that dwelleth in me, he doeth the works."

Our text is selected from the Gospel according to St. John, the appropriate reading for the feast of St. Philip and St. James, apostles, which occurs on May 1. St.
Philip, as we know, is the patron saint of this parish and his feast day coincides
with the seventy-eighth-anniversary celebration of St. Philip's Episcopal Church
in Brooklyn, which began with thirteen men and women who met together on
the 1st of May 1899 at the home of Esther A. Reese.

As we celebrate this significant event in the religious life of the Brooklyn
community, we reflect upon one of the most beloved passages in the New Testament, one to which we turn again and again in time of trouble. The occasion
is the final meal Jesus of Nazareth shares with his disciples before he goes out
to meet his death by torture and crucifixion, an execution reserved for the degraded criminals in the Roman Empire of the first century. The mood is one of
apprehension and uncertainty as the disciples become dimly aware of impending separation from their master and teacher. The words of comfort which Jesus
spoke to them on that solemn day have come down to us over the years—words

of reassurance when we are hesitant and unsure of ourselves, words of courage to strengthen our faith in a time of crisis, words of strength in the face of trials in which we are tested to the very limits of our capacity, and above all words of *hope* with which to meet that supreme crisis in the life of every human being— the crisis of our own death.

Is it not a paradox to speak of sorrow and death on a day of joyous celebration, of homecoming and reunion of family and friends? Have we not passed through the season of Lent, the Passion Week, and now stand in the afterglow of the Resurrection story? Is not the month of May in both religious and secular tradition a month which rings with anthems of rebirth, and when the very earth, in our part of the world at least, is a riot of color and fragrance—lilacs, tulips, azalea, and roses?

Yes, it is a paradox, but human life is full of paradoxes which exist alongside of one another—acts of absurdity in the most solemn of moments, courage and abject anxiety cropping up in the same personality, doubt and uncertainty at the very heart of faith, *humor* undergirding tragedy. Jesus Christ understood these paradoxes of the human condition, for was not his own life a paradox— colossal failure, defeat, and scandal preceded his victory over death.

Professor William Lyon Phelps once said, "You can learn more about human nature reading the Bible than by living in New York City," and there is great truth in this statement.[1] Our patron saint, Philip, living two thousand years ago, reflected in his own life the paradox of great faith and great doubt in the same personality. According to John's Gospel story, he was one of the first disciples in Galilee to be called by Jesus of Nazareth. He lived in the city Bethsaida, the city of Andrew and Peter. We are led to believe that he was a man of great faith, a seeker after righteousness, steeped in the religious traditions of the people of Israel, waiting for the fulfillment of the prophecy of the Old Testament— the coming of the Messiah.

When Jesus of Nazareth found him and said, "Follow me," he did not hesitate. He knew that moment for which he had been waiting had come. The impact of his encounter with Jesus was so compelling that he went to his friend Nathaniel, bursting with the news of his discovery. He said, "We have found him, of whom Moses in the law and the prophets, did speak, Jesus of Nazareth, the son of Joseph."[a]

Philip's conviction was so strong that he was not put off by Nathaniel's skepticism—a skepticism we so often encounter today among our friends in a world engulfed in secularism. When Nathaniel asked, "Can any good thing come out of Galilee?" Philip replied simply, "Come and see [for yourself]."[b] And Philip was not disappointed in his faith. Nathaniel went to see and had spoken only a few words with Jesus before he confessed, "Rabbi, thou art the Son of God; thou art the King of Israel."[c]

The other glimpses of Philip's character in John's version of the Gospel story suggest that he was one of Jesus's most trusted and reliable followers—in today's language, a facilitator, a coordinator, an enabler. (We sometimes speak of the office of a deacon as that of an enabler, one who serves others in the church and helps them carry out their parish objectives; one who looks after the ar-rangements for funerals, weddings, baptisms, programs of outreach, etc., and keeps up with the necessary details so that everything is carried out smoothly.) For example, when Jesus crossed the Galilee and went up into a mountain but saw a great multitude following him who had brought no food with them, Jesus turned to Philip to ask where they might buy bread to feed five thousand people. And certain Greeks attracted to Judaism joined the caravans of Jews who had come to Jerusalem to worship at the feast of the Passover just before Jesus was arrested and crucified. They had a great desire to meet and talk with this new prophet who was the subject of such controversy among the Pharisees, scribes, and Sadducees, and they went to Philip to act as their intercessor and obtain an audience with Jesus.

Yet during that final meal, when Jesus himself was troubled in spirit and in his human aspect needed the support and understanding of his followers, it was Philip—Old Reliable—whose faith seemed to falter at the crucial moment, who needed proof of God's presence at a time of impending separation: "Lord, show us the Father, and it sufficeth us."[d]

Jesus's answer revealed the hurt and disappointment we all feel when a close friend on whom we depend suddenly lets us down or fails to understand us: "Have I been so long [a] time with you, and yet you have not *known* me, Philip?"[e]

"Do you not believe that I am the Father and the Father is me? The words I speak unto you, I speak not of myself; but the Father that dwelleth in me, *he doeth the works.*"[f]

Although we are not told how Philip responded to this loving rebuke, we know from our own experiences how often, like Philip, our own faith falters, how we worry and fret and are filled with despair over the problems of our lives and the more intractable problems of the society in which we live. In times of national and international crisis, we too demand proof of God's love and providence. When we agonize over mankind's inhumanity and insensitivity to fellow human beings—the tyranny of the official South African government, which holds millions of Blacks and Coloreds in virtual peonage; the continual struggle against the persistence of discrimination because of race or sex or age or other stereotyped classifications within our own country; the neglect of our cities, which are falling into decay; the projection of blame upon the victims of poverty and exclusion; the frustrations of trying to keep our sanity in an uncaring society which seems addicted to the drug of material gain and cares little for the human factor—we too waver between belief and unbelief.

Out of the urgency of the moment, the knowledge of his own approaching passion and death, Jesus of Nazareth spoke the words which give us the key to the Christian way of life, the hope of overcoming the paradoxes of the imperfect human existence—"Not I, but the Father in me, he doeth the works."[g]

Much of our anxiety, our fear, our disbelief, our despair is rooted in our human tendency to rely upon our own strength and to fail to recognize our utter dependence upon God, the creator and preserver of our universe. When we fail, when we fall flat on our faces, we are tempted to question the wisdom, even the existence of God. Jesus Christ was able to say, "Let not your heart be troubled," to counsel serenity in the midst of social chaos, because he *knew* that all which was required of him was to bring his will into harmony with God's will, to live and act in utter obedience to God, even unto death. His power was the power of God working in him and through him, the response of the Christian to God's illimitable love and compassion. Living in accordance with God's will does not spare us from the pain of suffering ourselves or seeing others suffer; it makes us an instrument of God's power working to bring all creation into harmony and perfection in the fullness of time.

Surrendering our human wills to the Eternal Will is perhaps the most difficult task of the Christian life because all of us are so prone to say, "Thy will be done *my* way!" It is a human tendency to shrink from pain, discomfort, conflict. Even Jesus, at the threshold of his greatest witness to the power of God, prayed, "Abba, Father, all things are possible unto thee; take this cup from me," and then he added, "nevertheless not what I will, but what thou wilt."[h]

As Jesus spoke to Philip, I believe that God speaks to us through those we love and through the circumstances of their lives. In moments of personal crisis, we are most open to hear God's words, and in the circumstances of approaching death, particularly the death of a loved one, we seem to be in closest touch with the eternal—we stand at the very boundary between what we call finite life and what we believe is eternal life. At such moments we glimpse what is the fundamental purpose of our lives—the mission of love and service—without which all our achievements are in vain.

Let Us Pray.

O God, as we celebrate the seventy-eighth anniversary of the mission and outreach of St. Philip's Episcopal Church in Brooklyn, give us the courage and faith to go on, to carry our share of the burden through to the end, to live all the years of our life, faithful to the highest we have seen, with no pandering to the second best, no leniency to our lower selves, no looking backward, and no cowardice. Enable us to break the bread of life to suffering humanity, and to serve our world in the spirit of Jesus Christ our Lord.

Amen.

Notes

[a] John 1:45.

[b] John 1:46.

[c] John 1:49.

[d] John 14:8.

[e] John 14:9.

[f] John 14:10.

[g] Ibid.

[h] Mark 14:36.

Put Up Your Sword

Matthew 26:49-52

And he came up to Jesus at once and said, "Hail Master!" And he kissed him. Jesus said to him, "Friend, why are you here?" Then one of those who were with Jesus stretched out his hand and drew his sword, and struck the slave of the high priest, and cut off his ear. Then Jesus said to him, "Put your sword back into its place; for all who take the sword will perish by the sword."

Luke 22:51

But Jesus said, "No more of this!" And he touched his ear and healed him.

The story of the Passion grips us as perhaps no other event in human history because it packs into a few days all the drama and paradoxes of human experience and lays bare the barbarism as well as the compassion of the human situation. Passion Week begins with Jesus's entry into Jerusalem at the high point of his public ministry, a triumphant procession of royal acclaim, yet imbued with the symbol of deepest humility—the crowds going before him, spreading their garments and the branches of palm trees on the road, shouting, "Hosanna to the Son of David," or in St. Luke's Gospel, "Blessed is the King who comes in the name of the Lord! Peace in Heaven and glory in the highest!" to one clad in simple clothing and riding upon a lowly donkey.

Jesus's long anticipation of bringing his message to Jerusalem, to the capital of Judea, "the city of the Great King," is followed by rising political tensions and confrontation with the established authorities. It was a message about the Kingdom of God which threatened their power. His achievement of reaching the

great city is followed by sorrow, foreboding, apprehension, and fear. The tenderness of communion with intimate friends and disciples with whom Jesus has
shared hunger and thirst, companionship, the weariness of traveling the dusty
roads, the joy of healing—all this is followed by betrayal and desertion. The
peacefulness of prayer is shattered by illegal arrest; attempted resistance is
rebuked and followed by healing and a spirit of reconciliation. Finally, the ordeal of star-chamber proceedings, a "trial" of sorts on trumped-up charges; the
quick transformation of the mob from popular acclaim to bloodthirsty, "Crucify
him, Crucify him!"; the passing of the buck, from the Roman curator, Pontius
Pilate, to the Jewish rabble in the streets; the customary flogging and taunting
of a victim sentenced to death on the cross, a process calculated to humiliate
and degrade human personality to the utmost in preparation for the most cruel
and obscene execution known to the ancient world—a slow torturous death by
crucifixion.

   As we reflect upon this rapid succession of events in the closing chapter
of the life of Jesus of Nazareth, we are enabled to participate more fully in his
passion by reference to crude parallels and paradoxes in our own contemporary
existence: the triumphant return of the American former hostages from Iran
bringing an upsurge of national joy followed by the domestic tragedy of Atlanta,
which still continues; the fantastic spectacle of national, regional, and ethnic
pageantry at the Reagan inauguration followed by near-death in the streets
through the ubiquitous handgun wielded by a wandering "drifter." Within the
same week we witnessed on television the continuous replay in slow motion of
the attempted assassination of President Ronald Reagan and the grave wound-
ing of three public servants, and we observed the thirteenth anniversary of the
assassination of the late Dr. Martin Luther King Jr., which also followed a triumphant march and public acclaim. The fact that in the one case the act seemed
senseless and in the other it was politically inspired does not alter the horror to
those who value human life and personality.

   If I were the prophet Isaiah, I would be tempted to proclaim to our
president,

> Thus, saith the Lord, this is a warning. You are the leader of a great people
> who have lost their way and are worshipping the false gods of violence. As
> a leader, you have been altogether too tolerant of handguns, and now you
> are the victim of a handgun at the very moment inspired and vigorous
> leadership is crucial to the survival of freedom and human dignity. With an

estimated 50 million handguns circulating in private hands, the stage is set for anarchy and guerilla warfare in a major domestic catastrophe. Will you speak out or will you equivocate?

But since I am not the prophet Isaiah, I will leave the president to his trusted advisors and resort to prayer.

There are historical events of such magnitude that each of us living at the time recalls vividly where we were and what we were doing at the very moment of the event. In Baltimore, on Monday afternoon, March 10, 1981, I was at the office of the bishop of the Diocese of Maryland from 2:30 to 3:20 p.m. and learned that the president had been shot when Bishop Leighton showed me to his outer office at the end of our conference. As I left the building, I stopped in the chapel downstairs in Diocesan House to pray on behalf of our president.... In the hours which followed, I suspect that millions of people like myself became "instant Republicans" for the moment, for if the president of the United States, who was not in some far-off place but in the very seat of the national government, could not be protected from the evil hand of an assassin, no one of us could walk the streets in broad daylight without fear. And I think in those long hours of uncertainty, a whole nation was engaged in spontaneous prayer. Without detracting one whit from the superb medical skill of the George Washington University Hospital staff, I think the "extraordinary progress" of White House press secretary James S. Brady, a man pronounced dead on television—as well as the rapid recovery of President Reagan and the others—is the result of communal prayer power.

Jesus's long vigil of prayer in the Garden of Gethsemane prepared him for the ultimate ordeal of his life and mission. Through prayer he gained the strength to face his mortal enemies with calm and compassion, to say to a zealous defender who sought to protect him, "Put your sword back in its place. All who take to the sword will die by the sword."[a] He knew the basic truth that hostility breeds further hostility, that armed resistance aggravates the situation of violence and there are no victors in violent contests. He knew that the work of the Holy Spirit—redemptive love, reconciliation, and peace—cannot be accomplished when human hearts are choked and enflamed by brutal combat.

Let us suppose from the human side of the gospel that in that Garden of Gethsemane Jesus and his disciples, knowing that they had engaged in no unlawful act, had sought to defend themselves against the mob from the chief priests and elders armed with swords and clubs. The Roman soldiers probably would have intervened, doubtless there would have been a massacre and what would have come down to us in history—if, indeed, it were recorded at all—would have been another incident in Jewish resistance to Roman rule, not unlike the drama of *Masada,* presented on television during the past week, a powerful story of human heroism, it is true, but not the message of the glorious Resurrection. This is not to condemn the theme of *Masada*—the love of liberty so great that it was more precious to the embattled Jews than mere existence in abject slavery under Roman rule—but to say that Jesus of Nazareth pointed us toward a greater power than armed resistance.

The lesson of the cross is that the battle does not end with the Crucifixion. From the agony of that cross came the Christian faith, for the Crucifixion and the Resurrection are part of an inseparable event. As weak, sinful, ineffective, like Peter lacking in courage in moments of crisis, as we Christians so often seem to be and are, ask yourselves what would the world be like today without the Christian faith?

Morton Kelsey, an Episcopalian priest and lecturer, has said, "I know of no other religion that faces the problem of human agony and pain and suffering as does Christianity at its best. We Christians are not advised to get off a hopeless world and forget about its problems, but rather to turn toward the cross, pass through the suffering and come to a victory which transcends suffering."[b]

Jesus of Nazareth, the author of our faith, was no "meek" submissive person "turning the other cheek" in the pejorative meaning these words have been given in our contemporary life. It takes a strength rooted in divine power to keep one's eyes fixed upon the goal of redemptive love in the face of every humiliation known to mankind. Jesus risked everything on obedience to God's will and his nonviolence was self-conscious restraint, not acquiescence. Rather than suffer the political corruption of his mission to proclaim the Kingdom of Heaven, he accepted torture and death and left the outcome to God. Through his faith, through his sacrifice, this higher and better way is available to us. We do not need to accept the verdict that terrorism and the threat of nuclear holocaust are the determinants of modern existence. At this moment in history, the eyes of the world and the prayers of faithful people are riveted to the situation in Poland (just as they were riveted to the racial crisis in the southern United States during the 1950s and 1960s) because the international stakes are so high. As James Reston observed in the *New York Times,* in Poland the Soviet Union is confronted by a faith more powerful than its own. . . .

Noting that the Poles are fighting inch by inch for the freedom we Americans take for granted and each day "we do scores of things that the Poles are risking their lives to be able to do," the *New York Times* columnist concluded that "the Poles, by fighting, at such high cost to themselves, to regain their freedom, have offered us a chance to rediscover the meaning of our own."

This characterization of the Polish struggle for freedom and dignity has a familiar ring to *this congregation* at least. I have long believed that in the present world crises one of the greatest human assets the United States possesses is its people of African ancestry. No other sector of the population has had so recent a history of enslavement; has had to fight for its freedom inch by inch; has learned the lessons of survival—albeit at high cost; has demonstrated its faith in democracy for all its imperfections; has had to make its major gains through moral persuasion and peaceful nonviolent action; and through its resolute struggle for human dignity has ignited the flame of freedom in the hearts of other groups, for example, women, Hispanics, ethnic minorities, the aged, the handicapped, homosexuals, and so on. Despite violent episodes in our recent history and periodic withdrawals into our psychic ghetto, our greatest folk hero has become the late Dr. Martin Luther King Jr., who chose to walk in the footsteps of Jesus Christ and to preach a message of universal human relatedness. Symbolically, since the day of Jesus of Nazareth's crucifixion when a Black man from Cyrene was "pressed into service to help him" up the steep hill on the way to Golgotha, we have carried the cross of Christ.

In that thought, as we celebrate the Holy Eucharist once again today in remembrance of Christ's passion, let us in truth go forth into the world, rejoicing—and working—in the power of the Holy Spirit, for we are called as Christians and as the "meek" witness to reconciliation to God and our neighbor—the whole of humankind—through regenerative love to inherit the earth.

Amen.

Notes

[a] Matthew 26:52.

[b] Morton Kelsey, *The Cross* (New York: Paulist Press, 1980), x.

Sermon Given on May 2, 1982

1 John 3:4

To commit sin is to break God's law: sin, in fact, is lawlessness.

1 John 1:5–6

God is light, and in God there is no darkness at all. If we claim to be sharing God's light while we walk in the dark, our words and our life are a lie.

In this letter to a Christian congregation around the beginning of the second century, John seeks to arouse his listeners to the urgency of the choice they must make before the end of all history and the second coming of Christ. He speaks in contrasts—evil and sin are seen as darkness, lawlessness, rebellion against God. Righteousness is seen as light, obedience to God's law. Sinners are the children of darkness, the children of the devil. The righteous are the children of God. The reason that Christ appeared was to destroy the works of the devil.

In recent weeks we have heard the prophetic voices of our own time, speaking with the same urgency of the choice we must make between the works of darkness and the future of all humankind—presenting us with the image of the entire human race walking blindly in the darkness of ignorance or apathy toward a precipice—the abyss of a nuclear holocaust, the doom of the planet earth and every living creature upon it.

In his book *The Fate of the Earth,* Jonathan Schell reminds us that not only are we and all future generations threatened with extinction by the nuclear peril but that also we are authors of that extinction, particularly the populations of the superpowers who support the governments that pose the threat of it. He argues that "when we hide from ourselves the immense preparations that we have made for our self-extermination we do so for two compelling reasons. First, we don't want to recognize that any minute our lives may be taken away from us and our own world blasted to dust, and second, we don't want to face the fact that we are potential mass killers. The moral cost of nuclear armament is that it makes of all of us underwriters of the slaughter of hundreds of millions of people and the cancellation of the future generations—an action whose utter indefensibility is not altered in the slightest degree by the fact that each side contemplates performing it only in 'retaliation.'"[a]

Most of us in this congregation were not yet born or were very young children when the United States dropped the first atomic bomb on Hiroshima, Japan, August 6, 1945, and so can grasp the reality of that horror only in our imagination. In a single explosion of what today would be a relatively small nuclear device, an estimated 130,000 people were killed outright or died of injuries within three months. The center of the city was flattened, 68 percent of the buildings were destroyed or damaged beyond repair, and people within 1 mile of ground zero were subjected to deadly nuclear radiation, made even more deadly by the fact that it cannot be seen or smelled. At the time I was a graduate student at the University of California in Berkeley, and the personal agony of that faraway catastrophe was brought close to me by one of my room-mates. Her name was Miyeko; she was a Japanese American born in the United States and loyal to her country despite the humiliation she and her family suffered by being confined in an internment camp for nearly three years during World War II. Miyeko had only recently returned from the camp and was in the room we shared with a Jewish girl, whose family had escaped from Hitler's Germany, when the horrifying news of the bombing came over the radio. I will never forget the deep pain of that moment when Miyeko spoke through the silence almost as if to herself. She said, "My grandparents live in Hiroshima."

Today, nearly 37 years later, there are about 50,000 nuclear warheads in the world, having an explosive yield of 1.6 million times the explosive yield of the bomb dropped on Hiroshima. We are told that the Soviet Union has about 7,000 large nuclear weapons, each about 1 megaton in size or 80 times the explosive power of the Hiroshima bomb, and an estimated 113 20-megaton bombs capable of being delivered to the United States, each of which has at least 1,600 times the yield of the Hiroshima bomb, plus 13,000 smaller weapons. The burst of the Hiroshima bomb was about two miles; the burst of a twenty-megaton bomb would be twenty-five miles. We are also told that the United States has about nine thousand strategic nuclear warheads capable of being delivered to the Soviet Union by land, sea, or long-range bombers and about twenty thousand smaller nuclear weapons. A single U.S. nuclear submarine carries enough of these devices to destroy every city in the Soviet Union and the same is true of the capacity of a single Soviet submarine to destroy every city in the United States. Nuclear armaments are rapidly spreading to other countries and may soon be in the hands of terrorists. The Union of Concerned Scientists warns, "Each day 3 to 5 new nuclear warheads are being constructed on this small planet and every day brings us closer to the possibility that the terrible destructive force of nuclear weapons will be unleashed."[1]

Such destruction does not have to begin with a planned attack but may be precipitated by a tragic accident. At least three times during the last two years American nuclear forces have been placed on the early stages of alert— twice because of a computer malfunctioning and once because the wrong tape was inadvertently inserted into the warning system. Poised on the brink of suicide, human error as well as human design could seal the fate of humanity.

Ordinary people like ourselves have to close our eyes to the peril which hangs over our heads every minute of our lives and to leave the fateful decisions on nuclear armaments to our governments, but we can no longer plead ignorance nor avoid a response to this crisis in moral values. Just ask yourself what would be the effects of a single one-megaton nuclear bomb burst over the city of Baltimore. Scientific accuracy is such that the device would fall within three blocks of the targeted area. By conservative estimates, all living things within 1 mile from ground zero would be destroyed instantly by the blast and incredible heat. Almost every building within a radius of four miles would be flattened and most buildings within a radius of eight miles (or beyond the beltway) would be heavily damaged.

Winds would reach 400 miles an hour within 2 miles from ground zero, and 2 to 4 miles away winds would reach 180 miles per hour in the blast wave. Who could survive against such a terrific force? From 1 to 3 miles from the explosion 5 percent of the people would be killed and nearly half severely injured. From 4 to 7 miles out, few people would be killed outright but one-quarter would be injured.

Meanwhile, a huge fireball, which would blind temporarily and probably cause permanent eye damage to anyone looking at it from as far as fifty miles away, would grow to more than a mile wide and rocket upward to over ten miles.

For ten seconds it would broil the city below, charring and burning to death instantly any people close to the explosion. Anyone caught out in the open within a radius of nine miles would suffer third-degree burns and probably be killed. Anything flammable like newspapers or dry leaves within 9 miles would ignite, causing mass fires to break out in an area of more than 280 square miles. Minutes after the explosion the day grows dark as heavy clouds of smoke and dust fill the air. A deadly fallout of nuclear radiation would be carried on the wind for 150 miles, and for another 150 miles would cause serious radiation sickness. Nearly one-third of the population would be injured within the first few minutes, most suffering from burns and massive doses of radiation, but all the downtown hospitals would be destroyed and most of the doctors and nurses killed, so no medical help would be available. Power lines and communication would be destroyed, food and water would be contaminated by radiation. The notion of survival through evacuation or shelters is an illusion, as civil defense experts recently testified.

In a broad-scale nuclear attack, evacuation would be transporting people from one death to another, to say nothing of disrupted transportation of food and supplies. Shelters within the city would be useless; it is more likely that people inside them would be asphyxiated from smoke or cremated by the heat. Further away, anyone who did not seal himself or herself within a shelter with food, water, and supplies enough to last for several months would soon die of radiation sickness.

Even if people survived the first stages of the attack, they face the perils of widespread injuries and no medical help; of lethal doses of radiation and eventual death; of piled-up corpses which bring on swarms of insects—the carriers of epidemic diseases; the lack of sanitary facilities—no running water or garbage disposal; the flow of food and supplies nonexistent; the specter [of] starvation ever-present; and the long-term effects of genetic abnormalities ranging from severe birth defects to sterility and the inability to produce the future generation.

It has been asserted that three hundred weapons used by each side could effectively destroy every major city in the United States and Soviet Union and wipe out 60 percent of the population. But these are just the primary local effects. What of the global effects of a full-scale nuclear holocaust? First, there is the "delayed" or worldwide fallout, encircling the earth with radiation, which could kill animals, birds, fish, insects, plants, and trees as well as people. The contamination of the earth and water would run off to oceans, destroying oceanic life. The peoples living outside the targeted area would be threatened by radiation and the loss of food supplies. The lofting of millions of tons of dust and debris in the air is likely to produce a general cooling of the earth's surface and drastically alter the earth's climate. The final threat to human survival would be the partial destruction of the layer of ozone that surrounds the entire earth in the stratosphere and is crucial to life because it acts as a protective shield against the deadly levels of ultraviolet radiation present in sunlight. This projects the possibility of the complete extinction of the human species and other life, leaving a silent and empty planet.

By our silence and inaction, do we not participate in this ultimate evil, this vast collective sin of humankind—the final rebellion against God and God's creation? Is it not the very antithesis of the Christian catechism that "the chief and highest end" of being human "is to glorify God"? We are reminded of the symbolic warning in the book of Genesis: "The tree of knowledge of good and evil you shall not eat, for on the day you eat of it, you shall most surely die."[b] What is the Christian response to the warning of nuclear death?

Amen.

Let Us Pray.

Almighty and eternal God, who has entrusted the minds of human beings with the science and skill which can greatly bless or wholly destroy. Grant them also a new stature of spirit to match your trust; that they may use their skills not for the sins and cruelties of nuclear war but to your glory and the relief of hunger and suffering in the earth, through Jesus Christ our Savior.

Amen.

Notes

[a] Jonathan Schell, *The Fate of the Earth* (New York: Knopf, 1982).

[b] Genesis 2:17.

Sermon Given on April 29, 1984

John 20:29

Jesus said to Thomas, "Because you have seen me you have found faith.
Blessed are those who never saw me and yet have found faith."

John's Gospel story of Doubting Thomas is a familiar one to us, and so utterly
human that we can identify with Thomas in his crisis of faith. He was a loyal
and courageous disciple, but he was also practical and down-to-earth, and he
did not hesitate to question what he did not understand. His loyalty to Jesus
stood out among the other disciples. You will recall earlier in John's Gospel that
Jesus got into a heated controversy with the Jewish religious leaders in the
Temple at Jerusalem. The Jews were so enraged over Jesus's parable of the Good
Shepherd that they picked up stones to stone him. As the argument continued,
they tried to seize him but he escaped and sought refuge in a place across the
Jordan. He was there when he received a message from Mary and Martha from
Bethany that their brother Lazarus was very ill. Now Bethany was a little town
less than two miles from Jerusalem on the road to Jericho, and when Jesus proposed to go to Lazarus, his disciples feared for his safety and argued with him:
"Rabbi, are you going there again? Only a short time ago the Jews there wanted
to stone you."[a] When Jesus insisted that he was going back, it was Thomas who
spoke up. In spite of the dangers which threatened Jesus's life, Thomas told the
others, "Let us also go, that we may die with him."[b]

Loyal though he was in spirit, Thomas could not accept what was not made
clear to him. John's Gospel tells us that when Jesus and [his] disciples gathered

in the Upper Room at the Last Supper, Jesus knew that his fate was sealed and wanted to prepare his disciples for the separation. He told them that he was going away where they could not see him, "and when I go and prepare a place for you, I will come again and take you to myself, so that where I am you may be also and my way there is known to you."ᶜ Thomas was not satisfied with Jesus's attempt to console them; he wanted to know more. And so he questioned Jesus: "Lord, we do not know where you are going; how can we know the way?"ᵈ It was then that Jesus said, recognizing that his way was the way of the cross, "I am the way, the truth and the life; no man comes to the Father, but by me."ᵉ

So it is not surprising that Thomas should be the one to raise doubts when he came back to the group in the Upper Room on Easter night and the disciples told him they had seen the Lord. He had not been with the others when Jesus had first appeared to them behind barred doors, and this may have been the first time he had heard of Jesus's resurrection. He had not visited the tomb as Mary Magdala and the other women had on Easter morning, or when Mary of Magdala ran and told Peter and the other disciple whom Jesus loved, and they went into the tomb and found Jesus's body was no longer there. Nor had he heard the story of the two disciples on the road to Emmaus, told in Luke's Gospel, in which Jesus made himself known to them in the breaking of the bread. Now when he heard the news, it was so stupendous that his mind reeled from shock. Although Jesus had showed his hands and feet to the others with the marks of the Crucifixion still upon them, Thomas doubted their testimony. He said, "Unless I see for myself the print of the nails in his hands and put my finger into the holes they made, and unless I can put my finger into his side, I refuse to believe."ᶠ

A week later, the disciples gathered into the same Upper Room with the doors barred for fear of the Jewish leaders, and this time Thomas was with them. Again, Jesus appeared to them, and he said to Thomas, "Put your finger here and look at my hands; reach your hand here and put it into my side. Stop doubting and believe."ᵍ

We can imagine the awe of this plainspoken man as his disbelief dissolved in the reality of his experience that this was the same Jesus who had hung on the cross and whose side had been opened by the soldier's spear. In the revelation of that moment, he burst out, "My Lord and my God."

How like so many of us Thomas was—wanting to believe but doubting. "Seeing is believing," we say. "I'm not taking anybody's else say-so. I must see for myself." Jesus did not condemn his friend. He understood the depth of human doubt from his own agony on the cross, in the darkest hour of his existence, when he cried out, "My God, my God, why hast thou forsaken me?"[h] He said simply to Thomas, "You believe because you can see me, blessed are those who have not seen and yet believe."[i]

And this brings us to our own struggles with faith. There are those who assume it is wrong to doubt, that one is somehow less Christian if one doubts. But doubt is an element of faith; faith is not certainty that can be scientifically proved or else it would not be faith. Recall that the author of the letter to the Hebrews writes, "Now faith is the substance of things hoped for, the evidence of things not seen" (11:1, King James Version). Other translations are "the conviction of things not seen" or "being certain of the things we cannot see." The Easter story is a matter of faith. No one saw the Resurrection, but something happened of such magnitude that it transformed frightened men and women into bold, courageous witnesses willing to die to proclaim the Risen Christ. And the power of this witness has been so great that it is brought down to us over the centuries as if the event happened yesterday. It is a mystery that we cannot understand with our senses; we can only comprehend it through faith.

What John's Gospel story seems to be telling us is that God is seeking us always, just as Jesus sought out his disciples behind barred doors. Our response to God's seeking is faith. Faith is not easily held in the face of calamity. Sometimes when we are going through an ordeal, we feel so alone and we think God has forgotten us. Our faith weakens and we wrestle with doubts like Thomas and the other disciples who thought that all was lost when their teacher and friend was crucified. But the message of the Easter faith is that there is no Crucifixion without Resurrection. So often, when our faith has reached its lowest ebb and we don't know where to turn, God steps in and our prayers are answered—not always in the way that we prayed for but better for us than anything we could have planned for ourselves.

Through the life, death, and resurrection of Jesus of Nazareth, we learn that God never deserts us, even when our faith is weak and our doubt almost overwhelms us. Through our own suffering and trials of many kinds, we learn, as Peter's Epistle tells us, that we are under the protection of God's power until salvation comes. Peter was writing to the Christians of Asia Minor who were undergoing persecution to encourage them to stand fast in their faith in Jesus Christ. He declared, "Without having seen him you love him, though you do not see him now, you believe in him and rejoice with unutterable and exalted joy."[j]

On the evening of his resurrection, Jesus, the Risen Christ, spoke not only to Thomas but also to the multitudes of us who have followed over the centuries. "Because you have seen me you have found faith. Happy are they who never saw me and yet have found faith."

Notes

[a] John 11:8.
[b] John 11:16.
[c] John 14:3.
[d] John 14:5.
[e] John 14:6.
[f] John 20:25.
[g] John 20:27.
[h] John 27:47.
[i] John 20:29.
[j] 1 Peter 1:8.

Nursing Home Sermon

On Thursday of this coming week, the church celebrates one of the principal feasts of the Christian year—All Saints Day. As often happens it has been overshadowed by the secular festivity of Halloween which comes the night before, but we must not forget that it is a day of special commemoration of all faithful departed souls. We reaffirm that the Christian Church is the "communion of saints," a reminder that the church is much greater than the company of Christians now on earth but includes all those who have gone before us. We emphasize the unity and fellowship of all Christians in Christ, the living and the dead, the continuity of the people of God.

There is a tendency to think of "saints" as only those persons of exceptional holiness, and this is true in part because the church has set aside certain days of the year to honor those great saints whose lives and works are widely known in Christian tradition. According to scripture, however, the word "saints" refers to all people of God who have been sanctified by the Holy Spirit—the humble and anonymous as well as the famous. We are all saints if we are committed to Jesus Christ and continue to grow in grace through the Holy Spirit.

In our communion and fellowship with those who have departed this life, we also acknowledge the mystical unity of past, present, and future, the continuous working of the eternal God in creation, reconciliation, and consummation "in one great action of Holy Being." It is said that the God who creates us and reconciles us to himself "is also the destiny toward which all created things are drawn—a destiny not of death but of new creativity," of new beginnings.[a] We are reminded that we came from God. We belong to God and our true destiny

156

is with God. Remembrance of those departed ones for whom we pray that they may be granted continual growth in God's love and service and that they may go from strength to strength unites us with both our past and future.

All human beings need a sense of the past, a sense of roots and continuity. Professor Letty M. Russell of the Yale Divinity School has said, "Our hope is focused on the future, but draws strength and meaning from the events of the past and present. These events form the tradition which guides our actions and gives meaning to our existence."[1] She points to the *tradition* of God's action in Jesus Christ as part of God's plan to redeem all humanity, which guides and shapes the Christian faith.

Several weeks ago we witnessed the extraordinary power of the past and present in Christian tradition to move millions of people to a spontaneous outpouring of religious feeling. During the visit of Pope John Paul II to the United States, we saw the union of a man of great presence and personal magnetism with the most powerful symbol of the continuity of the Christian Church—the office of the pope—the most continuous high office in Western civilization, stretching back nearly two thousand years in a line of unbroken succession to Peter, disciple of Jesus of Nazareth. John Paul's radiant personality coupled with his prestige as spiritual leader of 700 million Roman Catholics around the world enabled him to make a deeply spiritual impact upon many people whom he touched. He telescoped history for them and gave some of them a momentary feeling of what it must have been like to have been a Christian during Jesus's time. Thus, an eighty-five-year-old woman said, "I feel almost as if I had shaken the hand of Jesus Christ. It felt just that powerful." One did not have to be a Roman Catholic or to agree with all the pope's pronouncements on dogma to feel the power of religious tradition.

Pope John Paul's visit was a dramatic public event, but there are the private events linked with our individual pasts which have shaped and given meaning to our lives. And these events are associated with our own heroes and heroines who have inspired us and strengthened our faith. In the words of Hebrews, "we are surrounded by a great cloud of witnesses" who are part of our history—our loved ones, our personal friends, those with whom we have shared fellowship in our church life, and the many who have touched our lives in various ways. While we tend to think of them as part of the past because they have been separated from us by death, in reality they point us toward the future because they have gone on before us. We believe that in Christ they have met and overcome that last great enemy—death.

All Saints Day reminds us that each of us must come to terms with the certainty of our own death. Because we are human and finite, it is only natural for us to fear the great unknown, the possibility of nothingness. Jesus himself was afraid, and the depth of his humanity is revealed in Hebrews: "In the days of his flesh, Jesus offered up prayers and supplications, with loud cries and tears, to him who was able to save him from death, and he was heard for his godly fear."[b] His humanity was again revealed on the cross when he cried out in his agony, "My God, my God, why hast thou forsaken me?"[c]

In this human cry is the universal fear of separation from God, of being cast into outer darkness. And it is here that faith enters. The Christian faith proclaims that the life, death, and resurrection of Jesus Christ reveals that God does not abandon us, that death does not have the last word. God is our future, always going before us, calling us to work toward perfection, sustaining us with infinite love in all of our suffering and even in death. It proclaims that death is not the end but the gateway to new life. We do not know what the future toward which we move will be, but faith calls us to place absolute trust in God's loving care. On All Saints Day we reaffirm the faith which led a great theologian when he was about to die to call his wife and confide to her, "Of all that I have read and pondered about death over the years, I feel certain of only one thing—that I shall be safe."

Let Us Pray.

O Almighty God, who hast called us to faith in thee, and hast compassed us about with so great a cloud of witnesses; grant that we, encouraged by the good examples of thy Saints, may persevere in running the race that is set before us, until at length, through thy mercy, we, with them, attain to thine eternal joy; through him who is the author and finisher of our faith, thy Son Jesus Christ our Lord.

Amen.

Notes

[a] John Macquarrie, *Principles of Christian Theology* (New York: Scribner and Sons, 1966), 357.

[b] Hebrews 5:7.

[c] Matthew 27:46.

The New Creation

2 Corinthians 5:17–18

And for anyone who is in Christ, there is a new creation; the old creation has gone, and now the new one is here. It is all God's work. It was God who reconciled us to himself through Christ and gave us the work of handing on this reconciliation.

These verses are part of Paul the apostle's letter to the churches of Corinth, in which he sets forth the heart of the gospel message of the ministry of reconciliation. New Testament scholars find no passage in his letters more important than the text we listened to in the Epistle this morning. Paul uses the words "reconcile" and "reconciliation" to describe the changed relations between God and man, which are the result of the death and resurrection of Jesus Christ. To Paul, mankind owes its salvation solely to the grace of God. Reconciliation is the work of God through a decisive act in history—the gospel is the mind-blowing proclamation that a man, human even as we are human, actually conquered death in order that we too might conquer sin and death.

No concept is more fundamental to the Christian faith. Reconciliation means in its essence an exchange of equivalent values, an exchange of sympathy and understanding, and thus a radical change of relations—a new stage of personal relationships in which a previous hostility of attitude or an estrangement has been replaced by mutual fellowship. Thus, in St. Paul's view, reconciliation is an act by which human beings are delivered from a condition of estrangement and restored to fellowship with God, and this act is accomplished by God through the power of the sacrificial death of Christ. According to New Testa-ment scholar F. J. Taylor, it includes other blessings such as peace with God, freedom from bondage to sin and death, fellowship with God and mankind, the notion of adoption as sons and daughters of God; and it "has as its goal the sanctification of believers in a life of ethical and spiritual progress toward per-fection."[1] In your parish theme of this Lenten season you reflect upon the Chris-tian [w]ay as a spiritual pilgrimage toward the New Jerusalem, toward the City of God.

> And for anyone who is in Christ, there is a new creation; the old creation
> has gone, and now the new one is here.[a]

The great stumbling block to wholehearted acceptance of the Christian faith lies in these words and their implications, particularly to contemporary human beings. How can a human being die and rise again? It is not the death of Jesus of Nazareth on the cross [that] baffles us. It is the Resurrection, the Risen Christ, which boggles the mind. If we could get past that stumbling block, we could really believe in the new creation, in the words "dying and rising with Christ," or "Behold, I make all things new." We could really believe that all things are possible with God. For many of us, in our pilgrimage toward eternity, our faith stops just short of this belief in the Resurrection, and yet this is the heart of the Christian gospel; this belief separates the Christian from the non-Christian. It is perhaps our inability to come to grips with this mystery that makes our ministry of reconciliation among human beings so imperfect and ineffective. There is no way around it: either we believe that Jesus Christ died and rose again; or we are something other than Christians.

Perhaps the most important concept I learned in my study of theology in seminary is that *doubt* is an element of *faith;* that if all things could be proven by empirical evidence, it would no longer be *faith.* Faith enters when reason falters. And it was Paul himself who saith, "Faith is the substance of things hoped for, the *evidence* of things unseen."[b]

However, because we are creatures of intellect, our faith in God and in Jesus Christ must appeal to reason. I must confess that I have been one of the doubters, and I continue to shuttle between faith and doubt, praying, "Lord I believe; help thou my unbelief."[c] It was reassuring to me to have my beloved professor of theology, Dr. James A. Carpenter, say that "none of us will know the truth until we get there."[2] How could I become a priest in Christ's church if I did not deal with this mystery? On the one hand I knew from my studies and reflection that "there could be no gospel, not one account, no letter in the New Testament, no faith, no Church, no worship, no prayer in Christendom to this day without the resurrection of Christ."[3]

On the other hand, the New Testament scholarship which has engaged some of the best minds for nearly two thousand years can conclude only with the observation that "it is impossible to gain a satisfactory idea of how the Easter events took place."

The debate among New Testament scholars has increased in volume and intensity in recent years as they try to come to grips with the core of Christian theology, representing both a hope and a mystery, which cannot be penetrated by direct evidence. Let me share with you the observations of two of these scholars, whose thinking helped me as I walked through the darkness of my own doubts. In his introduction to a series of studies called *The Significance of the Message of the Resurrection for Faith in Jesus Christ,* published in 1968, Professor C. F. D. Moule had this to say: "Among Christians who unite in affirming, as central to the Gospel, the final and absolute aliveness of Jesus after his death, the greatest cleavage in contemporary interpretations of this affirmation is between those, on the one side, *who [believe] that the resurrection is the expression of a faith already reached by the first Christians, rather than its cause, and those, on the other side, who hold the opposite, namely, that the resurrection was the cause of a faith which did not previously exist.*" In other words, the debate appears to be between those who seek to praise the Resurrection *within* human history and are thus confronted with insuperable difficulties described by the German scholar [Rudolf] Bultmann as the "incredibility of a mythical event like the resurrection of a corpse," and those who accept the Resurrection as an event *beyond* and *above* history.[4] Thus Neville Clark points out:

> It is obvious that the Resurrection itself is not a "historical" event in the ordinary sense of that term. The New Testament views it as the eschatological deed of God, which shatters history. The historian has to conclude that he has no framework, which will contain it, no corresponding happening with which he might compare it, no language which will capture it. In terms of historical investigation, the last and indisputable facts, which lie on either side of the resurrection are the death and burial of Jesus and the belief of the early church that he has risen. Between these two facts lies some reality which seems to defy definition but demand explanation.[d]

Paul's belief in the Resurrection seems to be rooted in his acceptance of the testimony of other eyewitnesses that they had seen the Risen Lord and in his own vision of the Risen Christ, although his letters never mention the Damascus Road experience. He says only in that stirring passage in 1 Corinthians 15:3ff:

> For I delivered to you as of the first importance what I also received, that Christ died for our sins in accordance with the scriptures, and that he appeared to Cephas [Peter], then to the twelve. Then he appeared to more than five hundred brethren at one time, most of whom are still alive, though some have fallen asleep. Then he appeared to James, then to all the apostles. Last of all, as to one untimely born, he appeared to me. For I am the least of the apostles, unfit to be called an apostle, because I persecuted the Church of God. But by the grace of God, I am what I am, and his grace toward me was not in vain.

Because of the passion of Paul's belief and the power of his pen, the Christian Church is universal, moving outward from a tiny Jewish sect to embrace every corner of the earth. It rests upon an idea so staggering that in spite of the demonic aspects of Christendom, the church has endured for twenty centuries. Why is this so? Is it merely religio-political power and wealth? Why, at the very moment that [the] God Is Dead syndrome sweeps over Christendom, do we have a prophetic movement arise and challenge the very foundations of the Roman Catholic and Anglo-Catholic traditions—namely, the struggle for the ordination of women to the priesthood? I have not yet read the Roman Catholic theologian the Reverend Dr. Hans Kung's 720-page bestseller, *On Being a Christian,* although I own a copy, but I submit that each of us could locate ourselves in one or more of the groups to whom he addresses the book. In addition to those who honestly want to know what Christianity, what being Christian, really means, he says that it is also written for those:

> Who do not believe, nevertheless seriously inquire;
> Who did believe, but are not satisfied with their unbelief;
> Who do believe, but feel insecure in their faith;
> Who are at a loss, between belief and unbelief;
> Who are skeptical, both about their convictions and about their doubts.

In the human condition, we share the contradiction between faith and doubt. As Paul Tillich says, "Man [generic humanity] is ultimately concerned about the infinity to which he belongs, from which he is separated, and for which he is longing."ᵉ Mankind cannot accept death as final—man cannot accept *nothingness, nonbeing.* Says Tillich, "The melancholy awareness of the trend of being toward nonbeing, a theme which fills the literature of all nations, is most actual in the anticipation of one's own death. What is significant here is not the fear of death, that is, the moment of dying. It is *anxiety* about *having* to die. . . . This anxiety is potentially present in every moment. It permeates the whole of man's being; it shapes soul and body and determines spiritual life. . . . The biblical record points to the profound anxiety of having to die in him who was called the Christ."ᶠ

But, as Christians we also share a hope that the sorrows and tribulations of our finite existence are not all there is to it; that we are on a pilgrimage toward some realm of being which is higher and better; that the Good News of the gospel is that there was one man in history so attuned to God that he overcame death and because of his overcoming—"the first fruits of them who slept"—it is possible for all other men, women, and children to overcome death and be transformed, into *what* we do not know, but into some stage of eternity for which our finite life has been the preparation.

And while we have only the testimony of those first-century witnesses and our response in faith to tell us this is true, we see all around us clues pointing in that direction: the evidence of the resurrection, rebirth, and renewal in God's creation—this year's springtime in particular, after an endlessly long and difficult winter we have just experienced. And who has watched a loved one die does not ask, "What happens to the beloved personality I knew? Is this really all there is to his or her existence? Is it my imagination that there seems to be a sudden burst of unexplainable creative energy in my tiny universe? When I look at the serenity of a beloved face from which all suffering has passed and I suddenly am struck by the thought, there is no death; there is nothing to fear," and I feel like rejoicing in the midst of the sorrow of separation, have I really come to experience what St. Paul meant when he said,

> And for anyone who is in Christ, there is a new creation; the old creation has gone, and now the new one is here. It is all God's work. It was God who reconciled us to himself through Christ and gave us the work of handing on this reconciliation.ᵍ

Amen.

Notes

[a] 2 Corinthians 5:17.

[b] Hebrews 11:1.

[c] Mark 9:24.

[d] Neville Clark, *Interpreting the Resurrection* (London: SCM Press, 1969).

[e] Paul Tillich, *Systematic Theology* (Chicago: University of Chicago Press, 1951), 1:14.

[f] Ibid.

[g] 2 Corinthians 5:17.

Sermon on Isaiah 9:2, 6, Luke 2:6–7

Isaiah 9:2, 6

The people who walked in darkness have seen a great light; on those who
live in a land of darkness, a light has dawned. . . . For unto us a child is born,
and to us a son is given, and dominion is laid upon his shoulders. And he
will be named Wonderful Counselor, Mighty God, Everlasting Father, Prince
of Peace.

Luke 2:6–7

While they were in Bethlehem, the time came for Mary to give birth. She
gave birth to a Son, her first-born, wrapping the baby in swaddling clothes,
she laid him in a manger, because there was no room in the inn.

More than any Christmas in recent years, a feeling of malaise seems to hang
over our world. A common complaint among people is "I just can't seem to get
myself together for Christmas. I just don't have the Christmas spirit." And indeed, all around us is misery—10 million people unemployed in our own country and another 2 million who have become discouraged and have dropped out
of the labor market; 30 million or more unemployed in Europe. Newspaper reports of forty thousand children around the world dying every day from hunger
and curable diseases; accidents and deaths of people close to us; frenzied preparations and decorations for a secular Christmas but without the joy of expectation; gloomy predictions of our economic life in 1983 and private charitable
agencies stretched beyond the limits of their resources trying to aid the home-

less, the hungry, the destitute in cities and towns throughout the nation—to say nothing of natural calamities, floods, storms, and fatal fires.

Yet we are here to give praise and thanksgiving for an event which changed the course of history—the birth of a savior. We have just reenacted the ancient story of salvation history. The birth of a child foretold by that great eighth-century B.C. prophet and poet Isaiah, and told in the incomparable poetic language of the New Testament physician and evangelist Luke. As I struggle with this sermon I am supported by the majestic strains of Handel's *Messiah* recorded by Sir Thomas Beecham and the London Philharmonic Orchestra and Chorus.

I am reminded that the dawning of the first century A.D. was very much like our own century—the disintegration of an old era and the beginning of a new; a period of wars and rebellions; political intrigues, assassinations, and crucifixions. The people of Palestine felt the oppression of Roman taxation, the bloody rule of old Herod the Great was ending. But not before he had the rabbis and other leaders of protest against his tyrannical policies burnt alive and with the approval of the emperor, Caesar Augustus, had his son and potential successor, Antipater, executed.

In their misery the people of Israel cried out for deliverance; they clung to their expectancy of a political messiah who would free them from the yoke of their oppression, but most people dreamed of a king like David of old, born in a royal palace in the capital city of Jerusalem, not an anonymous child born of modest parentage in a stable of a small town five miles south of Jerusalem with no one to attend his birth except his parents, Mary and Joseph, and the lowly sheep and cattle, and no one to announce it to the world except a few humble shepherds watching their flocks in the fields nearby.

Only two of the four Gospels tell of the birth of Jesus Christ—Matthew and Luke—and their accounts vary in several important details, written fifty years or more after the Crucifixion. They were second-generation Christians, relying upon oral tradition. It was [as] if those of you born after 1960 were trying to describe the Great Depression from what a few people remembered. But neither Matthew nor Luke was writing biography or history as we think of these forms today. They were writing a proclamation to the Christian communities of their time and place, telling *who* Jesus was and what God accomplished through him. Each approached his task differently. Matthew's account of Jesus's birth emphasized the political atmosphere—the visit of the Magi from the East asking, "Where is he who has been born King of the Jews?" Herod's fear that a rival king had been born and his order that all male children under two years old in Bethlehem be put to death; the flight of Joseph, Mary, and their baby Jesus to Egypt to live in exile until Herod the Great died and they felt it safe to return to Nazareth.

Luke, on the other hand, presents a picture of the profound simplicity of God's saving action. In Luke's eyes the savior of the world came in utter humility, [dis]regarded by the rich and powerful or the religious establishment and known only to a few rough shepherds, considered outcasts and unwelcome at the Temple because they were too poor and preoccupied with the business of earning a living to comply with the meticulous requirements of Temple worship.

Luke's account of the Holy Nativity emphasizes the paradoxes in human existence and that God's ways are not our ways. We rush about madly, caught up in the glitter and tinsel of secular Christmas, worry[ing] about our gifts and decorations, forgetting that the event which we celebrate was one of calm and inner serenity. Mary, the mother of Jesus, who had been told by the angel Gabriel that she would bear a child "who will be called Holy, the Son of God," went quietly about her business, making no elaborate preparations and carrying with her only swaddling clothes to wrap her baby when he was born.

The birth of Jesus Christ joined majesty and humility—the shepherds and the Heavenly Host. It replaced apprehension with reassurance of God's love for all humanity. "Do not be afraid, I bring you good news of great joy, a joy for all people. Today in the town of David a Savior has been born to you; He is Christ the Lord!"

The birth of a child is a miracle, a mystery, and yet the most natural act of humanity. It is also a gift of hope, symbolizing our claim to immortality, the ongoingness of the human race. The message of Christmas is a message of hope—a paradox—in the midst of despair it comes to tell of new life, new beginnings.

God is closest to us when we feel abandoned, when there is no room at the inn in the moment of personal crisis. Luke expresses this closeness in the soaring image: "Suddenly there was with the angel a great throng of the heavenly host, praising God and saying, 'Glory to God in the highest; and on earth, peace among those of good will.'"

The gift of Christmas is the birth of love and self-giving. The nameless shepherds had no gift but the gift of themselves to the Christ child, but it was enough. Symbolic of this self-giving is the story this past week of the unemployed father of eight from Harlem who had been looking unsuccessfully for work for almost a year. Coming home on the subway from his latest rejection he sees a blind man of seventy-five fall between the cars to the tracks just as the train is about to move. Forgetting his own misery, he thinks only, "somebody needs help," jumps down, and drags the man to safety under the narrow platform until the train stops. Overnight he becomes a hero with a job assured.

In the midst of the darkness of our time we celebrate the light of love, hope, and self-giving in the birth of our Lord and Savior Jesus the Christ.

Amen.

Forgiveness Without Limits

Matthew 18:21–22

Peter said unto Jesus, Lord, how oft shall my brother sin against me, and I forgive him? Till seven times? Jesus saith unto him, I say not to thee, Until seven times; but, until seventy times seven.

Peter's question to Jesus of Nazareth about how often he should forgive his brother who had wronged him brought forth a startling answer. Many rabbis of his time said three pardons of a wrongdoing were enough before seeking revenge. Others thought seven times were sufficient. Jesus, however, insisted that forgiveness has no limits—"seventy times seven." He shifted the emphasis from a matter of arithmetic—a given act at a given time—to the question of one's general attitude, one's willingness to forgive others at all times. And he made no distinction between the seriousness of wrongs. All are to be forgiven.

Jesus then went beyond Peter's question and told the parable of the Unmerciful Servant, which demonstrated that we cannot separate God's forgiveness of our sins from our willingness to forgive the wrongs of others. Jesus's stress on forgiveness of others was not only unusual for his time; making it a condition for God's forgiveness was revolutionary thinking. Old Testament writers had been concerned primarily with *God's* forgiveness of *man's* sinful acts. For them forgiveness is experienced as the free gift of a loving and merciful God to restore the fellowship between God and man which has been broken by man's transgressions. Jesus carried this thinking forward and applied it to broken human relationships. He saw that evil continues and grows more destructive unless fel-

169

lowship is restored through forgiveness. The inseparable link between loving God and loving one's neighbor is also present in Jesus's teaching that forgiveness of one's neighbor must have no limits and upon it rests man's salvation.

But isn't this demanding too much of us, we ask. Isn't it human to strike back against the mean, cruel, hurtful things which people do to us? Am I expected to forgive the person who tells a malicious lie on me, or carries on a whispering campaign which damages my character and reputation on my job or in my community? What about those in positions of power who block my advancement, frustrate my plans, cause me and my family suffering and loss? What of the disloyalty of a wife or husband which shatters a marriage? Or the betrayal by a friend on whom I have relied? Or the hostility of a church member which destroys my fellowship in the church?

Can we speak of forgiveness in the context of the crisis with Iran during the past week, when sixty American citizens are held hostage by angry Iranian mobs, paraded bound and blindfolded in public, and threatened with death? Does forgiveness have any meaning when we have suffered "national humiliation" and our "national pride" is at stake?

In these circumstances, forgiveness seems impossible to achieve if we think of it as a single dramatic act which we are called upon to perform at the very moment of wrongdoing. It is less impossible if we look upon forgiveness as a discipline, a lifelong process of continuous search for wholeness and for reconciliation in human conflict. Jesus understood that we do not have the power to forgive of our own volition. As we experience God's forgiveness of our own shortcomings, we are given the strength to forgive others. Jesus taught us to say in the Lord's Prayer, "Forgive us our trespasses, as we forgive those who trespass against us."

In biblical thought forgiveness "is the act of God's grace which re-reestablishes man in his true relationship to God" by removing the barriers of sin and guilt which have destroyed that relationship. The core of sin is our rebellion against God, pitting our own will against God, believing that we can work out our own destinies through our own knowledge and effort. When we become aware of our own helplessness against evil and suffering and turn to God, God is waiting to grant forgiveness. God's gracious act is not given to us because we merit it. In fact, as Dr. Hans Kung has said, "the sinner is accepted even before he repents. The sinner who has deserved every punishment is freely pardoned. . . . He need only accept the gift and repent." Through God's grace we are freed from the burden of sin and guilt and given strength to enter upon a new life: "It begins with unconditional forgiveness: the sole condition is trust inspired by trusting faith; the sole conclusion to be drawn is the generous granting of forgiveness to others."[1]

Forgiveness is putting aside any claim to retaliation and making possible the renewal of the relationship. It does not imply any relaxation of God's opposition to evil, nor does it avoid judgment. If I abuse my body, I suffer the judgment of illness and pain. The Prodigal Son who squandered his inheritance was forgiven and welcomed home by his loving father but he did not escape the judgment of poverty and shame. Forgiveness does not undo the past, but it clears the way to begin anew.

Jesus made it abundantly clear in the parable about the servant, whose own Lord forgave him a huge [debt] but who refused to forgive his fellow servants much smaller debts, that God will not forgive us if we are unwilling to forgive our brothers and sisters. It is not my understanding that God expects us to make special efforts in order to guarantee our own forgiveness. We do not forgive in order to roll up "brownie points" with God. My understanding is that God is always ready to forgive a penitent sinner but cannot enter an unforgiving heart. God has made us free to accept or reject divine grace and can grant forgiveness only to one who is prepared to accept it. The measure of forgiveness we extend to others is the measure of forgiveness we are prepared to receive. When we are self-righteous, thinking of our own hurt pride, and show a hard, retaliating spirit, we have no forgiving power and set up barriers to our own forgiveness. Not to forgive is to alienate ourselves from God. Only when we have the capacity to forgive are we set free "from the endless wear and tear of nursing grudges and remembering offenses."

In the present crisis with Iran, we could speak of forgiveness only in a most rudimentary stage of the process—restraint in the face of provocation and doing whatever can be done to keep channels of communication open between adversaries. So far our official responses are dictated by the fact that the lives of nearly fifty Americans are at stake. Here the hostages are visible, we see concretely the immediate cost of retaliation. But in every case of wrongdoing, in every human conflict, there are invisible hostages at stake—peace of mind, minimizing the harm and preventing it from spreading to others, the possibility of a creative solution which will bring about a richer fellowship. . . . Certainly one can never forget if that means erasing it totally from [one's] mind. But when we forgive, we forget in the sense that the evil deed is no longer a mental block impeding a new relationship. Likewise, we can never say, "'I will forgive you, but

I won't have anything further to do with you.' Forgiveness means reconciliation, a coming together again." Dr. [Martin Luther] King went on to say, "there will be no permanent solution to the race problem until oppressed men (and women) develop the capacity to love their enemies. The darkness of racial injustice will be dispelled only in the light of forgiving love."[2]

Dr. King's prophetic words come back to us as we reflect upon the city of Birmingham, Alabama. Would any one of us [have] predicted sixteen years ago—watching the horror of racial bombings of churches and homes—the killing of four little girls in Sunday School; the unleashing of angry police dogs, firehoses, and electric cattle prods against defenseless Black citizens—that today Birmingham would have its first elected Black mayor?

Can we avoid the problem of forgiveness in political conflict? Does the Iranian crisis have a lesson for us? We have seen the ugly mood on the faces of Americans clashing with Iranian demonstrators around the country and read angry letters to the newspapers calling for retaliation and demanding that the United States make a show of force. One wonders if these Americans are not more concerned with flexing their own muscles than they are with the immediate safety of the sixty American hostages being held in Tehran. The irony of the entire situation was reflected in a few poignant lines written by Ann Rivers to the *Washington Post*. She said, "What a horror to read that the Iranian protesters shouted, 'A peaceful death is too good for the shah.' Obviously none of these people has ever stood by helplessly as a loved one died from cancer. Believe me, peaceful is not the word to describe it." Thoughtful commentators like Carl Rowan and James Reston have commended President Carter for his patience and restraint in a gravely volatile situation, urging calmness and that we do nothing to provoke an attack upon the lives of the defenseless American hostages.[3] In this situation [as I noted before] the hostages are visible—we see concretely what is at stake. But in every act of wrongdoing, in every human conflict, there are invisible hostages at stake—peace of mind, minimizing the harm and preventing it from spreading to others, the possibility of a creative solution which will bring a richer fellowship than we could have envisioned. All of these are threatened when we react with an unforgiving spirit. Even when we can't forgive we can pray for our adversary.

Yes, forgiveness is costly and is not accomplished without pain. Someone has said, it is "giving ourselves to others with such openness that they may hurt us. In fact, being human, they probably will hurt us despite themselves. Therefore, we must give of ourselves, forgiving in advance the trust they may betray."[a]

This does not mean that we have to become a Mr. Milquetoast. It requires strength to forgive, the strength of that ultimate act of forgiveness—Jesus praying for his executioners as he hung on the cross—"Father, forgive them for they know not what they do." Jesus could not have uttered those words if the discipline of his entire life had not prepared him for that moment. Whatever the pain and cost, it is through the discipline of forgiveness that we ourselves are healed and become more whole.

Amen.

Notes

[a] James G. Emerson Jr., *The Dynamics of Forgiveness* (Philadelphia: Westminster Press, 1964).

On Suffering Souls

Palm Sunday Sermon

Mark 11:7–11

And they brought the colt to Jesus, and threw their garments on it; and he sat upon it. And many spread their garments on the road, and others spread leafy branches, which they had cut from the fields. And those who went before and those who followed cried out, "Hosanna! Blessed is he who cometh in the name of the Lord! Blessed is the kingdom of our father David that is coming! Hosanna in the highest."

It is both a great privilege and an unsettling experience to come back to my old neighborhood, where I lived many years ago as a college student going to Hunter College, and to share with you some reflections on the meaning of the celebrating of Palm Sunday in the Christian faith. I say "unsettling" because it is inconceivable to me that anyone can presume to preach the Word of God without a deep feeling of doubt of one's capacity to speak the truth and without a sense of deep humility in approaching those areas of fundamental meaning in our lives. For as professed Christians, everything in our existence dwindles in importance when we are stripped down naked and alone and must face ourselves and our God. And it is of this relationship between ourselves and our God which ministers of the gospel are called upon to speak.

Palm Sunday ushers in Passion Week in the Christian faith and this Palm Sunday 1974 marks the beginning of the Passover celebrations in the Jewish faith—the festival of the emancipation of the Jewish people from bondage in Egypt, the feast of the Unleavened Bread, which we know as *matzahs.* Last night,

177

in the company of two Roman Catholic nuns and the family of Charles E. Silberman, author of *Crisis in Black and White,* I participated in a celebration of the Passover Seder service. It included a ceremonial meal and lasted six hours. It began with the lighting of the candles and an invocation written by Arlene Silberman for the occasion. . . .[1]

As I listened . . . and reminded myself that I am only two generations removed from chattel slavery in the New World, I realized how much ancient Jewish tradition speaks to our contemporary situation, how integrally related are Judaism, the Roman Catholic and Anglican faiths; how much our Christian faith owes to its Jewish ancestor. Our prayers and liturgies, our celebrations of high holy days, our hymns of praise and thanksgiving, even aspects of our Eucharist—all are rooted in ancient Israelite customs. We are reminded that the primitive Christian church was a community of Palestinian Jews. We can therefore look upon the Passover Seder service, Jesus's entry into Jerusalem, the events of the Passion narrative, Our Lord's Last Supper, which some biblical scholars have identified as the Passover meal and others as the *Haburah* ([or] chaburah) [i.e., a small group of the like-minded] meal of common fellowship, and the Crucifixion of Jesus as part of a common historical heritage of both Jews and Christians.

And so, let's reflect briefly upon Palm [Sunday] in the context of ancient Jewish tradition of the first century and its meaning for us as Christians living in the twentieth century A.D.

As we know, the historical Jesus was a prophet of Galilee who went about teaching, healing the sick, and preaching of the Kingdom of Heaven. He lived in the early first century in Jewish Palestine, which was seething with revolt against "intolerable Roman oppression." He had already aroused the hostility of the Sadducees, the wealthy aristocracy of the Jewish temple, and of Herod Antipas, a petty Jewish ruler of Galilee who had beheaded John the Baptist. According to tradition, Herod saw Jesus as John the Baptist risen from the dead and was out to kill him.

As Luke relates the Gospel story, Jesus was aware that his life was in danger but he preferred to die in Jerusalem, for as he said, "It cannot be that a prophet should perish away from Jerusalem," a Jerusalem known for "killing the prophets and stoning those who are sent to you," in Jesus's words. As David Flusser, the distinguished biblical scholar, points out, "The ostensible reason for his pilgrimage was something else, however; the Passover was drawing near, and the Jews were accustomed to making a pilgrimage to Jerusalem to sacrifice the paschal lamb and celebrate their deliverance from slavery in Egypt. Jesus, too, had longed earnestly to eat this paschal lamb with his disciples; so his way to the cross began."[2]

The entry into Jerusalem was in keeping with tradition. As Jesus rode into the city, he was greeted with cries of "Hosanna!" which means "Save us," and with a verse from the 118th Psalm, "Blessed is he who enters in the name of the Lord!" These words were sung on pilgrimage festivals and were used to greet pilgrims as they arrived in Jerusalem. Strewing garments and leafy branches in Jesus's path may have been the people's way of honoring the prophet from Galilee, we are told.

And here we recall the prediction of Zechariah, the Old Testament prophet, that the Messianic King would enter Jerusalem as one who would come not as a triumphant military conqueror but as a man of peace riding not in a chariot nor on a war-horse but on an ass.

> Rejoice greatly, O daughter of Zion!
> Shout aloud, O daughter of Jerusalem!
> Lo, your king comes to you;
> Triumphant and victorious is he,
> Humble and riding on an ass,
> On a colt the foal of an ass. (9:9)

From his triumphal entry, as we have reenacted the story here this morning, Jesus the Messiah was condemned to suffer the most disgraceful death known to the Roman Empire. Among the Romans, crucifixion was a capital punishment inflicted only upon slaves and those who had committed the most heinous crimes, for robbers, thieves, and terrorists. According to some interpretations, Jesus was the victim of political intrigue because his message was so powerful as to constitute a threat to the established hierarchy.

What does this say to us as Christians? Is there something very extraordinary about this story? How often in our own lives have we experienced some great victory only to be followed by a devastating defeat or an intolerable event of sorrow and suffering? Does not our own racial history include an experience within our own memory, which suggests unavoidable parallels with the Gospel narrative of Passion Week?

Do you recall that as we approached the Easter season six years ago, our own Dr. Martin Luther King made a triumphal march in Memphis, Tennessee? That he had premonitions of his coming death and yet he accepted the challenge of continued nonviolent resistance to racial oppression and economic injustice? That on [the] day of his death he had planned to eat a meal of special delight with his disciple, colleague, and successor, the Reverend Abernathy? That with his death by an assassin's bullet, the dream of justice with reconciliation seemed to die and throughout our nation cities went up in flames?

Have we not seen over and over again in our time, our experience, and in the course of human history that those who set themselves against established tyranny and rigid conservatism suffer in varying degree vituperation, carping criticism, loss of job, petty harassment, and even martyrdom? Does not the re former, the agent of social change, the follower of [the] cross of Christ know daily small crucifixions of the spirit if not of the body along the way? And have we not asked ourselves, if this is to be the result of our effort, why bother? Are we prepared to meet the challenge of the prophet Micah (6:8) when he says, "And what does the Lord require of you but to do justice, and to love kindness, and to walk humbly with your God?" If crucifixion, symbolic or real, were indeed the end of our efforts we would be overwhelmed with despair. And all too often we are overwhelmed and discouraged in both our personal lives and our group existence when so many outward signs seem to point to failure and defeat, to loss of hard-won progress, to a reversal of our march toward freedom.

But the Christian hope and the Christian faith reaffirm constantly that the Crucifixion and the Resurrection are part of one continuous event—that humiliation, degradation, and death are followed by victory, the overcoming of death, by rebirth, and the making of all things new. This is the message of God's creation, and we see its signs all around us as the earth breaks free from "the tyranny of winter" and the green of spring comes forth. This is the promise of God our Creator and Redeemer, as revealed in the incarnation, the life, death, and resurrection of our Lord Jesus Christ, and the Holy Spirit, which abides among us. And it is this hope of triumph over evil in ourselves and in the world about us, of victory over sin and death, which constitutes Christian joy and which enables us across the ages to join with those who greeted Messiah at the gates of Jerusalem, singing,

> Hosanna!
> Blessed is he that cometh in the name of the Lord!
> Hosanna in the highest!

> Let Us Pray!

Faith Makes Us Whole

Mark 10:46–47

As he [Jesus] left Jericho with his disciples and a large crowd, Bartimaeus (that is, the son of Timaeus), a blind beggar, was sitting on the side of the road, [and] when he heard that it was Jesus of Nazareth, he began to shout and say, "Son of David, Jesus, have pity on me." And many of them scolded him and told him to keep quiet, but he only shouted all the louder, "Son of David, have pity on me."

This is one of the most exciting and inspiring stories of the New Testament, and it speaks especially to individual determination and [the] stubbornness of faith. Some weeks ago in our Sunday meditations we left Jesus of Nazareth on the road to Jerusalem, slowly but surely moving toward the climax of his earthly ministry. He was accompanied by his disciples and went through towns and villages preaching and bringing the Good News of the Kingdom of God, as Luke describes this pilgrimage, "and the twelve were with him and also some women who had been healed of evil spirits and infirmities" (Luke 8:1–3).

In Mark's narrative, Peter has answered Jesus's question, "Who do you say I am," by a profession of faith, "You are the Messiah. You are the Christ" (Mark 8:29). Jesus has prophesied that as God's servant, the Son of Man, he is destined to suffer grievously, then according to Mark, Jesus takes Peter, James, and John up on a high mountain where they can be alone and there in the presence of these three chosen disciples he is transfigured; his clothes become dazzlingly white, whiter than any earthly bleacher could make them (Mark 9:2–3). You will recall that in the Old Testament story of Moses, there was a similar incident. Moses went up on the mountain of Sinai and Yahweh appeared, descending in the form of a cloud. It was on this mountain that God made a covenant with Moses and gave Moses the Ten Commandments, which we call the Decalogue. And when Moses came down from the mountain of Sinai with the two tablets of the testimony in his hand, the skin on his face was radiant. After speaking with Yahweh, writes the author of Exodus, "and when Aaron and all the sons of Israel saw Moses, the skin on his face shone so much that they would not venture near him" (34:29–30). This tradition of the transfiguration of Moses has been carried forward to the New Testament figure of Jesus of Nazareth.

Then Jesus came down from the mountain and continued his way toward Jerusalem. During their journey Jesus made a second and third prophesy of his passion, and last Sunday's Gospel told us how James and John, the sons of Zebedee, hearing once more Jesus's prediction that he would be condemned to death but would rise again, asked him to do them a favor of allowing them to sit one at his right hand and one at his left hand when Jesus entered upon his glory. We can see that even among Jesus's closest disciples, the notion of political patronage was strong. James and John wanted to be "in on the ground floor" of the New Kingdom, so to speak.

Having admonished them and made it clear that loyalty and closeness to Jesus gave them no special privileges—"whoever wants to be great must be your servant, and whoever wants to be first among you must be slave to all" (Mark 10:44), the band of pilgrims crosses the Jordan River to the west bank and moves southward to the city of Jericho situated in the valley of the Jordan, about five miles from the northern end of the Dead Sea and about seventeen miles northeast of Jerusalem, an ancient city regarded as the oldest city in the world, going back at least to 7800 B.C., more than ten thousand years ago. Jericho was a place rich with the history of conquests by the Canaanites, by the Egyptians, by the Israelites ("Joshua fit the battle 'round Jericho . . . and the walls came tumbling down" sings the old Negro spiritual). During the prophet Elijah's time, there was a community of prophets at the place, and according to Old Testament tradition, Elijah, when about to be taken up to heaven, passed through Jericho with Elisha, and Elisha returned to Jericho after parting from Elijah. The road from Jericho to Jerusalem was the scene of the parable of the Good Samaritan, and in today's Gospel lesson it is the scene of a great demonstration of faith. The Jericho of the New Testament is today a village in the country of Jordan and has been renamed Ariha.

Now, let us picture the scene of encounter between Jesus of Nazareth and Bartimaeus on the road between Jericho and Jerusalem. The name "Jericho" means "place of fragrance," and [it lies] in the fertile valley five miles west of the River Jordan, some 825 feet below the Mediterranean Sea level. The city has a tropical climate—palms, balsams, sycamores, and henna flourished there. Luke tells of Zacchaeus, a man too short to see Jesus as he was going through the town of Jericho, surrounded by a crowd, climbing a sycamore tree to get a view of Jesus as he passed through (19:2). When I think of Jesus and the crowds attracted to him wherever he went, I think of the twentieth-century Eleanor Roosevelt whose magic created excitement whenever she appeared in public. There was something about her personality—a charisma—that made people want to get close to her. Once she was campaigning in Harlem toward the end of her life and she was riding in an open car; the crowds surged forward and her grandsons riding with her were afraid that she would be harmed, but the people of Harlem just wanted to touch her. "There's Eleanor," they said with complete unselfconsciousness, and she responded to them with like simplicity.

Bartimaeus could not see, but he heard the excitement of Jesus's passing, and that was enough for him. Only he, a blind beggar, according to Mark, recognized Jesus as the Messiah, the "Son of David." The gift of sight is perhaps the most precious of the five senses. To be imprisoned in a world of darkness, never to see the radiance of a sunset, the colors of flowers, or the colors of the clothes we wear, particularly if we are women; never to be able to read the newspapers, or a book, or even with modern talking books and newscasts for the blind, never to have freedom of choice but to receive what someone has selected for those who cannot see. This is one of the great afflictions of human experience. Having lived during early childhood in a household where my grandfather was blind and having a brother who was sightless for about ten years before his death, I am particularly vulnerable to the problems of blindness as well as to the beginning of cataracts, and can empathize with Bartimaeus, sitting there on the roadside, hearing the excitement of the crowd, recognizing the great healing power of Jesus of Nazareth and believing this was his one chance to regain or to receive his sight. Mark does not tell us whether he was blind from birth or from some tragic illness or accident. But Bartimaeus was one of those persistent, single-minded individuals who, in spite of his rags and his destitute condition, knew *who* he was and was not to be denied this opportunity to overcome a barrier which had blighted his life.

"Jesus, Son of David, have pity on me," he called out. Some of Jesus's followers—we all know the type—had a proprietary attitude toward him and wanted the beggar to shut up. We do the same thing when we talk about "Our Church," "Our Vestments," as if we were anything more than stewards of God's church. Had Bartimaeus been less determined or possessed a fragile faith, he would have been intimidated by Jesus's followers and his golden moment would have passed. But this blind beggar had a boldness which we can glory in; he had no superior except the God of all creation and he was afraid of no human being. "He only shouted all the more, 'Son of David, have pity on me!'" And when Jesus stopped and said, "call him," Bartimaeus was ready. "He threw off his cloak, sprang up, and came to Jesus" (Mark 10:50), and he knew exactly what he wanted. There was dignity as well as humility in his request: "Rabbi—Master, Teacher—I want my sight back" (Mark 10:51). The Revised Standard Version and Jerusalem Bible translations are less abrupt—"Master, let me receive my sight."

The clue to Jesus's power was the meeting of the mysterious cosmic force, which we call God, with the response of human faith. Not a passive faith, but an active faith, a reaching out, a taking of the first step. "And Jesus said unto him, 'Go your way, your faith has made you whole,' and immediately he received his sight and followed Jesus in the way" (Mark 10:52). Or "*on* the way," which means in Mark's theology, "on the way to the cross."

I have been deeply troubled by so many expressions of discouragement from members of this congregation. As an outsider who came into your midst by happenstance, I am only beginning to learn how much you have suffered from various trials and tribulations over the years, and many of the afflictions which have beset the Holy Nativity community have been beyond your control. And it may be that in your collective frustrations, you have lashed out against one another and hurt one another, as members of a close blood-related family strike out against those closest to them when they are hurt by the outside world.

The same God who healed Bartimaeus through Jesus of Nazareth can set the Holy Nativity community on the path to renewal and vigorous rebirth, but it requires faith and determination and a knowledge of *who you are and what is your mission.* In the northwest sector of Baltimore, blind Bartimaeus knew that with God all things are possible and refused to give up; he also had the energy to respond to God's call to follow Jesus Christ on the way. His healing and wholeness can be our healing and wholeness if we will only claim our heritage as children of God and sisters and brothers of Jesus, the firstborn of [the] New Creation.

Amen.

Sermon Given on August 5, 1984

As we reflect for a few minutes on the scripture readings [not provided by Murray] chosen for today, I want to share with you part of a letter I received not long ago from a young friend who grew up in church, served as acolyte, and has just graduated with honors from college as valedictorian of her class. As with many young people of her generation, she is undergoing a crisis of faith. She wrote me:

> Christianity, and faith in general, presents a real problem for me, perhaps due to the crisis that the world faces today. In what I realize is an age-old-cry, I just cannot accept that a God would subject his people to so much agony. I have little doubt that the world as I know it and love it won't survive another fifty years—I fear we will have blown ourselves to smithereens before then. . . . I also became very troubled because it seems that peace is an aberration in the world today. War and killing exist almost everywhere—why do we persist in destroying ourselves? . . . If there is a God who is testing us, we are sadly failing. . . . I do not believe my generation has any future, we will not survive.

The despair expressed by this young woman, a thoughtful, intelligent, honest individual who seeks to serve her community and is eager to make the society in which she lives a more compassionate and peaceful place, is the common despair of many people today who find little assurance in public morality or governmental policies that we will solve the problems of economic decline, environmental pollution, growing terrorism, and the threat of nuclear destruction. And even those of us who profess a strong Christian faith, if we are honest with ourselves, must confess that there are times when we are overwhelmed by the sorrow and suffering in our lives and the lives of those we love, as well as by the evils all about us in the world. We often feel powerless to cope with human problems too vast for our strength. As one Christian writer has put it, "Granted the world has always been violent, but when our civilization seems to lack the means to secure peace within itself, we seem hopelessly lost."[a]

The basic sin of humanity is forgetting that we are God's creatures and attempting to live as if we are the authors of our power and the determinants of our destiny. Our human arrogance and pride are the source of much of the fear and misery in the world today. We are indeed hopelessly lost if we assume that peace—or any of the blessings of life—can be achieved by our own power. Rather it is a gift from God, the source of our true security. As Christians, we must continually remind ourselves that God is eternally working in history to bring all creation to perfection, and that we are God's creatures and part of God's divine plan. When we attempt to rely on our own power and place God at the periphery instead of at the center of our lives, we are in rebellion against God's rule and not living in accordance with our true selves as God's creatures. We can live in peace and harmony with ourselves and others only when we know ourselves in relation to God. To learn to be God's creatures means that we must learn to recognize that our existence and the existence of the universe itself is a gift. As creatures, we cannot hope to return to God a gift of such magnitude. But we can respond with a willingness to receive the bounty of God's love. To accept the gift of God's love in creation is to learn to be at home in God's world even in the midst of uncertainty, knowing that God is in charge and whether in life or death, in this world or beyond, we are safe in God's care.

The theme of God's boundless love and mercy recurs throughout our scripture readings. In the Old Testament lesson, we encounter the God of the people of Israel whose land had been overrun and who were driven into exile. Nehemiah, a man of great faith, was serving in exile as a cupbearer to the Persian king Artaxerxes, and he persuaded the king to let him return from exile and rebuild the walls of the city of Jerusalem. Against fierce opposition and with only a few workers Nehemiah succeeded in rebuilding the city walls, then the people were called together in a general assembly and the priest Ezra led a public service of confession and praise to God, reviewing the history of God's covenant with the chosen people, God's presence in their suffering, God leading them to liberation from their bondage in Egypt, God's steadfast forbearance despite their blindness and disobedience. Ezra prays, "But thou art a forgiving God, gracious and compassionate, long suffering and ever constant, and thou didst not forsake them. Even when they made the image of a bull-calf in metal and said, 'This is your god who brought you up from Egypt,' and were guilty of great blasphemies, thou in thy great compassion didst not forsake them in the wilderness."[b]

The unfailing God of history is the God who sent his Son Jesus Christ, the firstborn of the New Creation, whose life and death and resurrection revealed the power of divine love to change the world. In today's Epistle we heard Paul's ringing hymn of faith in his letter to the Romans: "Then what can separate us from the love of Christ? Can affliction or hardship? Can persecution, hunger, nakedness, peril or the sword? . . . I am convinced that there is nothing in death or life, in the realm of spirits or superhuman powers, in the world as it is or the world as it shall be, in the forces of the universe, in heights or depths—nothing in all creation can separate us from the love of God in Christ Jesus our Lord."[1]

Paul was writing to reassure the early Christians who were beginning to suffer hardships and persecution because of their belief in Jesus Christ. The people feared that the trials and tribulations they faced would cause them to weaken in their faith. Paul had endured many hardships himself and from his own experience knew the power of adversity to defeat the human spirit and make people bitter. But he also knew that all the adversities which threaten our well-being are impotent against the greater power of God's love in Jesus Christ.

We have heard the saying that when the struggle becomes too much for us and we don't know where to turn in our difficulties, we must *let go and let God*. This does not mean that we use God as an insurance policy against adversity. In our human condition we cannot avoid suffering any more than Jesus of Nazareth could avoid death on the cross in the fulfillment of his mission on earth. What it does mean is that through the power of divine love working in us we can transform our sufferings into a blessing and turn evil into good.

Our own racial history affirms this great truth. When the late Dr. Martin Luther King Jr. began his nonviolent crusade against the humiliating system of racial segregation in the South almost two decades ago, he declared that the nonviolent resister could endure suffering in the cause of justice because he knows that he has cosmic companionship. He led his followers to accept the verbal abuse, the firehoses, the electric cattle prods, the beatings, the jailings, the bombings meted out to them when they challenged the foundations of Jim Crow because they were relying on a higher power than the evil forces which sought to destroy them. And, as we know, they were enabled to transform their suffering into a victory and overthrow the system of human degradation. Now, less than twenty years later, we have been privileged to see a product of that struggle— Jesse Jackson—defy custom and have a Black man taken seriously as a candidate for the presidency of the United States. However we choose to describe the political events which brought about this phenomenon, they are rooted in the transforming power of God's love working in history and memorialized in the words of our Negro National Anthem:

> God of our weary years, God of our silent tears;
> Thou who hast brought us thus far on our way;
> Thou who hast by thy might
> Led us into the light
> Keep us forever in the path, we pray.

And mindful of our human tendency toward forgetfulness of the source of our progress, even as the Israelites turned their backs on the God who led them out of Egypt, the anthem continues,

> Lest our feet stray from the places, our God,
>   where we met Thee,
> Lest our hearts, drunk with the wine of the world,
>   we forget Thee.

Finally, learning to be God's creatures is learning that when we are open to God, God uses us to accomplish miracles. My New Testament professor in seminary once described Jesus as a man God found he could use and used him to the hilt. This is the lesson in today's Gospel story. Jesus's disciples had only five loaves and two fishes to feed the multitude, but Jesus did not reject their offering. He blessed it and had the disciples distribute it among the people. Through God's power working in Jesus, more than five thousand men, women, and children were fed to their content, and there was such abundance that twelve great baskets of food were left over. However small and insignificant our contribution may seem in the face of vast human problems beyond our power to resolve, God takes our tiny gift, uses it, and multiplies it in ways we would not have dreamed possible.

The foundation of Christian hope is our faith in the limitless possibilities through God's love. We dare to trust in the mighty compassion of God as revealed in Jesus Christ, whose transforming spirit continues to work through human life and through creation. And we are called to be like God, to be perfect as God is perfect. This is our destiny, a perfection that comes by learning to be like this man, Jesus, whom God sent to be our forerunner in the kingdom of love.

Amen.

Notes

[a] Stanley Hauerwas, *The Peaceable Kingdom* (South Bend, IN: University of Notre Dame Press, 1983), 6.

[b] Nehemiah 9:17.

The Meaning of Baptism

We have just passed the celebration of New Year's, the going out of the old with all of its frustrations and sorrows and the ushering in of the new with all our hopes for better times as we face the uncertainties of the future. We now celebrate the Epiphany season in Christian tradition. The first Sunday after Epiphany is the festival of the Baptism of Christ, reminding us that Christian baptism signals a new beginning, a new life in Christ.

As we experience New Year's and Epiphany in close proximity, this year especially, it would not be surprising if we find that our hope struggles with apprehension and our faith with doubt, looking at the temporal world about us. We continue to worry about making ends meet as we read that grocery store prices rose nearly 15 percent in 1980 and will probably continue their upward climb in 1981. We hear of the threatened bankruptcy of [the] Social Security system, which would bring misery to millions of aged people, ourselves included, who may have no other source of income when they are no longer able to work. We wonder about the capacity of the incoming political administration to solve the stubborn problems of unemployment and inflation and fear that some of its heralded policies, if put into effect, may result in greater misery of the poor and needy. We listen to daily bulletins of robberies and burglaries in our cities and realize that any one of us is a potential victim of senseless murder. We are increasingly alarmed over hate-inspired violence against individual Blacks and reports of rising anti-Semitism. We watch anxiously the hazardous international situation threatened by the continued poverty, hunger, and oppression of many peoples in the world and aggravated by terrorism.

The drumbeat of anxieties pervades our daily lives, and who among us does not succumb to moments of downright despair at the suffering, conflict, and confusion over which we have little or no control? I am reminded of Dr. Hans Kung's observation that "suffering constantly proves to be the crucial test of trust in God and of basic trust.... Where is trust in God more challenged ... than in [the] face of all the suffering and evil in the world and in one's own life?"[1]

Christians are not immune from this doubt. Our faith is tested each day of our lives. But it is precisely in our moments of doubt and despair that the Gospel story of Jesus's baptism brings home to us the meaning of being a Christian. Here was a human being in whom the love of God was so manifest at the moment of his baptism that it was depicted as the Spirit of God descending upon him like a dove, and a voice from heaven saying, "This is my beloved Son, with whom I am well pleased." Jesus's experience was reminiscent of Isaiah's prophecy [in the Old Testament lesson]: "Thus says the Lord, 'Behold my servant, whom I uphold, my chosen, in whom my soul delights; I have put my Spirit upon him.... He will not fail or be discouraged till he has established justice in the earth.'"[2]

Matthew's Gospel proclaims Jesus to be the fulfillment in his person of the mission as the servant of God portrayed in Isaiah. He began his public ministry, according to Luke, with the words of Isaiah:

> The spirit of the Lord has been given to me,
> For he has anointed me.
> He has sent me to bring the good news to the poor,
> To proclaim liberty to captives
> And to the blind new sight;
> To set the downtrodden free;
> To proclaim the Lord's year of favor.[a]

Jesus's conception of Sonship was complete openness to God's love shining through him and obedience to God's will. His mission was to stand as God's representative in the midst of turmoil and [the] complexity of human existence, speaking and working with infinite love and compassion on behalf of the poor, the sick, the handicapped, and the oppressed, calling men and women to faith in a loving God.

Yet God's love did not exempt him from the suffering and evil inherent in the human situation. In human terms, the paradox of the Gospel story is that the path of the beloved Son, God's chosen one, led to the cross, to agony and a shameful death, the victim of senseless evil, forsaken by man and abandoned by God. Commenting on the Crucifixion, Peter Hodgson has said, "Jesus may have experienced the abandonment of God at the moment of death in peculiarly acute form just because his life had been lived in extraordinary immediacy to God. He had proclaimed the saving nearness of God's kingdom and often spoke of God in familiar terms as 'my Father.' To be abandoned by God in the full awareness of the gracious nearness of God, and to be delivered up to the death of a criminal, is the torture of hell; indeed [Martin] Luther interpreted the tradition of Christ's descent into hell as referring to his death in God-forsakenness."[3] When we contemplate the tragic circumstances of life in our own era, we are brought face to face with the question: Where was God at the time of Jesus's ordeal when his enemies cried, "If you are the Son of God, come down from the cross," and when the pious pillars of the establishment, the chief priests and elders, mocked him saying, "He saved others; he cannot save himself?" How do we answer this question?

"The answer of the Christian faith," says Hodgson, "is that God was there— in the depths of God-forsaken humanity, in the anguish of death, in the humiliation of the crucifixion, in the sinfulness of a despairing death cry. . . . God suffers death—(even the death of God's beloved Son)—not to let death prevail over it, to liberate from it."[4]

"This senseless death of Jesus Christ," [Hans] Kung tells us, "acquires meaning only with the resurrection of Jesus to a new life in God, as known by faith. . . . God's love does not protect us *against* all suffering. It protects us in all suffering." Wrestling with the problem of faith in threatening circumstances, Dr. Kung asserts, "it is only if there is a God that we can look at all this immense suffering in the world. It is only in trusting faith in the incomprehensible always greater God that man can stride in justifiable hope through that broad deep river; conscious of the fact that a hand is stretched out to him across the dark gulf of suffering and evil."[5] In [the] baptism, ministry, death, and resurrection of Jesus of Nazareth, God revealed an ever closeness to humankind, down here with us, suffering with us, loving and sustaining us in every personal and social crisis, and ultimately delivering us from the last enemy—death.

Christians believe, therefore, that while suffering and evil against which we struggle are constant facts of human existence, they do not have the last word. Christ points us toward a higher destiny beyond pain, suffering, and death, a destiny fulfilled in his resurrection and entry into new life with God. We reaffirm our hope in this human destiny when we participate sacramentally through baptism in Christ's death and resurrection. In the words of St. Paul, "We are buried therefore with him by baptism into Death, so that as Christ was raised from the dead by the glory of Easter, we too walk in the newness of life. For if we have been united with him in a death like his, we shall certainly be united with him in a resurrection like his" (Romans 6:4–5).

In baptism, by the power of the Holy Spirit, we become brothers and sisters of Jesus Christ, sons and daughters of God and inheritors of the Kingdom of Heaven. Following his example, we are anointed—we might even say "ordained"—into the general ministry of the church shared by all its members, the ministry of reconciliation. We are commissioned to labor for justice and peace, to work for the alleviation of suffering, but our hope is centered not upon our own efforts alone or upon human institutions, however powerful they may seem or benevolent their aims. "Hope," says one theologian, "is not self-fulfillment by one's own power. It is not addressed to man and his capabilities. It is focused upon God. Hope even implies a complete rejection of dependence on man and of confidence placed in man's capacities."[6] Remembering Jesus's words [John 5:19], "the Son can do nothing by himself, he can do only what he sees the Father [do]," and "Not I, but the Father in me, doeth the work."

We are called upon to walk in faith, meeting each situation in life, however gloomy the outlook, serene in our basic trust that the outcome of every struggle belongs to God. And although baptism occurs only once, the process by which we become liberated from the anxieties and fears of human existence is a lifelong effort as we strive to grow in Christ and to share in the divine promise: "You are my beloved child with whom I am well pleased."

Amen.

Notes

[a] Isaiah 61:1.

Can These Bones Live Again?

Today is Passion Sunday, on which the Christian world begins its commemoration of Passiontide, that two-week period in the life of Jesus of Nazareth which marked his final journey to Jerusalem, his triumphant entry, his increasing encounters with his enemies, the Last Supper with his closest friends and disciples, his agony in the Garden of Gethsemane, his betrayal by Judas, his arrest and abandonment by those on whom he had depended, Peter's denial, his trial and conviction before Pilate, his crucifixion—the shameful death reserved for the worst of criminals. All this culminating in the Resurrection of Christ the Lord on Easter morn.

The Old Testament lesson for today is a prophetic pointer toward this Christ event, which changed the course of human history. It is taken from the book of the prophet Ezekiel 37:1–7, which begins,

> The hand of the Lord came upon me, and he carried me out by his spirit and put me down in a valley full of bones.... They covered the valley, countless numbers of them and they were very dry.... He said to me, "Man, can these bones live again?" I answered, "Only thou knowest that, Lord God." He said to me, "Prophesy over these bones and say to them, 'O dry bones, hear the word of the Lord. This is the word of the Lord God to these bones; I will put breath in you and you shall live.'"

Whenever I read this passage in Ezekiel and reflect upon its impact upon my own life, the image comes to me of a little child in Durham, North Carolina, tugging at the hand of her aging grandmother, saying, "Come on in the house, Gran-ma, and I'll read to you in the Psalms. I'll even try to read a little about 'Zekiel in the valley of dry bones."

The recorded story of this child continues:

[She] had touched on Grandmother's favorite Bible selection(s). And she treasured that ragged old Bible Miss Mary Smith of Chapel Hill had given her more than any other article in the house. She said she got it when she was a little girl and was confirmed [at] the Chapel of the Cross. It was over one hundred years old. It was the one book Grandmother tried to read herself, peering through her glasses and spelling out the Psalms a word at a time. I had learned to read some of the Psalms by now and every Sunday evening I would read to Grandmother some of her favorite passages. She seemed so proud of having me read to her from the Big Bible that I loved it as much as she did. I liked the huge print and the way the verses were divided on the pages. I liked the sound of the words rolling off my tongue and I would let my voice rise and fall like a wailing wind, just as I had heard Reverend Small chant the Morning Lesson at St. Titus on Sundays. Grandmother had the utmost respect for the Holy Word.

Why Ezekiel? We who live in a technocratic age are prone to overlook our prophets and the prophetic incidents in our lives. Little did that child know then that someday sixty years later—when she was as old as her grandmother was at that time—she would be called upon [to] interpret those "dry bones," so vivid in her grandmother's prophetic vision, as a priest in Christ's Holy Catholic Church.

Ezekiel was a Hebrew prophet who lived at the time of Jeremiah. He was first and last a priest and poet. We are told that when Jerusalem was captured by Babylonian forces in 597 B.C., although the city was left intact, Ezekiel was among the leaders, including the king, taken away by their captors and forced to live in exile in Babylonia. His prophetic writings were addressed to his fellow exiles, and while he believed that God's judgment was being visited upon Israel for her failure to observe God's laws when the Babylonians finally destroyed Jerusalem in 587 B.C., he nevertheless had a vision of hope, of rebirth, and the eventual restoration of the exiles to their homeland.[a]

The persistent strength of the human desire for roots is seen in the continuing Middle East crisis today, some 2,500 years after those early dispersals of the people of the Kingdoms of Israel and Judah. What the loss of a sense of belonging meant to the Hebrew people of the Old Testament is embodied in the 137th Psalm:

> By the waters of Babylon, there we sat down;
> Yea, we wept, when we remembered Zion.
> We hanged our harps upon the willows in the midst thereof.
> For they that had carried us away captive required of us a song;
> How can we sing the Lord's song in a stranger land?
> If I forget thee, O Jerusalem, let my right hand
> forget her cunning . . . let my tongue cleave to
> the roof of my mouth.[1]

In our own immediate past history, there has been a symbolic reenactment of the exile of Israel. At the end of slavery in 1865, the North American South was the homeland of 90 percent of the people of color in the United States. As one of our poets cried out during World War II:

> We have no other dream, no land but this.
> With slow deliberate hands these years
> Have set her image on our brows.
> We are her seed; have borne a fruit
> Native and pure is unblemished cotton.[2]

For more than a century now a process of dispersal has been taking place, until today about half or more of our people live outside the South—their ancestors not captured and taken away but driven out by the intolerable conditions which they faced. Many of these migrants continued to look backward toward their roots, and their children have painfully discovered that the Babylon of the Spirit is everywhere in the United States. . . .

This image of Negro migrants in cities of the North during the Depression years of the 1930s has changed very little for all too many. The third generation of these exiles constitutes the "dry bones" still scattered about in the crumbling urban areas. We take considerable pride in the fact that one of our own modern Joan of Arc—Secretary of Housing and Urban Affairs Patricia Roberts Harris, who just happens to be an Episcopalian—is leading a historic campaign against entrenched economic interests to see to it that "these dry bones live." When her fellow Episcopalian Senator William Proxmire was giving Pat Harris a hard time during her confirmation hearings a year or more ago, I suggested to somebody in the White House that both of them were in need of some good Baptist "born-again" prayers. As I read the political barometer today, I wonder if the White House may not be in need of some of our good Episcopalian prayers, decorous though they may be. We may operate on the principle of the separation of church and state, but all we have to do is look at the White House today to see that the gospel and politics are all mixed up together!

We Negroes/Blacks of the South have long seen the parallel between our own enslavement in the United States and the Old Testament. Alex Haley's *Roots,* Margaret Walker's *Jubilee,* and my *Proud [Shoes]*—published in reverse order, in 1956, 1966, and 1976, respectively—in various ways have told the stories of Abraham and Hagar and Ishmael, the outcast, of the bondage of the people of Israel in Egypt, the Exodus, and the wandering in the wilderness. Martin Luther King Jr. glimpsed the Promised Land, and I think he may have been dreaming of a reborn South. Writers like Richard Wright, Ann Petry, James Baldwin, Toni Morrison, and poets like Langston Hughes, Gwendolyn Brooke, Countee Cullen have documented the exile years. Robert Hayden and I have attempted epic poetry telling the story from the slave-ships in Africa to modern times. And if you will forgive the self-reference, I would like to share with you what the younger generation of prophets thinks of us in our sixties. Several weeks ago I received a letter from a young Black woman seminarian studying at Colgate-Rochester Divinity School. She had been a pre-med student in college who finally chose theology instead of medicine. She wrote, "Before coming to Seminary learning of your ordination further inspired my own decision. I've long wanted to meet you—though you may find it amusing that in grade and high school, when reading your poetry, I assumed that like Hughes, Cullen, Dunbar and others, you too had long since passed away." Although her letter sent me into hysterics of laughter, it scared me into thinking I might "pass away" before I complete my mission in life—whatever that mission may be.

But there is another side to the story of exile. We must remember that not all of the people of Israel and Judah were deported to Babylonia. The Babylonian captors took the Jewish leaders—priests, prophets, skilled artisans, and so on. Those who were left behind in ransacked Jerusalem and the land of Palestine had to endure a half-century or more of military and political domination until a new leadership was developed and some of the exiles returned. They carried on life and inched ahead despite the suffering—both physical and spiritual—of being outcasts in the land of their roots.

Even in exile, however, Ezekiel saw the power of God's divine grace to raise up a "new and holy Israel" which would be reborn out of the "dry bones of an old battlefield." Unconsciously influenced by his vivid imagery of those dry bones and informed by the New Testament story of the Resurrection and the Christian hope of rebirth and renewal, our twentieth-century exile from the American South . . . I acknowledge the potential gloom and doom in my brother William Stringfellow's prophecy, his justifiable embarrassment at being an Episcopalian as he wrote in a recent issue of *The Witness,* our forward-looking church magazine which is leading the struggle for social justice—nevertheless my own life experiences lead me to follow in the footsteps of Ezekiel. For the Christ event has intervened between the exile and today. And the Christ event confirmed Ezekiel's vision.

Symbolically, I am a returning exile to the American South after an absence of more than fifty years. I am the fourth generation of a family who migrated here and cast its lot with southern people during Reconstruction. Many of my generation fled the South in the 1920s, 1930s, and 1940s. What does it say to you that a member of the fifth generation is now resettling in Atlanta, Georgia, and is representative of a modern trend?

Just before I left North Carolina in 1927 to live permanently in the North— I was a teenager, seventeen at the time—my Aunt Pauline, whom Durhamites may remember as Mrs. Pauline Fitzgerald Dame, my mother by adoption, brought me here to Raleigh to visit Bishop Henry B. Delaney, who had confirmed me at St. Titus when I was nine years old and who was then on his deathbed. At the end of our visit we had prayers and Bishop Delaney blessed me and said, "You are a child of destiny." For the next fifty years I pondered this prophecy of a holy man. Did he see then what I could not see—that God was calling me, even a woman, against the weight of every traditional theological argument and two-thousand-year tradition, to be a priest in Christ's Holy Catholic Church and to say to you today that out of these dry bones, the outcasts of the earth—even women—shall arise and the House of Israel shall be reborn?

Let Us Pray.

Almighty God, giver of all good things, we thank you for the faith we have inherited in all its rich variety. Help us, O Lord, to finish the good work here begun. Strengthen our efforts to blot out our ignorance and prejudice, to abolish poverty and crime. Hasten the day when men and women, Black, Red, white, and Yellow, will stand as equals and brothers and sisters before one another as they now stand in your sight. And hasten the day when all people, everywhere, with many voices, in one united chorus, will glorify your holy Name, through Jesus of Nazareth, the Crucified, the Risen Lord.

Amen.

Notes

[a] Keith W. Carley, *The Book of the Prophet Ezekiel* (New York: Cambridge University Press, 1974).

Thoughts on Dying and Death

Romans 5:1–6

We rejoice in our sufferings, knowing that suffering produces endurance, and endurance produces character, and character produces hope, and hope does not disappoint us, because God's love has been poured into our hearts through the Holy Spirit which has been given to us.

Because it is the Lenten season of the Christian year, our thoughts are directed toward the trials and temptations, the suffering passion and death of our Lord Jesus Christ. For the Christian, I believe that Lent, which usually begins sometime in February, is a time of testing, of trial and tribulation, of illness and death of loved ones, of misunderstandings within families, within Christian congregations, within the larger society. My best friend, Irene Barlow, used to say that February was the most difficult month of the year and that if one could just get through February, one might be able to survive. Five years ago on February 21, she died of a brain tumor; tomorrow, February 27, will mark the fifth anniversary of her memorial service. She had just passed her fifty-ninth birthday. And it was my experience with dying and her death as her trusted friend and power of attorney, in which as a lay Christian I was compelled to perform all of the services that we usually think a priest must perform for those who are dying— and after her death had to plan her memorial service—which led me to recognize my call to the ordained ministry.

Before this experience with my best friend, I had run from death, avoided funerals, refused to revise my last will and testament or to leave directions for my own funeral services. But I couldn't run out on my best friend, and so I had to do what was necessary because there was no one else to do it. Her mother was ninety-three, too frail and ill to take any responsibility. Her one surviving sister was in another state trying to take care of the mother. There were no relatives close by.

In my desperation to try to do the things my friend would have wanted me to do, I looked through her files and came upon a folder (she was the director of personnel of a Wall Street–type law firm) marked "LAST WILL AND TESTAMENT." In this folder were her directions, written ten years earlier, for her funeral service, the hymns she wanted sung, and a list of people to be notified. It was as if, even in death, she was guiding me in my most difficult task up to that time.

Because my best friend was also my contemporary, three years younger than I, standing at the top of her profession, and taken in the prime of life, I was compelled to think of my own mortality and to decide what I wanted to do with the years of life left to me—and it was in that moment of grief, of rebelling against God—"It isn't fair, God; she hasn't even reached her threescore years and ten"—that I recognized that I was called upon to serve others as she had served so many during her relatively short life. I realized that her work, her mission on earth, had been completed and that she was beyond pain; that God had more work for me to do. I also got the distinct feeling that only the *living* experience death as we think of it and dread it; that for those who go on, there is a release, something which is so mystifying to us in the finite life, we can only call in *faith,* the *eternal life.* I would like to share with you something I wrote about this experience one year later when I was in seminary studying for the ordained ministry. . . .

During the past week or ten days I have been thinking about death in a personal sense because, at last, I am trying to get together a last will and testament. I think what started my train of thought was a letter I received from a young woman seminarian who is now studying for the ordained ministry. She wrote, "Before coming to Seminary learning of your ordination future inspired my own decision. I've long wanted to meet you—though you may find it amusing that in grade and high school, when reading your poetry, I assumed that like (Langston) Hughes, (Countee) Cullen, (Paul Laurence) Dunbar, and others, you too *had long since passed away.*" Well, I thought to myself, before I long since pass away, I had better get my affairs in order. And so, I am trying to come to grips with my own death. Elisabeth Kübler-Ross, the physician-psychiatrist, tells us that

> dying is an integral part of life, as natural and predictable as being born. But whereas birth is cause for celebration, death has become a dreaded and unspeakable issue to be avoided by every means possible in our modern society. . . . It *is* hard to die, and it will always be so, even when we have learned to accept death as an integral part of life, because dying means giving up life on this earth. But if we can learn to view death from a different perspective, to reintroduce it into our lives so that it comes not as a dreaded stranger but as an expected companion in our life, then we can learn to live our lives with meaning—with full appreciation of our finiteness, of the limits on our time here.[a]

Someone has said, "live each day as though it were your last." Even though we may be Christians of great faith, nevertheless most of us fear suffering, fear the process of dying. Yet our most recent public example to approaching death in a joyful spirit is the beloved late senator Hubert H. Humphrey, whose life was a testament to blessedness. He lived in such a way that those who were closest to him saw his death not as an experience of unremitting sorrow but as an occasion for joy and the celebration of a blessed life of service to humanity.

It is human to fear death and to want to avoid it. In his great humanity, Jesus of Nazareth feared his coming death and prayed that God remove this cup from his lips. Some versions of the Passion are that he "uttered loud cries." None of us knows what death will be like; we have only our faith that God is with us in death as in finite life. I find myself consoled by the words of a brother priest, the Reverend Steve Garney, a worker-priest in New York City, who shared with me some of his thoughts and reflections upon death and dying when I most needed it. He wrote,

> Not that your death can ever be easy. The Christian, though, can always recognize it as probably his (or her) most real moment of identification with his (or her) Lord, the moment when everything that has belonged to (oneself) . . . is taken away either as chaff or to be transformed; and (one) . . . who had never really been able to give everything away as the Gospel had asked, can have the chance at least to accept this moment of extreme poverty as the occasion to receive the riches of the new life that Christ has promised to those who love him; the entrance into the great silent mystery of even greater human becoming, human loving and communion.

So, perhaps St. Paul was looking at that ultimate and universal human experience and our preparation for it when he said, "We rejoice in our sufferings, knowing that suffering produces endurance, and endurance produces character, and character produces hope, and hope does not disappoint us, Because God's love has been poured into our hearts through the Holy Spirit which has been given to us."[1] For Jesus of Nazareth, the Christ of faith, not only taught us how to live but he also taught us how to die.

Notes

[a] Elisabeth Kübler-Ross, *Death: The Final Stage* (New York: Simon and Schuster, 1975), 6.

Man in God's Image

Genesis 1:26–27

And God said, Let us make man in our image, after our likeness.... So God created man in his own image, in the image of God created he him; male and female created he them.

Galatians 3:28

There is neither Jew nor Greek; there is neither bond nor free; there is neither male nor female: for ye are all one in Christ Jesus.

Colossians 3:3, 11

Where there is neither Greek nor Jew, circumcision nor un-circumcision, Barbarian, Scythian, bond nor free but Christ is all, and in all.

The year 1963 was the year of concurrent social revolutions. The racial crisis flared up with [a] breadth and intensity anticipated by few Americans. Two sociology professors of the Florida State University, Lewis M. Killian and Charles M. Grigg, wrote recently, "Americans, white and black, may have to endure an ordeal of hatred and conflict before they ever learn to live with each other in peace.... Americans, particularly white Americans, must soon awake to the fact that the crisis in race relations is second in gravity only to the threat of nuclear war."[1]

At the same time, a quieter revolution was in progress. Public scrutiny of the American woman ranged from the significant report of President Kennedy's Commission on the Status of Women to "a flood of magazine articles and books." Of this revolution, Paul Foley wrote in the March 1964 *Atlantic Monthly,* "perhaps it is a time for women, married or unmarried, to arise as individuals committed to perfect themselves as human beings wherever they are, whatever they do."

What we are witnessing in our country today are upheavals reflecting in varying degrees of intensity the yearnings of the millions of individuals for self-fulfillment, however these yearnings may be couched in group demands. For, as one observer commented on the racial crisis, what is claimed "is not merely job opportunity, housing privilege, political status, or the freedom to use one's native talents in chosen professions and avocations but, even more, the right of the essential self, the rights of the soul to be itself and to become under the grace of God what it can be." Beyond all of the claims for political, social, or civic rights are "the rights of the person as a person."

Never have Christians had a greater opportunity or greater challenge to our faith than we now have. Ours is revolutionary, when it transforms, recreates, and forces us to choose standards of conduct which are higher and more exacting than those of the secular world of which we are a part.

As Christians, we are confronted with responsibilities from which none of us can escape. For our task is more than the dispensation of racial justice or taking a stand for human rights irrespective of age, sex, race, or culture. We have the responsibility of standing for the essential unity and oneness of humanity even in the midst of conflict and tension. Ours is the task of reconciliation, of restoring the harmonious relationship within the human family.

For this important task we are not without the necessary resources. Our text today, selected from the Old and New Testaments respectively, suggests two basic principles which are part of our Judeo-Christian heritage and which are highly relevant to the perplexing problems of group tensions and conflict in contemporary America. The first relates to the Judeo-Christian view of the nature of man and the basis of each individual's claim to dignity and respect. The second relates to the fundamental condition upon which all Christian fellowship must be predicated.

Dr. Kyle Haselden, formerly a minister in the South, of southern origins, and now editor of the *Christian Century,* has recently published a paperback edition of his remarkable study *The Racial Problem in Christian Perspective,* which I strongly recommend to you for fresh insights into our most baffling domestic problems. What makes Dr. Haselden's book so remarkable, among other things, is the fact that although he addressed himself to the Negro problem in the United States, his analysis might easily be applied to the problem of any group which has suffered the disadvantages of an inferior status. In many parts, strike the word "Negro" and insert the word "woman" and the analysis remains valid and pertinent.

He talks of three important rights of every human being: (1) the right to *have,* without discrimination; (2) the right to *belong,* without segregation; and (3) the right to *be,* to be one's individual, unique, irreplaceable self, without being stereotyped. Of the many theories advanced to support the claim to these rights, none is more compelling than Dr. Haselden's statement of the Christian view: "If we asked why all human life should be treated with respect, we are reduced in our answer to a Biblical claim that every man has within him and as an essential and indestructible part of his being a native dignity. It is common among Jews and Christians to refer to this essential dignity of man, the worth and sacredness of his personality, in the Biblical term *the image of God.*"[a] But, Dr. Haselden continues, "we see the worth of the naked and irreducible man by looking, not at him, but at his Creator. Man's dignity is conferred upon him: his worth is bestowed," not by man but by God. He is "unique among God's creatures not because he is a reasoning, tool making, cooking, or laughing animal, in these particulars distinct, but because God made him a special and preferred creature."[b]

We are reminded that the innate dignity to which we refer in the Christian faith when we speak of the *image of God* is the result not of man himself but of his Creator. This dignity is shared universally and in equal portions by all men and women, for "the Christian view knows no graded scale of essential and fundamental worth." There is no divine right of whites which differs from that of Negroes, no superior right of men which differs from that of women, no privilege or status of one that is higher than the other: "The glory of the 'image of God' is in God and only reflectively in the image. The sacredness of man has to do with what man is only secondarily; it has to do primarily with the fact that God has made him."[c]

Dr. Haselden maintains that apart from a faith in God who has created man, "loved him, sought him, and in the final gracious act suffered for him on a cross . . . all talk of human dignity and equality is ultimately unsupportable."[d] From this he concludes that

> We cannot acclaim the sacredness of any man until we acknowledge the sacredness of all men. . . . Cancel that innate worth of man anywhere and it is cancelled everywhere; deny it to one and it is denied to all. . . . We do not begin to comprehend the meaning of the phrase *in the image of God* . . . until

we can look at the derelict, the profligate, the prodigal as well as the saint and can know that there, however torn and faded it may seem, we are look- ing at the image of the Eternal. For the Christian therefore, the sacredness, the infinite worth, of individual personality has nothing to do with culture or intellect or color or race or morality or faith; but it has to do with God, with the God who in His will and wisdom created all men in His image and destined them for His likeness.[e]

"Consequently, in the Christian view no human life is worthless; every human being has upon it the indelible and dignifying stamp of the Creator. The fact that it is a human life, that fact alone, qualifies it to share equally in that elemental worth which belongs to all men. However worthless the particular life may appear by the standards of men, it has nevertheless an irrevocable value; to assault that value in any man but also to offend his Creator." For, we are told, God is no respecter of persons; his love is indiscriminate. Not only is every human being created in the *image of God* but each human being has individu- ality, he is an original without reprints, he or she is distinctive, "unrepeatable." "The individual defies definition by data drawn from the masses; behind him is no precedent, about him no duplicates, before him no replacement."[f] He defies a stereotype. The fundamental claim which every human being can make, whether Negro or white, man or woman, is "I am an individual and irreplace- able whom God loves; deal with me on the basis of what I am." The Christian ethic requires that in dealing with another human being, "color or the curl of the hair, culture or lack of it, literacy or ignorance, health or disease, morality or immorality are superficial and irrelevant distinctions which have no bearing upon the intensity or the range of the Christian's good will."[g]

This, then, is the Christian's obligation to all men and women. In the Christian fellowship, however, the standard is even more exacting. For there, there can be no ethnic or racial distinction, no economic or social classes, no cultural differentiations, and male and female are abolished. Dr. Haselden has suggested that perhaps Paul added the phrase "male and female" for emphasis as well as for its practical applications, for here is a radical, universal, cherished, and beneficial division of humanity which has its foundation deeper in nature than any other distinction, yet this difference too is abolished in Christ. Biolog- ically, in the creation, God said, "Let there be male and female"; spiritually, in Christ, God said, "Let there be neither male nor female."[h]

What we are told here is not that there are no human differences which are natural but that there are none which justify superior or inferior status; that the unifying power of our Christian faith—we "are one body in Christ, and *individually* members of one another"—transcends racial or other differences and makes us all one.

In short, we are required to have both a sense of identification and sense of inclusiveness. If we can apply these two principles as we go about our daily activities, we can help restore the unity of the human family. More than that, there is in store for us the joy that comes with seeing in the radiance of another human being's eyes the image of God reflected even as it is then reflected in our own eyes, as we learn the deeper meaning of loving our neighbor as our self.

Notes

[a] Kyle Haselden, *The Racial Problem in Christian Perspective* (New York: Harper and Row, 1964), 169.

[b] Ibid.

[c] Ibid., 171.

[d] Ibid.

[e] Ibid.

[f] Ibid., 172.

[g] Ibid., 186.

[h] Ibid., 193.

Getting Church Right

Christian Community

John 13:34–35

A new commandment I give to you, that you love one another, even as I have loved you. . . . By this love that you have one for another, everyone will know that you are my disciples.

John's Gospel version of the Last Supper conveys to us the poignancy of the moment in which these words are spoken. Jesus has ended his public ministry and has withdrawn into the intimate fellowship with his closest disciples to give them his final instructions and benediction before his arrest and execution. Parenthetically, it is very comforting to some of us that our beloved professor of New Testament emeritus, the Reverend Canon Pierson Parker, has suggested in a recent article in *The Living Church* that this intimate company who shared the last meal with Jesus may well have included both men and women.[1] In any event, Jesus's humanity, which enables us to identify with him as our brother as well as our Lord, is never more evident than at this time. He is sorrowful and troubled in spirit; he has just identified Judas as his betrayer, and Judas has gone out into the night to hand over his Master to death by crucifixion. With heavy heart Jesus now turns to those who are left and opens his heart to them. He knows that the time is short, and he has much to say. There is the urgency of imminent separation and there is the gentleness of a mother who has nurtured her brood as long as she can but must now leave them to fend for themselves. He calls them "little children."

One can understand why Julian of Norwich, the fifteenth-century mystic whose life and work our church celebrated on Sunday past, May 8, wrote in her reflections:

> The human mother will suckle her child with
> her own milk, our beloved Mother, Jesus, feeds
> us with himself and with most tender courtesy
> does it by means of the Blessed Sacrament.[2]

Although John's Gospel makes no mention here of bread and wine, the moment is a deeply sacramental one. Earlier Jesus has washed his disciples' feet. By word and example as the fateful hour draws closer, he is trying to impress upon them the essence of his ministry to them during their life together, and to ensure the foundation of the Christian community which will continue after his physical death.

We are able to enter more deeply into such a moment when we recall our own experience with dying and death. We tend to remember with greatest clarity what a beloved member of our family, or a dear friend, or even someone who we admired greatly, said and did in the closing chapter of that person's life. Most of you familiar with the civil rights movement of the 1950s and 1960s may have read of Fannie Lou Hamer, a great Christian, Negro civil rights fighter, and advocate of creative nonviolence in Mississippi. I met her only twice. The first time was in the summer of 1967 at an interracial education conference on the campus of a Negro junior college in a small town in Mississippi. That evening there was a sudden blackout of the electrical circuits, which seemed to affect only our section of the township. We sat up for most of the night singing softly and talking in anxious whispers, while headlights of our cars drawn together in close formation lighted up the buildings, grounds, and roadway entrance, to at least give us warning in the event of a surprise attack.

I saw her only once briefly after that, but the impact of Mrs. Hamer's life and struggles upon me were so great that I wept when I read of her death in March of this year.

During her long and valiant battle for human dignity in Mississippi, she was shot at, beaten, and thrown into jail but she held fast to her Christian faith. She explained, "I feel sorry for anybody that could let hate wrap them up. Ain't no such thing as I can hate anybody and hope to see God's face." A friend who visited her for the last time March 4, [1977], about ten days before she died, reported, "She was sitting in a wheelchair crying. She stated that she was so tired;

she wanted all of us to remember her and to keep up her work. She wanted us to understand that she had taken care of business. She felt that her house was in place, and that everything was in order with God." Knowing that her death was near, Fanny Lou Hamer was trying to pass on the faith which had sustained her in life.

Jesus's final commission to his disciples is "to love one another even as I have loved you." According to John, this is a new commandment, not the same as the Great Commandment of the Synoptic Gospels to love one's neighbor, nor like the command to love one's enemies, but the characteristic of the Christian community: "By this love that you have for one another, everyone will know that you are my disciples."[a]

How often in our own lives do we cry out in protest that this is an impossible standard, even though we may feel ourselves called to be one of Christ's disciples in a full-time ministry, whether lay or ordained? I have sometimes thought it easier to love our enemies than our fellow Christians. And sometimes I cannot tell the difference. For those whom I believe to be my enemies, my love may be remote and somewhat theoretical. I may categorize them as a faceless group and avoid dealing with them (and my conscience) as individuals. If personal contact is unavoidable, I may retreat into polite formality.

But we are less able to rationalize our attitudes and behavior toward those with whom we associate continuously in a professing Christian community. The closer our contact, the more transparent are our biases, arrogance, self-righteousness, super-sensitivity, anger, and lack of charity. Or, we may waver between being a "doormat" on the one hand and being harshly judgmental or abrasive on the other hand. In seminary, we can even become divided upon whether one kneels or stands, genuflects or bows, prefers Rite I or Rite II, is charismatic or not, and what are often divisions over form can deepen into divisions of substance. Or, we can lose sight of Christ's command in a bitter struggle over human-made traditions.

I recall my first year here at General [Theological Seminary] as a seminarian. I had just left an educational institution based upon the Judaic tradition although it was nonsectarian, and I longed to be part of a Christian community. During one of our small-group meetings in the Junior Tutorial, one of my classmates said, "It is wonderful to be in a place where we can talk about God without feeling self-conscious or apologetic." I immediately felt a bond of fellowship because he expressed my own feelings so exactly. Yet, before two years had passed, despite our common interest in poetry and liturgical music, or the fact that we attended the same classes, studied the same books, wrestled with the same theological doubts, worshipped together in the same chapel, ate in the same dining room, and suffered the same jitters over term papers and final exams, we had become strangers to one another—separated by our mutual alienation over the issue of ordination of women. My brother could not accept the idea that I could be authentically his sister priest. I, feeling that the integrity of my whole personhood was being drawn into question, was unable to reach out to him. Neither of us was able to enter into one another's pain, yet both of us were under the injunction to "love one another even as I have loved you." Fifteen years earlier we might have been just as deeply alienated over the issue of race.

Such alienations, particularly in a seminary community where devotion to Christ's teachings and way of life is the major preoccupation of its members, have sometimes led to disillusionment and despair—over ourselves and our fellow Christians. We become restive before the end of our training and are impatient to get out into our own parishes where we may think that as pastors and priests we will be able to develop Christian fellowship—only to find, of course, that the same human cussedness is everywhere in the church—in the vestry, the congregation, the bishop's office, the ministers' association, the diocesan convention, the General Convention.

More sadly, we may find ourselves isolated in a small parish, alone, struggling with staggering problems of competence and conscience, without the availability of experienced advisors, the presence of a group of peers with whom to share our apprehension, or the daily discipline of common worship to sustain us and give us spiritual strength. In these circumstances, we begin to appreciate more deeply Bonhoeffer's remark that "the Christian in exile is comforted by a brief visit of a Christian brother [or sister], a prayer together and a brother's [or sister's] blessing; indeed, he is strengthened by a letter written by a Christian."[b]

We also begin to understand dimly Bonhoeffer's reflection that a Christian community is *not based on human love*, or upon our own dreams of what such a community should be, but upon what Christ has done for all of us; that what determines our brotherhood or sisterhood is not our piety or spirituality, but we are by reason of Christ. He concludes, "We are bound together by faith, not by experience.... For Jesus Christ alone is our unity.... Through him alone do we have access to one another, joy in one another, and fellowship with one another."[c] We forget this at our peril.

Amen.

Notes

a John 13:35.

b Dietrich Bonhoeffer, *Life Together: A Discussion of Christian Fellowship* (New York: Harper and Row, 1954).

c Ibid.

Sermon on Acts 8:5

Acts 8:5
Philip went down to a city of Samaria and proclaimed to them Christ.

As we continue celebration of the Easter season and pursue the biblical account of the development of the post-Easter church, the story of Philip in today's Epistle has special significance for those of us who feel called to the ordained ministry. Traditionally, our service of ordination to the diaconate includes a reading of the Choosing of the Seven (of whom Stephen and Philip are the most prominent)—"men of good repute, full of the Spirit and of wisdom"—selected by the disciples of the early church in Jerusalem and consecrated by the apostles through prayer and the laying on of hands. The recent upheaval in our own communion over the issue of ordination of women recalls to mind [. . .] the earliest struggle for more inclusive representation in the leadership of the church.

I suspect that when most of us are ordained deacons, we are so relieved over having survived the rigorous period of preparation and testing of our vocation that our thoughts seldom go beyond the joyous event of the laying on of hands, the fact that our ministry is being affirmed by the church and we are given the "authority to proclaim God's Word and to assist in the ministration of his holy Sacraments." The bishop's charge—"You are to make Christ and his redemptive love known, by your word and example, to those among whom you live, and work, and worship"—takes on a deeper meaning as we encounter the myriad unanticipated problems of our ministry and discover the cost of discipleship. Today's Epistle speaks to the cost as well as the joy of ministry.

Following the ordination of the seven, we hear again only of Stephen and Philip. Stephen, a man of unusual faith and power, incurred the enmity of a Jewish cult, "The Freedman," and Jews from various foreign provinces who became enraged over his preaching Christ. He was stoned to death by an angry mob, his followers were persecuted, men and women were dragged from their homes and thrown into prison. Others, including Philip, were scattered throughout Judea and Samaria.

We are told only that Philip went down to a city of Samaria and are given no hint of the shock he must have suffered after the tragic events in Jerusalem—his close friend and co-worker brutally murdered, his own ministry destroyed. We can envision his state of mind as he fled the city, cut off from fellowship with the apostles who remained, no longer feeling the support of a believing community, and driven to find refuge among a people who were hated and despised by their Jewish neighbors, doubtless considered unlikely to receive the gospel. We can imagine the sorrow and loneliness of that journey in which doubt and uncertainty warred with faith and hope. What we do know is that Philip emerged from his ordeal with renewed power, an evangelist missionary, transforming the calamity in Jerusalem into the opportunity to proclaim the Risen Christ and spread the Christian gospel beyond the confines of that city. Out of his own suffering he brought hope and healing to the Samaritans: "The crowds, to a man, listened eagerly to what Philip said, when they heard him and saw the miracles that he performed . . . and there was great joy in the city."[a]

Here is an example of how God uses us to build the kingdom in ways we may never have contemplated when we sought the ministry, whether it be lay or ordained, of how the fullness of ministry may develop out of circumstances which appear at the time to represent failure of our mission. We may not experience the kind of sudden catastrophes which overtook Philip, but there will be times when we feel utterly alone, cut off from the fellowship and support of a seminary community, or even of other clergy, and facing situations which overwhelm us with a sense of our own inadequacy. If we are in parish work, there may be times when in spite of all our labors our hopes and plans are frustrated and we see little or no growth. Others will demand certitude from us when we ourselves live with uncertainty. Opportunities for service as we conceived it may be blocked; positions for which we prepared ourselves may be unavailable. If we are women clergy, we may have to struggle with the added pain of nonacceptance of our sacramental function. In our loneliness and frustration we may be tempted to question the authenticity of our calling.

It is comforting to know that we are not unique. I think of Dean [of General Theological Seminary] James C. Fenhagan's reference to the intense loneliness of the ordained ministry and to the anxiety of uncertainty. He reminds us that "the deeper answer to anxiety does not lie in increased certainty, but in the courage to live creatively in the midst of ambiguity and paradox." We hear resonance of Philip's journey to Samaria in Henri Nouwen's theme of the "wound of loneliness" in the life of the minister, and of making one's own wounds a source of healing to others "through a constant willingness to see one's own pain and suffering as rising from the depth of the human condition which all men [and women] share." Nouwen points to hope grounded in the Christ-event which enables us "to enter unknown and fearful territory," in his words "an act of discipline-ship in which we follow the hard road of Christ who entered upon death with nothing but bare hope," whose resurrection affirms "that there is light on the other side of darkness."[b]

Amen.

Notes

[a] Acts 8:6.

[b] Henri Nouwen, *The Wounded Healer* (New York: Random House, 1979).

The Prophetic Impulse

Luke 3:7–17

Then said he to the multitude that came forth to be baptized of him, O generation of vipers, who hath warned you to flee from the wrath to come? Bring forth therefore fruits worthy of repentance, and begin not to say within yourselves, we have Abraham to our father: for I say unto you, that God is able of these stones to raise up children unto Abraham. And now also the axe is laid unto the root of the trees: every tree therefore which bringeth not forth good fruit is hewn down, and cast into the fire. And the people asked him, saying, What shall we do then? He answereth and saith unto them, He that hath two coats, let him impart to him that hath none; and he that hath meat, let him do likewise. Then came also publicans to be baptized, and said unto him, Master, what shall we do? And he said unto them, Exact no more than that which is appointed you. And the soldiers likewise demanded of him, saying, And what shall we do? And he said unto them, Do violence to no man, neither accuse any falsely; and be content with your wages. And as the people were in expectation, and all men mused in their hearts of John, whether he were the Christ, or not: John answered, saying unto them all, I indeed baptize you with water; but one mightier than I cometh, the latchet of whose shoes I am not worthy to unloose: he shall baptize you with the Holy Ghost and with fire: Whose fan is in his hand, and he will thoroughly purge his floor, and will gather the wheat into his garner; but the chaff he will burn with fire unquenchable.

In every age of political and social crisis, human prophets appear to sound warnings of what is to come unless humanity changes its course. They may be humble, untutored individuals, like Amos, the sheep-farmer of the eighth century B.C. They may be learned public figures; they may be gentle poets, or wild creatures driven by some inner fire to burst suddenly upon the scene and command attention through some bizarre and often violent act. [. . .][1]

We usually think of prophecy as foretelling the future—prediction of things to come. But the biblical meaning of prophecy is the declaration of religious truth, speaking as the voice of God. It may have an element of prediction, but as R. B. Y. Scott writes in his study *The Relevance of the Prophets, 1944–1968,* "What is about to happen is *the necessary consequence of a moral situation.* At the same time it will be the concrete realization of the prophetic 'Word' which expresses in relation to that situation the righteous will of YAHWEH, When God is about to act he (God) makes known his purpose."[a]

John the Baptist, subject of today's Gospel reading, in biblical tradition was the last of the great Hebrew prophets before the Messiah, standing on the boundary between the old epoch and the new ushered in by Jesus of Nazareth, proclaimed as the Messiah. He was the immediate forerunner of Jesus. The name "John," so popular in the New Testament, which records at least nine men of that name, is derived from the Hebrew word *Yohanan* which means "Yahweh (God) has been gracious." (Jesus, from the Hebrew *Jeshua* or *Joshua* means "Yahweh is salvation.")

John was born in the hill-country of Judea, the son of elderly parents and heir of priestly tradition. His father, Zechariah, was a priest and his mother, Elizabeth, was the daughter of a priestly family and cousin to Mary, the mother of Jesus. Born within six months of each other, the destinies of these two young men were linked together by a common religious commitment. Both emerged from obscurity in their late twenties or early thirties; both had short, dramatic public ministries. Both ran afoul of the establishment and were executed within a few years of one another—John beheaded around A.D. 28 by order of Herod the Jewish tetrarch who ruled over Galilee, and Jesus around A.D. 30 by crucifixion under the Roman governor of Judea Pontius Pilate.

John's dramatic appearance on the banks of the Jordan River was seen by some of the people of his time as a throwback nearly one thousand years to the ninth-century B.C. prophet and reformer Elijah the Tishbite, described as "a wild figure, clad only in a leather loin-cloth and a cloak of hair" who appeared suddenly before Ahab, the king of Northern Israel, protesting the pagan ways of the people who had deserted their God who had led them out of bondage in Egypt. To the consternation of King Ahab and his court, Elijah predicted that there would be a terrible drought upon the land, then escaped across the Jordan River before he could be apprehended and holed up in a desolate spot where, according to biblical tradition, he was fed by ravens and drank from a brook until it dried up.

John the Baptist too was a wild and lonely figure, dressed in camel-skin and living on a diet of locust-beans and wild honey, very much like the Bedouin tribes in the North African desert today. His message was repentance and water baptism as the Hebrew symbol of the cleansing of sin. Unlike his cousin and successor Jesus, he did not speak of forgiveness but preached wrathful judgment. "You brood of vipers," he told the crowds of people, "who warned you to flee from the wrath to come?" Or in today's English Version, "You snakes! Who told you that you could escape from God's wrath that is about to come?"[b] Here John was referring to desert snakes scurrying from their holes when the dry brush of the desert caught fire. "And don't start saying among yourselves, 'Abraham is our ancestor,'" in other words, John was warning the people that they could not rely upon a mistaken interpretation of themselves as God's elect, God's chosen people. "Do the things that will show you have turned from your sins."

As in the first century, so today—this very week past—we had a dramatic warning from another bizarre, strange creature, coming out of obscurity and for twelve suspense-filled hours holding an entire nation spellbound, as his solitary figure, dressed in helmet and armored suiting and threatening to set off a thousand pounds of dynamite with the detonator in his hand to blow up the Washington Monument from his white van, walked back and forth at the foot of the monument. All Norman Mayer, sixty-six years of age, wanted apparently was "a national dialogue on the nuclear weapons question."[2] For weeks he had picketed the White House and was ignored, of course, and he chose the empty threat of violence to one of America's "sacred icons" to get attention. His leaflets, according to the Associated Press, bemoaned a "failed civilization . . . on the verge of annihilation" through nuclear war. Was his act of madness any more insane than that of the United States House of Representatives voting $231 billion for the lethal weapons in the face of millions of unemployed workers, people being evicted from their homes and wandering the streets in search of shelter, and other symbols of a deep and pervasive economic crisis? Every Christian today must ask himself or herself, "How can I talk of loving God and my neighbor and simultaneously support or acquiesce in the MX missile?"

Nearly fifteen years ago, another prophet was gunned down, Martin Luther King Jr., who devoted most of his career to the development of nonviolent solutions to social conflict. In his final book, *Where Do We Go from Here: Chaos or Community?,* he wrote, "Therefore I suggest that the philosophy and strategy of nonviolence become immediately a subject for study and for serious experimentation in every field of human conflict, by no means excluding the relations between nations. It is, after all, Nation-States which make war, which have produced the weapons that threaten the survival of mankind and which are both genocidal and suicidal in character."[3] Norman Mayer too spoke of the "Genocidalists" and demanded that the dialogue on nuclear weapons be "the first order of business on every agenda of every organization in the U.S.A.—schools, churches, business, fraternal, unions, sports, ETC. No association exempted, local state and national elected bodies must comply."

I do not know whether Norman Mayer spoke out of religious conviction. The paradox and tragedy of his life was that although he threatened violence, there were no instruments of violence in his van. The police found no TNT. In totally opposite ways, he and Martin Luther King Jr. proclaimed the identical message, and both met the fate of John the Baptist, Jesus of Nazareth, and all the martyred prophets between the first and twentieth centuries.

As we approach the celebration of the birth of the Prince of Peace, what is our individual response to the death of Norman Mayer?

Let Us Pray.

Eternal God, in whose perfect Kingdom no sword is drawn but the sword of righteousness, no strength known but the strength of love. So mightily spread abroad your Spirit, that all peoples may be gathered under the banner of the Prince of Peace, and your Kingdom may increase until the earth is filled with the knowledge of your love. Through Jesus Christ, our Lord and brother.

Amen.

Notes

[a] R. B. Y. Scott, *The Relevance of the Prophets, 1944–1968* (New York: Macmillan, 1978).

[b] Luke 3:7.

Atonement

Luke 10:29
But he, willing to justify himself, said unto Jesus, And who is my neighbor?

The lawyer who posed this question to Jesus of Nazareth wanted him to elaborate upon the meaning of the familiar Old Testament commandment (Leviticus 19:18): "You shall not take vengeance or bear any grudge against the sons of your own people, but you shall love your neighbor as yourself." Jesus's listeners were Jews, and for ancient Israelites a neighbor meant anyone who belonged to the Jewish community. In time it included Gentiles known as proselytes, those who converted to the Jewish faith. Few Jews of Jesus's time would have applied the term to Romans, Greeks, and Syrians who lived in their land. Widespread public opinion also resisted the idea that the commandment to love extended to one's personal enemies.

We have similar difficulty defining and applying the Christian understanding of "neighbor" in our own complex modern society. We wrestle with the practical problems of giving aid to all those we know to be in need and of giving of ourselves beyond a limited circle. Racial, religious, class, or national loyalties tend to separate us from others, and our feeling of responsibility for the neighbor's welfare tends to lessen in proportion to the remoteness of our immediate common interests. Ours has been described as an impersonal society in which people living in the same apartment house or in the same block as we do may be as distant from our active concern as those living in a far-off country. Frequently, we are so preoccupied with our own affairs we are unwilling to become involved in the troubles of others, particularly when we think it is dangerous to intervene. How often have we stifled the impulse to pick up someone standing in the rain at a bus stop because it is inconvenient to pull over in traffic, or have driven past a stalled car on the roadside because we are afraid we might get mugged, or we refuse to sign a petition on behalf of an apparently worthy cause because we do not know the people sponsoring the campaign.

Jesus, of course, might have answered the lawyer's question by saying simply, "Your neighbor is any person in need." Instead, he told a parable in which the identity of the needy man was irrelevant—merely "a certain man" who fell among thieves. He focused upon the responsibility of those in a position to give aid and in the telling of the story pointed up the requirements of a good neighbor, which Dr. Martin Luther King Jr. once described as the capacity for *universal, dangerous,* and *excessive* altruism—making concern for others the first law of one's life.

Jesus's listeners were familiar with the dangers of the seventeen-mile-long road from Jerusalem to Jericho, filled with sudden curves from which a lonely traveler could be ambushed, and notorious as a haunt of ruthless bandits. They may have assumed that the nameless man who was beaten, robbed, stripped naked, and left to die was a Jew like themselves. The priest and Levite, representing the highest religious leadership, "passed by on the other side" without even stopping to investigate. They were not necessarily heartless men; perhaps they were afraid to get involved. To linger on that perilous road was to risk one's own life. Since a priest was forbidden to touch any corpse except that of a blood relation, and a Levite as a member of the lower clergy was also required to maintain strict ritualistic purity when engaged in his duties, it was easier for them to assume that the man was probably dead anyway and nothing was to be gained by stopping.

If Jesus had merely wanted to demonstrate human kindness, he might have used the figure of a Jewish layman as the third person to come along, but he chose to present the one who did stop and give aid as a Samaritan—a shocking image to his audience and one who belonged to a race considered inferior and utterly despised by Jews. The Samaritans were a people of mixed Assyrian-Jewish blood who lived in the territory between Judea and Galilee and practiced a debased form of Jewish religion. Over the centuries a bitter hostility had developed between the two peoples. Jews had destroyed the Samaritan temple in Samaria, and in turn Samaritans had desecrated the Jewish temple in Jerusalem by scattering human bones in the sacred places. Jews publicly cursed Samaritans in the synagogues and prayed God they would have no share in eternal life. A Jew would not believe the testimony of a Samaritan or accept any service from him. We recall in John's Gospel that the woman at the well questioned Jesus, "How is it that you a Jew, ask a drink of me, a woman of Samaria? For Jews have no dealings with Samaritans." The picture of a *good* Samaritan was inconceivable to Jesus's listeners. He would be at least expected to show compassion in the circumstances, for why should a half-breed stranger risk his life for a man, if a Jew, would have treated him with contempt as the scum of the earth?

It was clear from Jesus's parable that the Samaritan took no thought of the race, religion, or class of the stricken man. He saw only a fellow human being in distress, and while he had as much to fear as any other lone traveler on the Jericho Road he risked the dangers of delay to rescue the victim. He poured on medicinal oil and wine and bound up his wounds, placed the injured man on his own breast, and walked beside him until he brought him to an inn. There he nursed him through the night. When he was ready to leave next morning, he made sure the man would be cared for. He gave the innkeeper enough money to cover the man's needs for several days and arranged to pay any additional expenses incurred when he passed by the inn on his return journey.

Jesus stunned his listeners and turned their conventional ethics upside down through his detailed description of a radical act which has been described [according to Charles W. F. Smith] as "not a matter of simple compassion but a much more important matter of obeying the fundamental will of God," recognizing that every human being is the object of God's love.[1] "*Just so,*" says John Dominic Crossan commenting on this parable, "does the Kingdom of God break abruptly into human consciousness and demand the overturn of prior values, closed options, set judgments and established conclusions."[a]

Christ's radical imperative of neighborly love continually confronts us, demanding that we reexamine our long-held biases and established conclusions in our political and social as well as our interpersonal relationships. And while it is painful to give up the comfort of exclusiveness and recognize the claims of others upon us, as Christians we are commanded always to keep before us the ever-widening concept of neighbor, however imperfectly we embrace it. The urgency of this imperative is reflected daily in news events which make it terrifyingly clear that all of the world's people are so interdependent the existence of war, revolution, terrorism, or famine in any part of the globe has immediate and fateful consequences for us here at home.

Perhaps we have been witnessing the Kingdom of God breaking into human consciousness and demanding the overturn of prior values and closed options in the recent turbulence surrounding the resignation of U.S. ambassador Andrew Young. Ambassador Young, as we know, resigned under pressure following disclosure of his unauthorized conversation with [a] PLO [Palestinian Liberation Organization] observer at this UN [United Nations] in violation of U.S. policy not to negotiate with the PLO because of its refusal to recognize the state of Israel's right to exist as defined by Security Council Resolution 242. It is generally conceded that the legitimate aspirations of the Palestinian people for autonomy must be dealt with in any settlement of the Mideast crisis, but objection to the PLO as spokesman for the Palestinians is that it is dominated by its terrorist factions whose objective is to destroy Israel.

What is glossed over in much of the political discussion is that there is a fundamental relationship between Andrew Young's action and his Christian understanding of what it means to be a good neighbor in the hazardous field of international relations. An ordained minister, he is rooted in the Martin Luther King Jr. tradition of nonviolence in the struggle for social justice. Dr. King emphasized that the principle of love stands at the center of nonviolence—love as *agape,* which does not mean "some sentimental or affectionate emotion, but understanding, redemptive good will"; which does not discriminate between worthy and unworthy people, or any qualities they possess, but is an entirely "neighbor-regarding concern"; which discovers the neighbor in every person it meets. Said Dr. King, "The Samaritan was good because he responded to the human need he was presented with." He declared that in the last analysis, "agape means a recognition of the fact that all life is involved in a single process, and all men (and women) are brothers (and sisters)." Shortly before his death Dr. King published his book *Where Do We Go from Here: Chaos or Community?* in which he proposed "that the philosophy and strategy of nonviolence become immediately a subject for study and for serious experimentation in every field of human conflict, by no means excluding the relations between nations."[2]

I believe this was the moral imperative which led Andrew Young to risk a meeting with the representative of the forces whose ultimate cooperation is crucial to peace in the Middle East. He was faced with the need to bring the issues of the Palestinian people more clearly into the open where it could be publicly discussed. Like the priest and Levite on the Jericho Road, he might have avoided trouble by a narrow interpretation of his diplomatic function. Or he might have overestimated his political influence and simply resigned, stating his disagreement with his nation's policy. Instead, he acted when and where he had the most leverage and in accordance with what he believed to be in the best interest of his country. He took the initiative and risked his job to open up communication when, as he said, he found himself as president of the UN Security Council "faced with an issue which required communication and understanding."

No other incident has jolted American consciousness, broken an embarrassed silence, and stimulated a new dialogue on the issues at stake as quickly as Andrew Young's action and its aftermath. There is the beginning of a new consensus affirming the political and moral soundness of Mr. Young's position. As William Raspberry has said in the *Washington Post,* there is a "new freedom to say what one truly thinks about Israel which extends to whites as well (as Blacks). As a result, the whole Mideast debate will never again be the same."

Typical of this emerging consensus is the thoughtful statement of former Undersecretary of State George N. Ball who said, "Though the circumstances are regrettable, Ambassador Young's resignation could still yield rich benefits if it focuses attention on his central position (on which he was correct and, hence, unforgivable) that no durable Arab-Israeli peace is possible without PLO participation in the negotiations." Pointing out that because the Israeli Army had permitted no political organization in the occupied areas of the West Bank and Gaza Strip and there are no alternative Palestinian spokesmen, Mr. Ball concluded, "We have no option but to engage the PLO's most moderate elements in conversations."

The Andy Young affair has set off a chain reaction the political consequences of which we cannot now foresee, but it points beyond itself to a reality more fundamental than the immediate issues of Black-Jewish relations or Black support for the reelection of President Carter, important as they may be. The ultimate model for human relations is that the neighbor is universal and must everywhere be the object of our compassionate concern. Christ calls us continually to choose whether we will follow the path of the priest and Levite or that of the Good Samaritan on the Jericho roads of life. "Then said Jesus unto him, Go and do thou likewise."

Amen.

Notes

[a] John Dominic Crossan, *In Parables: The Challenge of the Historical Jesus* (New York: Harper-Collins, 1973).

The Holy Spirit

John 26:26

When the Comforter is come, whom I will send to you from the Father, even the Spirit of truth, which proceedeth from the Father, he will testify of me; and you shall also bear witness, because you have been with me from the beginning.

On this Sunday after Ascension Day, we also celebrate the seventy-sixth anniversary of Calvary Protestant Episcopal Church. An anniversary is [a] joyous occasion in which we look back to our beginnings and give thanks for blessings which have brought us thus far, and we recommit ourselves to God as disciples of his Son Jesus, the Christ, to carry on the mission and outreach of this church. We recall that first meeting of nine people held in a private home on Florida Avenue in 1902, and of the faith which enabled this tiny Christian mission to grow into a robust parish.

In reading the history of this church, I learned that it took its name from Calvary Church in New York City. This tradition has a special meaning for me because Calvary in New York was the church in which Mrs. Eleanor Roosevelt was christened as an infant back in 1884 or 1885. It is also the church I attended when I was in New York, and it [was] there in 1973 that I first talked with my friend the rector, the Reverend Tom Pike, about the possibility of entering the ordained ministry.

Our Gospel text this morning takes us back to the very beginnings of the Christian community to which we belong. Jesus is in the Upper Room sharing his last meal with his closest disciples before his arrest and crucifixion. His earthly mission is drawing to a close, and he knows that he must rely upon these few disciples, weak and fearful though they may be, to carry on the work he has begun. The atmosphere is not one of joyous celebration but one of heavy-heartedness. Jesus knows that very soon he will be separated from his disciples and that they will be scattered in confusion, shattered by grief, and overwhelmed with fear. Patiently, in the few minutes they have left together, he tries to summarize his teachings, to comfort them and give them courage and hope so they will be able to withstand the tribulations, the persecutions, which lie ahead. He must make them understand that they will not be alone; that the Holy Spirit will be with them and remain with them always. The word "Comforter" is a translation from the Greek word *Paraclete,* which also means "Counselor," "Advocate," or "Helper." Jesus also refers to it as the Holy Spirit.

During his earthly ministry, *Jesus* has been with [the] disciple[s] as their counselor and helper, teacher, guide. Now that he will no longer be with them in the flesh, the Holy Spirit will come in [his] place. At one point he tells them, "The Paraclete, the Holy Spirit, whom the Father will send in my name, will instruct you in everything, and remind you of all that I told you" (John 14:26). The Spirit is the bequest of the glorified Christ to all who believe in him.

In our church life, we tend to emphasize the gift of the Holy Spirit on very special sacramental occasions—at baptism or at confirmation or at an ordination. But we must remember that the Spirit of God's presence is with us at all times and in all places, in every possible situation—at home, in school, at work, in politics, in social life, in the marketplace, in joy, in the depths of sorrow, sin, sickness, and despair—the ever-present companion, friend, and helper, the Eternal One working in and through every moment of history in the affairs of mankind.

Whether we are consciously aware of it or not, God is with us every moment of our lives in everything that we do. I think sometimes we shrink from the idea of the nearness of God because we think of it as such a fearful and awesome thing. But God is not alien or distant from us; his Spirit is as close as the touch of a loved one's hand.

Remember the Psalmist in the 139th Psalm:

> Whither can I go from your Spirit?
> Where can I flee from your presence?
> If I climb up to heaven you are there;

If I make the grave my bed, you are there also;

If I take the wings of the morning;

And dwell in the uttermost parts of the sea;

Even there your hand will lead me;

And your right hand will hold me fast.[a]

I, personally, am not a good flyer and when I am in a plane I have to remind myself that God is there just as much as when I am on the [ground] driving my own car. When we feel alone and desolate, it is not God who has shut us out but *we* who have tried to shut out God. When we are open to the presence of the Holy Spirit, we feel a certain serenity in the midst of conflict, trouble, or confusion. God's power works in us and through us, to guide us in our critical decisions, to comfort us when we are bereaved, to strengthen us when we are overcome with fear and apprehension. As one Christian writer has said, "There is a wonderful, loved, protected feeling that embraces one who realizes that God is always near."

To dwell in the Holy Spirit is to dwell in Christ. The Spirit replaces the visible presence of Jesus, and the church is the Spirit-filled community bound to one another in Christ. In our communion we share the supreme gift of the Spirit expressed in the benediction, "The grace of our Lord Jesus Christ, and the love of God, and the fellowship of the Holy Spirit, be with us all evermore."

When we speak of the "fellowship of the Holy Spirit," we are speaking of God's faithfulness in all situations. The Psalmist says, "Even though I walk in the valley of the shadow of death, I fear no evil, for thou art with me, thy rod and thy staff, they comfort me."[b] Any one of us who has stood by the side of a beloved relative or friend who is dying understands the meaning of this verse. We also speak of God's responsiveness—and it is this responsiveness which is the foundation of our faith in prayer. Prayer is our attempt to bring our whole being before God—our thankfulness, our needs, our hopes, our fears—in the expectation that God will respond to our needs. So often we find that when we rest our lives and our plans in God, things work out for us better than any plans we can make for ourselves. Things fall into place.

We also believe that God understands us better than we understand ourselves. God understands our needs, and sometimes, in retrospect, we realize that something we have greatly desired has been withheld from us in God's wisdom for our own best interest.

The "fellowship of the Holy Spirit" also speaks to us of the forgiveness of

God. Mankind was created for community with God. We are likened to the eternal in the midst of transitory existence. Yet in our willfulness, all too often we live in ignorance of and estrangement from God. When we become aware of our estrangement, we are conscious of sin. And when we are separated from God, we are also separated from our fellow human beings. It is the alienation from God which brings about enemies and conflicts between human beings. Through God's grace and forgiveness, we are healed of our sinfulness, the estrangement is overcome, and we are restored to community with God.

Jesus said, "Love one another even as I have loved you," and this is the standard for the Christian community.[c] Through faith in the Risen Christ and in his message of love and his sacrifice, we are bound together in at-one-ment with God and at-one-ment with one another.

Above all, it is the assurance of being united with Jesus and his life, which overcomes death. Mankind has never been able to come to terms with death; it calls into question all our human values and would make our earthly existence seem futile if we did not have this hope through our faith in Christ of the new life after death. We do not know what life after death will be like, but in faith we can say with the devout theologian who spent his life studying the Holy Scripture and when he was nearing death was asked about the life beyond, he replied, "I do not know, I know only that I shall be safe."

The Holy Spirit, then, as Jesus promised his disciples, is God's eternal presence with us always, coming to us as he came to us in Jesus of Nazareth, loving us, sustaining us, guiding us, forgiving us, never letting us go, transforming our lives, and leading us toward the consummation of God's ultimate plan for all his creation. When the Spirit dwells in us, we are able to let go [of] our own self-centeredness and yield ourselves up to the workings of the love of God, knowing that we shall be safe.

Let Us Pray.

Almighty and everlasting God, behold us your children gathered once again to give praise and thanks for this holy house dedicated to your service. Mercifully grant, that recalling our own dedication as living temples of your Holy Spirit, we may be enabled to govern our souls and bodies according to your commandment and to the glory of your holy name; through Jesus Christ our Lord.

Amen.

Notes

a Psalm 139:7–10.

b Psalm 23:4.

c John 13:34.

Sermon Given on April 3, 1983

Luke 24:5

Why search among the dead for one who lives?

In Luke's Gospel, these words ascribed to two men in dazzling garments announce the resurrection of Jesus to the sorrowful women standing dumbfounded in the empty tomb on that first Easter morning. Although details vary in other Gospel accounts, the message is essentially the same. In Matthew the women are told, "Do not be afraid; for I know you seek Jesus who was crucified. He is not here; for he has risen. Come and see the place where he lay."[a] Similar words are found in Mark. In John's Gospel, Jesus himself appears to Mary of Magdala saying, "Go to my brothers, and tell them that I am ascending to my father and your father, my God and your God."[b]

These pronouncements constitute the central claim of the Christian faith which we celebrate at Easter—"The one who was dead now lives; Christ is risen. The Lord is risen indeed." It has been rightly said that "there would be no gospel, not one account, no letter to the New Testament, no faith, no Church, no worship, no prayer of Christendom to this day without the message of the resurrection of Christ."[1]

During the past week, Christians throughout the world through worship services, prayers, and meditations have reenacted the swift rush of events leading up to this astounding message. Coming to us hallowed by tradition over the centuries, we can experience only vicariously its impact upon those first witnesses who heard it. They were caught up in the turmoil of these events which

233

swept them from an ecstasy of joy into the depths of human despair. The week had begun with Jesus's triumphant entry into Jerusalem, as joyous crowds scattered palm branches before him and lifted their voices in praise: "Blessed is he who comes in the name of the Lord. Hosanna in the highest!" Within a few days the atmosphere had changed to snarling crowds shouting, "Crucify him! Crucify him!" The public ministry of Jesus of Nazareth, which began with his proclamation, "the Kingdom of God is near," had ended in total disaster, his message a failure, himself utterly repudiated. The man who had preached God's loving mercy and forgiveness, who had healed the sick, cast out demons, restored the blind to sight, fed the hungry, and raised the dead—the man upon whom his followers had pinned all their hopes—had died in public disgrace, the shameful death of a criminal, utterly alone, jeered by the crowds, deserted by his closest companions, and seemingly abandoned by God.

The disciples who had been with him throughout his ministry had scattered and fled in terror at the time of crisis. During the agony of Jesus's crucifixion, they had stood far off and even left his burial to others. Only one man, according to Luke, Joseph of Arimathea, who was not a close disciple, had the courage to dissent from the Jewish Sanhedrin's action in turning Jesus over to Pilate. Only Joseph of Arimathea came forward after Jesus's death, got permission from Pilate to take his body down from the cross, then wrapped it in a linen sheet and laid it in a tomb.

In Luke's account, only the women who had followed Jesus from Galilee, then followed him to the cross and mourned him there, were devoted enough to follow to the end, take note of the tomb, and observe how his body was laid. Then they went home and prepared spices and perfumes to return to the tomb as soon as the Jewish Sabbath ended, so that they might perform love's last service to their Lord in death.

Because of their faithfulness to Jesus, even after his death and burial, in Gospel tradition women held a central place at the very "foundations of Christian faith and witness." According to Mark and Luke, Jesus's resurrection is first announced to women. Matthew reports that Jesus first appeared to Mary of Magdala and the other Mary. In John's Gospel, he first appeared to Mary of Magdala alone and she ran bursting with the news, "I have seen the Lord!" All four Gospels agree that women (or a woman) were commissioned to go and tell Peter and the other disciples that Jesus is not dead but risen.[c]

That women should be reported as the first bearers of the Easter message is one of the remarkable features of the Gospel accounts of the Resurrection, for as we know, in Jewish custom women were not authorized or considered qualified to teach or give reliable testimony. In fact, Luke reports that when they told the disciples all they had heard and seen at the tomb, the women's words "seemed to them an idle tale, and they did not believe them."

It is not surprising that the disciples would dismiss the women's testimony about so stupendous an event. For them Jesus's death was final; all hope was gone; God had deserted him; the power of evil had prevailed. They were not prepared to accept on hearsay an action of God which, in the words of Hans Kung, "bursts through and goes beyond the bounds of history," an action incomprehensible to human experience.[2]

Yet, the very sequence of events in the Gospel narratives reminds us that God's wisdom is not the world's wisdom, and that God has often used the most unlikely human instruments to demonstrate divine power. St. Paul pointed this out later to the church of Corinth. Reflecting upon Christ's death on the cross, he wrote, "God purposely chose what the world considers nonsense in order to put wise men to shame, and what the world considers weak in order to put powerful men to shame. He chose what the world looks down on, and despises, and thinks is nothing, in order to destroy what the world thinks is important" (1 Corinthians 1:27–28).

The women's faith in the Easter message which changed human history was later confirmed by the testimony of the male disciples who told of various encounters with Jesus. What happened to bring about such a radical change in the lives of these disciples and transform them from cowering, frightened men who had lost all hope into bold proclaimers of the Risen Christ and founders of the Christian Church?

Since there is no recorded witness to the Resurrection, it has been of utmost importance to Christian faith to understand how the disciples interpreted their experiences. For many people in the modern world, a stumbling block to faith in the Resurrection has been the assumption that resurrection, in the New Testament sense of the term, meant literally bringing Jesus's dead body back to life. But we have come to understand that this is not the biblical meaning. As one biblical scholar has put it, the

> appearances reported by the disciples were not encounters with Jesus as he had been before his death. . . . Jesus manifested himself to his disciples as one who now belonged to an order of things different from the world of

their ordinary experience. . . . In meeting and knowing the risen Jesus . . .
they had been seized up, if only for a moment, into a new life. . . . They had
seen the Kingdom of God, the New Age of Promise. It was realized and
fulfilled in Jesus himself; and in meeting him, they too had a taste of it. . . .
Whatever the death of Jesus might seem to have meant, God had not in fact
rejected him. On the contrary, he had affirmed Jesus' ministry and fulfilled
his promise—in however unexpected and unforeseen a way. The Kingdom
of God was not a dream but a reality. It could be met in the person of the
Risen One.[d]

Throughout history, humanity has been preoccupied with fear of the finality of death, and there is the strong human tendency to cling to this life at
whatever cost. But the Easter faith proclaims that God, not humankind, has
the final power over evil, suffering, and death; that death is not the end but
the "transition to God," breaking through that final frontier to a new dimension of existence which we speak of in faith as "eternal life." The Easter event
marked the beginning of God's new creation and Jesus was the first representative of the new human being, the first-born from the dead. Death has not been
canceled—for there can be no resurrection without the cross—but death has
been overcome.

God's act in raising Jesus from the dead is a promise to all humanity
which gives meaning and hope to our lives in the living Christ. We cannot escape the cross, but in following Christ and placing our whole trust in God's love
and forgiveness, we hope to pass through the cross and share with Christ in new
life with God. We do not know what that new life will be; faith is not certainty
which can be proved, or it would not be faith. Perhaps the Easter faith is most
simply expressed by a man named Heinrich Rendtorff who, when he was dying,
called his wife and asked her to listen very carefully. He told her, "These last
nights I have been thinking over and testing everything that we can know and
everything we have been told about what will happen to us when we die. And
now I am certain of one thing. I shall be safe."[e] In God's love, with the Risen
Christ going before us, we shall be safe.

Amen.

Notes

[a] Matthew 25:5–6.
[b] John 20:17.

[c] Evelyn Stagg and Frank Stagg, *Women in the World of Jesus* (Louisville, KY: Westminster/John Knox, 1978), chap. 6.

[d] Richard A. Norris, *Understanding the Faith of the Church* (New York: Seabury Press, 1979), 134–135.

[e] Gunther Bornkamm, *Jesus of Nazareth* (New York: Harper and Row, 1975), 181.

Sermon on Matthew 5:20

Matthew 5:20

Jesus said unto his disciples, Except your righteousness shall exceed the righteousness of the scribes and Pharisees, ye shall in no case enter into the kingdom of Heaven.

Few of us familiar with the Gospel tradition of the bitter controversies between Jesus of Nazareth and the scribes and Pharisees of his time would want to identify ourselves [with] Pharisees. Yet we must remember that these angry confrontations throughout his public ministry were not with lawless criminals and moral outcasts but with the most respectable, law-abiding, devout, church-going elements in Jewish life—a description which certainly parallels values we hold in high esteem today.

The Pharisees were men of great piety and strong religious faith. Unlike the reactionary, elitist Sadducees, who represented wealth and vested interests, they were the progressive party of the Jews of Palestine and immensely popular with the people. The scribes, most of whom were Pharisees, were the legal scholars, experts in the interpretation and application of the Mosaic Law to the many details of daily living. They lectured in the synagogues, traveled in the best society, and had seats in the Sanhedrin, the highest Jewish assembly for government.

The Pharisees shared many of the beliefs which Jesus held, for example, a belief in the Resurrection, which the Sadducees ridiculed. They were eager for a spiritual renewal of Israel, and they also looked for the coming of the Messiah. Their great passion was to study, honor, and obey the Law of Moses and to preserve the distinctive identity of the Jewish people and their religious heritage. As the late Dr. Harry Emerson Fosdick of New York's Riverside Church once wrote, "If he (Jesus) visited special censure on them it was because in them he saw the best hope of his people and to their reform dedicated his attention. . . . The great heritage of Jewish religion in Jesus' day was in the keeping not of the Sadducees, Zealots, or Essenes but of the Pharisees; to them in criticism and appeal his attention was given; and to them, as the crowds must have sensed, he was closer than to any other group in Israel."[1] We recall that Nicodemus, who supported Jesus, was "a man of the Pharisees," that according to tradition his own brother James was an ardent Pharisee who became head of the first Christian church in Jerusalem, and Paul said of himself, "I am a Pharisee, a son of Pharisees."

Why, then, did Jesus feel so strongly that unless his disciples' standard of right living was higher than the standard of the scribes and Pharisees they would never enter the Kingdom of Heaven? Was he demanding the impossible?

Jesus saw among the scribes and Pharisees the faults common to many devout, respectable, church-going people—more dangerous than the transgressions of moral outcasts because they are seductive and lead to self-deception. These are the sins of false pride, self-righteousness, complacency, and a sense of superiority, leading people to believe that because of their virtuous conduct they are more meritorious than others and are entitled to greater privileges.

The Pharisees took pride in their meticulous religious observances; they were fastidious in their ritualistic handwashing, fasting, praying, and observance of the Sabbath. They were preoccupied with applications of the law in minute detail. They were generally better off than the poor, uneducated masses of people whose harsh living conditions made it difficult to follow the complicated religious rules and regulations. They lacked compassion and had nothing but contempt for those who were not scrupulous [to] tithing, dietary rules, and ritual cleanliness.

Jesus had no patience with a legalistic morality, which seemed primarily concerned with outward and ritualistic purity but neglected the need for inward transformation. He called the Pharisees hypocrites and told them, "You cleanse the outside of the cup and plate but inside they are full of extortion and rapacity."[a] He also opposed their claims to superiority. In his eyes the Pharisees were inordinately fond of show; they wanted to be seen doing their deeds of piety; their prayer garments were ostentatious—their phylacteries (or prayer aprons) were broader and their tassels longer than those of others; they wanted the best seats in the synagogue and the place of honor at feasts.

Pride in learning led to scorn for the unlettered. Pride in keeping the law led to instinctive judgment and condemnation of the despised and disreputable, as in the case of the woman caught in adultery whom the Pharisees brought to Jesus saying the Law of Moses commanded that she be stoned. Jesus replied, "Let him who is without sin cast the first stone."[b] As Jesus saw his mission, [he] "did not come to judge the world but to save the world."[c] His attitude, as Dr Fosdick pointed out, was that "the sins of the flesh are bad . . . but the sins of the spirit are worse: harsh legalism, contemptuous condemnation without trying to understand its victim, concentration on the law's letter with no care for the personality involved and for what yet by God's grace be done in her, pride without pity, judgment without mercy."[d]

In contrast to the Pharisees who despised sinners and did not reach out to them, Jesus taught an all-inclusive love, that God cared for sinners, valued them and their potential, and constantly sought them out. When the Pharisees asked his disciples, "Why does your teacher eat with publicans and sinners?" Jesus answered, "Those who are well have no need of a physician, but those who are sick; I have come not to call the righteous, but sinners to repentance."[e] He told the parables of the Lost Sheep and the Lost Coin and said there is more joy in heaven over finding one lost soul than over ninety-nine "righteous persons who have no need of repentance."

The lack of humility among the Pharisees was offensive to Jesus. He knew that unless we are continually aware of our own waywardness and of God's gracious acceptance of us and forgiveness of our sins, we are unable to forgive others. Jesus coupled humility with servanthood. When his disciples argued among themselves as to which of them was the greatest, Jesus told them, Whoever would be great among you must be your servant, and whoever would be first among you must be your slave."[f]

To illustrate his lesson of humility he told the parable of the Pharisee and the Publican "to some who trusted in their own righteousness and despised others." The Pharisees and the tax collector went up into the temple to pray. The Pharisee stood and said this prayer to himself: "I thank you, God, that I am not grasping, unjust, adulterous like the rest of mankind, and particularly that I am not like this tax collector here. I fast twice a week; I pay tithes on all I get."[g] The tax collector stood some distance away, not even daring to raise his eyes to heaven, but beat his breast and said, "God be merciful to me, a sinner." "This man," said Jesus, "went home again as right with God; the other did not. For everyone who exalts himself will be humbled, but the man who humbles himself will be exalted."[h] Jesus's emphasis upon humility and servanthood may be especially disturbing to an oppressed group, which traditionally has been assigned to a servile position. We may ask: In [the] face of racial or sexual arrogance, should we not reject notions of humility and servanthood? Should we not foster pride in ourselves in order to overcome the negative self-images inherited from centuries of being downgraded? And should we not value those sturdy traits of decent living, respect for learning, and responsible citizenship which will enable us to move into the mainstream of our society?

The answer is: of course, we should do all these things . . . affirming one's self-worth as a child of God, and affirming the humility and servanthood which Jesus exemplified in his own life. Black theologian J. Deotis Roberts reminds us that "God's address to the despised and rejected is aimed at restoring the dignity of those made in his likeness."[2] Reinhold Niebuhr has said, "Religion is at one and the same time, humility before the absolute and self-assertion in terms of the absolute."[3] Jesus's criticisms were aimed at the *excessive* pride in self in which we elevate ourselves *above* others rather than share a common brotherhood and sisterhood with all human beings. As Dr. Roberts says, "Pride in goodness on the part of blacks is just as harmful to them as it is to whites who are the prime targets of their criticism. . . . Sin is universal and therefore must be faced frankly."[4] One of the perils of the concept of the oppressed as chosen of God is that it may lead to an attitude not unlike that which Jesus condemned in the Pharisees, as illustrated by the words of one angry Black theologian who wrote, "The divine election of the oppressed means that black people are given the power of judgment over the high and mighty whites."[5]

The humility and servanthood of which Jesus spoke and exemplified do not mean servile-ness. As Letty M. Russell points out, "The role of servant in both the Old and New Testament is not an indication of inferiority or subordination. . . . The privilege of God's gracious choice is a privilege of *election for service.* . . . This service to others on behalf of God was not a form of subordination to other people, but rather a free offering of self and acceptance of service and love in return."[i]

Jesus's standard of righteousness confronts each of us with searching clarity. It is as sinful for the oppressed not to be able to forgive their oppressors as it is for the oppressors not to be able to repent: "God has forgiven us our sins not because we deserve or have earned his forgiveness, but because he loves us in spite of our fallenness."[j] What Jesus was saying to his disciples and what he says to us today is that we can never be good enough, that we can never be satisfied with ourselves, that our pilgrimage is toward perfection, never to be achieved on this earth but never to be abandoned. Only as we recognize our continual need to repent and to forgive can we be saved from the deadly sins of the spirit.

Amen.

Notes

[a] Matthew 23:25.

[b] John 8:7.

[c] John 3:17.

[d] Harry Emerson Fosdick, *The Man from Nazareth as His Contemporaries Saw Him* (New York: Harpers, 1949).

[e] Mark 2:17.

[f] Matthew 20:26–27.

[g] See: Luke 18:11–12.

[h] Matthew 23:12.

[i] Letty M. Russell, *Human Liberation in a Feminist Perspective: A Theology* (Philadelphia: Westminster Press, 1974), 140.

[j] J. Deotis Roberts, *Liberation and Reconciliation: A Black Theology* (1971; reprint Louisville, KY: Westminster/John Knox, 2005), 61.

Salvation and Liberation

There is today fermentation at work in Christian theology which may well signal a rebirth of religious consciousness and a reintegration of faith at new levels of understanding. This fermentation has important implications for religious communities growing out of the Judeo-Christian tradition, despite their divergences in doctrine and symbolism, for they share a common search for salvation from the forces of alienation and violence in today's world. . . .

Since the late 1960s, in response to the human liberation movements of oppressed peoples around the world, Catholic and Protestant theologians in Europe, Latin America, and the United States have been evolving what is variously called theology of liberation, political theology, theology of hope, and theology of revolution. Black theology and feminist theology, arising out of the parallel struggles of Blacks and women, are native to the United States.

The central question for all of these theologies of liberation is, What does the Christian faith have to say that will give strength and hope to those who struggle against the "Powers and Principalities"—the institutionalized evils and injustices which destroy the humanity of whole peoples and which are virtually immune to individual morality? Some writers, convinced that the Christian Church is too deeply implicated in supporting the status quo to be a force for liberation, have gone beyond Christianity and seek new religious symbols. Most, however, have remained within the Christian tradition while developing new concepts and challenging the content of orthodox doctrines at crucial points. . . .

I can touch only briefly upon some of the common perspectives of this new development but think they may find resonance in your own religious experience.

Liberation theologies are not overall systems of dogma. They grow out of specific contexts. As Letty Russell says, they "try to express the gospel [of salvation] in the light of the experience of oppression out of which they written, whether that be racial or sexual, social or economic, psychological or physical."a In their efforts to illuminate the human situation, they undertake social and historical analysis and draw upon many disciplines instead of one particular theological tradition. They develop through a method called *praxis,* continuous action concurrent with reflection, and to this extent they are experimental and open-ended. They are concerned with the relation of faith to social change and are oriented toward the transformation of the world in history. The "shared efforts [of men and women] to abolish the current unjust situation and to build a different society, freer and more human," as Gustavo Gutierrez, the Latin American theologian, puts it, or in [Rosemary Radford] Ruether's words, "an overthrowing of this false world which has been created out of man's self-alienation, and a restoration of the world to its proper destiny as the 'place where God's will is done on earth, as it is done in heaven.'"b,c This restoration refers to the physical environment as well as social organization.

There is a decided shift from an other-worldly to a this-worldly emphasis. Some of these theologians envision, ultimately, a new human being in history. Ruether speaks of "a movement of the whole globe toward a new unity" through the spread of "a revolutionary momentum, in the form of a demand for the improvement of life. . . . Development toward a new planetary humanity goes hand in hand with the revolt of every oppressed group, in demands for national, class, racial, and sexual integrity and identity."d Along with this emphasis is the effort to reexamine and reinterpret the Christian faith so that it has relevance for people committed to the search for liberation in today's society.

The new society envisioned is one in which diversity is valued and is so structured as to encourage each individual to develop to the fullness of his or her own potential. Dr. Major J. Jones, writing on Black theology, says, "We move, as if we were indeed under some power of the future, toward some larger context wherein every person, race, or ethnic group shall take comfort in the fact of separateness or difference. . . . There will be pluralism in ideologies, interests, aims and aspirations, and personhood, and no one will for any purpose be denied opportunity to achieve or be excluded from community."1

Feminist writer Sheila D. Collins speaks of a "wholeness of vision" which "does not imply an eradication of differences between the sexes" but which "may lead to a multiplication of differences. Only through an affirmation and celebration of our differences can we come to an understanding of the ties that bind the whole creation together."[e] A wholistic ethic [in a pluralistic world] affirms singleness within community, diversity within unity, the validity of *both/and* rather than *either/or.*

This vision of a new humanity in history, it seems to me, reflects a broadening of the common ground shared by humanists and those who accept the divinity of Jesus Christ. . . . Liberation theologians maintain that our perceptions of God are shaped by the culture in which we live and by historical experience. Theologies change as cultural experience changes. A major critique of traditional Christian theology by Blacks and women is that, historically, theologians have been white and male and that the historical experience of Blacks and women have been excluded. To this extent these groups find some traditional doctrines and interpretations inadequate for self-understanding.

For example, consider the impact of traditional Christian doctrines which stress obedience, meekness, humility, and suffering servanthood. Many oppressed people are turned off by these doctrines, seen to be expressions of their own powerlessness and used to invoke divine approval for patterns of dominance and submission in human relationships, as in the experience of Blacks during slavery. "Servanthood," as Letty Russell points out, "presents problems for women and other oppressed groups who have been condemned to play a servant role not of their own choosing. For these groups humanization is experienced, not so much through service, as through bonding together in supportive communities that can provide new identity and hope." Russell finds that even when the biblical image is clarified to indicate [that] the true meaning of servanthood is not inferiority or subordination but "the privilege of God's gracious choice" of one to act as "an instrument of divine help to someone else's need," the debasing connotation of this term is not dispelled for women and other groups struggling against roles of subordination in church and society.[2] Black theology sees that much of its task is to reclaim a people from humiliation and therefore it is less concerned with "such unrelated subjects as humility before man and guilt before God."[f]

Traditional Christian spirituality looks upon anger and pride as negative qualities, but as Ruether asserts, they are crucial "virtues" in the salvation of the oppressed community. In this context, anger "is felt as the power to revolt against and judge a system of oppression to which one was formerly a powerless . . .

victim. Pride is experienced as the recovery of that authentic humanity and good created nature 'upon which God looked in the beginning and, behold, it was very good.'[g] Stress is placed upon the second half of the commandment to love one's neighbor *as one's self.* Only as we love ourselves are we prepared to love our neighbor. Love of self, here, is not seen as selfishness but as self-respect.

More radical feminist theologians like Sheila D. Collins challenge Christianity as practiced by the official church as a "death-loving rather than a life-affirming religion, as attested to by its heavy emphasis on the Crucifixion and the atonement rather than on Jesus's life and ministry and the concrete, time-realized hope and courage he gave to those with whom he came in contact."[h]

A second important perspective of liberation theologies is that of salvation as a social and historical event. Salvation is interpreted as a deliverance from sin and from political and social oppression. Russell speaks of the "broadening of the understanding of individual salvation in the afterlife to include the beginnings of salvation in the lives of men and women in society."[i] Emphasis is placed upon the longed-for eternal life as a quality of existence in the *here and now.* Salvation is stressed not as an escape into "heaven" but rather "the power and the possibility of transforming the world, restoring creation and seeking to overcome suffering." Gutierrez, a Roman Catholic, speaks of the growth of the Kingdom of God as "a process which occurs historically *in* liberation, insofar as liberation means a greater fulfillment of man. . . . Without liberating historical events, there would be no growth of the Kingdom."[j]

Sin also acquires a different meaning in this perspective and is seen to include corporate or social evil as well as individual transgression. This view attempts to correct tendencies within the traditional church to concentrate upon sin as "an individual, private, or merely interior reality" necessitating a "spiritual" redemption while ignoring the presence of sin in institutional structures which alienate and oppress people and prevent their communion with God and with one another. Rosemary Ruether charges that the concentration on individualistic repentance and "private confession" has, in effect, "involved people in a process of kneeling down to examine a speck of dirt on the floor while remaining oblivious to the monsters which are towering over their backs" and which cannot be overcome individually.[k] Dr. J. Deotis Roberts of Howard University School of Religion argues that while we should not abandon the quest for strengthening the inner spiritual life, the Christian faith today must be understood in a highly political context and that the only gospel suitable for the new consciousness "is one that opts for radical and massive change in oppressive attitudes and structures of power."[1]

The analysis confronts us with our own participation in collective evil and our responsibility to change the social structures which bring it about. From Gutierrez's perspective, conversion to Christ means commitment to one's neighbor and to "participate in the struggle for the liberation of those oppressed by others."[3] Dr. Martin Luther King Jr., explaining how he came to embrace nonviolent boycotts and demonstrations in the struggle against racial segregation, said that he became convinced that to accept passively an evil system was as immoral as active perpetuation of it, "thereby making the oppressed as evil as the oppressor," and that in order to be true to one's conscience and to God, a righteous person has no alternative but to refuse to cooperate with an evil system.

The process of liberation is said to begin with an awareness of restrictions, alienations, and limitations, and moves on to affirm liberation from these restrictions and toward a vision of wholeness and unity. Heightened consciousness impels action because we are no longer willing to accept the old order of things. Self-affirmation involves throwing off old stereotypes of one's self imposed by the dominant culture and achieving self-esteem through self-definition. A major concern of Black theology has been to redefine the term "Black" and to transform it into a symbol of "new self-understanding of persons in black skin who are equal in nature and grace with all humans."[m]

Self-definition for women involves recognition that the chief source of their limitations has been the Judeo-Christian tradition and the culture to which it has given rise. As Ruether and others point out, religion is the single most important factor in shaping and enforcing the image and role of women today in society, and has reflected sexual domination and subjugation in both its doctrines and practices as a social institution. Witness the present revolt of women in Iran who fear that fundamentalist Islamic elements will rob them of their social gains and reduce them to second-class citizens.

The most devastating critique of the Judeo-Christian faith has come from feminist theologians who point to its images of an exclusively male God as Father, King, Lord, and Master, and assert that it has projected a patriarchal worldview in which subordination of women has been the model for the oppression of other groups. . . . This challenges biblical religion at its root and forecasts attempts to correct the content of Judeo-Christian symbolism and imagery which, if the church were to take [them] seriously, as one feminist theologian suggests, it might find itself turned completely inside out.

Finally, theology of liberation also calls for a redefinition of [the] task of the church in the world. It asserts that salvation is not limited to the action of the church but is a reality which occurs in history. Therefore, the church must cease looking upon itself as the exclusive place of salvation and orient itself to a new and radical service to the people. As a sacramental community and a sign of the liberation of humanity and history, the church in its concrete existence should be a place of liberation which reflects in its own structure a witness to the salvation whose fulfillment it announces. True renewal of the church must be on the basis of an effective awareness of the world and a commitment to it. . . . In short, liberation theology, born in world crisis and developing in the turmoil of transition, may prove to be a catalytic force for changes in the Christian tradition as profound as those of the Protestant Reformation of the sixteenth century. It has accepted the challenge to redirect the Christian faith so that the church in fact as well as in proclamation becomes a witnessing community to the new age.

Notes

[a] Letty M. Russell, *Human Liberation in a Feminist Perspective* (Philadelphia: Westminster Press, 1974), 54.

[b] Gustavo Gutierrez, "Introduction," in *A Theology of Liberation* (Maryknoll, NY: Orbis Books, 1973).

[c] Rosemary Radford Ruether, *Liberation Theology* (Boston: Paulist Press, 1972).

[d] Ibid.

[e] Sheila D. Collins, *A Different Heaven and Earth: A Feminist Perspective on Religion* (King of Prussia, PA: Judson Press, 1974).

[f] Major J. Jones, *Black Awareness: A Theology of Hope* (Nashville: Abingdon, 1971), 13.

[g] Ruether, *Liberation Theology.*

[h] Collins, *A Different Heaven and Earth.*

[i] Russell, *Human Liberation in a Feminist Perspective.*

[j] Gutierrez, *A Theology of Liberation.*

[k] Ruether, *Liberation Theology.*

[l] J. Deotis Roberts, *A Black Political Theology* (1974; reprint Louisville, KY: Westminster/John Knox, 2005), 27.

[m] Roberts, *A Black Political Theology,* 24.

The Second Great Commandment

Mark 12:28–31 (see also Luke 10:25–28 and Matthew 22:34–40)
And one of the scribes came up and heard them disputing with one another, and seeing that he answered them well, asked him, "Which commandment is the first of all?" Jesus answered, "The first is, 'Hear, O Israel:
The Lord our God, the Lord is one; and you shall love the Lord your God
with all your heart, and with all your soul, and with all your mind and with
all your strength.' The second is this, 'You shall love your neighbor as yourself.' There is no other commandment greater than these."

In Luke's account of the Great Commandment, a certain lawyer stood up and
put Jesus to the test, saying, "Teacher/Master, what must I do to inherit eternal
life?" The answer to both ways of putting the question is the same. Two commandments from the Mosaic Law found in Deuteronomy (6:4–5) and Leviticus
(19:18) are combined into one, and Jesus made it clear that in the totality of
human existence we are all bound together inseparably in our relationship to
God, to our own selves, and to one another.

In spite of this clear teaching, some people experience their religious faith
primarily as private salvation. They come to church seeking comfort and strength
to meet their own personal problems and they view the prime business of their
church as concern for the spiritual needs of its members and question its outreach to the social problems of society. They are desperately trying to love and
serve God, but the second half of the Great Commandment does not have the
same urgency for them as the first half. On the other hand, there are those who

seldom go to church and profess no strong religious faith but devote themselves to humane causes and to the service of others. They too are trying to split what is essentially a single commandment and to give their allegiance to only one-half of God's command.

For the Christian, however, as Jesus taught us, wholeness of being and salvation depend upon our continual awareness of and response to the insep-arability of love of God and love of neighbor. This is what John had in mind when he wrote in his first Epistle, "No one has seen God; but as long as we love one another God will live in us and his love will be complete in us" (1 John 4:12). He also asked, "If a man who was rich enough in this world's goods saw that one of his brothers was in need, but closed his heart to him, how could the love of God be living in him?" For John, "Our love is not just words and talk, but something real and active; only by this can we be certain that we are chil-dren of truth and able to quiet our conscience in his [God's] presence" (1 John 3:17–18).

Pivotal to my relatedness to God on the one hand and to my neighbor on the other is my relationship to myself. Unless I love and accept myself, I am not free to love and accept my neighbor. Loving myself in this context simply means self-respect, a self-regard born of the realization that I am the object of God's limitless love and mercy, part of his creation. Self-acceptance does not mean uncritical self-approval but self-understanding, awareness of my strengths and weaknesses, and the blessed assurance that God-in-Christ is working in me and through me toward the perfection of my life. When I can believe as St. Paul did "that neither death, nor life, nor angels, nor principalities, nor things present, nor things to come, nor powers, nor height, nor depth, nor anything else in creation, will be able to separate us from the love of God in Christ Jesus our Lord,"[1] I am liberated from self-preoccupation which blocks my capacity to care for others.

We are not commanded to *like* everyone with whom we come into contact. What is required of us is not admiration, approval, or even personal affection but *caring,* empathy, seeking to understand, identifying with another's common humanity, and being concerned for another's well-being as if it were our own. In this sense the command is absolute. We are not free to pick and choose those we accept and those we reject. Every other human being is our neighbor. When Jesus was asked, "Who is my neighbor?" he answered with the parable of the Good Samaritan and used a member of a despised race to illustrate the relationship.

As we know from biblical tradition, the Jews had no dealings with the Samaritans and held them in contempt. Their animosity had persisted for centuries because the Samaritans were a mixed people not of pure Hebrew blood and they worshipped idols along with the worship of Israel's God, Yahweh. The man from Jerusalem on the way to Jericho who had been beaten, robbed, and left to die was presumably a Jew. The priest and the Levite were exemplars of Judaism, and as men whose profession was religion, they would be expected to have compassion for human need. Yet they passed by on the other side.

By contrast, the Samaritan would not be expected to concern himself with a member of a hostile race. He owed nothing to the Jew and would have an understandable reason for not becoming involved. Yet he ignored traditional differences of race and religion. He saw only another human being like himself, suffering and alone. He went beyond mere passing concern; he not only cared for the man's wounds and brought him to the inn but also took responsibility to see that the Jew's needs were cared for until he recovered and could take charge of his own affairs. The measure of neighborly love was compassion for a stranger whom he did not know and had no reason to like.

Few of us would deny our responsibility in such a situation. What may be more difficult for us to accept is our ongoing responsibility for whole communities of people victimized by an uncaring social system; beaten down by oppression, poverty, and neglect; and robbed of their chance to share in the benefits of the richest nation on earth. All too often in our modern society we have erected the idol of competition in place of the God of Love and tend to blame the victims for their dire state.

As Christians, and especially as Episcopalians who take great pride in the aesthetic beauty and dignity of our worship services, we are in constant danger of falling into the error of the people of Israel of the eighth century B.C. Remember how the Lord God said to them through the prophet Amos, "I hate, I despise your feasts, and I take no delight in your solemn assemblies. . . . Take away from me the noise of your songs; to the melody of your harps I will not listen. But let justice roll down like waters, and righteousness like an ever-flowing stream" (6:21, 23–24). Of what significance, then, are our liturgies and anthems of praise in the eyes of God if our response to his infinite love does not also move us to identify with the oppressed wherever they may be and to work unceasingly to transform our society so that all may be free to share in the bounties of God's creation?

The message of the gospel of Jesus Christ is that there can be no individual salvation for us apart from our commitment to the well-being of our neighbor.

Each of us is responsible before God for "the least of these." But serving "the least of these" is not easy. Often we are so harassed by our own problems of living that we do not make the effort to understand the causes of wretchedness and misery we see around us. Or there is the temptation to give ourselves undue credit for our good fortune and to say, "We made it. Why can't they?" And in this separation of the human family into "we" and "they," we have already passed by on the other side.

Or our generous impulses toward social justice may be stifled by fear. We are afraid to speak out or take a stand—it may be too costly; we may offend those whose friendship or approval we value, or who can threaten our comfort and security. Or we may be paralyzed to act because we are torn between competing loyalties, or because we are confused by complex issues and simply do not know the best action to take.

Each of us faces these crises of conscience from time to time, and we are driven back to questions of our relation to God and to ourselves. In such a crisis I have to ask myself, Have I not elevated my fear of human judgments and human institutions above my faith in God's great providence? Do I believe that manmade social barriers are more powerful than prayer? When I am confronted with a social controversy, do I tend to rely solely on my own wisdom and strength and become frightened and irresolute when it fails me? Do I tend to think of God's presence only in the reverent atmosphere of church services or when I am engaged in formal personal prayer, and lose sight of that presence in every human encounter of my secular pursuits?

In community action as in all our other concerns, those words of family prayer are particularly appropriate: "O God . . . Grant us, in all our doubts and uncertainties, the grace to ask what thou wouldst have us do, that the Spirit of Wisdom may save us from all false choices, and that in the light we may see light, and in thy straight path may not stumble; . . . Preserve us from faithless fears."[2]

Who of us is not assailed by doubts, uncertainties, the danger of false choices, faithless fears, when we take stands on such issues as busing for equal educational opportunities, affirmative action for equal employment opportunities, open housing in our own neighborhoods, large public expenditures to bring about full employment and to open opportunities for the disadvantaged, equal rights, capital punishment, prison reform, abortion, and so on?

Yes, loving one's neighbor involves risk, the risk of pain and unpopularity, the risk of being wrong, the risk of sacrifice and defeat, the risk of distrust and even abuse from those whom we want to serve. Yet I believe that in facing these issues we are required to ask only, "God, what is my responsibility to this situation? What would you have me to do?" We are required only to act to the best of our ability in response to our prayer for guidance in any given situation and to leave the outcome to God.

We are now approaching the season of Advent in which we reflect upon the coming of Jesus as the Christ and ask for God's "grace to cast off the works of darkness and put on the armor of light, *now* in this time of mortal life." The universal significance of the Christ event, says Paul Tillich, is "salvation . . . overcoming the split between God and man, man and his world, man and himself."[a] As baptized Christians, we all have a ministry, whether we are laypersons or clergy: "to represent Christ and his Church; to bear witness to him wherever we may be; and, according to the gifts given us, to carry on Christ's work of reconciliation in the world."

The repeated lesson of history is that reconciliation between human beings is possible only when they are all treated as equals and can come together in an atmosphere of mutual trust and respect. Our ministry is to witness to the Christ in every human being and to those conditions in which human dignity can take root and grow. And although we may not experience the triumph of our own efforts, we need not despair. In recent history we have seen the power of the Holy Spirit working through the civil rights movement led by the late Dr. Martin Luther King Jr. to overturn an entrenched system of racial segregation which degraded one-tenth of our population and spiritually deformed the other nine-tenths. Even more recently, we saw the power of silent prayer at work in the 1976 General Convention of our own Episcopal Church. It immediately preceded the crucial vote in the House of Deputies on the ordination of women to the priesthood, and when the decision was made those who had won were able to share the pain of those who had lost and to commit themselves to the task of healing and reconciliation in our church.

Loving our neighbor is being open to God's purposes working in us and through us. However difficult this may be at times, we can say with St. Paul, "And let us not grow weary in well-doing, for in due season we shall reap, if we do not lose heart."[b]

Let Us Pray.

O God, you have made us in your own image and redeemed us through Jesus your Son. You have bound us together in a common life. Look with compassion on the whole human family. Take away the arrogance and hatred which infects our hearts. Break down the walls that separate us. Unite us in bonds of love. In all our struggles for justice, help us to confront one another without hatred or bitterness, and to work together with mutual forbearance and respect, to the end that all those who are oppressed may enjoy with every one of us a fair portion of the benefits of this rich land which you have given us; through Jesus Christ our Lord.

Amen.

Notes

[a] Paul Tillich, *Systematic Theology* (Chicago: University of Chicago Press, 1957), 2:192.

[b] Galatians 6:9.

Reflections on the Special
General Convention

This memorandum is prayerfully submitted, and is more in the nature of a prophecy than appeal.

Future of the Protestant Episcopal Church USA

The future of the Episcopal Church in the United States cannot be looked at apart from history. Traditionally, it has been an elite body exercising power and prestige out of proportion, perhaps, to its actual members. The early history of the United States will reveal a substantial number of Episcopalians who were presidents, Supreme Court justices, governors, and other rulers of the nation.[1]

Much of the corporate wealth of the country has been and continues to be in the hands of Episcopalians. The Episcopal Church, therefore, is symbolic of the Protestant establishment and is one of the most visible targets of revolutionary, alienated elements in the population.

Moreover, the history of Episcopalianism in the United States reveals a consistent policy of subordination, not merely of Negroes/Africans/Afro-Americans/Blacks, but also of women. The slavocracy of the South was largely Episcopalian. Professor Emeritus F. S. C. Northrop, of Yale Law School, makes this point clearly.[a] "White supremacy" in the United States has been, in substance, *white male supremacy,* as indicated increasingly through the studies of observers and scholars (Gunnar Myrdal, Ashley Montagu, Caroline Bird, Helen M. Hacker, and others). It is no accident that the region of the United States most recalcitrant on the issue of equality for Negroes has also been most conservative on the issue of the rights of women—the South and, more particularly, the Old South. Episcopalians have been prominent among the resisters to desegregation in Mississippi, Tennessee (Sewanee), and elsewhere.

The Episcopal Church USA has begun to recognize its failure to fulfill its Christian mission in the case of Negroes; what it has not fully recognized is its equal and far more extensive failure to fulfill its mission with respect to half or more of the human race, namely, women.

Moreover, what may not be clearly apparent to the male hierarchy of the church—both clergy and layman—is that there is in progress a women's revolution, not yet of the momentum of the Black revolution but clearly evident to all those who are following the trends of the worldwide human rights revolution.

The church, through its highest law-making body, the General Convention, has also failed to understand the most elementary principle of the present world revolution in human rights, namely, that *human rights are indivisible,* and that institutions and governments cannot recognize and implement the rights of one disaffected group over another without arousing resentments, creating divisiveness, and exacerbating the very turmoil the church seeks to resolve.

In this context, the recent simultaneous actions of the Special General Convention with respect to Negroes/Blacks and women highlight the church's violation of the elementary principle of indivisible human rights. It has gained time at the expense of the most subordinated and disfranchised group, and the very grave question arises as to whether the church may not have lost more than it has gained. Furthermore, the church has somehow failed to implement the New Testament mandate that in Christ we are all one and we are all equal, that in the Kingdom of Heaven there is neither Greek nor Jew, Black nor white, male nor female. Hampered by its Judeo-Catholic parentage, the Episcopal Church has perpetuated the patriarchal concept of the place of women in society and in the church. The male hierarchy has assumed a "business as usual" attitude toward recognizing the right of women to be seated as delegates in the General Convention; to vote; to be ordained and serve as priests; to serve as lay readers, crucifers, acolytes, and in all other positions in the church without regard to sex. What is not apparent at present, but may become increasingly clear, is that the same impatience which motivates Negroes/Blacks to decide to wait no longer—having waited 350 years (1619–1969)—now motivates a substantial and growing number of women of the church having waited almost two hundred years. There is grave danger that the male hierarchy of the church will fall victim to the unwise assumption that the majority of the women of the church will wait longer. History shows us that it is not majorities which bring about radical changes but organized and determined minorities which exercise power out of all proportion to their numbers.

Present Trends in the Episcopal Church USA

I am not aware of any statistical studies which will confirm this observation, but it seems safe to say that there are at least three dissatisfied groups in the Episcopal Church today—youth, racial and ethnic minorities, and women. Walk into any Episcopal service and you will note the decreasing proportion of young people in relation to their proportion in the population. You will find in many of these churches a middle-aged congregation with a preponderance of women. The younger, more able, more trained and active women are not in the church. Some of them have difficulties with the theological dogma of the church, as did Dr. Pike.[2] Some of the very young women are doubtless drawn to the new female liberation movement which has flowered in the Boston metropolitan area but has echoes throughout the country. Abby Rockefeller, daughter of David Rockefeller, Radcliffe-trained, is one of the prime movers of this revolutionary development. As in the Black revolution, which began under the leadership of the Negro middle class and penetrated to the masses of ghetto-dwelling Negroes, the female liberation movement has sprung up in the wake of efforts of more moderate elements of women's groups and is frankly revolutionary, antireligion, anti-Church, antifamily, and raises the question, Are men the enemy? It advocates judo and karate as methods of self-defense, questions the institutions of marriage as well as the family as instruments of the enslavement of women, and some of its theoreticians advocate that women not marry but live single lives and become self-sufficient until such time as the establishment has been destroyed.

One does not have to agree with the tactics of the younger, alienated women to recognize that they have attracted more public notice and potentially are a greater threat to traditional institutions as presently organized than moderate women like Dr. Cynthia Wendel, who served on President Kennedy's Commission on the Status of Women and who is an outstanding Episcopalian, and others of her caliber. The longer the church delays full recognition of women's legitimate rights as *persons,* the larger this alienated group will become, the greater its threat to established procedures and the more powerless will become women who are desperately trying to bring about reforms within these procedures.

Although the church now has a residue of faithful women who are still willing to do the thankless supportive work of the church—dinners, altar guilds, choir mothers, and so on, these needs do not satisfy women capable of leadership and the shaping of policy. Nothing less than full sharing of power in every phase of church life will satisfy the needs and legitimate aspirations of these women. They will either share power *within* the church or they will be outside of the church as part of its formidable opponents. Any lawyer who follows the trends is aware of the numerous cases presently in the lower federal courts brought by women challenging almost every phase of remaining inequality under the law. Moreover, the movement for an Equal Rights for Women Amendment has leapfrogged over the generation of women of which I am a part and gathered unanticipated support from the younger, more radical women. A Human Rights for Women tax-exempt fundraising corporation (comparable to the NAACP Legal Defense and Educational Fund, Inc.) has just been organized in Washington, DC. Its directors include Alice Paul, leader of the suffragist militant wing which went to jail in World War I, and some of the radicalized young feminists which broke away from Betty Friedan's National Organization for Women.[3]

I do not suggest that Episcopal women are in the forefront of these more radical movements; I do suggest that the younger generation of women who will replace my generation will be deeply influenced by these developments. To the degree that their disaffection leads them to be outside of the church, to that degree the church's important work traditionally done by women will shrivel.

Students of reform or revolutionary movements have pointed out that such movements of various groups feed one another. The activities of the American labor movement in the 1930s stimulated the beginnings of the Black revolution; the successes of the civil rights movement [of the] 1940s–1960s have stimulated the beginnings of the women's revolution. The flow of pamphlets, law review articles, newspaper stories, magazine articles, and books about the changing attitudes of women has increased two- or threefold during the past decade. Women, like Negroes, are beginning to recognize that they have been the victims of stereotypes, of feelings of inferiority, of a manmade—fundamentally, a white-man-made—"brainwashing." Daily, women are proving [this] by performance capacities which give the lie to these stereotypes. The more thoughtful women are beginning to realize their potential political and financial power. Moreover, they are beginning to realize that it is not necessary to convince all women of the need to make a bid for power; *an organized, determined minority can do the job.*

People in close contact with the more group-conscious women of the church are acutely aware of a growing dissatisfaction based upon an awareness of what seems to be male hypocrisy with respect to the Black revolution while ignoring the less stridently articulated needs and aspirations of women. As I have pointed out in another context, many of these women are presently withholding their United Thank Offerings and urging other women to do so. If this movement should spread, if a Woman's Caucus should be organized within the church—and this is not beyond a strong possibility—the church might find itself the target of a woman's boycott far more threatening than any challenge which Black churchmen can mount, for women can be decisive with respect to the church's business lifeblood—funds, contributions.

Prospect of a Woman's Boycott

It requires little imagination to envision what would happen if a successful woman's boycott were mounted in the church. All women would have to do would be to refuse to make their individual pledges and to withhold their UTO funds.[4] Local vestries would be unable to raise their budgets. Priests would not receive their full salaries. The charitable work of the church would be threatened. The work of the Executive Council would almost grind to a halt. The church would be unable to fulfill its commitment to the Black Union of Clergy and Laity and would then be the target of further recriminations. Or suppose the Women's Caucus organized a few stay-at-home Sundays. Who would be present to listen to the priests' message? Who would do the thousand-and-one humble services that keep the church going? The House of Bishops and the House of Deputies would have no recourse other than to recognize that they brought such a state of affairs upon themselves by their short-sightedness in dramatizing their unfairness to women at the Special Convention in South Bend.[5] Had their refusal to seat a woman delegate occurred in any other circumstances, women might have let it pass and waited until the General Convention in 1970. In the inflamed circumstances in which it did occur, the law-making body of the church has outraged many women of the church and brought down upon its head resentment from all sides: resentment on the part of women who hold incipient prejudices against Negroes/Blacks; women who have done yeoman service in the civil rights movement and have learned well the tactics of struggle; women who have been urging the church to abandon its antediluvian policies and move into the twentieth century.

The Role Women Can Play: An Alternative

Mindful of the fact that power is seldom shared without a struggle, nevertheless I hold fast to the view that it is not all racism and/or sexism which motivates the actions of the power structure of the church. It is blindness, lack of imagination, and lack of experience. A white male Episcopalian is called upon to stretch his imagination to its ultimate boundaries to understand what it means to be a Black in a white world, or to be a woman in a male-dominated world. Too many males have assumed that, because many women do not articulate their grievances, they are content with their lot. Too many men have failed to see what is at stake. In the case of women, as in the case of Negroes, Spanish-surnamed people, American Indians, [Asians], or the poor, the issue is of human dignity and the God-given right to share in the shaping of one's destiny. Too many men have fallen victim to their own manmade stereotypes: women are too emotional, and so on. The performance of the male clergy and laity at the Special Convention in South Bend should destroy that stereotype once and for all. (Absent observers reading the news reports can be forgiven if the convention gave the impression of a bunch of hysterical fishmongers.)

If the church can face fully the implications of the Second Great Commandment—love thy neighbor as thyself—it can meet the challenge which women now present. For women, like Negroes or any other group which suffers minority or subordinated status, are looking for recognition of their *personhood,* which has no sex.

If the House of Bishops and the House of Deputies have the courage to face fully this challenge and bring women into full partnership with men in the church, then I believe that the church will unleash a burst of creative energy that can work miracles both within the church and in the church's impact upon the larger society and its problems. For the problem of race does not begin with the relationship of white to Black. It begins with man's relationship to his most intimate counterpart—woman.

Women have had a unique historical experience, as different from that of men as the Black experience has been from that of whites. Women have not had the need to express an aggressive manhood; they have, by cultural conditioning, been compelled to be intuitive, creative, innovative, and to look at the whole. They may well be society's greatest asset in bringing about reconciliation of the races on the basis of equality and fraternity (sorority). A society in which the major policy decisions are made by only one-half of the human race is an incomplete society; it lacks the insights and creativity of the other half. Integration of the races is impossible to achieve until there has been or simultaneously takes place integration of the sexes. By such integration, I do not mean identity of functions or approaches. I mean bringing the whole together in all of its various parts: At-one-ment, as my former rector, Reverend E. L. Henderson of Durham, North Carolina, and later Washington, DC, used to say.

Many women have great empathy for disadvantaged minorities because they have experienced a minority status themselves. As such, they can perform the important function of interpretation, they can bridge gaps, they can point out the obvious, they can civilize and humanize the process of resolving human conflict. They have not been conditioned to physical warfare, thank God. For these and other reasons, women can make a unique and necessary contribution to binding up the wounds and reducing the hostilities of racial conflict. But they cannot do this unless they themselves are liberated and are able to exercise their power creatively.

The alternative to continued delay on the issue of full equality for women in the church is the very real danger of contributing to a head-on collision of the militant Blacks' movement and the militant women's movement, a result which can undo all the church thinks it has done to resolve the racial problem. Alternatively, there can be a coalition between these militant groups to mount a concerned assault to destroy the system to which the mature American is committed. It is in the interest of avoiding both of these alternatives that I submit this analysis for your prayerful consideration.

Notes

[a] F. S. C. Northrop, *Philosophical Anthropology and Practical Politics* (New York: Macmillan, 1960).

What the Protestant Episcopal Church of the USA Could Be Doing the Next Century

1975–2075

I begin with the Tillichian proposition that human existence is ambiguous and contradictory, that the church in its human aspects reflects this ambiguity; that it is both holy and demonic; and that we, individually and collectively, are both sacred and profane.[1] However much we strive to overcome these contradictions and ambiguities, our small victories are transitory and fragmentary. What is a major social reform for us in our time may well be overturned by the next generation; thus, *our responsibility is for our own time and our own era.* All we can hope to do with respect to PECUSA [Protestant Episcopal Church of the USA] during the next century is to set in motion some processes which we pray will have continuity throughout the coming decades. We must begin, not so much with the focus of the church as with focus of the individual member(s) of the church—*What should be my focus as a Christian and a member of the Protestant Episcopal Church USA for those years left of my human existence?*

Accordingly, I shall try to limit myself to my individual responsibility, which I share ... in the hope that each of you will be moved to make self-reference that will result in collective inspiration and guidance from the Holy Spirit.

As an individual approaching the "golden years" of life (variously known as the "youthful aged," the "healthy aged," "senior citizen"), I want to bring to bear upon the society in which I live, including my church, the culmination of what Midge Decter calls "the distillation of the twin refineries of experience and intellection."[2] In my case, this means, "What have I learned as a Negro—*repeat 'Negro'*—a woman, a professionally trained lawyer, author, and teacher—living in the United States from the second to seventh decade of the twentieth century—that is of value to pass on, particularly with respect to the Anglican Communion?"

Of the many experiences, it seems to me that the two greatest gifts of God to the human race are good health and imagination. I identify imagination with *imago dei,* the image of God, and with the bestowal of the Holy Spirit. Imagination in the human sense permits us to have a vision—of the life to come after death; of life in our human existence for decades to come; of the possibility of transforming ambiguities, contradictions, anger, hostility, human limitations into positive and creative acts touched by the Holy Spirit. What, then, do I imagine creatively for PECUSA in the decades to come?

Here, I focus upon two groups with which I am most closely identified by accident of birth: women and "people of color." I use the quaint nineteenth-century term "people of color" because it seems to me to be the only inclusive term that will accommodate the wide variety of persons in the United States who, historically, have been variously identified as Africans, Afro-Americans, Negroes, Colored, blacks (or Blacks). *I categorically reject the term "black" or "Blacks" as a term of identification for the reason that:*

1. It fails to describe the multiple origins of a large sector of the "people of color" in the United States, of which I am one.

2. It is a term of polarization, for example, *black and white,* and symbolically underscores the separation of the races—a condition antithetical to the church as the Body of Christ.

3. It does not take into account the fact that Americans of whatever sub-culture or ethnic background are more related by blood, culture, political, sociological heritage than they are separated one from another.

4. It negates the dignity associated with upper-case identifications, for example, Christian, Jew, Puerto Rican, black, Japanese (note this series which now regularly appears in print in the USA).

5. Given the instability of identification of persons of color throughout the history of the USA, it is no more than a passing phase of identification and is quite likely to be rejected by a future generation as *my* generation rejected "Colored" in favor of "Negro."

6. If we are thinking forward in terms of a century, we should ally ourselves with what we hope the future to be. I hope the future will eliminate the terms "black" and "white" from our nomenclature. (I'd much prefer "pink" and "blue" people, or "chocolate" and "strawberry"—any term not so loaded with emotions and biases.)

7. Notwithstanding the levity of the above paragraph, what I am trying to get across is that *we begin now* in our thinking, our acting, and in our terminology to act out the slogan "liberation and reconciliation" in our church and in our society. For me, this means avoiding terms of polarization and selecting terms, as far as possible, which have positive or even pleasant associations.

Even as I inveigh against the terms "black" and "white," I understand how "black" has become the current term of identification. It represents the effort of members of an embattled and alienated minority group to develop self-esteem and pride by identifying with and transforming a term freighted with the most virulent kind of racism into an acceptable identification. The fact is, however, that "black" too becomes a stereotype. One way of testing this assertion is to ask the members of the committee what images come to mind when an individual is described as (a) a Negro civil rights worker? (b) a black militant? Are the two images the same? Or, in another category, (a) a women's libber? (b) an ardent feminist? Or, (a) a "gay" person? (b) a homosexual? (c) a bisexual? Underlying this discussion is an attempt to illustrate how prone all of us are to categorize, label, stereotype, and put into boxes *individuals.*

In sum, my focus as a Christian and a member of PECUSA must be on *individuals,* and only incidentally upon their multiple identifications. This conclusion is supported by my reading of the Second Great Commandment as well as of the Fourteenth Amendment to the U.S. Constitution: "Thou shalt love thy *neighbor* as thyself." "No State shall . . . deny to any *person* within its jurisdiction the equal protection of the laws."

Once I began to look at people as *individuals,* their stereotyped classifications begin to fall away; I become more cautious of making generalizations; I address myself to that individual's unique personality, needs, background, or expectations. The fact that a particular individual has golden hair or ebony skin becomes incidental to the fact that he/she is my spiritual brother or sister—a child of God. When I begin to internalize this fraternal/sororal relationship, I am less inclined to think "we" and "they." When I am forced to use terms of classification, I say "my black brothers" or "my white brother," or "my black sister," my "white sisters," and so on. The modification "brother" or "sister" expresses the closest possible human relationship aside from parent-child relationships. It suggests the equality of siblings while allowing for the conflicts within a family of siblings. Those of you who have sisters and brothers know that persons born of the "same father and same mother" (a term used by some Africans to distinguish between a biological brother or sister and a *tribal* brother or sister) can be as alienated from one another as different races. You also know that one can have spiritual brothers and sisters who are closer to oneself than one's biological siblings.

All of this is to say that the *key* to the reconciliation of the races (or the sexes) is my sense of *relatedness* to an individual of another social classification. The *key* also lies in one-to-one relationships—the development of reciprocal affection and esteem between two individuals that spills over into group relationships. To make an extremely personal reference, it is this sense of relatedness which impels me to reject a choice of priorities between the Black Caucus and the Women's Caucus in our Anglican Communion—an unpopular position which subjects me to many misunderstandings but the only one I can live with in accordance with my understanding of Jesus Christ's teaching in the Second Great Commandment.

If any of the above discourse makes sense, how do I reflect it in my day-to-day actions within my church? One way is to reject the segregation of the races in separate "black" or "white," or "predominately black," "predominately white" congregations. I will automatically begin to seek small ways in which this separation can be overcome. For me, personally, I saw a great vision of what our church *could* be on July 29, 1974, at the ordination of the eleven women priests at the Church of the Advocate in Philadelphia. This ordination ceremony was historic in more than one aspect. It took place in the heart of the ghetto, and a "black" congregation and church was the host. Symbolically, the rejected opened their arms to the rejected. (I went to this ordination ceremony in fear and trembling, in almost panic, having the same fears and apprehensions as one about to break a tribal taboo. Therefore, I was completely unprepared for the resultant joy and sense of the Holy Spirit I experienced.)

The congregation and participants were completely integrated both as to race and sex—even down to the little girl acolytes in their hot red robes on a July day with a temperature in the nineties who went out among the congregation carrying canteens of cold water and paper cups. What distinguished it from other "integrated" congregations I have experienced is that this time it was the ghetto—not the suburb—congregation that was the host. There was a reciprocal equality of status, and the ghetto congregation left no stone unturned to welcome, embrace, make comfortable, and *serve* the two thousand predominately "white" visitors who attended the service. For a congregation who are largely the descendants of slaves in the United States, this voluntary *service* spoke volumes to me.

The liturgical service had the earmarks of a great religious festival, a family reunion of all ages, sexes, and colors—all within the framework of our disciplined Anglican communion. Jocularly, the remark was made that "God's frozen people—we Episcopalians—got religion today." Another remark: "God was very busy today."

Given my ambivalence about attending this service in the first place, I reflected upon the change of attitude it wrought in me—very much like a "conversion." In an electrifying flash of insight I saw the coming together of two groups who have been submerged in both our society and our church—no other two groups in the United States could have brought it about. The ordination of *women* was the focus of the event, the ghetto congregation played the role of "sponsoring host." "The stone(s) which the builders have rejected shall become the cornerstone(s)." It was the reversal of traditional roles which contained the "magic" of the experience—a glimpse into the future, the potential of two rejected groups for the enrichment of our Christian witness and our secular society.

As I move closer toward the ordained ministry, I find myself resolved to do all in my power to break down the barriers of race and sex between people. I conceive of individuals, perhaps two by two, spending one Sunday per month visiting other churches—ghetto residents in the suburbs, suburb residents in the ghetto (note how quickly we substitute one stereotype for another). Yesterday, July 20, the Reverend Dr. Annette Ruark, ordained deacon on June 14, 1975, and I visited two services in Harlem—morning Eucharist at St. Philip's (Episcopal) and 11 o'clock service at St. James Presbyterian (where I have preached on four previous occasions). The Reverend Dr. Ruark looks like Alice in Wonderland—golden-haired, moon-faced, and so on. Our color contrast identified us racially. Our clerical (seminarian's and deacon's) collars signified our identity of vocation and purpose. It was a completely spontaneous experience and seemed Spirit-led. What did we find? The two supply priests at St. Philip's were of European extraction. One woman member of the St. James Presbyterian choir, also of European extraction, is a misplaced Episcopalian, drawn to St. James because of the musical talent of Mrs. Dorothy Maynor Rooks, minister of music (and a former coloratura), and the masterful sermons of the pastor, Dr. Shelby Rooks, a scholar, poet, prophet, and above all a magnificent preacher.[3] We were welcomed with open arms by both congregations.

Here we have it. In the next century PECUSA can become enriched and can make its Christian witness by the fullest utilization of two of its most neglected assets—its women and its ethnic minorities. We are *not* the Church of England, although it is our parent church become our sister church. We are part of the New World drawing from all races and cultures. We are *not* Roman Catholics, although some of us are oriented toward Rome. We are *not* Eastern (Russian, Armenian, etc.) Orthodox, who still think that women are unclean and may contaminate the "temple of God" at certain times. We are *not* Methodists, Baptists, Presbyterians, and so on and so forth—but we are integrally related to all of these. We can stand at the center of the ecumenical movement, drawing all communions closer together. We are the descendants of planters, slaves, immigrants, indigenous Americans, and so on, and if we are sufficiently creative, we will be flexible enough to reflect the range of our unique heritage, cross-fertilizing one another and breaking out of our cocoon into Christian joyousness. We will not really care whether one bows or genuflects at the cross, whether one stands or kneels at the Eucharist, whether we use the Book of Common Prayer or the Second Service; whether the priest wears a chasuble or a plain surplice when celebrating—all these are matters of personal taste, and have nothing to do with *salvation,* which is what we *should* be about.[4] We will be as comfortable in a "low church" as in a "high church"—grateful and rejoicing in the range of our liturgical expression—in the pageantry *and* the simplicity. We will begin to incorporate Negro spirituals into our musical expression, or Indian chants, or Hispanic tempos—while not veering too far from our basic liturgical discipline. We will also be as comfortable in a "black," "brown," "yellow," "pink," or "blue" church as in a church with an absence of color. Only as we express our common humanity can we hope to express the Glory of God!

If this memorandum has concentrated on the first person singular, it is because I dare not speak for anyone but myself in such profound matters. *I have dared* to let my imagination run riot in the hope of showing what an exciting experience a Christian witness can be in the closing decades of the twentieth century. I hope somehow that this excitement can be infectious and that its contagion can contribute in some small way to the rebirth and renewal of the Anglican Church into which I was born and in which I have remained by choice. *Praise Be to God!*

Law and Religion

Impact on the Relation Between the Sexes

Introduction

Religion and law throughout history have been dominant forces in defining the relations between men and women and in enforcing their respective roles in society. The two systems have interacted and reinforced one another in this area. Both systems share common characteristics of ritual, tradition, authority, and universality which are designed to induce belief in the sanctity of their proceedings. While these common elements contribute to stability of the social order, they also present formidable barriers to change. This has been particularly true with respect to the sexes.

Historically, the relationship between men and women has been one of domination/subjugation. As modern-day feminists point out, the oppression of women by men is undoubtedly the oldest form of oppression in human history and has been peculiarly resistant to change. Formulations embedded in both religion and law which have supported and perpetuated the inequitable relationship between the sexes continue to influence the culture long after the historical conditions which gave rise to the inequalities have all but disappeared. . . .

Our discussion will focus upon the role of the Judeo-Christian tradition in defining the respective roles of men and women in society and will touch briefly upon the corresponding role of the Western legal system in this respect. Our emphasis upon the image and role of women is largely influenced by the fact that traditionally the female has been defined not as an independent entity but in her relation to the male, who has been considered normative for society. The issues of male-female relationships arise today within the framework of the revitalized women's movement, which has supplied the initiative and impetus to bring about changes in the relations between the sexes and uses the status of women as its point of departure. As women begin to define their own identities and to assume new roles in cultural and social life, correlative changes will doubtless occur in the traditional identities and roles of men.

The Judeo-Christian Tradition

Patricia Martin Doyle, writing on women in religion, has said that the question "how shall we evaluate and reform religious life in terms of the full dignity, equality and liberation of men and women" constitutes "the most important and radical question of our time and for the foreseeable future," precisely because it concerns religion and therefore the most deeply held motivations, beliefs, and life orientations. "To raise the issue of women in religious systems therefore challenges the most important and profound aspect of life," she declares.[1]

Rosemary Ruether, a leading liberation theologian, asserts that "religion has been not only a contributing factor, it is undoubtedly the single most important shaper and enforcer of the image and role of women in culture and society." She points out that traditionally religion has been both highly political and highly sexual in its imagery, but that Judaism and Christianity have been distinctive "in their elevation of an exclusively male, patriarchal God, without female consort as the sole ruler of the heavens, and a corresponding repression of female imagery of the divine and of female roles in religion." This imagery "in turn has had a profound effect on the way in which actual men and women have been able to experience their respective existences." Thus, says Dr. Ruether, in a marked degree religion has been the "ideological reflection" of "sexual domination and subjugation," and "it has been religion, as a social institution, that has been its cultural sanctioner."[2]

The Judeo-Christian religion which has shaped Western civilization was born in a patriarchal culture in which the male was recognized as head of the family and tribe. The wandering life of the semi-nomadic ancient Hebrew tribes and their final settlement in Palestine, observes Sheila Collins in *A Different Heaven and Earth,* "depended on the physical strength and leadership of strong males. In the popular mind, their tribal god, over a long period of time, came to take on the character of a male leader, or potentate, who enforced rules and regulations, maintained discipline, sat in judgment over disputes, and led the tribe into battle."[3]

Old Testament history also reflects a bitter struggle carried on by the leaders of Israel against the feminine idols of the Canaanite religion, which centered on the Mother Goddess. The political and religious struggle for dominance in Palestine offers a further clue to the intense maleness of the Israelite God, Yahweh, who eventually emerged triumphant. According to Ruether, the feminine symbol was transformed in ancient Judaism. Yahweh is seen as the Father God and Israel collectively as his wayward bride. The life-giving force of the nature mother is suppressed. In the creation story in Genesis the natural order of life in which women give birth to men is reversed, and Eve is born from Adam's rib. Ultimately, "maleness is identified with intellectuality and spirituality; femaleness with the lower material nature . . . dependent upon and morally inferior to males."[4]

The predominant metaphors for God in the Bible are masculine—God as father, husband, lord, warrior, king. Although Professor Phyllis Trible's research indicates "there are also to be found in the Old Testament metaphors expressing the image of God as female—metaphors such as God the pregnant woman . . . the mother . . . the midwife . . . and the mistress," these images have not been emphasized in the Judeo-Christian tradition.[a]

The projection of the image of God as male served to reinforce the superior position of males in patriarchal culture. As Ruether puts it: "Traditional theological images of God as father have been the sanctification of sexism and hierarchicalism precisely by defining the relationship of God as father to humanity in a domination-subordination model and by allowing ruling-class males to identify themselves with this divine fatherhood in such a way as to establish themselves in the same kind of hierarchical relationship to women and lower classes."[b]

A recent example of an appeal to male imagery of deity to support the hierarchical relation of men to women in the Roman Catholic Church was Michael Novak's concluding paragraph in his column "Should There Be a Unisex Clergy?" which appeared in the *Washington Star* on November 3, 1979. Said Mr. Novak: "The image of God the Father and the image of the son were not, one thinks, chosen in a state of absentness. They are not a sign of sin, least of all the sin of sexism. God who made humankind made us male and female, different. To respect the difference is no sin. To overlook it is to blind oneself."

Here we see the continued impact of a religious tradition in which, as Collins points out, women were perceived "as secondary creatures to males, who assumed more and more of the characteristics the society had projected onto their God."[c] Biblical scholar Phyllis Bird notes that except for a handful of exceptional women, "the Old Testament is a man's 'book,' where women appear for the most part simply as adjuncts of men, significant only in the context of men's activities . . . a collection of writings by males from a society dominated by males. These writings portray a man's world. They speak of events and activities engaged in primarily or exclusively by males (war, cult, and government) and of a singularly jealous God, who is described and addressed in terms normally used for males."[d]

Thus, Christianity inherited an Old Testament religion conceived in ancient Hebrew culture in which a woman was in many respects regarded as the chattel of her husband. In the Tenth Commandment of the Decalogue, she is included along with her husband's servant, maid, ox, ass, or any other of his possessions. With a few exceptions like Deborah, Miriam, and Huldah, women were excluded from political and religious authority. "Only males could speak to and for God, and only males were the rightful inheritors of the Jewish name and tradition—the true Israelites."[e] Women were not part of a congregation. Only ten males could bring a congregation into existence.

Paul K. Jewett, in his biblical study *Man as Male and Female,* calls attention to the three doxologies a Jewish male was required to utter each day: Praise God that he did not create me a heathen! Praise God that he did not create me a woman! Praise God that he did not create me an illiterate person! "This prayer," says Jewett, "was faithfully offered for centuries in the synagogue, in the hearing of women, who were taught to pray simply: Praise God that he created me. . . . In the Jewish conception of the relation between man and woman the man was obviously superior as a person, the woman inferior. Therefore the man was to rule, the woman to obey, in all things."[f]

This hierarchical relation between man and woman became sanctified in the biblical story of creation. Let us bear in mind, however, that there are two creation myths in Genesis which have led to divergent views on male-female relationships. The later myth, thought to have been written around the fifth century B.C., appears in chapter 1 of Genesis, and the priestly author implies no inequality between the sexes. Male and female were created together as man; both were made in the image of God and were given joint stewardship over the earth. So God created man in his own image, in the image of God he created him; male and female he created them.

The second and older myth in Genesis 2 and 3, written around the ninth century B.C., tells the story of Eve's creation from Adam, assigns responsibility for the fall of man to Eve's susceptibility to evil, and furnishes the theological basis for male domination and female subordination as God's plan in the order of creation.

Recent biblical research offers a different emphasis on the Adam and Eve myth. It is said that a careful reading of the original Hebrew text of Genesis 2 shows that *Adam,* the first of God's creation, is generic, if not androgynous, that is, including within itself both sexes. After God builds woman, the Hebrew changes, "and specific terms are used for male and female. Man as male does not precede woman as female but happens concurrently with her."[g] However, we must deal with the myth as it has come down to us through church tradition.

In the New Testament texts, we discover how these two versions of creation were used to reach contradictory results. Jesus's liberated attitude toward women was a radical departure from Jewish tradition and was in harmony with Genesis 1. He treated them as persons in their own right, fully human and equal to men in every respect. "No word of deprecation about women, as such, is ever found on his lips," says Jewett. When he defended the right of women to stand on an equal footing with their husbands in the matter of divorce, he declared, "but from the beginning of creation, 'God made them male and female.'" A modern commentator observes, "Jesus contributed to the self-esteem of women he met by treating them as important and significant in parables, in teaching, in action, and in his final revelation of his resurrection."[h]

Because of Jesus's teachings and encouragement of women disciples, there was greater openness to the participation of women in the earliest days of the Christian community. Christian meetings were often held in the homes of women rather than in the Temple. In these early church houses women were no longer excluded from the congregation or segregated from men in worship. Women were accepted as prophets and teachers. Paul refers to several women as his co-workers and to at least one woman as a deaconess. In his letter to the Galatians Paul affirmed the equality of women and men in Christian life: "In Christ there is neither male nor female."

Why, then, did Paul revert to a strong antifemale bias in his later writings? Some scholars have conjectured that some of Paul's antifemale statements were insertions by later editors as the church became more conservative. The most common explanation is that while Paul intellectually and spiritually embraced the vision of a new personhood of men and women equal in Christ, he remained emotionally and culturally bound to Jewish tradition. Thus, when he had to deal with practical problems of order in the infant church, he fell back upon the

Adam and Eve version of creation to support his contention that women should play a subordinate role in the religious community and he related this role to the divine hierarchy. To summarize Paul's arguments:

1. Woman should be subject to man because man, created first, is directly in the image and glory of God, whereas woman, created after man and for him, is in the glory of man.

2. In the divine order of creation, God is the head of Christ, Christ is the head of every man, the husband is the head of the wife.

3. Woman, because of her weaker nature, was deceived by the tempter while the man was not. Therefore, no woman should aspire to teach or have dominion over the man but should learn from him in quietness with all subjection.[5]

The later Christian Church thus inherited two widely divergent messages: in theory, the spiritual equivalence of men and women in Christ; in practice, the subordination of women buttressed by confused and sometimes distorted theological and anthropological statements.[i]

During the patristic period, some Church Fathers equated the sinfulness of woman with her primary responsibility for the original fall of man as a daughter of Eve. For example, Tertullian, called the Father of Latin theology, writing in the third century, said of women: "Do you not know that each of you is also an Eve? . . . You are the devil's gateway. . . . You are the first deserter of divine law, you are the one who persuaded him whom the devil was too weak to attack. How easily you destroyed man, the image of God! Because of the death which you brought upon us, even the Son of God had to die."[j]

Ruether's assessment of this period is that male-female dualism was assimilated into soul-body dualism in patristic theology with the result that the spiritual image of God in man became essentially male, and female was equated with the lower, bodily nature. The woman was created as a helpmate to man "solely for the task of procreation, in which she is alone indispensable. For any spiritual task, another male would be more suitable. So the purpose of woman's existence was defined essentially in terms of childbearing. Other than this there is no reason for the existence of woman."[k] Augustine concluded that the male alone possesses the full image of God. The woman, when taken by herself, does not possess this complete image of God, but only when taken together with the male who ranks above her and "is her head." "Woman is therefore defined as a relative being who exists only in relationship to the male, who alone possesses full autonomous personhood," says Ruether. She adds, "This view of woman is perhaps the ultimate core of misogynism."[l] In the view of the Church Fathers the inferiorities of bodily weakness—pettiness, maliciousness, sensuality—which are contrary to salvation are feminine *by nature,* "whereas all the virtues that are associated with salvation—chastity, patience, wisdom, temperance, fortitude and justice—are distinctively masculine."[m]

According to the Fathers, a woman could rise above her lower nature by assuming the role of a virgin and living according to the spirit. She must transcend her female nature and live "in manly vigor." She must abase her physical appearance, strip herself of all adornments, "wear unshapely dress and a veil that conceals her face and limbs, so that she will no longer appear as an attractive female body before the eyes of the male."[n] As Eleanor C. McLaughlin points out, "Thus only the female, whose whole existence and finality are bound up in her auxiliary procreative function, must deny what the society defined as her nature in order to follow the religious life. . . . For the female, virginity is not an affirmation of her being as a woman but an assumption of the nature of the male, which is identified with the truly human: rationality, strength, courage, steadfastness, loyalty."[o]

The great medieval theologian of the thirteenth century Thomas Aquinas followed Aristotle's biology in his assertion that the female is a "misbegotten" or "defective" male, the result of an accident to the male sperm which otherwise would have produced another male. He also followed Augustine's view "that the male possesses the image of God in a way different from and superior to the image found in the female." McLaughlin notes that Aquinas assumed without discussion that a woman was inferior and subordinate by nature to the man in the moral as well as the physical and intellectual realms: "Even that which is peculiarly the woman's, the generative function, is inferior to its male counterpart, for the man is the active and fecund force, the woman but a passive and receptive instrument."[p]

Thomas Aquinas also dealt specifically with the question why Jesus Christ took on human flesh in the male form. Thomas's answer was that Christ assumed specifically a male sexuality because the masculine sex is stronger and more perfect and because the roles of the Redeemer as pastor and defender are incompatible with the subordinate status of the woman. Throughout church history and even today the maleness of Christ is pointed to as the reason for exclusion of women from the priesthood. The priest is said to act "as the instrument of Christ's work, an extension of the humanity of Christ, whose duties are incompatible with the subordination peculiar to the female sex." But, as Mc-Laughlin observes, Thomas's rationale focuses largely "not on female disabilities with respect to the divine nature of Christ but on biological and sociological grounds for a male priesthood," reflecting the patriarchal character of medieval and feudal family structures, and therefore are not properly speaking theological arguments.[q]

Christian theology also produced a schizophrenic view of woman, symbolized by the contradictory images of the "carnality" of the fallen Eve and the purity of the Virgin Mary. In medieval theology, as Christ was seen to be the new Adam, so Mary was said to be the new Eve beginning the work of salvation as Eve began the work of sin. But, as McLaughlin insists, the cult of Mary did little to improve the image of women. The emphasis upon Mary's sinlessness tended to remove her from the human sphere and prevented her from functioning psychologically as a model for female personhood. "As the embodiment of the ideal of virginity, Mary did function as a symbol of female equivalence in the order of creation, a model for the nun and the chaste wife," says McLaughlin. "But that equivalence was, in heaven as in this world, always qualified by the subordinate, auxiliary, and ultimately inferior character of female personhood relative to the masculine norm."[r]

The ultimately catastrophic effect of a theology which emphasized the proneness of woman to evil is seen in the witch craze of the fifteenth, sixteenth, and seventeenth centuries. H. R. Hays, in his detailed study *The Dangerous Sex: The Myth of Feminine Evil,* asserts that the Christian Church constructed a systematic demonology, pointing to the Bible as proof of the existence of witches belonging to the kingdom of the devil. The ecclesiastic documents on the subject projected the fantasies of a male celibate clergy motivated by fear of and hostility toward women. The strong antifemale bias of that era is revealed in the leading handbook on witchcraft, *Malleus Maleficarum,* issued by two Dominican monks around 1484, with the approval of Pope Innocent VII, the full legal support by the king of Rome, and the reluctant endorsement of the faculty of the University of Bologna. Explaining why women tend to become witches, the *Malleus* declared, "Perfidy is more found in women than in men. . . . Since they are feebler in body and in mind, it is not surprising they should come under the spell of witchcraft. . . . [Furthermore, the woman] is more carnal than man as is clear from her many carnal abominations. . . . All witchcraft comes from carnal lust which in women is insatiable. . . . For although the devil tempted Eve, yet Eve seduced Adam."[s]

When we consider that the interrogators, torturers, executioners, judges, and other officials of the Inquisition were males; that most of the victims of witch burnings were females; and that an estimated more than a million women died during the witchcraft hysteria, it is understandable that some modern historians compare the Inquisition to the Nazi Holocaust.

The notion that woman is inferior to man carried over into the Protestant Reformation. Martin Luther held that woman was created for the benefit of man; her principal function was to bear children and to be in subjection to man in all things. Apparently recognizing the inconsistency between his concept of the universal priesthood of all believers and his view of woman's incapacity to rule or to exercise spiritual leadership, Luther conceded by way of exception that in times of necessity, when a male was not available, a woman might assume the office of ministry. Calvin, although more moderate than Luther on the subject, also equated woman's subordination with the order of creation.

While Protestantism found biblical sanction for the patriarchal structures of the day, it has been pointed out that Protestant doctrines of Christian vocation and [the] priesthood of all believers applicable to the laity, both women and men, along with a new view toward marriage, which sought to reform abuses, laid the groundwork for a change of the image and role of women in the direction of greater freedom and responsibility, both immediately and over the centuries.[t]

In sum, male-female dualism, absolutized in Judaic-Christian theology, has penetrated all Western cultural institutions and reinforced ideologies advanced to exclude women from positions of authority and prestige. Although women have made considerable progress in the secular world during the past two centuries, and it is no longer popular to argue that females are inherently inferior to males, the strongly male-oriented symbolisms continue to be present in Bible readings, liturgies, and the hymnody of modern churches. Moreover, as Paul K. Jewett has correctly observed, while "today no responsible theologian would say that the woman is a 'kind of appendage' or 'lesser helpmeet' to the man, yet the doctrine of hierarchy is still affirmed." Jewett points to the theology of Karl Barth, a leading Protestant theologian of the 20th century, whose "thinking in this whole area points in the direction of the full equality of the man and woman in the fellowship of life, yet argues for female subordination." Instead of the view that the woman is inferior, Barth stresses the fact that she is different. Jewett is convinced that as long as the religious argument for the subordination of the woman to the man is maintained, it cannot be separated from the traditional theological grounds on which this subordination is based, namely "the superiority of the man as the image and glory of God in whom the discretion of reason predominates."[u]

While many of the views reported here may seem laughable to a late twentieth-century audience, church historian Eleanor C. McLaughlin has voiced her continual amazement at the extent to which medieval attitudes about the female in relation to the male are still with us today, not merely in Christian tradition but also in "our secularized society, which in its assumptions about the woman and all her works has deep and unconscious roots in medieval culture." She argues that the medieval church's view of woman "in all its ambivalence, ambiguity, and even sometimes perversion, must become part of our consciousness if we are to overcome and build creatively on the past."[v]

The Law and Relations Between the Sexes

Turning briefly to the impact of law upon relations between the sexes, we call attention to the strong influence of Christian tradition upon Western legal institutions. Professor Harold Berman of Harvard Law School points out in his little book *Interaction of Law and Religion:*

> The canon law of the later Middle Ages was the first modern legal system of the West, and it prevailed in every country in Europe. The canon law governed virtually all the aspects of the church's own army of priests and monks and also a great many aspects of the lives of the laity. The new hierarchy of church courts had exclusive jurisdiction over laymen in matters of family law, inheritance, and various types of spiritual crimes, and in addition it had concurrent jurisdiction with secular courts over [certain types of] contracts, property . . . and many other matters.[w]

The patriarchalism which permeated Christian theology also undergirded the legal relationships between men and women. We will content ourselves with a few examples taken from the American experience. The legal status of men and women was determined by the English Common Law system imported into the Anglo-American colonies. Under the early Common Law, a woman was considered her husband's chattel, "something better than his dog, a little dearer than his horse."[x] At one time it was legally permissible for a man to chastise his wife with a stick no larger than his thumb, although by the mid-seventeenth century it was held in the Massachusetts Colony that she should be free from corporal punishment by him. During marriage, a woman's legal identity merged completely with that of her husband who had sole control over her personal property, her wages, and the custody of their children. In other words, during marriage, or coverture, a woman was said to be civilly dead. The notion that women and men stand as equals before the law was no part of the original understanding. In the words of Thomas Jefferson: "Were our state a pure democracy, there would still be excluded from our deliberations women, who, to prevent deprivation of morals and ambiguity of issues, should not mix promiscuously in gatherings of men." The same ambiguities found in theology were present in the law. Notions of woman's inherent physical and intellectual inferiority to man fused with rationalizations that she was a "favorite" of the law and that restrictions on her liberty were intended for her "protection and benefit." Thus, on the one hand, an argument opposing woman's suffrage was that a woman's brain was smaller in capacity and therefore inferior in quality to that of a man, the same argument used to resist equality for Blacks. On the other hand, in the late nineteenth century the myth of female purity was invoked to discourage women's activities outside of the home. It was now argued that the woman-centered home was the "sanctuary" where all moral and spiritual values were located and that these Christian virtues would be destroyed if she ventured into the man's "world of hard practical aggressiveness, devoid of sentiment and morality." Rosemary Ruether reports that this "mythology led the Catholic Bishops of Massachusetts, in opposing woman's suffrage in 1920, to declare that for women to enter the realm of politics was tantamount to becoming 'a fallen woman.'"

For more than a century after the adoption in 1868 of the Fourteenth Amendment guaranteeing to "all persons" equal protection of the laws, the Supreme Court of the United States frustrated women's attempts to apply that amendment to discriminatory sex-based distinctions in state laws and policies. Theology was invoked to support the validity of such discrimination. In 1873, the Supreme Court upheld the power of the state of Illinois to refuse Myra Bradwell a license to practice law solely because she was female, although she had passed the state bar examination. The high Court affirmed the judgment of the state court, which had declared in its opinion "that God designed the sexes to occupy different spheres of action, and that it belonged to men to make, apply, and execute the laws, was regarded as an almost axiomatic truth." Mr. Justice Bradley of the Supreme Court, joined by two other justices, observed in a concurring opinion:

The paramount destiny and mission of woman are to fulfill the noble and benign offices of wife and mother. This is the law of the Creator . . . and, in my opinion, in view of the peculiar characteristics, destiny and mission of woman, it is within the province of the legislature [we note that the legislature is all-male] to ordain what offices, positions, and callings shall be filled and discharged by men, and shall receive the benefit of those energies and responsibilities, and that decision and firmness which are presumed to predominate in the sterner sex.

A review of the judicial record up to 1971 led two male law professors to conclude that one of the forms of rationalization commonly used by the courts at all levels to uphold sex discriminatory state legislation was "express reliance on a mythology of male-supremacy, which confines women to a subordinated social role and then patronizingly 'protects' them against even their own attempts to change that role." And law professor Leo Kanowitz pointed out in his study "Women and the Law," published in 1969:

As long as organized legal systems, at once the most respected and most feared of social institutions, continue to differentiate sharply, in treatment and in words, between men and women on the basis of irrelevant and artificially created distinctions, the likelihood of men and women coming to regard one another primarily as human beings and only secondarily as representatives of another sex will continue to be remote. When men and women are prevented from recognizing one another's essential humanity by sexual prejudice, nourished by legal as well as social institutions, society as a whole remains less than it could otherwise become.

It was the realization of how deeply embedded in the legal system are hundreds of gender-based inequalities—all products "of a long prior history of open subjugation of women by men"—and the reluctance of the courts to strike down these inequalities which finally convinced the feminist movement in the 1970s that only the adoption of the Equal Rights Amendment would set forth an unequivocal constitutional standard of equality of the sexes before the law.

Some Concluding Observations

In concluding our discussion, let me point out that while the present controversies over the Equal Rights Amendment, abortion rights, and ordination of women to the priesthood are the most visible reflections of continued ambiguities in the relations between men and women in both law and religion, a less publicized development is taking place which may profoundly influence future relations between the sexes. I refer to the emergence of feminist theology concurrent with the revival of the women's movement in the 1960s, which shares with other contemporary theologies of liberation commitment to radical political and social change, seeking to transform the structures of society in order to build a more humane world.

Feminist theology seeks a new worldview. As Ruether and others have pointed out, it recognizes that the issue of sexism "crosses and includes every field of human specialization" and encompasses the entire human situation. Women are a part of every race and class. True liberation of women, therefore, must envision a radical reconstruction of society which will eliminate racism, economic exploitation, imperialism, and other forms of oppression and alienation, as well as hierarchical relationships based upon sex. Such a vast undertaking, says Ruether, requires that the theologian move beyond the purely "religious" sphere and draw upon many fields of human experience.

Thus, some feminist theologians are addressing themselves to the present world crisis in human values and the extent to which this crisis is rooted in the patriarchal worldview and its one-sided development of male-oriented cultural patterns—aggressiveness, competition, militarism and war—which have reached the limit of their utility. Erik Erikson, among other contemporary commentators, has asserted that "the special dangers of the nuclear age clearly have brought male leadership close to the limits of its adaptive imagination," a situation which necessitates "nothing less than a redefinition of the identity of the sexes within a new image of man." Patricia Martin Doyle adopts Erikson's approach in her analysis of the psychological and cultural implications of women in religion. She contends that the result of male-dominated ideologies and identities is a dangerous imbalance, "a framework [which] even—or perhaps, especially—infects the perception of God, so that the Ultimate is invoked to substantiate a destructively masculine world. . . . Women need to cultivate and help formulate new identities and new ideologies in the light of the new valuations and understandings of women in the world, not only for themselves but for the sake of a new and more holistic image of both women and men and a new understanding of the meaning of life." She argues, "Cultivation of the feminine in religious symbolizations and consciousness, in future ideologies and identities, is urgently needed if humanity is to be saved from possible catastrophe and become more whole."[z]

Rosemary Ruether also stresses the need through modern research to "re-shape patriarchal religion" and "establish the basis for a new humanity beyond patriarchy."[aa] From this perspective, feminism has a potentially revolutionary quality which cuts across political ideologies and systems and seeks a worldview which can release human creativity—male and female—for the regeneration of society. It points beyond the present global crisis and signals a new civilization.

Notes

[a] Phyllis Trible, *God and the Rhetoric of Sexuality* (Minneapolis: Fortress Press, 1978), 22.

[b] Rosemary Radford Ruether, *New Woman, New Earth: Sexist Ideologies and Human Liberation* (1975; reprint Boston: Beacon Press, 1995), 63.

[c] Sheila D. Collins, *A Different Heaven and Earth: A Feminist Perspective on Religion* (King of Prussia, PA: Judson Press, 1974), 64.

[d] Phyllis Bird, "Images of Women in the Old Testament," in *Religion and Sexism: Images of Women in the Jewish and Christian Traditions,* ed. Rosemary Radford Ruether (1974; reprint Eugene, OR: Wipf and Stock, 1998), 41–42.

[e] Collins, *A Different Heaven and Earth,* 65.

[f] Paul K. Jewett, *Man as Male and Female* (Grand Rapids, MI: Eerdmans, 1975), 93.

[g] Marianne H. Micks, "The Case for Women's Ordination," in *The Ordination of Women: Pro and Con,* ed. Michael P. Montgomery and Nancy S. Montgomery (New York: Morehouse Barlow, 1975), 5.

[h] Alicia Craig Faxon, *Women and Jesus* (New York: HarperCollins, 1973), 106.

[i] Constance F. Parvey, "The Theology and Leadership of Women in the New Testament," in Ruether, ed., *Religion and Sexism,* 146.

[j] Cited and quoted in Jewett, *Man as Male and Female,* 156.

[k] Rosemary Radford Ruether, "Is the Church Misogynist?" in Ruether, *Liberation Theology* (Boston: Paulist Press, 1972), 99–100.

[l] Ibid., 100.

[m] Rosemary Radford Ruether, "Misogynism and Virginal Feminism in the Fathers of the Church," in Ruether, ed., *Religion and Sexism,* 159.

[n] Ibid., 160–161.

[o] Eleanor Commo McLaughlin, "Equality of Souls, Inequality of Sexes: Woman in Medieval Theology," in Ruether, ed., *Religion and Sexism,* 234.

[p] Ibid., 216–218.

[q] Ibid., 220.

r Ibid., 220, 246–251.

s H. R. Hays, *The Dangerous Sex: The Myth of Feminine Evil* (New York: Pocket Books, 1964), 193.

t James Dempsey Douglass, "Women and the Continental Reformation," in Ruether, ed., *Religion and Sexism,* 314.

u Jewett, *Man as Male and Female,* 85.

v McLaughlin, "Equality of Souls, Inequality of Sexes," 214–215.

w Harold Berman, *Interaction of Law and Religion* (Nashville: Abingdon, 1974), 58,

x Quoted from Alfred Lord Tennyson, "Locksley Hall" (1842).

y Leo Kanowitz, "Women and the Law," *Case Western Reserve Law Review* 21 (1970): 4.

z Patricia Martin Doyle, "Women and Religion: Psychological and Cultural Implications," in Ruether, ed., *Religion and Sexism,* 23–39.

aa Rosemary Radford Ruether, "Preface," in Ruether, ed., *Religion and Sexism,* 11–12.

Challenge of Nurturing the Christian Community in Its Diversity

Last week Canon Casson spoke of the tragedy of the People's Temple cult at Jonestown, Guyana, a Christian community which started out with a vision of a new equalitarian society and ended in the horror of mass murder and suicide.[1] He talked of Jonestown as a mirror of ourselves and a warning of what can happen when people give up the struggle to direct their own lives and have such little self-esteem that they submit their destinies in abject conformity to a human savior with a drive for power over others.

It seems fitting that this week we consider the challenge of nurturing the Christian community in its diversity, of developing the freedom and autonomy which affirms life and creativity instead of death and destruction. One of the dimensions of hunger is the universal human longing for acceptance and inclusion in the actions which affect our lives, for the recognition of our individuality and personal worth. This hunger transcends the basic struggle for physical existence, for when our personhood is respected we are lifted up and experience an abundance of life even when we are enduring hardships. We achieve our sense of personhood in relation to God and to other human beings. When we realize that we are made in the image of God, we glimpse a vision of our true selves. But since we live in a human society, it is only in community with others that we find affirmation of our sense of being and personal worth. When Paul wrote, "In any and all circumstances I have learned the secret of facing plenty and hunger, abundance and want," he was making a statement of self-affirmation growing out of his life in Christ and his loving relationship to the Christian community at Philippi.[a]

We saw this aspect of human need sensitively portrayed in the television showing of "Backstairs in the White House," the story of the humble household workers who served the First Families through the successive administrations of eight American presidents. There is a poignant scene of an encounter between President Franklin D. Roosevelt and Lillian Rogers, a young Black maid who does sewing for the First Family. The president, confined to his wheelchair and rolling it through a corridor, happens to catch sight of young Lillian hobbling on her crutch into a closet to get out of sight. He is curious about her strange behavior. He doesn't know that she is obeying a rule laid down by his predecessor that all household employees are to disappear whenever they hear the bell signal that the president or the First Lady is passing through. President Roosevelt has Lillian called out from the closet. When he looks at her he realizes she is a fellow victim of polio. In that moment their common humanity bridges the vast differences of race, social position, and political power. He acknowledges their kinship by saying, "You and I know what it's all about, don't we?" and she replies with complete understanding, "Yes, Mr. President."

Mr. Roosevelt then tells her that from now on she is to use the presidential elevator whenever she has to go up or down stairs, and when she leaves his presence the expression on her face is one of heightened self-esteem and her head and shoulders are thrown back in an attitude of self-affirmation.

True community is based upon equality, mutuality, and reciprocity. It affirms the richness of individual diversity as well as the common human ties which bind us together. The marks of a community of faith are communion, participation, mutual trust, sharing, and fellowship. A community of faith is both social and sacramental. As Professor Letty M. Russell of Yale Divinity School defines it, "Communion is participation with Christ in his work as the representative of God's love to others, and sharing with his community in common actions of celebration, reflection, and service to the world." This is what we do in our Lenten season in a special sense, for following our celebration of the Holy Eucharist and sharing of [a] common meal, we reflect together on how we can respond to world hunger for human dignity as well as physical sustenance.

Let me put this question in the words of two European theologians, Elisabeth Moltmann-Wendel and Jürgen Moltmann, who say,

> Just as the call for salvation from transitoriness to attain immortality could
> be heard in every corner of the ancient world, today a cry for liberation is
> shouted by the oppressed, the humiliated, and the offended in this inhuman

world. . . . Will men and women experience the compelling force of God's liberation "on earth as it is in heaven" in Christ, in the proclamation and in the powerful manifestation of the Holy Spirit? . . . This seems to be the decisive question now, not only for Christians—so often of little faith—but also for humanity as a whole—which seems to have lost its sense of direction.[2]

The questions we have asked ourselves about the church are also being asked by a growing number of theologians: What has our faith to say about the social injustices and inequalities which are systematic, which cannot be overcome by our individual efforts, and which destroy the humanity of whole peoples as well as the possibility for any meaningful community? How can we remain Christians with despair as we struggle against oppressive institutions in which the church itself has been deeply implicated and has helped to perpetuate? These have been burning questions for Blacks, women, and the poor in the United States as they seek to improve their position in society.

Over the past ten or twelve years, a number of theologians arising from the ranks of women, Blacks, and Third World peoples have begun to reexamine and reinterpret the Christian faith so that it has relevance for people committed to the search for liberation in today's world. These religious scholars are developing theologies of liberation. They interpret salvation as hope for deliverance not only from sin but also from social and political oppression, the institutionalization of sin. They speak of salvation which begins in the here and now and they relate the gospel to the efforts of men and women to abolish the present unjust order and build a freer, more humane society. They try to express the gospel in the light of experience of oppression . . . whether it stems from racism, sexism, economic exploitation, imperialism, or authoritarian dictatorship. Thus, Black theology, which has been developing since the late 1960s, addresses itself to what it means to be a Black Christian struggling against racism in white-dominated America. Feminist theology deals with the experience of women in male-dominated church and society.

These theologies perform the valuable function of subjecting the Judeo-Christian tradition to critical analysis. They seek to correct distortions of interpretation of the faith and to reclaim the prophetic mission of the church by transforming its structures so that in its own life it is a witnessing community to the vision of the new humanity which the gospel proclaims. Because these theologies are concerned not only with the removal of institutional barriers to wholeness of being but also with what Russell calls "the reality of the ultimate intention of God that all people be reconciled with one another," they speak to our search for a Christian community which responds effectively to the problems we face in today's world. They offer us fresh ways to think about God, God's nature and will as revealed to humankind.

First, theologies of liberation emphasize that our perceptions of God are shaped by the culture in which we live and by our experience. A major criticism of traditional Christian theology is that, historically, its theologians have been white and male. The concrete experiences of Blacks and women have not been included in theological undertakings, and to this extent these groups find theological interpretations insufficient for their self-understanding.

For example, consider the doctrines of obedience, meekness, humility, and suffering servanthood. Many oppressed people are turned off by these doctrines because they see them as expressions of their own powerlessness. They have often been used to invoke divine sanction for patterns of dominance and submission in human relationships. This was apparently what happened at Jonestown. Jim Jones, who called himself "Father," began to identify himself as the savior and to require absolute obedience to his commands. It was certainly the experience of Blacks during slavery. Letty Russell points out that "servant-hood presents problems for women and other oppressed groups who have been condemned to play a servant role not of their own choosing. For these groups humanization is experienced, not so much through service, as through bonding together in supportive communities that can provide new identity and hope."[b] Even when the biblical image of servanthood is clarified to indicate that inferiority or subordination is not the true meaning but rather "the privilege of God's gracious choice" of one to act as "an instrument of divine help to someone else's need," yet the degrading connotations of the term are not dispelled for women and other humiliated groups struggling against roles of subordination in church and society.

Dr. Major J. Jones, a Black theologian, has said that much of the task of Black theology is to reclaim a people from humiliation and therefore it may "neglect such unrelated subjects as humility before man and guilt before God." This is not to deny our human sinfulness but to point up the abuses of doctrines when used to justify the oppression of others.

Traditional Christian spirituality looks upon anger and pride as negative characteristics, says Dr. Rosemary Ruether, but they "are the vital 'virtues' in the salvation of the oppressed community. Anger, here, is felt as the power to revolt against and judge a system of oppression to which one was formerly a powerless and buried victim. Pride is experienced as the recovery of that authentic humanity and good created nature 'upon which God looked in the beginning and, behold, it was very good.'"ᶜ

A second important characteristic of theologies of liberation is the stress upon the corporate nature of salvation and sin and its relation to community. The building of community can only begin, says one theologian, when we take seriously the understanding of salvation as a social as well as an individual event and begin to deal with all the various social obstacles to communication. This is a broadening of the understanding of salvation in the afterlife to include the beginnings of salvation in the lives of men and women in our present world. The emphasis is upon salvation, not as an escape into "heaven" but rather "the power and possibility of transforming the world [in which we live], of restoring creation and seeking to overcome suffering." This means that we don't simply endure evil or, on the other hand, withdraw from the world as the people did in Jonestown, but accept the challenge of continuous struggle to change it.

Sin also takes on a different meaning in this perspective and is interpreted to include corporate or social evil as well as individual transgression. This view attempts to correct tendencies within the church to concentrate upon sin and repentance as an individual matter while ignoring the institutional structures of alienation and oppression which, in Rosemary Ruether's words, "blot out the face of God's good creation." She says that concentration on individualistic repentance and "private confession"—she speaks out of a Roman Catholic background—has had the effect in Christianity of involving people in the process of kneeling down to examine a speck of dirt on the floor while remaining oblivious to the social monsters who are towering over their backs. They are what St. Paul meant by "Powers and Principalities," and human beings cannot overcome them individually, yet privatistic religion which argues that "politics has nothing to do with religion" serves to exclude such institutional monsters as racism, sexism, and oppression of the poor from the very definition of sin and repentance. This analysis confronts us with our own participation in collective evil and our responsibility to change the social structures which bring it about. Dr. Martin Luther King Jr. explained how he came to embrace nonviolent demonstrations, boycotts, and civil disobedience in the struggle against racial segregation. He said he became convinced that to accept passively an evil system was as immoral as active perpetuation of it, "thereby making the oppressed as evil as the oppressor," and that "in order to be true to one's conscience and to

God, a righteous [person] ... has no alternative but to refuse to cooperate with an evil system." Dr. J. Deotis Roberts of Howard University School of Religion argues that while we should not abandon the quest for strengthening the inner spiritual life, what we need today is an understanding of the Christian faith in a highly political context and that the only gospel suitable for this new consciousness "is one that opts for radical and massive change in oppressive attitudes and structures of power." This is what the Reverend Walter Fauntroy meant when he told a television interviewer several nights ago that he attempted to translate the gospel he preached on Sunday into his political activity in Congress on Monday.

A third point to be made about theologies of liberation is the vision of a new earthly society in which diversity is valued and which is so structured as to encourage each individual to develop to the fullness of his or her own potential. This vision of the possibility of a new earth and a new human being gives the hope which fuels our efforts toward social change. It forces us to stretch our minds beyond the harsh realities of our present state and impels us toward the future even as we try to cope with poverty, the drug scene, crime in the streets, inflation, and the threat of nuclear war. It foresees a society in which differences of race or sex or ethnic background will be affirmed and celebrated. As Dr. Jones put it, "There will be pluralism in ideologies, interests, aims and aspirations, and personhood; and as one will for any purpose be denied opportunity to achieve or be excluded from community."[d]

Where and how [can] we begin to fulfill this vision? It is said that the process of liberation begins with an awareness of the alienations, divisions, and constrictions which limit our lives, and moves on to affirm our liberation from these constrictions and toward a vision of wholeness and unity. For oppressed people this process involves throwing off the debasing stereotypes imposed upon them by the dominant society and engaging in self-definition and the achievement of self-esteem. The new self-image moves them to action because they can no longer tolerate the old conditions. We have seen this process at work in the heightened Black awareness of recent years and in the consciousness-raising activities of feminist groups.

This new self-awareness affects our relationships with others. It pours new meaning into the commandment to love one's neighbor as *one's self.* Dr. Roberts points out that it is because we love self that we can express love on a higher moral level toward others. Self-love in this sense is not selfishness but self-respect. Only when we love ourselves properly are [we] prepared to love others.

Self-hate is at the bottom of much of the crime and violence in an oppressed community. I recall that during the 1960s the crime rate dropped markedly among Negroes in communities engaged in nonviolent protest demonstrations.

Self-definition for women is an enormously complex process. Not only do they represent half of humanity in every race and class but in our culture, the Judeo-Christian tradition, and the civilization to which it has given rise constitute the principal source of their constriction and limitation. Religion is said to be the single most important factor in shaping and enforcing the role and image of women in culture and society, and has reflected sexual domination and subjugation in both its doctrines and its practices as a social institution. The first overt protest against the new regime in the revolution in Iran has come from women who fear that fundamentalist elements of Islamic beliefs will be used to rob them of gains and reduce them to second-class citizens.

Women must still struggle against the contradictory images which have come down to us through Judeo-Christian doctrines: woman as the temptress, the cause of humankind's fall; woman as the body-negating virgin who attains virtue only at the sacrifice of her sexuality; woman as wife-mother whose destiny determined by the divine order of creation is to bear children and be subordinate to her husband. Embedded in the history of Christian doctrine is the view that woman is incapable of autonomous personhood and is secondary to the male who alone possesses the full image of God. The residual effects of this doctrine are still present today in the theological arguments against the ordination of women as priests in the church.

Women also find that the pervasiveness of male language in biblical imagery, in liturgy, and in hymns reflects a patriarchal worldview and presents formidable barriers to a sense of community and mutuality in the church. Biblical images of an exclusively male God as Father, King, Lord, Master present problems for women not only because these images do not represent the full human experience but also they have served as divine substantiation of the exclusion of women from full participation in religious life and their subordination to men in society. Ordination experience language, as Ruether points [out], is the principal indication of "the power of the ruling group to define reality in its own terms and demote oppressed groups into invisibility. Women, more than any other group, are overwhelmed by a linguistic form that excludes them from visible existence."[3] Making the church a more inclusive community involves transforming our imagery as well as church structures to reflect the experience of women as well as men.

In short, our salvation begins with our quest for liberation and a search for our true personhood, a wholeness of being. In this search, our vision of new possibilities and a new human being is centered in Jesus Christ because we believe that in Jesus of Nazareth God revealed to us what it is to be fully human. We enter into community with others based upon our new self-understanding, and we struggle to transform ourselves, our church, and our society in order to actualize [the] vision.

In the process we glimpse only fragmentary moments of the community we seek and fleeting images of our authentic selves. We are held in tension between the "now" and the "not yet." We are buffeted between advancing and receding waves of fellowship and withdrawal, or reconciliation and alienation. The human lifespan is so short we experience only tiny segments of social change in a single lifetime. I think of Elizabeth Cady Stanton and Susan B. Anthony whose entire lives were dedicated [to] woman's suffrage but both of whom had been dead for nearly two decades or more before the Nineteenth Amendment became part of the Constitution. I think of President Kennedy who initiated the Civil Rights Act of 1964 but did not live to see it enacted into law. I think of Dr. Martin Luther King Jr., who did not survive to see the partial transformation of the South and the acceptance of desegregation by people today who shouted "Never!" when he was alive. And of former Israeli prime minister Golda Meir, who I think passionately wanted peace but died a few months before the treaty between Israel and Egypt was signed. I think of my own beloved aunt whose call to the ministry could not be fully consummated. The closest she came was as the wife of a priest, and she died twenty-one years before I was ordained in the same diocese where she and her husband last served.

No one knows how the oppressed people of the earth can move together and eliminate the barriers of race, sex, and class which rob human beings of their freedom, says Letty Russell, but we believe that we are not acting out of our own power but under the power and plan of God. And, as Dr. King once said, we can have deep faith in the future because we know that in our struggles for justice we have "cosmic companionship." Dr. Ruether's reflection on the tension between what "is" and what "will be" seems an appropriate conclusion to our discussion. She said, "To remain in this tension in fidelity is to live by faith; to keep our hope for the Kingdom in the midst of inconclusiveness and our love for the brothers and sisters in the midst of brokenness. In this faith we can also begin to celebrate now."[4]

Notes

[a] Philippians 4:12.

[b] Letty M. Russell, *Human Liberation in a Feminist Perspective* (Philadelphia: Westminster Press, 1974), 140.

[c] Rosemary Radford Ruether, *Liberation Theology* (Boston: Paulist Press, 1972), 12.

[d] Major J. Jones, *Black Awareness: A Theology of Hope* (Nashville: Abingdon, 1971).

Women and Women's Rights

Minority Women and Feminist Spirituality

Some time ago, I did a comparative study of Black theology and feminist theology, seeking insights into the dual burdens of race and sex. I discovered that although the two theologies arose out of parallel liberation movements in the United States and that certain historical similarities in the subjugation of Blacks and women suggest a basis for solidarity and fruitful dialogue, considerable tension existed between the two.

Black theology, rooted in the male-oriented Black Power movement, which began in the late 1960s, regarded the emerging women's movement as a competitive diversion. Its exponents ignored feminist theology and did not address themselves to the special problems of Black women.

On the other hand, the revived women's movement, led by predominantly white, middle- or upper-class women, had not successfully incorporated the aspirations of poor and minority women into its struggle. Both groups tended to concentrate upon a single factor of oppression without adequate consideration of the "interstructuring" of racism, sexism, and economic exploitation. I noted that focusing on a particular factor of oppression could obscure the goal of universal liberation and reconciliation which lies at the heart of the Christian gospel.

Some feminist theologians, aware of this danger, stressed the necessity for an inclusive approach, broad social analysis, and self-criticism which recognizes and opposes the oppressive practices within one's own group. This feminist analysis also points to the fact that women constitute half of every social class and their common concerns necessarily embrace the whole spectrum of the human condition. This offers possibilities for joint action which can begin to transcend barriers of race, sex, and economic class. At the time of the study I also noted that the interlocking factors of racism and sexism within the Black experience await analysis.

With these findings as a point of departure, the question arises, What promise does feminist spirituality in the context of the women's movement hold for minority women—and specifically Black women—in their struggles for liberation? In the broad sense, spirituality refers to that which gives meaning and purpose to our lives, our vision of wholeness of being. Theologian Letty Russell speaks of the spirituality of liberation which focuses upon partnership in situations of oppression. "Feminist theologians," she notes, "have sought to articulate the groaning of women and to build solidarity among those working to anticipate the new meaning of human wholeness."

When I seek to apply this model, however, I find that the severe tensions existing between Black women and white women stand as barriers to the solidarity which feminist spirituality envisions. What follows is an attempt to highlight some of these tensions in the hope that an analysis will produce insights that point the way toward reconciliation and collaborative effort.

Alienation of Black Women

A typical expression of the deep-seated alienation Black women continue to feel toward white women twenty years after the rebirth of the women's movement is that of Dr. Deborah Harmon Hines of Meharry Medical College, Nashville, and national president of the Union of Black Episcopalians. Speaking on "The Black Women's Agenda" at a conference of the Episcopal Church's Task Force on Women in 1981, Dr. Hines declared, "The Black women that I work with, seek advice from, socialize with, go to church with, come from a wide variety of backgrounds, economic strata, educational levels, work, family and leadership experience. These women unequivocally see their roles as maintaining, strengthening and uplifting our race, our families, our culture and heritage, our men and ourselves. And these women see racism as our archenemy in this struggle."

Dr. Hines spoke of the degrading images—"Aunt Jemima," "Jezebel," and "welfare seeker"—with which Black women have to contend and charged that "my White step-sisters are often as guilty or guiltier than their men folk in perpetuating these myths about Black women." She went on to say,

Black women find it extremely difficult to ally themselves with those who have not been part of the solution, but a part of the problem. Black women find it extremely difficult to ally themselves with those who say, "We have all suffered the same," when we know it isn't so. Black women find the situation intolerable when we are told (by White women) what we should do in our struggle, and not asked what we want to do. Until our step-sisters stop super-imposing their needs onto us, we have nothing to say to them.[1]

This sentiment expressed by a Black professional woman who is a deeply committed Christian is echoed in various ways by other Black women and is cause for deep concern among those of us who work for solidarity among women as a necessary expression of our feminist spirituality. Its implications go to the core of our beliefs and actions and must be confronted honestly, however painful this may be.

A review of recent literature in which Black women have sought to define themselves and their priorities reveals the consistent theme that Black women are the victims of multilayered oppression. The "Black Feminist Statement" formulated by the Combahee River Collective states, "We believe that sexual politics under patriarchy is as pervasive in Black women's lives as are the politics of race and class. We also find it difficult to separate race from class from sex oppression because in our lives they are experienced simultaneously."[2]

To a much greater extent than white women, Black women are victimized by racial-sexual violence which has deep historical roots in slavery and continues today in rape, forced sterilization, and physical abuse in family relations. They constitute the most disadvantaged group in the United States as compared to white men, Black men, and white women. They are found in the most menial, lowest-paying jobs, and are disproportionately represented among poor, female-headed, and welfare families. Black women and their families suffer from inadequate health care, high rates of infant mortality, and other health hazards associated with poverty and powerlessness.

As Deborah Hines indicated, Black women have had to struggle against myths and humiliating stereotypes which undermine a positive self-image. The Black matriarchy myth, which became popular in the social science literature of the 1960s, has depicted Black women as having an unnatural dominant role in family life, which has had damaging effects upon Black society. The ill effects attributed to the alleged existence of a matriarchal family structure included juvenile delinquency, self-hatred, low intelligence, cultural deprivation, crimes against persons, and schizophrenia among Blacks, according to one reviewer. The sharp rise in numbers of female-headed families in the Black community has reinforced this stereotype.

This matriarchy myth has come under heavy criticism during the past decade, particularly by Black women scholars. Dr. Jacqueline J. Jackson of Duke University Medical Center has pointed to the demographic factor of a significant sex-ratio imbalance in the Black population. She noted that in 1970, there were about ninety-one Black males for every one hundred Black females in the United States. The growing excess of Black females over Black males has been reflected in every census since 1860 but has become increasingly acute. By 1976, the U.S. Census reported that there were 80.7 Black males for every 100 Black females over twenty-four years old.

This cannot be explained solely on the ground that Black males have been overlooked in the census count. Jackson finds that this sex-ratio imbalance is directly related to the high proportion of Black female-headed families and has defined these families as an adaptation to larger social structural forces. The limited availability of marital partners for Black women is also a factor in expressions of hostility toward white women who enter into sexual or marital relationships with Black men.

In their embattled struggle for day-to-day survival, Black women's attitudes toward the women's movement have ranged from indifference and outright rejection to suspicion to cautious approval of certain of the movement's goals coupled with aloofness and strong criticism of perceived racism and classism within the movement itself.

Gloria I. Joseph and Jill Lewis of Hampshire College, in a penetrating analysis of conflicts in Black and white feminist perspectives, maintain, "The White women's movement has had its own explicit forms of racism in the way it has given priority to certain aspects of struggles and neglected others, and it has often been blind and ignorant of the conditions of Black women's lives."[3]

While they acknowledge that many of the issues raised by white women do affect all women's lives—for example, contraception, abortion, forced sterilization, rape, wife battering, inequities in law, health care, welfare, work conditions, and pay—they point out that "because of the inherently racist assumptions and perspectives brought to bear on these issues in the first articulations by the White women's movement, they were rejected by Black women as irrelevant, when in fact the same problems, seen from different perspectives, can be highly relevant to Black women's lives." "Too frequently," they assert, "participants in the struggles of parallel liberation movements are blinded to each other and have only a limited understanding of each other's priorities."[4]

One area of misunderstanding has been in the perception of male/female relationships. According to the Joseph and Lewis study, "The differences recognized in the sexual relationships between Black women and Black men in contrast to White women and White men relate to the question of power. . . . To categorically lump all men together and attribute the same sense of power to both Black and White men is racist in the same sense that the crucial role of white-skin privilege in our society is being disregarded. It is incumbent upon White feminists to recognize the very real differences that exist between White men and Black men when their degree of power is considered."[5]

While white feminists necessarily have directed their energies against a system of male domination, Black males and females are bound together in a political struggle against white racism which has traditionally repressed in the most brutal manner assertions of power by Black males. Black women, feeling a strong need to support their men, have often perceived the women's movement to be a "divisive" tactic which would alienate them from their partners in their effort to throw off white domination. Black women face the dilemma of the competing claims of the Black liberation movement and the women's liberation movement, each of which is a separate entity based on its own distinctive realities. The Black woman cannot participate fully in both, but she cannot afford to ignore either movement.

Toward a Resolution

The rise of Black feminism within the past decade is an important development but it is not yet clear what direction it will take to resolve the Black woman's dilemma. Some Black women's groups have developed coalitions with white women on specific issues. Several Black feminist groups have sprung up as a third movement exclusively devoted to the concerns of Black women, but their isolation and aloofness raise questions as to their effectiveness. Dr. Constance M. Carroll, president of Indian Valley College, Novato, California, urges an alternative course which is a

> productive but difficult and lonely road if the Black woman is to achieve concrete benefits at the end of her struggle. She must be the gadfly who stings both movements into achieving their goals—prodding the women's

movement into confronting its racism and working doubly hard for the concerns of Black women, and prodding the less volatile Black movement into confronting its inherent sexism and righting the injustice it has done to Black women. She must become the sorely needed bridge between them if their goals are to be translated into reality.

Some Black women are beginning to follow this course—reexamining their position and becoming more vocal in their feminism, within the Black movement at least. Several Black women theologians have launched a critique of Black theology. The most pointed criticism has come from Jacquelyn Grant, doctoral candidate at Union Theological Seminary. She observes that "some theologians have acquiesced in one or more oppressive aspects of the liberation struggle itself. Where racism is rejected, sexism has been embraced. Where classism is called into question, racism and sexism have been tolerated. And where sexism is repudiated racism and classism are often ignored." She declares bluntly, "The failure of the Black church and Black theology to proclaim explicitly the liberation of Black women indicates that they cannot claim to be agents of divine liberation. If the theology, like the church, has no word for Black women, its conception of liberation is inauthentic." Grant also questions the thesis that the central problem of Black women is related to their race and not their sex. She says, "I contend that as long as the Black struggle refuses to recognize and deal with its own sexism, the idea that women will receive justice from that struggle alone will never work."[6]

Significantly, these and similar criticisms have influenced Black theologian James H. Cone to reexamine his views. In his recent book, *My Soul Looks Back,* Cone confesses, "When I began writing about Black theology, the problem of sexism was not a part of my theological consciousness. When it was raised by others, I rejected it as a joke or an intrusion upon the legitimate struggle of Black people to eliminate racism."[7]

Cone traces his reeducation, which began at Union Theological Seminary where he was exposed to the women's liberation movement. He says,

> While White women forced me to consider the problem of sexism in a White context, Black women forced me to face the reality of sexism in the Black community. . . . As I listened to Black women articulate their pain, and as I observed the insensitive responses of Black men, it became existentially clear to me that sexism was a Black problem too. . . . Black women theologians appear to be developing a new comprehensive way of thinking about

theology, church, and society. While Black male theologians focus almost exclusively on racism, White feminists primarily on sexism, and Third World theologians or Latin Americans concern themselves with classism, Black women are seeking to combine the issues of race, sex, and class, because they are deeply affected by each.[8]

Further indication of Cone's movement toward a more comprehensive approach is his reflection upon the doctrine of "woman's place," and the doctrine of "Black people's place," which leads him to ask, "Is it not possible that the two doctrines are derived from the same root disease? This does not necessarily mean that the struggles of White women are identical with Black people's liberation. It does mean that oppressions are interconnected."[9]

Cone's new insight affirms the central theme of my presentation. As feminist theologian Rosemary Ruether has urged, it is "essential that the women's movement reach out and include in its struggle the interstructuring of sexism with all other kinds of oppression, and recognize a pluralism of women's movements in the context of different groupings." White feminists need to recognize that racism is also a feminist problem and begin to deal with it as a necessary development of feminist consciousness. As Ellen Pence, a white feminist, has put it:

> Knowing that we grew up in a society permeated with the belief that White values, culture, and lifestyle are superior, we can assume that regardless of our rejection of the concept we still act out of that socialization. The same anger and frustration that we have as women in dealing with men whose sexism is subtle, not blatant, are the frustration and anger women of color must feel toward us. The same helpless feelings we have in trying to expose that subtle sexism must be the feeling of women of color in working with us.[10]

The women's movement has rich resources at its disposal to deal seriously with this issue. One of these is the experience women have gained in consciousness-raising, which can now be used to explore the ways in which racism has dehumanized women of all races and classes in the United States. This is already being done by small groups of Black and white women in face-to-face discussions, especially in the academic field.

Finally, if feminist spirituality includes the vision of wholeness of being, then those who follow that vision have the task of reeducation within the women's movement, which involves both a search for greater understanding and a capacity for self-criticism of the racism and classism which alienate us from one another. Feminist theology points the way toward this imperative. Marianne H. Micks reminds us that "human selfhood before God is historical selfhood" and speaks of the need to "stretch ourselves, go beyond ourselves, as we enter the spaces of our common past which many of us have never visited. If we are to understand each other today," she says, "we must know more about Native American experience, Black experience, and the experience of many additional ethnic groups."[11]

I submit that our openness to self-criticism is an antidote to the guilt which often paralyzes our actions and makes us resistant to change. I also believe that the sharing of personal histories and feelings in face-to-face contact brings an understanding which we cannot achieve merely through the absorption of historical and statistical data. Both are important steps in the healing process which builds mutual trust and the basis of genuine solidarity as we strive together in our daily lives to make real our vision of human wholeness.

Resources

Cone, James, and Gayraud Wilmore, editors. *Black Theology: A Documentary History, 1966–1979.* Maryknoll, NY: Orbis Books, 1979.

Hull, Gloria T., Patricia Bell Scott, and Barbara Smith, editors. *But Some of Us Are Brave: Black Women's Studies.* Boston: Feminist Press, 1982.

Joseph, Gloria I., and Jill Lewis. *Common Differences: Conflicts in Black and White Feminist Perspectives.* Garden City, NY: Anchor Press, 1981.

Micks, Marianne H. *Our Search for Identity: Humanity in the Image of God.* Minneapolis: Fortress Press, 1982.

Ruether, Rosemary Radford. *New Woman, New Earth: Sexist Ideologies and Human Liberation.* New York: Seabury Press, 1975.

Russell, Letty. *Growth in Partnership.* Philadelphia: Westminster Press, 1981.

Wallace, Michelle. *Black Macho and the Myth of the Superwoman.* New York: Dial Press, 1979.

Willie, Charles, Bernard Karamerand, and Bertram Brown, editors. *Racism and Mental Health.* Pittsburgh: University of Pittsburgh Press, 1972.

The New Feminism

Reform or Fundamental Social Change?

Introduction

Our gathering tonight in one respect is the celebration of a historic milestone in the history of feminism in the United States: . . . one week ago, on March 22, the final approval by Congress of the Equal Rights Amendment, which now awaits ratification by three-fourths of the state legislatures [and] represents forty-nine years of continuous effort by women in their struggle for equality in this country. Like the first women's rights conference in Seneca Falls, New York, in 1848 which launched the movement for the right to vote, but only one woman of those who attended that conference lived to see the Nineteenth Amendment become part of the Constitution, few of those courageous women who began the campaign for the Equal Rights [Amendment] in 1923 lived to see it through Congress. It is appropriate for us to pay tribute to those women—living and dead—who carried forth the tradition of equal rights, passed it along to others, until the first major hurdle has been overcome.

It is the Equal Rights Amendment which links us with the earlier feminism, for it was a few of those women leaders who had the wisdom to recognize that the battle had only been partly won. In 1920, after women achieved the vote, most of them thought great changes would come with this new political power, but as historian William O'Neill has said, "Enfranchisement did not mark the beginning of women's real emancipation, but its end." There followed a period of forty years in which the women's movement was dormant and some of the gains generated by that earlier momentum were lost. We hear again today some of the identical complaints voiced in the Declaration of Sentiments adopted by the Seneca Falls Conference in 1848, namely, that women living in a society dominated by males and defined only by their relationship to males are "aggrieved" and "oppressed," that they lack confidence in their own powers, have [lost] self-respect, and have been conditioned to dependency.

Now, however, we face the prospect of a national commitment of constitutional proportions to the equality of women. The amendment declares, "Equality of rights under the law shall not be denied or abridged by the United States or by any State on account of sex." The reemergence of a vigorous feminist movement in the 1960s, the speed with which it has moved into the public consciousness, is reflected in the final vote of the Senate last week—84 to 8—and by a vote of 354 to 24 in the House of Representatives last October.

Meanwhile, the debate continues as to the meaning of this new phenomenon. There are those who, like Professor Joseph Edelson writing in the *New York Times Magazine* of March 19, 1972, suggest that women's liberation may be merely a passing fad instead of "the beginnings of something which will change our lives profoundly," although he admits that he does not know what the future holds for the movement. There are others who have taken a deeper look and are less pessimistic. Authors [Judith] Hole and [Ellen] Levine of that excellent study *Rebirth of Feminism* (1971) look at it from the inside and conclude, "The feminist movement has emerged during a period of general social dislocation, rapid and virtually unchecked technological innovation and widespread attacks on the traditional power structure. Precisely because feminism, however, challenges the most basic assumptions about the nature of men and women that underlie all value systems and institutions, it may well inspire social change more radical and fundamental than any other political movement." Both views, however, recognize that there is a potential in the "New Feminism" which transcends social reform and raises fundamental questions. As one who has been both a participant and an observer for more than a decade, I propose to examine some of the social forces which created the "New Feminism," some of its present manifestations, and its implications for the future.

Relationship of Feminism to Other Social Movements

First, we take note that the women's movement in the United States is part of a worldwide stirring among women in which one-half of the human race is seeking to throw off the oldest form of inequality in human relationships. It is also one of many movements which, taken together, constitute an international revolution in human rights which began to accelerate after World War II and the ideals of which were expressed in the United Nations Universal Declaration of Human Rights in 1948. The declaration, prepared by the UN Commission on Human Rights chaired by our own Eleanor Roosevelt, reaffirmed the dignity and worth of the human person and the equal rights of men and women. Second, the movement is part of the continuing struggle in our own country to extend recognition and implementation of human dignity to every sector of the population. Social movements to achieve fundamental rights for various groups have often moved along parallel lines, cross-fertilized one another, and at times formed coalitions to reach common goals. We are all aware of the interaction between the abolitionist and feminist movements of the early nineteenth century. The labor struggles of the 1930s doubtless helped to stimulate the civil rights movement of the 1940s and 1950s. The racial crises of the 1960s not only brought to the forefront the injustices of racism but also set in motion active concern for inequities experienced by other groups in the population.

As a civil rights activist in my youth, who was both a Negro and a woman, it did not take me very long to see the similarities between racism and sexism. As time passed, however, and the issues of civil rights became more urgent, increasing numbers of white women began to see these similarities. It became apparent that while women in the United States are a numerical majority, as a group their ascribed position in society has been one of subordination to men as a group, and this ascribed status has many parallels to that of a racial minority.

Many women, of course, reject this parallel and do not feel themselves discriminated against. Obviously, they are not segregated in ghettoes as women and, as women, they do not suffer the cumulative deprivations of racial discrimination. They live in close proximity to men and are represented evenly with men in every social class, and have a derivative status based upon that of the men with whom they are closely associated as wives, mothers, or daughters. They identify their interests with their dual status [which] tends to obscure the fact that apart from their men they are members of a distinct class in the society which is discriminated against as a class.

The parallels, however, are compelling. Both women and Negroes in the United States have had a long history of disabilities imposed upon them by law and custom. Both groups were traditionally denied the elementary rights of citizenship—the right to vote, to serve on juries, and to hold public office. The Common Law made married women so completely dependent upon and subordinate to their husbands that defenders of the institution of slavery often justified it by asserting that in theory and often in fact women were also slaves. In 1873, the Supreme Court held in the case of *Bradwell v. Illinois* that a state was not prohibited by the Fourteenth Amendment from denying [Bradwell] admission to practice law on the theory that, as a married woman, her inability to enter into independent contracts might hinder her relations with her clients.

Legal commentators (and recently the California Supreme Court) have recognized the common elements of discrimination based upon race and sex. Sex, like race, is an unalterable biological characteristic which defines one's status from birth and from which status one cannot escape at will. The visibility of the physical characteristic helps to perpetuate group stereotypes and prejudices against the entire class irrespective of the wide variations among the individuals within the class, thus making the discrimination more difficult to eradicate.

Moreover, underlying the legal distinctions created on the basis of race and sex has been the common assumption of the inferiority of the group set apart. Sometimes identical arguments have been used to justify the discrimination in both cases. It was widely asserted in the nineteenth century that Negroes on the average had a smaller cranial capacity than white people and that women had a smaller brain than men. In each case it was argued that members of the group were not competent to exercise wisely the franchise or to participate in public affairs.

Finally, we note that the forms of discrimination have often been similar. While sex distinctions have been more subtle than those of race and often justified on the basis of "protection" of the "weaker sex," nevertheless they have usually resulted in an inferior status for women. Recently, the Supreme Court upheld a three-judge federal court ruling in Alabama in the case of *Forbush v. Wallace* that a married woman must use her married name in obtaining a driver's license, although Wendy Forbush and her husband, Ronald P. Carver, had agreed upon their marriage that she would continue to use her maiden name in her business and personal dealings. In 1972, the Supreme Court perpetuates the old Common Law notion that a married woman's legal personality merges with that of her husband and that the husband is the head!

Contemporary pressures for women's studies in schools and colleges confirm the fact that the contributions of women to the history and development of the United States, like those of racial minorities, have been ignored. As Barbara Harrison wrote in the *New Republic,* "We were stuck with a male version of history that made it appear as if women agitated [for] her suffrage and for prohibition; and women worked in defense plants during World War II. That version of history would not do."[1]

Like racial stereotypes of a generation ago, sex-role stereotypes depicting women in passive roles still dominate children's textbooks, and the mass media are the target of continuing feminist protest against the portrayal of women as "sex objects" defined by their attractiveness to men rather than as individuals in a variety of roles. And of course we know that women as well as racial minorities have been victimized by inequities in higher education, unequal job opportunities, unequal pay, concentration in lower-paying less prestigious jobs, exclusion from or gross underrepresentation in the major processes of decision-making in government, industry, religion, academia, and other social institutions.

We are now learning that systematic discrimination against a group has similar effects, whether the basis of the discrimination is race, sex, or alienage. The victims are deprived of an acceptable self-concept, they are inhibited in the full development of their personal capabilities, they react in frustration and anger, and they represent a massive waste of human resources. The social cost of sex discrimination is even greater than that of discrimination against minorities because it affects half of the population in every sector of society. Yet because women have been isolated from one another, despite their numerical potential, until very recently they have not been able to develop the solidarity and the political strength which would facilitate a national consensus that inequality based upon sex is immoral, indefensible, and unjust and must be outlawed in all of its manifestations.

Social and Economic Forces

My third observation is that while the New Feminism is not popularly called women's liberation, and the dramatic episodes which brought it to the public's attention are of very recent origin, historical forces were at work which signaled the revival of a women's movement in the early 1960s. Urbanization, technological advances, a steady increase in numbers of college-trained and professional women, increasing longevity, the Pill, the trend toward earlier marriages and smaller families, and the dramatic change in the economic role of women set the stage for the present movement. Labor-saving devices, packaged foods, the mass production and distribution of goods and services reduced the onerous burdens of housekeeping and took over many of the economic functions which women had formerly performed in their homes. An increasingly smaller segment of a woman's life was devoted to childbearing and childrearing. When a woman faced the prospect of thirty-five years of life after her children had grown up and left home she could no longer accept unquestioningly the notion of her total fulfillment through motherhood. Moreover, technological changes created millions of new jobs and stimulated a massive movement of women into [the work] force.

The shift of mothers and housewives from household activities awakened millions of women to the possibilities of development. Since we live in [a] cash economy, a paycheck helps to give one a sense of worth and it fosters independence. At the time of the adoption of the Nineteenth Amendment in 1920, only 1 of every 5 workers was female. By 1970, the 31.2 million working women constituted 38 percent of all workers. Census figures in 1970 revealed that 45 percent of all adult women were working or looking for work compared with 37 percent in 1960, 34 percent in 1950, and only 12 percent in 1920.

Since 1940, women have contributed the greatest share of growth in the job market. During the 1960s they filled nearly two-thirds of the new jobs which developed. The old myth that "a woman's place is in the home" was shattered by the reality that married women, particularly older married women, have become a permanent and growing part of the job market. In the year ending March 1969, for example, married women represented more than 45 percent of the 1.8 million increase in the labor force while married men accounted for only 22 percent of the increase. Most of these women were working to support themselves and others. Of the 37 million women who worked at some time during 1968, 17 percent were widowed, divorced, or separated from their husbands, and another 23 percent were single. Nearly one-third had husbands whose earnings were barely equal to or fell below the estimated average low income for an urban family. And we must not forget that women are the responsible economic heads of 11 percent of all families in the United States.

As Dr. Alice Rossi has pointed out, when women began to find themselves a permanent part of the workforce, "their daily experiences forced awareness of economic inequities on the grounds of their sex" and "gradually provided the momentum" for the events of the 1960s. Their focus upon job discrimination was the impetus for the establishment of the new women's civil rights organizations.[2]

The catalytic event which triggered these social forces into action, I submit, was the work of President Kennedy's Commission on the Status of Women and its seven consultative committees in 1962 and 1963. As Dr. Margaret Mead and Frances Bayley Kaplan, who edited the commission's publications, wrote, "The time was ripe for a new stocktaking. It was highly appropriate that President Kennedy should ask Mrs. Eleanor Roosevelt with her world orientation to chair the commission that would bring the status of women up to date. It is appropriate, too, that this should be Mrs. Roosevelt's last service to the women of America, to whom she so long had been an inspiration." The impact of Mrs. Roosevelt's personality and leadership upon those of us who worked with her cannot be overestimated. Those of you who have read *Eleanor and Franklin* [by Joseph P. Lash, published in 1984] can appreciate Dr. John Kenneth Galbraith's comment that Joseph Lash "makes clear how much of the women's movement of our time is a rediscovery of Eleanor Roosevelt." Over a period of twenty-two months the commission brought together the heaviest concentration of experience and talent—male and female—which up to that time had ever met under governmental auspices to think through some of the issues of vital concern to women. No other instrumentality at the time could mobilize such a diversity of experience from all parts of the country. I look back upon it as the first high-level "consciousness-raising" sessions in the nation, albeit sponsored by the federal government. The commission's various reports generated new currents of thinking, and the nucleus of men and women who worked with the commission fanned out over the country, providing a network of informal communication and making possible a climate of opinion in which issues of women's rights could be raised as matters of legitimate public concern. State commissions on the status of women, which followed upon the commission's report, helped to broaden the discussion at the local level.

It should be noted here that the commission's findings and recommendations and Betty Friedan's *The Feminine Mystique* were both published in 1963 and found a widely responsive audience. It is also important to note that a number of the key women in the campaign to get Congress to adopt the Equal Rights Amendment had their first experience of working together in the President's Commission on the Status of Women.

However, women quickly recognized that government sponsorship was not enough; they would have to build a strong independent movement of their own to achieve their goals. Thus, in 1966, the National Organization for Women (NOW) came into being. Since then women's organizations dealing with various approaches to their problems have proliferated. They range from such structured groups as WEAL (Women's Equity Action League), FEW (Federally Employed

Women), Human Rights for Women, the Professional Women's Caucus, and its counterpart caucuses in learned societies, academic groups, church organizations, civil rights and civil liberties organizations, Black and Third World groups, to various women's liberation bodies, often unstructured, and to spontaneous small groupings of women springing up throughout the country in "consciousness-raising" sessions.

In 1971, two significant developments occurred. One was the organization of the National Coalition for Research on Women's Education and Development to coordinate and disseminate research findings with respect to the educational, occupational, and related developmental needs of young and adult women and to generate new research particularly in the biological and behavioral sciences in these areas. The other is the formation of the National Women's Political Caucus, which at last report had stimulated local women's political caucuses in forty-six states to mobilize women as an independent political force.

Gains of a Decade

The gains for women resulting from this activity over the past decade have been astonishing to some of us who met to consider the status of women in 1962. Two major pieces of federal legislation—the Equal Pay Act of 1963 and the sex provisions of Title VII of the Civil Rights Act of 1964—set a national policy of equal employment opportunity without regard to sex. The new 1972 Equal Employment Opportunity Law extends coverage to employers of fifteen or more employees and to state and local governments. It also empowers the EEOC to go into the federal courts to seek enforcement of the provisions of the act. In 1967, President Johnson amended Executive Order 11246 by Executive Order 11375 to prohibit employment discrimination based upon sex in the federal civil service and by federal contractors and subcontractors. Academic women, noting that colleges and universities receive federal grants in the form of contracts, have utilized these executive orders and brought complaints against hundreds of institutions of higher learning seeking redress for long-standing inequities in matters of hiring, promotion and tenure, and salary scales. The threat of withholding federal funds from universities, notably Columbia and Harvard, has stimulated many institutions to undertake a review of their policies with respect to minorities and women and to begin to bring themselves into compliance with HEW's [Health, Education, and Welfare] regulations through the development of affirmative action plans.

At the state level gains have been made, particularly in the field of employment opportunity. Forty states and the District of Columbia now include "sex" as a prohibited basis of discrimination in their fair employment practices legislation. Now thirty-four states and the District of Columbia prohibit sex-based discrimination by private employers.

Women have also engaged in intensive litigation in the courts to challenge inequality: exclusion from a state university, restrictive state labor laws which conflict with federal policy of equal employment opportunity, longer prison sentences for women than for men for the same offense, exclusion from jury service, denial of admission to taverns and bars, the validity of criminal abortion laws, and so on. Finally, in November 1971, for the first time in our history, in the case of *Reed v. Reed,* the Supreme Court held that the Fourteenth Amendment's Equal Protection Clause applied to discrimination based upon sex when it invalidated an Idaho statute which gave preference to males over females in the administration of estates. In reciting these gains, I do not overlook such discouraging setbacks as President Nixon's veto of child care legislation, or the action by the House of Representatives exempting undergraduate institutions from a provision in the Higher Education Bill (H.R. 7248; S. 2552) banning sex discrimination in federally assisted education programs. I do, however, suggest an irreversible trend.

Implications of the New Feminism

The question remains as to the implications of the New Feminism. Will it suffer a decline, as did the movement in 1920, when legal equality becomes a reality? First, as I have already suggested, this movement is the culmination of many historical forces and cannot be dismissed as merely a passing fad. The range and pervasiveness of women's activities today tend to negate this assumption. The New Feminism has not only developed innovative and experimental approaches to women's problems by small groups operating outside of the established structures and therefore more open to new ideas, but also has tremendous impacts upon traditional women's organizations such as the YWCA, Church Women United, [and] business and professional women's groups, to name a few, which have been engaged in tooling up their programs to meet the new aspirations of women. The Equal Rights Amendment is viewed as only one of many avenues of attack upon sex inequality, and the campaign for its ratification is being carried on simultaneously with other activities at many levels.

Second, the view that many women are "turned off" by some of the rhetoric and the more bizarre manifestations of that branch of the movement called women's liberation, which the mass media have fully exploited, tends to overlook the less visible process of women's growing awareness of themselves as a force in society. Increasing numbers of women (and men) are affected by the movement, whether or not they are involved. It is significant that Professor Edelson reported on March 19 that his sampling of cosmopolitan, suburban, and well-educated women found that only 3 percent had any interest in an identification with the movement, [while] the Louis Harris poll publicized on March 24 shows that today women "back efforts to strengthen and change women's status in society" 48 to 36 percent with 16 percent uncertain, while a year ago they narrowly opposed such efforts 42 to 40 percent. Harris also noted that the biggest gains were among married women, college graduates, suburbanites, and those between the ages of eighteen and twenty-nine, which include the very groups that Professor Edelson found were alienated by the terms in which the issues were raised.

Third, it is obviously misleading to assume that some of the rhetoric which the movement has produced accurately defines its total character. Precisely because women are one-half of the population they reflect the whole spectrum of attitudes in the society at large. Moreover, like other groups which do not have access to the media to state their claims, some women have resorted to overstatement and shock techniques to gain the public's attention. And it has often been the publicity given to such dramatic episodes which made possible the gains of more moderate women's representatives at the bargaining table and in their legislative lobbying.

The cumulative impact of the "consciousness-raising" sessions of women talking together about their common problems, breaking out of their isolation, and beginning to develop a sense of mutual respect, solidarity, and sisterhood should not be underestimated. As Jo Freeman has put it, "The rap group [for women—not meaning the linguistic dimension of hip hop culture] is what the factory [was] for workers, the church [was] for the Southern civil rights movement and the campus [was] for the student."[3] This process has helped to give the New Feminism a dynamic potential unlike that of any other movement. It is infectious, crossing class, race, and sex lines and resulting in hundreds of thousands of small individual acts which have contributed to rapidly changing attitudes. Through it many women have had a liberating experience and found new meaning to their lives. It has gradually matured to effective political action on the one hand and a more serious study of women's role in society on the other hand. Since 1969, nearly seven hundred courses in women's studies have been added to the curricula of several hundred colleges and universities, and many more have been developed which have not been reported. Serious women scholars are turning their attention to the position of women in literature, history, economic and political life, the church, and in the various disciplines, and are producing long-needed materials written from women's perspectives.

This fundamental reexamination of the role of women in every aspect of society and of the relationships of women and men in every societal institution has revolutionary implications of massive proportions. For women are now seeking to define themselves and to determine for themselves what roles they shall play. They are saying that whatever may have been the historical reasons for the so-called division of labor between the sexes, today a society dominated by the values of one sex is in dangerous imbalance. It may well be that our present inability to cope with racism, war, and poverty stems in large part from our failure to come to grips with the broader and more fundamental aspect of human relations—the relationship between the sexes as equal participants in the decisions which ultimately determine the fate of humanity. The avowed goal of the New Feminism is to destroy the rigid sex stereotypes in which both men and women have been forced, to liberate all the human values latent in each individual, and to bring these values to bear upon the pressing social problems we face. It is this aspect of the women's movement and the promise it holds for transforming our society which makes it the most exciting and perhaps the most significant development of our time.

Black Women, Racism, and the Legal Process
in Historical Perspective

Introduction

Black women in the United States have had a unique experience in that they have been victims of both racial and sexual bias deeply embedded in the legal process and stubbornly resistant to change. The historical conjunction of these two evils aggravated their degraded status. During two centuries of chattel slavery, they suffered brutal sexual oppression characterized by the most violent invasions of personal dignity and privacy a woman can experience.

In the law of slavery, a slave woman was likened to a "brood mare" and her children, referred to as "increase," were held to belong to the owner "like that of other female animals." Forcible rape of a female slave by a man other than the owner was not a criminal act but a trespass upon and injury to the property of another for which the master could recover civil damages. The slave woman had no recourse if the forcible rape was committed by her master. Since the slave had no rights except the right to exist, invasions of her person which did not destroy her existence were beyond the purview of the criminal law. For the slave woman, therefore, the slavery experience was a continual negation of her personal integrity; her worth was measured primarily as a breeder and an object of white male sexual exploitation.

The effects of this experience are still felt today. Despite achievements and the fortitude which Black women have exhibited in the face of multiple oppressions, they remain the lowest and most vulnerable social and economic group in the United States. A century after the abolition of slavery, Black women in the South were still battling in the courts to remove the public indignities growing out of the degraded past. It was necessary to appeal to the nation's highest tribunal to enforce common courtesy in the judicial process. Thus, in 1964 the Supreme Court in *Hamilton v. Alabama* (376 U.S. 650) reversed the conviction of Miss Mary Hamilton for contempt of an Alabama court. Miss Hamilton was held in contempt by a white Alabama judge when she refused to answer the questions of a white prosecuting attorney who insisted upon addressing her as "Mary" although he addressed white witnesses as "Mr." or "Miss."

It is against this background that I propose to discuss Black women intimately involved in the legal process as advocates or jurists, seeking to combat racism and achieve equal justice. The great civil rights lawyer Charles H. Houston wrote in 1935, "The social justification for the Negro lawyer as such in the United States today is the service he can render the race as interpreter and proponent of its rights and aspirations." In attempting to fulfill this role, Black women lawyers, like their male counterparts, have faced the difficulty of limited opportunities to become lawyers and the dual pressures of having to earn a living and simultaneously becoming involved in civil rights matters which make extensive demands upon their time and limited resources. In addition, however, Black women lawyers have had to struggle against formidable sex-based discrimination in a male-dominated profession and in a legal system traditionally hostile to their acquisition of power and prestige. Let us look at this struggle in historical perspective.

Black Women and the Legal Process in Historical Perspective

Two events a little more than a century apart symbolize the long and difficult road Black women lawyers have traveled. In 1872, Charlotte E. Ray became the first Negro woman to graduate from a university law school in the United States. Taking her degree from Howard University School of Law, she went on to be admitted to practice in the District of Columbia. Her achievement followed by twenty-eight years that of the first three Black males to become attorneys in 1844. One hundred five years later, in 1977, Patricia Roberts Harris, a lawyer, became the first Black woman to be appointed to the president's cabinet, a powerful position involving the dispersal of billions of dollars in federal expenditures. Between those two events, however, is the history of a heroic struggle for survival, marked by a few significant breakthroughs which provided role models for future generations of Black women aspiring to enter the legal profession.

During the late nineteenth century and first three decades of the twentieth century, the outlook for Black lawyers generally was not very promising. The disfranchisement of Negro males in the South following Reconstruction, the rampant racism in southern courts, and the total lack of legal education for Blacks in that area until 1935, according to Dr. Horace Mann Bond, "almost completely extinguished the prospects for a Negro lawyer in the South." Able law school graduates in that early period, unable to establish themselves at the bar, were often reduced to earning a pittance by surreptitiously drafting wills, deeds, and contracts for white lawyers. As late as the early 1960s a member of a successful Chicago firm voiced the opinion that there is a "deep-seated feeling on the part of both Negroes and whites that a white lawyer can obtain better consideration for them from courts, administrative agencies, and government than a Negro lawyer can."

If the Black male lawyer found it difficult to gain a foothold in his profession and received only "the crumbs of litigation" during that period, Black females shared with white females the possibility of outright exclusion from the legal profession. In 1873, one year after Charlotte Ray graduated from law school, the Supreme Court with only one dissenting vote upheld the power of the state of Illinois to deny a woman a license to practice law solely because she was female (*Bradwell v. Illinois,* 83 U.S. 130). In the now-notorious concurring opinion of Mr. Justice Bradley joined by two other justices, the widely held male chauvinistic attitude toward women was elevated into law. Mr. Justice Bradley declared,

> The civil law, as well as nature herself, has always recognized the wide difference in the respective spheres and destinies of man and woman. Man is, or should be, woman's protector and defender. The natural and proper timidity and delicacy which belongs to the female sex evidently unfits it for many of the occupations of civil life. . . . The harmony, not to say identity, of interests and views which belong, or should belong, to the family institution is repugnant to the idea of a woman adopting a distinct and independent career from that of her husband. . . . The paramount destiny and mission of woman are to fulfill the noble and benign offices of wife and mother. This is the law of the Creator. And the rules of civil society must be adapted to the general constitution of things, and cannot be based upon exceptional cases.

As late as 1894, the Supreme Court refused to order the commonwealth of Virginia to admit to practice a woman who had already been admitted to the bars of the Supreme Court and the District of Columbia. In [*In*] *re Lockwood,* 154 U.S. 116, Virginia's statute provided that any "person" admitted to practice in another state or in the District of Columbia could practice law in Virginia, but Virginia's highest court construed the word "person" in the statute to mean "male" and the Supreme Court refused to disturb that ruling. Thus, until well into the twentieth century, women's entry into the legal profession was governed by the varying policies of the several states and admissions practices of individual law schools. Prestigious Harvard Law School, for example, did not admit women students until 1950.

Meanwhile, the few Black women who dared to challenge this traditional attitude felt keenly the rejection because of their sex in circles generally regarded to be liberal on racial issues. Sadie T. M. Alexander, the first Negro woman in the United States to earn a PhD degree and who in 1927 became the first Negro woman to be admitted to the bar of the state of Pennsylvania, once told me of a humiliating experience she had when she accompanied her husband, Raymond Pace Alexander, on his class reunion visit to Harvard Law School. A successful practicing lawyer in Philadelphia, she went with him to an alumni seminar. When the professor saw her, he interrupted his lecture and invited her to leave the room.

Despite barriers of race and sex, Black women slowly persevered in the law. In the first half of the twentieth century their numbers remained small and they were isolated from one another, having to make their way through sheer grit and steely determination. The 1950 census reported only 83 Negro women employed as lawyers and judges in the United States. By 1960, according to census data, 176 of the 2,180 Negro lawyers and judges were women. Their proportion of all female lawyers (2.36%) was higher than the proportion of Black male lawyers to their white male counterparts (0.95%). Some of these woman pioneers achieved visible success. In 1939, Jane Bolin, a graduate of Yale Law School, became the first Black woman judge in the United States when the then-Mayor Fiorello LaGuardia appointed her to the Court of Domestic Relations of the City of New York. (At the time I was a young unemployed teacher working [for the] WPA but I am sure her appointment helped to encourage me to enter law school two years later.) According to Gilbert Ware, between 1939 and 1974, twenty-eight Black women became judges. We might also note that today there are at least five Black women federal court judges (exclusive of the District of Columbia), four of whom were among the twenty-two Blacks appointed recently to the federal bench by President Carter.

Sadie T. M. Alexander made a significant contribution to the forward thrust of civil rights as one of the two Negroes appointed to President Truman's Committee on Civil Rights in 1946. (The second Negro was the late Dr. Channing Tobias.) The committee's report, "To Secure These Rights," issued in 1947, was the first official federal document to recommend unequivocally the elimination of segregation based on race, color, creed, or national origin in American life. The existence of this report was a powerful stimulus to the movement to outlaw racial discrimination. Also in 1947, Jean Capers, a lawyer of Cleveland, Ohio, became the first Negro woman to be elected to a municipal city council. The late Ruth Whitehead Whaley, the first Negro woman to be admitted to the New York bar (c. 1925), went on to become secretary to the New York City Board of Estimate. Edith Sampson, later a judge in the Municipal Court of Chicago, was the first Negro woman to be named a delegate to the United Nations by President Truman in 1950. In 1953, Carmel Carrington Marr was appointed legal advisor to the U.S. Mission to the United Nations.

These success stories of an earlier period forecast the emergence of increasing numbers of Black women attorneys as a potent force in the legal process today, commanding strategic positions in many areas of public life. To fully appreciate their achievements, however, we need to know something about the concrete conditions they faced during the period when they lacked most of the supportive structures which facilitate success at the bar as well as the legal protection now afforded by Title VII and affirmative action programs.

A Marginal Existence

Prior to the 1950s, Black women received little encouragement to enter the legal profession. They were conspicuously absent from the organized legal efforts of [the] NAACP to achieve justice through the courts. Despite the facts that women were deeply involved in the civil rights movement as local leaders and that Howard University School of Law produced a generation of lawyers prominent in the struggle led by [the] NAACP, one has only to look at the pictures of successive graduating classes on the walls of Howard Law School to document the absence or rarity of women students until recent years. Significantly, only two Black women attorneys are mentioned as having a visible role in the civil rights struggle in Richard Kluger's book *Simple Justice,* a detailed history of civil rights litigation culminating in *Brown v. Board of Education.* These two are Marjorie McKenzie Lawson and Constance Baker Motley.

In this respect, Howard Law School was typical of law schools generally. As a student there in the early 1940s, I recall that while the atmosphere was not hostile to women, male condescension was never far from the surface. On my first day in class as a new student, one of my professors acknowledged the presence of the two women in class—the only women registered in the entire school—with the half-joking remark, "I don't know why women bother to come to law school, but since you're here I guess we'll have to put up with you some-how." His comment brought loud laughter from the male members of the class and suggested a predisposition not to take women seriously. It certainly did not increase our self-confidence. In fact, before the end of the school year, my woman classmate had dropped out, leaving me to spend the remainder of my law school career as the lone and sometimes embattled female among male professors and students.[a]

However excellent her academic record, following graduation from law school a Black woman had fewer options than her male classmates. Clerkships to judges, jobs as "house counsel" to corporations, or opportunities to work in large firms which provided broad legal experience were virtually closed to her even when these jobs were beginning to open up to Blacks. She discovered that sex stereotypes limited her opportunities when race was not a factor. Shortly after being admitted to the New York bar, I was interviewed for a job with a small liberal white firm. My credentials were satisfactory, and two of the four partners were anxious to take me on as an associate. I did not get the job be-cause the other two partners had decided to hire no more women. They gave the reason that the woman associate hired the previous year "did not work out." As I recall, Roger Wilkins eventually got the job.

Many Black women attorneys, unable to make entry into the profession, ultimately had to settle for employment in other fields where they were often overqualified for the work they were doing and felt a sense of personal failure. I remember particularly the sad case of a brilliant young attorney who had put herself through law school by working at odd jobs and by virtually starving her-self. I learned there were times during her struggle when she had no food to eat and had to drink salt and water to relieve the gas pains. In spite of all her effort and her ability, in order to survive she had to take a nonlegal job in the adver-tising department of the *New York Times*.

Typically, a Black woman attorney in those days, like her male counterpart, entered private practice by becoming an employee or associate of one or more Black attorneys with a rapidly growing practice. Because she had little bargaining power the risk of exploitation was high. She was more likely to get low pay, do the "dirty work," [and] have few professional privileges and less opportunity for advancement than a male attorney starting out in the profession. Before I passed the bar in New York in 1947, I worked as a law clerk for a Black male attorney with a lucrative practice but received only twenty-five dollars a week, hardly a subsistence wage even in those days. Even after admission to the bar, I earned only forty dollars a week and was not even permitted to have my name printed on the door as an associate attorney.

The alternative for a woman who resisted exploitation was to strike out on her own with all the accompanying hazards of little financial capital, a small clientele, and few of the resources necessary to compete successfully. The result was a marginal existence which subjected her to intolerable economic pressures. If she were fortunate, she might be able to afford a tiny cubbyhole in another lawyer's suite. More often than not she lacked facilities for research and investigation, had to do her own typing, and be her own law clerk. Some women had to run their law practice from their homes, or even from their pocketbooks if engaged in criminal practice, sometimes being compelled to interview their criminal clients on the courthouse steps. I know of one instance where a woman's net income from her law practice averaged less than $2,000 a year during the 1940s—less than the allowance for a person receiving public welfare. She had to supplement her earnings by typing manuscripts and doing research for other lawyers.

Such precarious conditions not only affected the quality of a woman's practice but also made her vulnerable to ethical improprieties. As a young lawyer I had the painful experience of representing a woman colleague in a hearing before the grievance committee of the Bar Association. She had borrowed money from a woman client and had failed to repay it. After numerous requests proved futile, the client filed a complaint with the Bar Association. The facts were not in dispute; my problem was to get the affluent white male attorneys who composed the grievance committee to appreciate what it meant to be a marginal Negro attorney practicing in a poor community and dependent upon a clientele most of whom could not even afford the fees necessary to cover the barest expenses of their cases. Fortunately, my colleague received nothing worse than a strong censure from the Bar Association, and from the comments of committee members to me later I gathered it was the first time they had been made aware of the appalling condition of Black lawyers struggling against the cumulative effects of poverty and discrimination.

In addition to sometimes overwhelming economic problems, the Black woman attorney had to maintain her personal dignity in a system where the expression of combined race-sex stereotyped attitudes assaulted her self-esteem and demeaned her professional status. A biased judge might embarrass her publicly before clients, witnesses, court personnel, and other attorneys, and she risked being held in contempt of court if she protested on the spot. In her exposed situation she was easily the target of thinly veiled male derision.

I recall one particularly galling incident in my early days of practice when the attorney for whom I was working asked me to appear in magistrate's court to represent two young women from Spanish Harlem who had been arrested and charged with prostitution. The entire legal process in such cases was insulting to women. The male customers were not charged but were coerced into cooperating with the government as witnesses for the prosecution. The first white male witness in this case testified as to the details of the sexual transaction and his payment of money, and he was then asked to identify the woman with whom he had engaged in sexual relations. Unhesitatingly, he pointed directly at me seated at the defense table beside my two clients! As far as he was concerned one colored female looked like another. The court personnel saw it as a huge joke and tittered audibly, the flustered prosecutor hastened to try and rehabilitate the witness's testimony, the judge denied my motion to dismiss the charge on the ground of failure to identify the defendant, and the hapless woman went to jail. I can laugh about it thirty years later, but at the time it was a crushing blow to my self-image.

Racism and Sexism

The conditions I have described illustrate the climate in which earlier generations of Black women fought to gain a foothold in the legal profession. They survived and established themselves by developing extraordinary competence, tenacity, and toughness. A significant outcome of exposure to a legal process administered by an overwhelmingly white male hierarchy and to numerous sex-based inequalities in substantive law has been recognition of the interrelation of racial and sexual bias and the urgent need of Black women to be protected from both evils.

This experience is now being widely shared by other Black women as a result of changes brought about through the movement for Black liberation. Black women traditionally have viewed racism as the chief handicap, but as Diane K.

Lewis noted in 1977, "As blacks began to participate in the wider society they moved into a public arena sharply characterized by sex inequality."[1] She points to a significant conclusion made by sociologist Jessie Bernard in a study of the earnings and occupations of Black and white men and women for the period 1939–1974, namely, that "racism tends to be more serious for black men than for black women . . . (and) sexism tends to be more serious for black women than racism."[2]

To test this conclusion, we need only to ask ourselves how much more devastating would be the impact of inflation and recession upon Blacks today if governmental policies of equality of opportunity and affirmative action in education and employment operative over the past fifteen years had contained no provision prohibiting sex-based discrimination. Protection against discrimination because of sex as well as race is crucial to the survival of Black families, given the fact that Black working wives contribute a larger proportion of family income than white working wives and the additional fact that more than one-third of all Black families in the United States are headed by women.

Black women, unlike Black males or white females, do not have the option of concentrating primarily upon racial or sexual issues or of giving priority to one or the other. As members of two subordinated groups—Blacks and women—they are strategically placed and can see more readily the negative impact of sexism upon the overall efforts of Blacks to combat the effects of racial bias. Sylvia Crudup Cole noted recently in the *Crisis* (August–September 1979) that sexism "contributes directly to limited opportunities for the race" and threatens racial unity necessary to advance the group as a whole. In sum, Black women are learning that since half of the Black population is female and that it is virtually impossible to separate the effects of racism and sexism in their experience, they face the historical task of working to eliminate sex-based inequality as crucial to recovery from the total racial experience.

Notes

[a] 1983 inaccurate: at least two women were enrolled during my senior year.

References

Bond, Horace Mann. "The Negro Scholar and Professional in America." In *The American Negro Reference Book,* edited by John P. Davis, 548–587. Hoboken, NJ: Prentice-Hall, 1966.

Cole, Sylvia Crudup. "Sexism and Its Impact on Minorities." *Crisis,* August–September 1979, 304–305.

Kluger, Richard. *Simple Justice: The History of* Brown v. Board of Education *and Black America's Struggle for Equality.* New York: Knopf, 1976.

Lewis, Diane K. "A Response to Inequality: Black Women, Racism, and Sexism." *Signs: Journal of Women in Culture and Society* 3, no. 2 (Winter 1977): 339–361.

Murray, Pauli. "The Negro Woman's Stake in the Equal Rights Amendment." *Harvard Civil Rights Civil Liberties Review* 6 (1971): 253–259.

Tollett, Kenneth S. "Black Lawyers, Their Education, and the Black Community." *Howard Law Journal* 17 (1972): 328–331.

Ware, Gilbert, ed. *From the Black Bar: Voices for Equal Justice.* New York: G. P. Putnam's Sons, 1976.

Coping with Racism and Sexism

Black Women's Perspectives

Introduction

When the women's movement resurfaced two decades ago, I was among those who joined with Betty Friedan to found the National Organization of Women. In NOW's statement of purpose we declared that "the time has come for a new movement toward true equality for all women in America." We also affirmed our belief "that human rights for all are indivisible" and expressed our intention "to give active support to the common cause of equal rights for all those who suffer discrimination and deprivation, and we call upon other organizations committed to such goals to support our efforts toward equality of women."[a]

As one who had to cope simultaneously with the twin evils of racial and sexual bias and who had been a civil rights activist in my student days, I saw the women's movement as essential to the liberation of women of color. My perspective was then, as it is now, the indivisibility of all human rights and the need to develop strong bonds of cooperation between Black and white women. In 1970, I wrote, "Because black women have an equal stake in women's liberation and black liberation, they are key figures at the juncture of these two movements. White women feminists are their natural allies in both causes. . . . By asserting a leadership role in the growing feminist movement, the black woman can help keep it allied to the objectives of black liberation while simultaneously advancing the interests of all women."[b]

Today, unfortunately, as I review the developments of the intervening years and examine the recent writings of a number of Black women scholars and educators, I must confess these brave hopes of the 1960s have not been realized.

Instead of the solidarity we envisioned, one finds severe tensions and misunder-standings existing between Black women and white women which stand as bar-riers to the full development of the women's movement as a genuinely liberating and humanizing force in our society.

These tensions arise from sharp differences in perspective, which tend not to be openly discussed until they explode in angry confrontations. Since they are forcefully articulated by Black women in academic fields, it seems ap-propriate to consider them in a conference of women educators, not only be-cause of your role in shaping future leadership but also because of your strate-gic position in the women's movement. Women educators have furnished much of the scholarship, which has helped to give shape and direction to feminism, enabled it to define its goals, and supplied it with the intellectual resources for effective attacks on sex-based inequalities. You have the professional skills to engage in self-criticism of the women's movement and to initiate corrective ac-tion where needed.

At the risk of traversing familiar territory, I propose to reexamine the com-plexities of being both Black and female in the United States, how this embat-tled position affects relationships between Black women and white women, and the need for a reorientation of feminism to come to grips with the underlying causes of conflict. Hopefully, this review will produce fresh insights and stimu-late imaginative approaches to a problem which continues to be of grave con-cern to us all.

Alienation of Black Women

Black women in the United States are unique in the sense that they carry the burdens of two deeply entrenched, interlocking systems of racial and sexual in-justice as well as being among those least protected against economic oppression. Their pressing needs and special problems are often overlooked, ignored, or inadequately understood within both the women's movement, which they per-ceive as predominantly white and middle-class, and the Black movement, which is male-oriented. They "fall between the cracks," so to speak, and this situation has created among Black feminists especially a deep sense of isolation and alienation, reflected in the poignant statement, "We realize that the only people who care enough about us to work consistently for our liberation is us."[c]

Alienation from white women is aggravated by the belief on the part of many Black women that racism is the "archenemy" in their struggle to maintain and strengthen their families, their culture, and heritage, and that white women are deeply implicated in the racial oppression that crushes the lives of Black people. This bitterness, for example, surfaced in a conference of the Episcopal Church's Task Force on Women in 1981, when Dr. Deborah Harmon Hines, assistant professor of anatomy at Meharry Medical College, Nashville, Tennessee, speaking with great feeling, charged, "My white step-sisters . . . are often as guilty as or guiltier than their men-folk" in perpetuating degrading myths and stereotypes of Black women. Dr. Hines went on to say,

> Black women's goals and agenda are very different from that of white women. Black women's goals have been defined by our roles, very few of which white women share. . . . Black women find it extremely difficult to ally themselves with those who have not been part of the solution but a part of the problem. Black women find it extremely difficult to ally themselves with those who say, "We have suffered the same," when we know it isn't so. Black women find the situation intolerable when we are told (by white women) what we should do in our struggle, and not asked what we want to do. . . . Until our (white) step-sisters stop superimposing their needs onto us, we have nothing to say to them.[d]

The ever-present racial factor is a major source of tensions in relationships between Black women and white women, creating responses that are ambivalent, often hostile, suffused with distrust, and seldom without reservations. The comment of Dr. Constance M. Carroll, a Black educator and active participant in the women's movement, now president of Indian Valley College, Novato, California, is enlightening. Dr. Carroll, writing on Black women in higher education, acknowledges that Black and white women share certain formulae followed by those who wish to succeed in a man's world, that is, you must be better qualified than the men, you must be more articulate, more aggressive, have more stamina and more patience, and above all remain feminine and not appear threatening. Then she adds, "However, Black women have an extra step in the syllogism which white women do not have, that is, *they must be better than white women.* It is this seldom discussed fact which has generated bitterness toward white women in general. In a power ladder, the white woman is seen to be two steps removed from power, but the Black woman is three steps removed. The Black woman cannot help being cautious in allying herself with a 'privileged competitor.'"[e]

Anthropologist Diane K. Lewis helps to clarify the inherent ambiguities and contradictions of the Black woman's position.[f] She notes that because the models of the women's liberation movement "usually focus exclusively upon the effects of sexism, they have been of limited applicability to minority women subjected to both racism and sexism." Furthermore, Black women, due to their membership in two subordinate groups that lack access to authority and resources in society, are in structural opposition with a dominant racial and a dominant sexual group. In each subordinate group they share potential common interests with group co-members, Black men on the one hand and white women on the other. Ironically, each of these is a member of a dominant group: Black men as men, white women as whites. Thus, the interests which bind Black women together with, and pull them into opposition with, co-members crosscut one another in a manner which often obscures one set of interests over another. Historically, their interests as Blacks have taken precedence over their interests as women.

This duality of interests is keenly felt by Black women professionals in academic institutions where their numbers are small and they are isolated, invisible, and often demoralized. As one Black woman administrator voiced the situation, "they have neither race nor sex in common with white males who dominate the decision-making stratum of academe. Black males in academe at least share with white males their predominance over women. . . . Black women have had very few models or champions to encourage and assist them in their development," and "have had to develop themselves on their own, with no help from whites or Black men. This has taken its toll on Black women in all areas of life and work."[g]

Black feminists Gloria T. Hull and Barbara Smith, writing of their academic experiences, speak of "the inherently contradictory and antagonistic nature of the conditions under which we work" in the white-male academy.[h] "Often our position as Black women is dishearteningly tenuous within university walls: We are literally the last hired and the first fired. Despite popular myths about the advantages of being 'double-tokens,' our salaries, promotions, tenure and general level of acceptance in the white-male 'community of scholars' are all quite grim. The current backlash against affirmative action is also disastrous for all Black women workers, including college teachers."[1]

In addition to professional isolation and economic insecurity, Black academic women are further demoralized by the general invisibility of Black women in the content of courses in Black studies and women's studies now being taught in colleges and universities and in some secondary schools.[i] They charge that women's studies have "focused almost exclusively upon the lives of white women," while Black studies, "much too often male-dominated, also ignored Black women. Because of white women's racism and Black men's sexism," these critics argue, "there was no room in either area for a serious consideration of the lives of Black women.ʲ And even when they have considered Black women, white women usually have not had the capacity to analyze racial politics and Black culture, and Black men have remained resistant to the implications of sexual politics."[2]

Hull and Smith, analyzing data on women's studies published in 1972, found that of a total of 4,658 women's studies courses taught by 2,964 teachers, approximately 45 (or less than 1 percent) of the courses focused upon Black women. The largest concentration of courses focusing upon Black women was found in Afro-American and Black Studies departments; only about three courses on Black women were being taught for Women's Studies departments. Since that time, corrective action was taken, and Florence Howe's report on women's studies in 1976 indicated that, largely through the initiative of women's studies, "separate courses on Black women, Chicanas, Third World women, etc. . . . taught by minority women, have appeared on most campuses with the cooperation and cross-listing of various ethnic studies programs." This general oversight led to the emergence in the late 1970s of a demand for Black women's studies as an autonomous discipline and to the publication by the Feminist Press in 1982 of a volume entitled *But Some of Us Are Brave: Black Women's Studies,* containing relevant essays, bibliographies, and syllabi on Black women.

The sharpest criticism is aimed at white feminist scholars who undertake major studies on women writers or women's imagination through the centuries, for example, but fail to recognize the rich cultural diversity among women and to include contributions of Black or Third World women. These omissions place white feminist authors in the same category as male authors whose writings assume the male experience to be the norm for human existence, an assumption which infuriates feminists. Alice Walker, winner of the 1983 Pulitzer Prize for Fiction, commented acidly on one of these feminist studies: "The index alone was sufficient proof that the work could not be really serious scholarship, only serious white female chauvinism."ᵏ

Differences in Black Women's and White Women's Perspectives

A major difference in perspective, as these criticisms reveal, is how Black women and white women perceive their problems and rank their priorities. The fact that Black women traditionally have given priority to their racial struggle and have tended to see white women as beneficiaries of white racism often polarizes the two groups despite other concerns they share as women. When Black women embrace feminism, they necessarily see their two struggles as inseparable and deplore the blindness of their white cohorts to their own responsibilities in this inescapable struggle. In the words of one Black women's group,

> One issue that is of major concern to us . . . is racism in the white women's movement. As Black feminists we are made constantly and painfully aware of how little effort white women have made to understand and combat their racism, which requires among other things that they have a more than su-perficial comprehension of race, color, and Black history and culture. Elim-inating racism in the white women's movement is by definition work for white women to do, but we will continue to speak to and demand account-ability on this issue.[1]

Another area of misunderstanding has been in the perception of male/female relationships in the context of liberation movements. The main thrust of femi-nism has been against dominant male power, but Black males and females are bound together in a struggle against a racial system which historically has bru-tally suppressed assertions of power by Black males. Black women feel com-pelled to support their men in this struggle, as white women have had no need to do. In the process they have emphasized racial solidarity in male-female rela-tionships and tended to subordinate their own need for autonomy. Many Black women have looked upon the women's movement as a "divisive" tactic which would alienate them from their male partners and weaken the Black struggle. Dorothy Height, president of the National Council of Negro Women, reflected this perspective in the early days of the new feminism when she declared: "Negro women have the same problems and hopes as other women, but they cannot take the same things for granted. . . . If the Negro woman has a major underlying concern, it is the status of the Negro man and his position in the community and his need for feeling himself an important person, free and able to make his contribution in the whole society in order that he may strengthen his home."[m] It is one of those ironies of history that Black males gained a newfound sense of power through the militant civil rights movement in the 1960s at the precise historical moment that male dominance came under heavy attack. Feminist writer Celestine Ware noted that the new Black militancy and pride, "in the minds of many, became confused with a return to a world defined and ruled by men. Some black men wish, by becoming militant, to assume the powers of

white men in an earlier, simpler century."[n] Nevertheless, despite the internal
frictions caused by this development, Black women's concern for the status of
Black men continues to be a powerful factor in their resistance to the women's
movement. And, as Gloria I. Joseph and Jill Lewis of Hampshire College have
written, "It is incumbent upon white feminists to recognize the very real differences that exist between white men and black men when their degree of power
is considered. The white-skin privilege cuts across any categories of class in a
racist society, as does male privilege in the white dominant culture."[o]

Black Women, Victims of Multilayered Oppression

The most fruitful way of looking at the position of Black women is the approach of an emerging Black feminism, which defines Black women as victims
of multilayered oppression and seeks a comprehensive analysis of what theologian Rosemary Radford Ruether has described as "the interstructuring of race,
sex and class." This was the point of departure of "A Black Feminist Statement"
issued in 1977 by the Boston-based Combahee River Collective, which declared
in part: "We believe that sexual politics under patriarchy is as pervasive in
Black women's lives as are the politics of race and class. We also find it difficult
to separate race from class from sex oppression because in our lives they are
experienced simultaneously. . . . If Black women were free it would mean that
everyone else would have to be free since our freedom necessitates the destruction of all the systems of oppression."[p] The convergence of these multiple systems of injustice in the lives of Black women places them at the bottom of the
economic and social ladder, the most disadvantaged subgroup in the United
States, compared to white males, Black males, and white females. They are disproportionately represented in the most menial, lowest-paying, non-unionized
jobs and among the unemployed, poor, and female-headed families. They are
especially vulnerable to racial-sexual violence, which has deep roots in slavery
and continues today in rape, forced sterilization, and physical abuse in family
relations. Black women and their families suffer from inadequate health care
and various health hazards associated with poverty and powerlessness. They have
twice as many heart attacks as white women and their death rate from hyper-
tension is seventeen times that of white women.

The demographic factor of an acute sex-ratio imbalance between Black
males and females (Census figures report eighty-one Black males to every one
hundred Black females over twenty-four years of age) severely limits the avail-

ability of marital partners among the Black female population and contributes to the high incidence of female-headed families condemned to poverty.

Black women battle continually against a host of demeaning, often contradictory, myths and stereotypes, which deny their worth as human beings and undermine their self-respect—for example, "Aunt Jemima," "mammy," "whore," "bitch," "welfare seeker," "Jezebel," "matriarch," "Sapphire," and so on. They are made to feel servile, unattractive, and sexually promiscuous on the one hand, and "deviant," "domineering," "emasculating" women on the other hand. Sociologist Elizabeth Higginbotham, commenting on the Black matriarchy myth which gained popularity in the 1960s and which attributed various social pathologies to the alleged existence of a Black matriarchal family structure, has said, "Black women have not been praised by dominant-culture sociologists for their strong role in aiding family stability; on the contrary, they have been strongly criticized."[3]

Black Women's Dilemma

We see, then, that Black women endure in aggravated form a range of social and economic disabilities not fully shared by Black men or white women. As Joseph and Lewis point out, in defining their priorities and seeking allies in their struggle, Black women face the dilemma of the competing urgencies of two parallel movements, each of which is a separate entity based on its own distinctive realities. "Yet an individual cannot be two separate entities."[q] The Black woman cannot participate fully in both movements. "Her choice lies between two equally unsatisfying alternatives, for to choose one and omit the other is detrimental to her being as a black woman. She cannot afford to ignore either movement."[4]

The frustrating results of attempted choices are reflected in Dr. Carroll's observation that while the Black woman "has learned that involvement in the black movement has not led to a significant advancement of black women, strategically her association with the women's movement places her in an extremely awkward position and often damages her credibility among her black friends and colleagues." She says, "I have often been criticized for 'deserting' the black cause and lessening the chances for black advancement in working for the cause of women. Yet, once in the women's movement, I find that many of my concerns and different needs are ignored, overlooked and rarely discussed due to the powerful myth of an all-embracing sisterhood."[r] Carroll recognizes that as a goal, the attempt of the women's movement to speak to the concerns of all women "represents the true cross-cultural and cross-racial orientation which was and is the basic unifying force in the movement."⁴ She believes, however, that with regard to Black women, "the women's movement has attempted to transcend rather than confront the racial tensions and complexities resulting from the black woman's involvement in the women's movement."⁵

Black women have tried to resolve their dilemma in various ways; some by working as individuals within the feminist movement, some by raising issues of sexism within Black organizations, some by forming coalitions with white feminists on specific issues, some by setting up separate feminist groups devoted exclusively to the concerns of Black women. Carroll warns against the isolation of a third interest group and believes that the only feasible alternative for Black women is to "be the gadfly who stings both movements into achieving their goals—prodding the less volatile black movement into confronting its inherent sexism and righting the injustice it has done to black women. The black woman must work doubly hard in both movements; she must become the sorely needed bridge between them if their goals are to be translated into reality."⁶

Implications for the Women's Movement

These challenges point to an imperative need to enlarge the concept of feminism and, as Rosemary Ruether has urged, to "reach out and include within its struggle the interstructuring of sexism with all other kinds of oppression," as well as to "recognize the pluralism of women's movements in the context of different groupings."⁴ Ruether has been strongly critical of the tendency of both the Black movement and the women's movement to ignore the structures of oppression within their own groups and to attempt to reduce "oppression" to a single-factor analysis. "To recognize structures of oppression within our own group," she believes, "would force us to deal with ourselves, not simply as oppressed or oppressors, but as people who are sometimes the one and sometimes the other in different contexts."⁷

This brings us, finally, to the question of racism within the women's movement, which has alienated so many Black women, and to the responsibility of white feminists, including women educators, to deal with it. Catherine Stimpson once wrote, "Our racism may be the curse of white culture, the oath of an evil witch who invades our rooms at birth. . . . Whatever the cause, the virus has affected us all." The term "racism" is emotion-laden because it attempts to describe a complex system of attitudes, individual acts, institutional patterns, and brutalizing violence as well as verbal and nonverbal subtleties. It is applied to unconscious behavior as well as intentional conduct.[u]

Nevertheless, the use of the term need not induce resentment or paralyzing guilt but rather act as a spur to healthy self-examination as women have done when exploring the ways in which they themselves have acquiesced in their own subjugation. Ellen Pence, confronting this issue, says, "There are many times when white women are put in a real bind so that no matter what we do we are accused of being racists. There are times when racism is inappropriately used as an issue when the disagreements are clearly philosophical. But those, often very legitimate, resentments we have cannot become a justification for perpetuating our racism. The confusion we feel about when and how this movement is racist will not be cleared up until we understand racism as our issue and our responsibility and begin addressing it among ourselves rather than depend totally on Third World women to raise and clarify the issue for us."[v]

Once the challenge of racism as a feminist issue is accepted, the women's movement has valuable resources at its disposal and can develop innovative responses as has been done in working on issues of sexism. An important resource is the experience women have gained from consciousness-raising, a tool which can now be utilized to explore in depth the various ways in which racism has stultified the lives of women of all races and classes in the United States. Small groups of Black and white women, especially in the academic field, have already begun to use this approach, and one of these groups reports that consciousness-raising is a particularly appropriate and useful feminist form for exploring our racism because it is based upon ways women have always talked and listened to one another.

This group recognizes that while it is essential to have a theoretical and analytical comprehension of the political and historical causes of racism, understanding merely on an intellectual level does not always help to make face-to-face meetings with women of color meaningful or productive. The consciousness-raising format "encourages personal sharing, risk-taking and involvement, which are essential for getting at how each of us is racist" in our daily lives, and it also "encourages the 'personal' change that makes political trans-formation and action possible." In these face-to-face discussions, the sharing of personal histories and feelings helps to dissolve hostility and build trust. The report concludes that through the consciousness-raising process, "the women's movement has begun to address racism in a way that no previous movement has, because we have a growing understanding that our racism often manifests itself in how we interact with other women."ᵂ This group finds that the process can lead to an exploration of class discrimination as well as a greater understanding of the interconnections between racism aimed at all people of color and bias against various white ethnic groups who are not Anglo-Saxon Protestants. It empha-sizes that CR about racism is not merely talk, talk, talk, and no action but the essential talking that will make action possible. . . . Actions can grow out of the CR group directly. For example, the group can find out about and publicize the resources which exist in their area, such as other CR groups, study groups, Third World women's groups, and coalitions between Third World and white women. The group can compile reading lists about Black women, racism, and white women's antiracist activity. It can spread the work about the CR process through writing articles, and by giving workshops and talks. . . . It is important to show other women what is possible.

Conclusion

I want to end on this positive note, a suggestion, which has exciting possibilities. Women educators can hasten the process of reorientation through teaching and writing, through careful attention to curricula content and materials, through professional associations with Black and Third World women, and through initiating exploratory consciousness-raising discussions in the workplace. Most essential is a continuous dialogue between white women and women of color, carried on in a spirit of sharing, of listening to and learning from one another, and of seeking greater self-knowledge. For, as Ruether has said, "In the long run, only this more complex self-knowledge gives us hope that liberation movements will not run merely to the reversal of hatreds and oppressions, but rather, to a recovery of a greater humanity for us all."ˣ

Notes

ᵃ Betty Friedan, *It Changed My Life: Writings on the Women's Movement* (New York: Random House, 1976), 87, 89.

ᵇ Pauli Murray, "The Liberation of Black Women," in *Voices of the New Feminism,* ed. Mary Lou Thompson (Boston: Beacon Press, 1970), 101,102.

ᶜ The Combahee River Collective, "A Black Feminist Statement: The Combahee Collective," in *But Some of Us Are Brave: Black Women's Studies,* ed. Gloria T. Hull, Patricia Bell Scott, and Barbara Smith (Old Westbury, NY: The Feminist Press, 1982), 16 (hereafter HSS).

[d] Deborah Harmon Hines, "Racism Breeds Stereotypes," in "Black Women's Agenda, Part I," *Witness* 65, no. 2 (February 1982): 5–8.

[e] Constance M. Carroll, "Three's a Crowd: The Dilemma of Black Women in Higher Education," in HSS, 125–126.

[f] Diane K. Lewis, "A Response to Inequality: Black Women, Racism and Sexism," *Signs: Journal of Women in Culture and Society* 3, no. 2 (1977): 339–344.

[g] Carroll, "Three's a Crowd," 118–119.

[h] Gloria T. Hull and Barbara Smith, "Introduction," in HSS, xxiv.

[i] Ibid., xx.

[j] Ibid., xxvi.

[k] Alice Walker, "One Child of One's Own: A Meaningful Digression Within the Work(s)—An Excerpt," in HSS, 38–39.

[l] The Combahee River Collective, "A Black Feminist Statement," 21.

[m] Quoted in Celestine Ware, *Woman Power: The Movement for Women's Liberation* (New York: Tower, 1970), 80–81.

[n] Ibid., 90.

[o] Gloria I. Joseph and Jill Lewis, *Common Differences: Conflicts in Black and White Feminist Perspectives* (Garden City, NY: Anchor Press/Doubleday, 1981), 280.

[p] The Combahee River Collective, "A Black Feminist Statement," 16.

[q] Joseph and Lewis, *Common Differences,* 38.

[r] Carroll, "Three's a Crowd," 122–123, 125–126.

[s] Ibid., 126–127.

[t] Rosemary Radford Ruether, *New Woman, New Earth: Sexist Ideologies and Human Liberation* (New York: Seabury Press, 1975), 125, 132.

[u] Catharine Stimpson, "'Thy Neighbor's Wife, Thy Neighbor's Servants': Women's Liberation and Black Civil Rights," in *Women in Sexist Society: Studies in Power and Powerlessness,* ed. Vivian Gornick and Barbara K. Moran (New York: Basic Books, 1971), 474.

[v] Ellen Pence, "Racism—A White Issue," in HSS, 47.

[w] Tia Cross et al., "Face-to-Face, Day-to-Day—Racism CR," in HSS, 52, 53–54.

[x] Ruether, *New Woman, New Earth,* 132.

Black Women

A Heroic Tradition and a Challenge

We are greatly privileged to come together tonight in a joyful expression of thankfulness for Mrs. Virginia Coffey's fifty-three years of exemplary service to the Cincinnati community. Over the years this rare individual has inspired and given purpose to the lives of thousands of young people and adults who have felt the warmth of her presence. In everything she has done—as public-school teacher, YWCA executive, Girl Reserve and Girl Scout director, community worker, and human relations specialist—she has consistently directed her talents and energies toward an overarching goal—the growth and enrichment of human personality and community life. Mrs. Coffey personifies a unique leadership in the rhythm of continuity and social change, seeking always to preserve those universal values which enhance the quality of life, while simultaneously working to transform social institutions and make them responsive to the aspirations of those who have been excluded from the benefit of our society.

We do not intend to embarrass Mrs. Coffey by dwelling at length upon her contributions, for I suspect she is very much like another great American in her own estimate of her community activities. Once Mrs. Eleanor Roosevelt explained her tremendous involvement in individual and social needs by saying that she was merely doing the things which came to hand. Doing the things which come to hand, of course, is the very quality which gives extraordinary significance to a life. It is the acceptance of individual responsibility to tackle the complex human problems which confront us every day that changes the face of any community and makes it a more humane place in which to live.

What we propose to do is to call attention to the heroic tradition in which

Mrs. Coffey stands and to relate this experience to some of the new challenges facing us today. Mrs. Coffey has brought to her life's work a historical perspective, which comes to those who have lived through many phases of a struggle. Born around the turn of the twentieth century, barely two generations removed from the turmoil of the final struggle over slavery in the United States, and growing up in a period which Dr. Rayford Logan has called the "nadir" of Negro history—the lowest ebb since emancipation—she has drawn strength from the past and used it to help build for the future.[a] She and her contemporaries inherited the tradition of the indomitable courage of Black women in the nineteenth century, which illuminates the long and torturous climb of America's Black people out of the depths of degradation. Her own life is a vital link in a continuing human drama of epic dimensions.

Perhaps I will be forgiven for confining my remarks to the role of Black women in this drama. With notable exceptions, women generally have been invisible in American history, and Black women have suffered even greater obscurity. Their contributions have been ignored for the most part and are only now beginning to be discovered in scattered social documents. Many of the women we encounter in these fragmentary references are anonymous, but the few glimpses we get of them tell a story of remarkable courage and the triumph of the human spirit over the most dismal circumstances. Some commentators have said of Black women that no other women in history have struggled for so long against so many formidable barriers and have done so much with so few resources. It is certainly true that many Black women through determination, spiritual resiliency, and abiding faith have helped themselves and their families, in the words of Dr. Andrew Billingsley, "to take advantage of the most minimal scraps of opportunity and convert them into outstanding achievement."[1]

If one could characterize in a single phrase the contribution of Black women to America, I think it would be "survival with dignity against incredible odds." The dramatic exploits of Harriet Tubman and Sojourner Truth in the nineteenth century are well-known examples of their will to survive, but they are the great peaks rising from a mountainous terrain of less visible heroines in everyday life.

Flashes of this quiet heroism appear in accounts of slavery. One tells of an unnamed slave girl in South Carolina during the Civil War who was a waiting maid and helped her mistress dress in the morning. During this morning activity, her master would give his wife the latest war information from the battlefronts and, knowing the slave girl could not read or write, he would spell important news so that she would not understand what he was saying. But she had trained herself to remember the letters in sequence and could spell whole sentences without missing a single letter. As soon as she could get away from her duties she would run to her uncle who could read and translate. Through her ingenuity the slaves on the plantation were kept informed of war developments.

During slavery the thirst for knowledge rivaled the longing for freedom and often involved as great a risk. The story of a daring slave woman named Milla Granson in Natchez, Louisiana, throws light upon this determination to learn at all costs. Slave laws generally prohibited education of slaves (and often free Negroes as well) and provided punishment up to forty lashes on the naked back. In Louisiana, the law against distributing books or printed material to slaves included the death penalty. In the face of this law, for several years Milla Granson, who had learned to read and write from the children of her master . . . ran a secret midnight school for slaves which opened around eleven or twelve at night and closed at 2 a.m. She would take twelve pupils at a time, teach them all she knew, then take on another twelve, until she graduated hundreds. Some of these slaves wrote their own passes and took off for Canada and freedom. The powerful motivation and dedication in this little midnight school flourishing in the darkest of moments of slavery challenge us to find solutions for the learning problems of our children today.[2]

Out of the slavery period comes another portrait of extraordinary effort, which belies the recurring racial stereotype of people who do not want to work. A slave woman who lived in Kentucky and whom we know only as Jackson worked for seven years to purchase her freedom by washing and ironing at night after her mistress's work was done. During this period she did not permit herself to undress except to change her clothes. She got her sleep in little naps over her ironing board. After she bought herself she continued at the same pace to buy freedom for her son and daughter. Before she could earn all of the purchase price her health broke down and her master got into debt and had to put her sixteen-year-old daughter up for sale. She went from door to door in her community until she found a kind buyer who would hold a mortgage on her daughter until she could raise the balance. Then she came here to Cincinnati, made contact with abolitionists, and eventually got the funds to pay off the mortgage and bring her daughter to this city where they could begin a new life.[3]

These personal stories highlight a history in which each generation has contributed resolute women to the struggle for freedom, education, and full citizenship. Despite all the strictures of race and sex and their precarious economic position, hardworking Black women in the nineteenth century played an important role in helping to create and sustain the first Black churches and other Black institutions. Long before the Civil War, these women formed benevolent organizations in local communities in the North to support a church, a school, an orphanage, or an old people's home. They joined female antislavery societies, raised funds for the abolition cause, and circulated antislavery literature and petitions. When the Civil War came, these women's groups organized relief for the Black regiments and the freedmen.

During this same period, Black women pioneered in breaking down barriers to higher education and professional training. The first Black woman college graduate, Mary Jane Patterson, took her degree in 1862 at Oberlin College. She was followed by Fannie Jackson Coppin, who graduated from Oberlin in 1865 with a distinguished record, who had been born a slave but whose aunt had worked for six dollars a month until she could buy the little girl's freedom and help her go to school. Between 1864 and 1870, three Negro women graduated from women's medical colleges and became physicians. The first Black woman law school graduate, Charlotte Ray, took her law degree from Howard University in 1872, although it was not until 1897 that the first Black woman lawyer was admitted to a state bar.

Difficult as problems of poverty, family disruption, unemployment, and discrimination seem to us today, it is hard for us fully to appreciate what it must have been like for Black people during Reconstruction and its aftermath, particularly in the South—the overwhelming poverty, the severe racial restrictions under which they lived, and the systematic terrorism directed against Black family life. Black men bore the brunt of white racial violence in the South, but Black women were not immune. Of 3,513 Negroes lynched between 1882 and 1927, 95 were women. Yet in spite of the chaos and terrorism which followed the war, there were sustained efforts at self-help in many Black communities, and Black women played a significant role in the establishment of schools for Black youth and in bringing to bear the first rudiments of social work upon the chaotic conditions.

Postwar migrations of Negroes from the rural South into urban Black communities and the needs of so many destitute people who had to depend solely upon private relief gave rise to a strong national Black women's club movement which eventually merged into the formation of the National Association of Colored Women in 1896, with a membership of 300,000. Historian Gerda Lerner points out that while this movement, like the white women's club movement, was led by middle-class women who were educated; unlike its white counterpart the members of the Black women's clubs were often working women, poor women, and tenant farmwives. They were concerned with education, self-improvement, and community improvement. They placed strong emphasis upon race pride, defense of the Black home and community, and race advancement, says Dr. Lerner.[4] Through their local clubs they worked on such matters as woman suffrage, child welfare, health conditions, conditions of rural life, mother's meetings and night school, gainful occupation and business, and so on. They exerted significant leadership in the fight against lynching, for equal accommodations, and for integration into national life.

In less than a generation following universal emancipation, Black women were distinguishing themselves in many areas: as prominent educators and founders of schools, as physicians, dentists, journalists, writers, teachers, missionaries, antilynching crusaders, women's rights advocates, an opera singer, a successful banker, a cosmetics manufacturer, and two founders of the NAACP. Two of these women have cast long shadows over our own era, extending to the mid-twentieth century. One, Mary Church Terrell, at the age of ninety was responsible for the important Supreme Court decision in 1953 which resulted in the desegregation of public accommodations in Washington, DC. She died the next year. The other was Mary McLeod Bethune, the most influential Black woman in the Roosevelt era, founder of Bethune-Cookman College and of the National Council of Negro Women.

Mrs. Bethune's account of how Bethune-Cookman College campus got started captures the spirit of these women to whom we owe so much. She began her school in 1904 with a total capital of $1.50, an enrollment of her own son and five little girls whose parents paid 50 cents weekly tuition, in a shabby four-room cottage which rented for $11.00 a month. She says of this experience:

> Though I hadn't a penny left . . . I had faith in a living God, faith in myself, and a desire to serve. . . . We burned logs and used charred splinters as pencils, and mashed elderberries as ink. I begged strangers for broom, a lamp, a bit of cretonne to put around the packing case which served as my desk. I haunted the city dump and trash piles behind hotels, retrieving discarded linen and kitchenware, cracked dishes, broken chairs, pieces of old lumber. . . . I wore old clothes sent me by mission boards re-cut and redesigned for me in our dressmaking classes. . . . As parents began gradually to leave their children overnight, I had to provide sleeping accommodations. I took

corn sacks for mattresses. Then I picked Spanish moss from trees, dried and cured it, and used it to substitute for mattress hair.

Two years later, when Mrs. Bethune's school had expanded to 250 pupils, she realized that the only solution to their problem was to stop renting and buy and build their own college. Nearby was a field used as a garbage dump, which the owner was willing to sell for $250. Mrs. Bethune says, "He finally agreed to take five dollars down, and the balance in two years. I promised to be back in a few days with the initial payment. He never knew it, but I didn't have the five dollars. I raised this sum selling ice cream and sweet potato pies to the workmen on construction jobs, and I took the owner his money in small change wrapped in my handkerchief."[5]

Against this background we see the driving force behind the dramatic achievements of Black women of our own time illustrated in the August [1975] special issue of *Ebony* magazine. In less than a generation Black men and women have moved from naked protest against exclusion from national life into opportunities which lead into the mainstream. Many younger people who rightfully accept these opportunities as a matter of birthright may not appreciate the cost of this struggle or the fact that they are standing on the shoulders of these giants of our past. The capacity of those pioneers to convert adversity into achievement has great relevance today because, while opportunities have increased, new perils confront us.

The struggle for equality demands more sophisticated tools than in the past. It requires high competence, technical expertise, knowledge of the political process, the ability to tap [into] and utilize a variety of social resources, [and] experience in planning, implementing, and evaluating the multiple strategies to improve the overall situation in the Black community. While many Black people have been able to take advantage of the new opportunities and move up the economic ladder, far too many have been so crippled by the cumulative effects of discrimination and poverty. They have fallen further behind in a society which has very little use for those who are unskilled and untrained.

Problems of unemployment, bad housing, segregation, drug abuse, and crime have . . . impacted . . . our central cities and are destroying large numbers of our children. There are today 9 million people living below the poverty level in these cities, more than a decade ago. The moral crusade, which aroused broad social concern and made possible the changes of the 1950s and 1960s, has all but vanished, and civil rights so painfully won are increasingly threatened by political indifference or outright hostility as well as judicial retrenchment. We are reminded that this is Full Employment Week and that Coretta Scott King, issuing a call to action several weeks ago, declared, "We are witnessing nothing less than the repeal of the civil rights acts of the 1960s and the gutting of the promises of justice."

In these circumstances, the position of Black women today is both inspiring and profoundly disturbing. The tradition, which has spurred Black women to notable efforts, has always struggled in hand-to-hand combat with cruel realities. As Professor Joyce Ladner wrote in *Ebony,* two major forces have characterized the lives of Black women: high achievement and excellence by a limited few, and a cycle of poverty engulfing the lives of many.[b]

On the one hand, Black women have made impressive gains in recent decades, and particularly since 1963. In 1940, three of every five Negro women workers were employed in low-paying private household service, and only 6 percent held white-collar jobs. By 1974, they had reduced their household employment to 11 percent and increased their white-collar employment to 42 percent. For younger Black women under thirty-five, household employment was down to 6 percent and white-collar jobs were up to nearly 55 percent.

We know, of course, that Black women are increasingly visible in skilled crafts, the professions, business, communications, government, and politics, and are slowly penetrating fields from which they were formerly excluded. They are moving into higher levels of government and corporate management. There are now 675 Black women elected officials throughout the country, four of whom are in Congress. These women are the brightest beacons of hope lighting the road to the future.

On the other hand, as a group Black women remain on the bottom of the rung of the economic and social ladder. They are the group most vulnerable to unemployment, low income, and poverty. Their relative wages are consistently lower and their rate of unemployment consistently higher than those of Black men and white women. In 1973, half of all Black women working full time earned (in round figures) less than $4,500, compared with $7,300 for white women, $10,500 for Black men, and over $14,000 for white men. The National Urban League reported recently that one of every four Black women today cannot find a job.

The depressed economic position of Black women is of special concern to the Black community for two reasons: (1) traditionally, Black women have worked and contributed to family income in greater proportions than their white counterparts and their contribution has been crucial; (2) the disproportionate responsibility Black women carry as family heads, the large number of children in these households, and the alarming increase of Black single-parent families headed by women in recent years. In the seven-year period ending in 1974, Black families headed by women jumped from 28 percent to 35 percent, and two of every five Black children under eighteen (3,178,000) were in these female-headed families. The trend is continuing. Mid-August figures released by the Census Bureau indicate that 48 percent of the 1.3 million Black households established since 1970 are maintained by a woman with no husband present. (Contrast: 15 percent of 7.8 million white households established during [the] same period headed by a woman.)

Female-headed households, generally, are more vulnerable to poverty than other households, and this is even more pronounced in the case of Black families headed by women. At the same time that Black families headed by males have experienced improvement in employment and earnings over the past decade, those headed by females were sinking deeper into poverty. By 1974, the proportion of Black families headed by males and living in poverty had dropped from 55 percent to 33 percent while poor Black families headed by females increased from 45 percent to 67 percent. By 1975, two-thirds of nearly 4 million Black poor children were living in households headed by women. Moreover, seven of ten of these poor Black mothers had two or more children to support, and only about one-third of these family heads had completed high school. Thus, hundreds of thousands of Black women are trapped in a self-perpetuating cycle of poverty, handicapped by limited education, restricted job opportunities, carrying the heavy burden of nurturing future Black America with the fewest resources to cope with the multiple problems all this entails.

The Black female-headed family is not unique but represents an aggravated symptom of our present society. A similar pattern is beginning to appear in the white population. One important factor in the accelerated increase of Black families headed by women is the steadily decreasing number of males in proportion to females in the Black population. 1974 census figures indicated there were 1,050,000 more Black females than Black males fifteen years of age and over. In the age group most likely to be engaged in childrearing, the twenty-five to forty-four age group, the ratio was less than eighty-four males to every one hundred females. This excess of Black females has been present in every census count since 1860, but it has now become acute. Dr. Jacqueline Jackson's studies conclude that Black males have been growing scarcer and scarcer over the past fifty years and that this is not a case of being more likely to be missed in the census count but that they are simply not there. In the white population, an excess of females has appeared in recent decades and the trend is more gradual.

This shortage of adult males combined with other social and economic forces which have assaulted the Black family has grave implications for the Black community and especially Black women. Many face the prospect of never marrying. It increases the pressures to which they are subjected in sexual and marital relations and the likelihood of being separated, divorced, or widowed during a part of their lives, and of having to bring up their children alone. This increased family responsibility comes at a time when traditional support structures have declined. The extended family system, which has played such a vital role in the past, has been weakened under the impact of migration and urbanization, which have tended to disperse family groupings. The influence of the church has also decreased.

The problems which face the Black community as a whole crystallize around the fate of the Black family, which has become an issue of crisis proportions. For Black women and Black girls growing up, this poses special problems with respect to planning education, careers, marriage, and family. The survival of Black family life is a matter of [the] highest priority for the Black community. If Black children are to develop into responsible and productive adults, then new supportive structures must be developed to strengthen the Black family at every level and new mechanisms of self-help devised for Black women struggling alone. While this issue presses most heavily upon Black women, its ramifications extend to the entire society, and how it is resolved will determine the fabric of this society.

It is here that Virginia Coffey's example of leadership comes into clearest focus. Steadfastly over the years, Mrs. Coffey, you have clung to your tradition and met challenge after challenge with vision, imagination, fortitude, and disciplined faith. You have fought against discrimination and poverty with dignity and grace. You have moved on the frontiers of social conflict in a continuous effort to bring together community resources to strengthen family and neighborhood life, to meet the needs of those with the fewest opportunities, and to develop cooperative relationships among people of many backgrounds. You have taken on the most difficult of assignments and performed them with distinction. Above all you have constantly reinvested yourself and the fruits of your personal achievements in your community to open the way for others.

May the spiritual light which guides you and the faith which sustains you continue to enrich this community and enable those who follow you to carry forth your tradition in meeting the challenges which lie ahead.

Notes

[a] See Rayford Logan, *The Negro in American Life and Thought: The Nadir, 1877–1901* (New York: Dial Press, 1954).

[b] August 1975.

Women on the Move

To me, the name YWCA has been almost synonymous with the concept of "Women on the Move." As I reflect upon my own experiences with the Y, which goes back to 1929, the year in which the Great Depression of the [Herbert] Hoover and [Franklin D.] Roosevelt eras began, I think of it as the sanctuary, the nurturing shelter, and the training ground for many pioneer women leaders of this century. Although some of our most militant feminists today may think that the women's movement sprang out of the civil rights, peace, and student movements of the 1960s, those of us who have been around for a long time know that many of the women who became prominent in government, the professions, and politics a generation ago emerged out of a YWCA background.

I was interested to see what Judith Hole and Ellen Levine, authors of *Rebirth of Feminism* (1971), had to say about the YWCA. Their summary is instructive. They write, "The YWCA was formed in 1867 to provide meeting places and centers of activities, both educational and recreational, for young women. Its stated purpose was to 'labor for the temporal, moral, and spiritual welfare of self-supporting young women.'" Although the YWCA's membership and scope of activities have altered considerably over the years, the group has been unable to shake its image of a nonpolitical organization of "prim and polite working girls." They conclude, "The YWCA has been in existence for more than one hundred years. During much of its history, it has not participated actively in movements for social change. Although the ultimate impact of [the] contemporary women's movement on the Y's activities cannot be known, its 1970 platform indicates that a significant step has been taken in [a] new direction."[a] These young historians of feminism do not distinguish between the role of acting as an *organizational agent* of social change and the role of *nurturing* the *individual agents* of social change, and I believe that it is latter role which the YWCA has performed so admirably during the years in which the ground for the New Feminism was being prepared. Let me share with you my own personal experience with the YWCA.

In the spring of 1929—nearly a half-century ago—I was a headstrong, irrepressible, rebellious late-teenager finishing my freshman year at Hunter College's Brooklyn Annex in New York City, ready to take my first step toward becoming an emancipated minor and to throw off the restraining influences of the family of close relatives with whom I lived in Queens. Our beloved Susie A. Elliott, now retired dean of women, Howard University, who is here today, was then the director of Emma Ransom House connected with the West 137th Street Branch of the YWCA in Harlem. Like other migrants from the South in those days, I was attracted to the Big City and particularly to Harlem. Through her good offices I got a room at the Emma Ransom House residence, a part-time job running the elevator and switchboard, and later a full-time job as dishwasher and steam table runner in the YWCA cafeteria. However, Mrs. Thayer, who used to be one of my many bosses in the cafeteria, is also in the audience today. (Asked Ms. Elliott and Ms. Thayer to stand and take a bow. Heavy applause.) Through the YWCA I was saved from being cast adrift and exposed to the hazards which threaten homeless young women from small towns who seek their fortunes in large metropolitan areas.

Think what the YWCA must have meant to a country bumpkin in those days—the privacy of one's own room in a protective environment, attractive surroundings in which to entertain one's boyfriends, the freedom to come and go as one chose, so long as one was in by midnight, a cafeteria where one could get nutritious inexpensive meals, a swimming pool next door, an employment office, and a beehive of community activities all concentrated in one spot. The Emma Ransom House even provided inadvertently a strong church-going impulse. My room on the fourth floor rear corridor faced the back windows of Abyssinian Baptist Church on West 138th Street, whose young assistant minister at the time was the future congressman Adam Clayton Powell Jr. Although my parish was St. Philip's Episcopal Church on West 134th Street, [I] soon found that if I *didn't* go to my own church on Sunday mornings I couldn't escape a *partial* attendance at Abyssinian. The choir and organ boomed out and filled my room with such churchly sounds it was impossible to sleep late, so it was better to get up and go to church. (Laughter)

Writing of this period of history in my autobiography, I have said,

> Working and living at the Y. brought me in contact with other self-support-ing young women who welcomed an attractive protected residence. I was also exposed to a number of professional Negro women whose careers in-spired me; white haired, youthful Cecelia Cabiness Saunders from South Carolina, whose leadership and efficient management as executive director of the Y. branch had attracted a top-notch staff; Anna Arnold Hedgeman, the membership secretary, who would go on to pioneer in politics, and pub-lic service, education and religion; Margaret Douglas, teacher and camp di-rector, who would become the first Negro woman assistant superintendent in the New York City public schools; Viol Lewis Waiters, who would climax her Y. leadership experience by working in industry during World War II as consultant to management on the problems of working women and mi-norities; Dorothy Height, who would follow in the tradition of our beloved Mary McLeod Bethune as president of the influential National Council of Negro Women and become a powerful leader in national affairs; Louise E. Jefferson, a young commercial artist from Washington, D.C. who would wind up her career as production manager of Friendship Press, and whose Friendship Maps and photographic exhibits on Africa would gain national and international attention in the 1960's and 1970's; the late Juliette Der-ricotte, international student secretary of the YWCA, later Dean of Women at Fisk University, whose untimely death (following an automobile accident in the South while being carried to a colored hospital miles away because a local white hospital had declined to admit her) had much to do with my passionate struggle against racial segregation.[1]

I could extend this roster to include many others, but this sampling indi-cates some of the role models which helped to shape my formative years:

> None of these women would have called themselves feminists then; yet most of them had grown up in the atmosphere of the Women's Suffrage movement at its climax; they were strong independent personalities who, because of their concerted effort to rise above the limitations of race and sex in the 1930's and to help younger Negro women do the same, shared a sisterhood not unlike the sisterhood of the reborn feminist movement of the 1960's

and 1970's. To the extent that I am known as a feminist pioneer in this re-born movement, they provided me with a direct link to the earlier tradition and helped to inspire me toward professional achievement of excellence with efficiency.[2]

Against this background, what can we say about the role of the YWCA of the late 1970s when [the] women's movement has swelled into an international tide of social change? What role can this 110-year organization play in the world-wide thrust toward indivisible human rights? As the oldest women's organization in the field, born in the vortex of Reconstruction after a searing civil war which had torn our country apart, is there any unique contribution which the YWCA can make which is not preempted by younger and seemingly more activist women's organizations?

I think there is such a unique role, and it is suggested by the one word in the title which differentiates the YWCA from most other women's groups—Young Women's Christian Association. The YWCA must continue to provide the nurturing role, the feeding of the devotional life of young women standing in the Christian tradition [to] assume a leadership function in the spiritual awakening which I believe is taking place in this nation today. It is the one women's organization above all others which can fly at its special masthead the two basic principles of the Christian tradition—loving God our Creator with all our hearts, souls, and minds, and loving our neighbors as ourselves. (We Christians are also beginning to "come out of the closet.")

I need not tell this audience that it has been the mass abdication from these principles which permitted the seeds of terrorism to flourish and burst upon this city last week. The Christian tradition is one of creative nonviolence in the resolution of human controversy, exemplified by the life *and* death of Dr. Martin Luther King Jr. When Dr. King was assassinated in 1968, a vacuum of leadership was created. Many of his followers have gone into politics; a younger, more militant generation (among whom were some false prophets) arose to preach "liberation by any means necessary" (without qualification), and we have witnessed riots, bloodshed, senseless killings in the inner city, lawlessness, terrorism.

To me, an essential part of the process of liberation from racism, sexism, ageism, or any other "-ism" which alienates human beings from one another is the simultaneous process of reconciliation wherever possible. It is the recognition that violence is not only physical but also psychic or spiritual. The younger generation speaks of "vibes"—*good vibes* and *bad vibes.* My barber told me the other day, "Thank God for President Carter; I love that man because he gives me such *good vibes!*" Individual vibrations radiating from human beings can be loving and friendly or hostile.

I submit, therefore, that in addition to the nurturing, devotional role of sisterhood which is built into the YWCA tradition—and which I believe is analogous to the radical feminist theologian Mary Daly's term "the sisterhood of man," although she might disagree—the YWCA can take the initiative in reviving and reconstructing the tradition of active and creative nonviolence as a process in what is now called the "Struggle for Liberation."[3] If you will forgive the personal reference, whatever activist reputation I have [has] been built upon [what] my friend Dr. Caroline F. Ware calls "sweeping out the corners," looking around and doing what nobody else is doing and yet which needs to be done.

The YWCA does not need to duplicate the work of other women's organizations. As a Christian laywomen's group, it is more free to be inclusive than denominational churches bound by their credos and canons of discipline. It can be truly ecumenical, crossing the lines of all faiths; it can be a bridge between the sacred and the secular—the outreach and mission of the Christian faith—not by proselytizing but by witnessing, embodying in its individual members the vitality which comes with the rebirth and renewal of the Christian way of life.

The field for further development of creative nonviolence in individual as well as institutional relationships is wide open and ripe for renewal. What if the YWCA made this a pilot project for a two-year study and experimentation? What if the Washington Metropolitan Area YWCA began with an intensive examination of the last week's events?[4] How can we prevent such a disaster from striking this city again? What are the alternatives? What can individual citizens do? How can we match a faith which ends in terrorism with a faith which proclaims rebirth, renewal, and reconciliation? A faith which delivers what it proclaims? How can this faith transform the city of Washington from a fortress against robbers, thieves, murderers to an open city in which trust and friendliness replace suspicion and fear? How can we turn the question of the responsibility of "they" into the responsibility of "we"? We must start *somewhere* to turn our own country around, and Washington is as good a place as any to begin. My student days here at Howard University School of Law bring back memories of creative and effective nonviolence in the desegregation of lily-white Washington restaurants. The leaders of the Howard University student campaigns were predominately women in 1943 and 1944 because the male students for the most part were caught in World War II military conscription. Out of that experience, I began to realize that women are the *natural* leaders of a movement for practical nonviolence in everyday struggles. We do not have a tradition of *armed combat.* We are not associated with the strategies of war and conquest. We do not have male egos to protect. (Laughter and applause) Our historical role has been a nurturing one; of necessity, as mothers, homemakers, wives, we have had to be concerned with the best interests of *all* the members of the family. If our contemporary feminism means anything at all, it should mean that our objective in our own liberation as women is to make our society more humane, and this means a total rejection of the instruments of a[n] expression in a male-dominated society which have led to violence and armed conflict. The consequences of this rule by only one-half of the human race are obvious—humanity is at a crossroads. Either we reject the instruments of psychic and physical violence and replace them with practical alternatives, or we shall be parties to the destruction of the human race—or certainly its retrogression to bestiality more horrible than we can presently imagine.

The great women pioneers of creative nonviolence of our own era are still within our memory. Mrs. Eleanor Roosevelt, whom I think of as the mother of the contemporary women's rights movement, did not actively oppose violence in wartime, but her whole life was one of compassion and working for peace and reconciliation within the framework of individual human rights. In the civil rights struggle, we remember Ella Baker, former NAACP coordinator of branches and the godmother of SNCC [the Student Nonviolent Coordinating Committee]; Daisy Bates, former Arkansas state president of [the] NAACP, who led the Little Rock struggle for segregation without the loss of a single life, as I recall; Gloria Richardson, who faced down the mobs in eastern Maryland in the early 1960s; Coretta Scott King, who was the partner and strong right arm of Dr. Martin Luther King Jr.; and many others. Their lives present us with the challenge of taking up the banner of creative nonviolence, adapting it to new situations, and going forward with it. The United States is at peace for the first time since World War II, and now is the time to perfect instruments of nonviolence in local situations, so that the models developed can be projected onto the national and international scene.

I close with a tribute to an apostle of nonviolence, Fannie Lou Hamer, of Ruleville, Mississippi, who died Monday, February 14, of cancer at the age of sixty. Thomas A. Johnson of the *New York Times* writes what may well serve as her epitaph and benediction: "Although she was beaten, arrested and shot at, Mrs. Hamer did not allow herself to hate whites, explaining many times, 'I feel sorry for anybody that could let hate wrap them up. Ain't no such thing as I can hate anybody and hope to see God's face.'"[5] I met Mrs. Hamer at an interracial educational conference in Mississippi in the summer of 1967, and we sat up most of the night talking anxiously while headlights of our cars lighted up the buildings and grounds during an unexplained blackout of the electrical circuits. Our paths crossed once more in Chicago, and I felt close enough to her to send her my periodic Round Robin letters, including one for Christmas 1976 and the announcement of my ordination to the Episcopal priesthood. Therefore, I feel a personal loss and a personal response to the report of her close friend June Johnson, who invited her for the last time on March 4. Mrs. Johnson said, "She was sitting in a wheel chair crying. She states (here speaker's voice broke and she wept in public. Everyone said it was a very moving moment.) was so tired, she wanted all of us to remember her and to keep up the work. She wanted us to understand that she had taken care of business. She felt her house was in place, and that everything was in order with God, because she was a very religious person."[6]

Mrs. Fannie Lou Hamer's work is done. Ours is not. The most fitting memorial we can set up in her name is to grant her last reported request—"*to remember her and to keep up with the work.*"

O God, our Creator, Preserver, and Savior from eternal darkness and death, we thank you for [the] life of Fannie Lou Hamer, a fallen leader in the ongoing struggle for human freedom and salvation; we are grateful for the example she set as a "light unto the world," [a] "city set on a hill"; and we ask that we may be given the strength and purpose to follow in her footsteps; to take up the candle of neighborly love and creative nonviolence she lighted in the darkness of Mississippi; to nurture the flame and help to make it glow throughout our nation and the world, in the name of him who taught us that the love of God and the love of neighbor are more powerful than material weapons, that creative imagination is more effective than brute force, and that active good, however long suffering, will ultimately triumph over evil—our Savior and brother, Jesus Christ. Amen!

Notes

[a] Judith Hole and Ellen Levine, *Rebirth of Feminism* (New York: Quadrangle Books, 1971).

Chronology

1910 (November 20) Born in Baltimore, Maryland.[1]

1911 (July 9) Christened Anna Pauline Murray at St. James Episcopal Church in Baltimore.

1919 Confirmed by Bishop Henry B. Delany of North Carolina.

1920–1926 Accompanies her uncle Reverend John Small on his trip to his various mission charges in southern Maryland. She serves as his organist during these trips.

1921–1925 Serves in various capacities (e.g., altar guild) at St. Titus in Durham, North Carolina.

1926–1929 Is a member of All Saints Church in Queens, New York.

1927 Called a "Child of Destiny" by Bishop Delany on his deathbed.[2]

1928 Attends Abyssinian Baptist Church while living at the 137th Street YWCA in Harlem.

1929 Attends St. Philip's Church in Manhattan.

1930s Leaves the church until the late 1930s and wrestles with issues such as the Virgin Birth, the Trinity, and so on.[3]

1930s (late) Reenters the church, joining St. Martin's Church in New York.

1948–1959 Attends St. Philip's Church in Brooklyn.

1955 (October 26) Aunt Pauline dies.

1959–1960 Transfers church membership to St. Marks-in-the-Bowery, New York.

1966 (March) Rebels against a policy excluding women from providing the Eucharist. Begins pushing for increased roles for women in lay ministry.

1966 (October) Committee to Study the Place of Women in the Ministry files its report in which the church is urged to give attention to the question of ordaining women.

1968 (July 4–20) Invited to be a resource person at the Fourth Assembly of the World Council of Churches in Uppsala, Sweden.[4]

1970 (April 24–26) Participates in the formation of a resolution (The Resolution of Concerned Women: Prologue to a Golden Age in Human Relationships) calling for equality in ordained ministry, theological education, and church leadership roles.

1970 (September 19) Special Commission on Ordained and Licensed Ministry in the Episcopal Church meets in Baltimore to study the issue of women's ministries.[5]

1970 General Convention held in Houston ignores the September 19, 1970, report.

1970 Stops attending church for almost one year because of the Episcopal Church's unwillingness to ordain women.

1973 (February 21) Irene ("Renee") Barlow dies, and Murray is unable to perform her last rites.

1973 (March 30) Murray makes an official request to Bishop John Burgess to be admitted as a postulant for Holy Orders and ordination (to the diaconate).

1973 (June 16) Murray is admitted as a postulant of the Diocese of Massachusetts.

1973 (July 10) Murray notifies Episcopal Divinity School that she will attend General Theological Seminary.

1973 (September) Begins a year as a special student at General Theological Seminary after resigning from Brandeis University.[6]

1973 (October) General Convention in Louisville fails to approve ordination of women.

1974–1975 academic year Teaches "The Spirited Person" at the New School in New York, using ethics to tie together her theological orientation and mundane concerns.

1974 (February 15) Bishop Morris F. Arnold recommends her for candidacy to Holy Orders.

1974 (March 2) Bishop Arnold admits Murray as candidate for Holy Orders.[7]

1974 (March 3) Gives first sermon (Emmanuel Church, Boston).

1974 (July 29) Attends irregular ordination of eleven women deacons (Merrill Bittner, Alla Bozarth-Campbell, Alison Cheek, Emily Hewitt, Carter Heyward, Suzanne Hiatt, Jacqueline Means, Marie Moorefield Fleisher, Jeannette Piccard, Betty Bone Schiess, Katrina Martha Swanson, and Nancy Hatch Wittig) to priesthood in Philadelphia, at Church of the Advocate.[8]

1975 (June 18) Writes to the vestry of Emmanuel Church indicating plans to transfer her candidacy to the Diocese of Washington, DC.[9] The transfer is never completed.

1975 (August 11) Requests permission to spend senior year at Virginia Theological Seminary.

1976 (January 26–February 1) Takes General Ordination Examinations.[10]

1976 (March 8) Passes her examinations.[11]

1976 (April 26) Examination by Standing Committee related to ordination.

1976 Spends the academic year at Virginia Theological Seminary and does field education in ministry at St. Philips Chapel–Aquasco in Prince George's County, Maryland.[12]

1976 (May) Receives Master of Divinity degree from General Theological Seminary.

1976 (June 9) Ordained a deacon in Massachusetts.

1976 (Summer) Serves as associate chaplain at Bellevue Hospital (New York).

1976 (September) Ordination of women approved during General Convention in Minneapolis.

1977 (January 1) Ordination of women effective as of this date.

1977 (January 8) Ordained a priest in National Cathedral, Washington, DC, consecrated by Bishop William F. Creighton.[13]

1977 (February 13) Celebrates first Holy Eucharist as a priest at Chapel of the Cross in Durham, North Carolina, her family church. She is the first woman to do so.

1977–1978 Volunteer chaplain, Wisconsin Avenue Nursing Home, Washington, DC; associate clergy at St. Stephen and Incarnation, Washington, DC.

1979 (Fall) The Society for the Study of Black Religion meeting at Howard University gives part of its program to the theme "Black Women in Religion."[14]

1979–1981 Ministers at Church of the Atonement, Washington, DC, as associate clergy, part-time.

1980 (August 11) Conducts her first wedding as a priest.

1981 (March 13) George Bush acknowledges receipt of Murray's sermon titled "The Light of the World."

1982 (November 16) Sends check for $25 to join the Union of Black Episcopalians.

1981–1982 Serves as supply priest for Church of the Holy Nativity, Forest Park, Baltimore, Maryland.[15]

1982 (December 31) Resigns from Church of the Holy Nativity and retires from the post.[16]

1983 (November 19) Retires from active church ministry.

1984 Serves as supply priest for the Church of the Holy Cross in Homewood, Pennsylvania, while the rector is on vacation.

1985 (July 1) Dies in Pittsburgh.

Editor's Notes

Editor's Introduction

1. In part, this "new" interest grows out of the natural maturation of womanist and feminist scholarship—and the generative call for recognition of intersectionality. With respect to the former in particular, the method of study—what I would name a type of archeology of voice—first comes across within the more obvious sources of womanist thought and behavior. It is only as these sources are explored that the presence of other, less widely celebrated figures emerge. Hence, Ida B. Wells-Barnett received attention prior to Ann J. Cooper, and so on. Nonetheless, Murray is an acknowledged pioneer in recognition of and response to racism and sexism as connected modes of discrimination.

2. Although I am critical of what I consider a lack of attention to Murray's religious-theological sensibilities, what I have attempted to describe does not constitute a complete omission on the part of scholars. Yet most tend to address her activism and legacy without giving sustained attention to her religious life and the manner in which this religious-theological identity informed and shaped her "secular" activities. Our understanding of American religious thought and life, as well as African American religious thought and life more specifically, could be greatly enhanced through scholarly attention to Murray's religious-theological writings and her ministry. I first articulated a sense of Murray's theology in "Religion and 'America's Problem Child': Notes on the Development of Pauli Murray's Theology," *Journal of Feminist Studies in Religion* 15, no. 1 (Spring 1999): 21–39. I further develop this attention to her theology in *Becoming "America's Problem Child:" An Outline of Pauli Murray's Religious Life and Theology* (Eugene, OR: Wipf and Stock/Pickwick, 2008). This introduction draws from that book. In addition, I am not the first to recognize the importance of Murray's religious identity. Several articles and dissertations have been written on Murray, including Flora Renda Bryant's "An Examination of the Social Activism of Pauli Murray" (PhD dissertation, University of South Carolina, 1991), and Darlene O'Dell's "Sites of Southern Memory: The Autobiogra-

phies of Katharine Dupre Lumpkin, Lillian Smith, and Pauli Murray" (PhD dissertation, College of William and Mary, 1997).

3. For early examples, see Delores Williams, "Womanist Theology: Black Women's Voices," *Christianity and Crisis* 47 (March 2, 1987): 66–70, and Katie Cannon, "The Emergence of Black Feminist Consciousness," in *Feminist Interpretation of the Bible,* ed. Letty M. Russell (Philadelphia: Westminster Press, 1985), 30–40.

4. However, her sexuality appears to be a dimension of her self-understanding that did not receive the same explicit attention given to her race and class. Unpacking her vocation and theological assertions around issues of sexuality remains an area left to be done by those who read Murray. Material in the Murray Papers at the Schlesinger Library suggests that she began questioning her sexuality at the age of nineteen. A memo to Dr. Helen Rogers dated March 8, 1940, indicates that Murray believed her collapse (of February 23–26, 1940, triggered by the disappearance of a friend) might have involved frustration over questions of sexuality and work. See box 4, folder 71, Murray Papers, Schlesinger Library, Harvard University, Cambridge, MA (hereafter Murray Papers). Folder 72 indicates that her condition was diagnosed as being related to a thyroid condition.

5. Introduction to the Reissue of Murray, *Proud Shoes,* 5, box 79, folder 1381, Murray Papers.

6. Murray, *Song in a Weary Throat,* 57.

7. Box 84, folder 1456, p. 10, Murray Papers.

8. Ibid., 70.

9. Murray was a strong supporter of legislation for a Martin Luther King holiday. On October 23, 1983, she wrote to President Ronald Reagan urging him to support the proposed holiday. See "October 23, 1983, Letter to President Reagan," box 94, folder 1634, Murray Papers. Regarding King, readers will be interested in her sermon "Martin Luther King, Jr.," found in box 64, folder 1091, Murray Papers. Caroline Ware's publications include *Greenwich Village, 1920–1930: A Comment on American Civilization in the Post-War Years* (London: Octagon Books, 1977), and *The Cultural Approach to History* (New York: Columbia University Press, 1940).

10. For some information concerning Murray's perspective on Eleanor Roosevelt, see "Servanthood—Eleanor Roosevelt," box 65, folder 1106, Murray Papers.

11. Murray, *Song in a Weary Throat,* 192.

12. Murray, *Dark Testament;* Pauli Murray, *Proud Shoes* (New York: HarperCollins, 1987).

13. Krishnalal Jethalal Shridharani, *War Without Violence: A Study of Gandhi's Method and Its Accomplishments* (New York: Garland, 1972).

14. Readers will find it interesting to read this incident in light of Murray's "Tribute to Mrs. Rosa L. Parks," a speech given on November 7, 1965, to Key Women, Inc., box 88, folder 1530, Murray Papers.

15. See Murray and Kempton, *"All for Mr. Davis."*

16. Prior to law school, Murray entertained the idea of graduate training at the University of North Carolina. Such an arrangement would have allowed her to pursue her intellectual interests and manage family obligations in Durham. However, the University of North Carolina did not admit African Americans. Events, including a Supreme Court decision involving the University of Missouri Law School requiring educational opportunities for Black Americans equal to that of white Americans, put pressure on the University of North Carolina. Word of Murray being denied admission spread well beyond North Carolina. However, this interest in her situation did not force the university to change its admissions policy. Admission of African Americans to the University of North Carolina occurred after 1951. Ironically, Murray was offered an honorary degree from the university in 1978, a gesture she rejected because of the university's failure to fully implement aggressive desegregation policies and procedures in compliance with federal government requirements.

17. Murray's article "An Alternative Weapon," published in *South Today* (Winter 1942–1943): 53–57, provides a sense of her early commitment to nonviolence. Copy available in box 84, folder 1462, Murray Papers.

18. See, for example, "A Decade of Women's Rights," June 28, 1972, box 89, folder 1552, and "The Women's Revolution—Prologue to a Golden Age in Human Relationships," October 16, 1971, box 89, folder 1549, Murray Papers.

19. Murray, *Song in a Weary Throat,* 255.

20. Pauli Murray, "An American Credo," *Common Ground* 5, no. 2 (Winter 1945): 24, copy in box 84, folder 1463, Murray Papers.

21. One gets a sense of her thought on this issue of cooperation in a 1947 speech given during Brotherhood Week, sponsored by the Long Island Council of the National Council of Negro Women and the Long Island Women's Division of the American Jewish Congress. See "Brotherhood in Action," box 87, folder 1516, Murray Papers.

22. "Reflections on the Special General Convention," 1969, box 95, folder 1666, Murray Papers.

23. While critiquing the church, Murray continued challenging African American (male) leaders who did not take as seriously the "Women's Rights/Women's Liberation Movement." She hoped for an effective coalition that would link this movement with the efforts of other marginalized groups. Yet in order for this coalition to

take form, gender equality could not be ignored. For an example of her thought on this, see "September 9, 1970, Letter to Bayard Rustin," box 99, folder 1771, Murray Papers.

24. "A Group of Concerned Women Gathered Together at Graymoor, April 24–26, 1970," box 95, folder 1666, Murray Papers.

25. "Images of Black Women," box 118, folder 2102, Murray Papers.

26. Murray, *Song in a Weary Throat,* 370.

27. Ibid., 369.

28. Ibid., 370.

29. "Letter to Members of the Vestry, March 27, 1966," box 67, folder 1148, Murray Papers.

30. See "To Those Who Loved Irene Barlow," March 7–13, 1973, box 6, folder 161, Murray Papers.

31. Murray provides information concerning the role of Irene Barlow's death in the formation of her sense of ministry in a sermon given on February 26, 1978, box 64, folder 1095, Murray Papers.

32. Hiatt, "Pauli Murray."

33. Murray, *Song in a Weary Throat,* 304.

34. It is interesting to note Murray's fear in relationship to a sermon given December 18, 1977, "The Conquest of Fear." The outline is available in box 90, folder 1566, Murray Papers.

35. One also gets a sense of this in her ordination examination, in her written account of "My Future Role in the Ministry and the Criteria by Which Its Effectiveness Will Be Judged, Set III Part A., pg. 1–3," box 23, folder 476, Murray Papers.

36. "Supplemental Statement to 'My Reasons for Seeking the Sacred Ministry,' April 29, 1973," box 95, folder 1668, Murray Papers. Of particular interest is her "Self-Evaluation," prepared in 1976 as part of the process for ordination, box 27, folder 525, Murray Papers.

37. Murray to Ernest Pollock, March 22, 1974, box 23, folder 466, Murray Papers.

38. Murray, *Song in a Weary Throat,* 425.

39. It was clear to her the law alone did not have the moral authority necessary for transformation on a large scale. On the other hand, church ministry involved an exemplifying of the "morality of the law" combined with a Christian way of life as moral principle. This synergy of moral postures allowed a demonstration of both the law and faith at their best.

40. Lawrence H. Fuchs, chair of the American Studies Department at Brandeis,

wrote one of the letters of support for her candidacy for Holy Orders. "Letter from Fuchs," box 95, folder 1668, Murray Papers.

41. See Murray to Lawrence H. Fuchs, April 18, 1973, box 45, folder 806, Murray Papers.

42. "Letter to Bob Godley, April 11, 1979," box 23, folder 466, Murray Papers. In addition to a hearing problem detected around this time, Murray's aggressive manner in the classroom might have stemmed from the lessons learned in law school, where she had a difficult time gaining opportunities to speak as the only women in her entering class.

43. Murray, *Song in a Weary Throat,* 183–184.

44. "Letter to Ernest Pollock (March 21, 1974)," box 23, folder 466, Murray Papers. His letter was sent on March 19, 1974.

45. See, for example, "May 1975 Letter to Professors Wright and Shriver and Dean Foster of General Theological Seminary," box 27, folder 525, Murray Papers.

46. On her General Ordination Examination short answers, Murray gave some definition to this particular brand of ministry—i.e., the unfolding of rights and grace, based on human need and her own experience of mortality—within the context of discretely religious engagements.

47. "Untitled, Set II Part A., pg. 10," box 23, folder 476, Murray Papers.

48. "Letter to Cecil Woods, Dean of Virginia Theological Seminary," box 27, folder 538, Murray Papers, emphasis added.

49. Of interest is Murray's paper "Reflections upon the Christian Ministry and Theological Education," written as part of the requirements for the Master of Divinity degree from General Theological Seminary, box 63, folder 1075, Murray Papers.

50. Murray, *Song in a Weary Throat,* 435.

51. "December 20, 1973, Letter to Family and Friends," box 99, folder 1773, Murray Papers.

52. And by prophetic she meant a critique of existing arrangements and a call to proper thought and action as a way of avoiding "destruction."

53. "Letter to Turner, October 31, 1982," box 118, folder 2100, Murray Papers.

54. "March 7, 1973, Letter from Bishop John M. Burgess of Massachusetts," box 95, folder 1667, Murray Papers.

55. "Untitled, Set II Part A., pg. 7," box 23, folder 476, Murray Papers.

56. One gets a sense of King's personalism in the multivolume set *The Papers of Martin Luther King, Jr.* (Berkeley: University of California Press, 1995–); also see Lewis Baldwin, *There Is a Balm in Gilead: The Cultural Roots of Martin Luther King, Jr.*

(Minneapolis: Fortress Press, 1991), and James H. Cone, *Malcolm and Martin and America* (Maryknoll, NY: Orbis Books, 1991). For Tillich, see his three-volume *Systematic Theology* (Chicago: University of Chicago Press, 1967–1976).

57. The Black Manifesto is available in a variety of locations, including the *New York Review*, July 10, 1969, https://www.nybooks.com/articles/1969/07/10/black -manifesto/.

58. Although she used the term "Black" on occasion, Murray had a clear preference for "Negro" over "Black" or "African American." The latter two, she believed, were too limiting in that they did not do justice to the complex identity held by her community. She gave attention to this issue in "What PECUSA Could Be Doing the Next Century, 1975–2075," in *Ruach: The Newsletter of the Episcopal Women's Caucus,* box 67, folder 1148, Murray Papers. She also explained her use of "Negro" in "Explanation of Use of the Term 'Negro' Instead of 'Black,'" 65th Annual Founders' Day Luncheon Speech, Baltimore Alumnae Chapter, Delta Sigma Theta, Inc., January 28, 1978, box 129, folder 2337, Murray Papers.

59. For a good introduction to Black theology as Murray encountered it, see James H. Cone and Gayraud S. Wilmore, eds., *Black Theology: A Documentary History, 1966–1979* and *Black Theology: A Documentary History, 1980–1992* (Maryknoll, NY: Orbis Books, 1993).

60. During the early years of Black theology, William R. Jones provided an important critique of the implicit theodicy found in Black theological thought. It is likely that Murray would have been familiar with this text, in light of her reading habits. But its humanist orientation would have been unappealing to her. See William R. Jones, *Is God a White Racist? A Preamble to Black Theology* (Garden City, NY: Anchor Press, 1973).

61. Some of this information is drawn from Pinn, "Religion and 'America's Problem Child,'" 28–30.

62. J. Deotis Roberts, *Liberation and Reconciliation: A Black Theology* (Philadelphia: Westminster Press, 1971); see also "Letter to J. Deotis Roberts, May 20, 1975," box 99, folder 1776, Murray Papers. Readers should also read an extended essay written by Murray addressing her understanding of Roberts's thought: "J. Deotis Roberts on Black Theology: A Comparative View," box 23, folder 474, Murray Papers.

63. "Continuity of Values amid Pressures for Change," Commencement Convocation, University of Florida, Gainesville, June 10, 1978, box 89, folder 1554, Murray Papers.

64. For a sense of this agenda for feminist theology, see Sheila Briggs and Mary McClintock Flukerson, eds., *The Oxford Handbook of Feminist Theology* (New York: Oxford University Press, 2011).

65. Some of the information on Murray's theological insights regarding feminist and Black theologies is drawn from Pinn, "Religion and 'America's Problem Child,'" 29–30.

66. More to the point, in a letter to Corona Machemer, Murray indicated that as of November 24, 1982, she hoped to complete the sequel to *Proud Shoes* and make progress on other projects including a collection of sermons and an account of her time in ministry. "Letter to Corona," November 24, 1982, box 83, folder 1446, Murray Papers.

67. Caroline F. Ware, "Epilogue," in Murray, *Song in a Weary Throat,* 436.

68. Marcia Y. Riggs and Barbara Holmes, eds., *Can I Get a Witness? Prophetic Religious Voices of African American Women: An Anthology* (Maryknoll, NY: Orbis Books, 1997), xiv.

The Dilemma of the Minority Christian

This sermon was given on May 19, 1974, at St. James Presbyterian Church of New York City. The manuscript is housed in box 64, folder 1089, Murray Papers.

1. First made available in 1957. Currently this album is available as *Marian Anderson: Johann Sebastian Bach Arias and Great Songs of Faith* (Classical Roots, 2013).

2. Martin Luther King Jr., *Where Do We Go from Here: Chaos or Community?* (1967; reprint Boston: Beacon Press, 2010), 46.

3. Matthew 26:52; David Levering Lewis, *King: A Biography* (Chicago: University of Illinois Press, 1978), 180.

Father's Day Sermon

This June 15, 1975, sermon was delivered to the members of St. Philip's Church in New York City. At this point, Murray was closing in on the completion of her seminary work. This document is housed in box 64, folder 1090, Murray Papers.

1. She is referencing the life of Jesus for whom, as far as the official biblical story goes, there is a gap between those ages.

2. For information on this novelist, see the Evelyn Underhill Association website, http://evelynunderhill.org/.

3. I have been unable to locate the exact source of this quotation but it is likely *Meditations Based upon the Lord's Prayer* (London: Longmans, Green, 1940).

4. See note 3, above.

5. See note 3, above.

Sermon Given on January 4, 1976

This untitled sermon was given at St. Philip's Church in Aquasco, Maryland. It is found in box 64, folder 1091, Murray Papers.

1. Found in the 1928 Book of Common Prayer, "Prayers and Thanksgivings," http://justus.anglican.org/resources/bcp/1928/BCP_1928.htm.

The Gift of the Holy Spirit

On May 29, 1977, Murray gave this sermon at Trinity Episcopal Church in Washington, DC. The manuscript is in box 64, folder 1093, Murray Papers.

1. Whitsun is the day Anglicans acknowledge as the seventh Sunday after Easter, the celebration of Pentecost.

2. King was referencing Isaiah 40:4–5.

3. Karl Barth, *The Faith of the Church: A Commentary on the Apostles' Creed According to Calvin's Catechism* (1958; reprint Eugene, OR: Wipf and Stock, 2006).

Sermon Given on December 25, 1977

Murray gave this sermon at the Wisconsin Avenue Nursing Home in Washington, DC. It is found in box 64, folder 1099, Murray Papers.

1. This line is found in a variety of devotional materials, including "A Devotional Program Dedicated to the Life and Times of Jesus Christ (Series 1 of 3), Written by Doris Aldean Wright," https://archive.org/stream/DPD2JC1/DPD2JC_1_djvu.txt.

2. From James Allen Francis, "On Solitary Life: An Essay on the Life of Jesus Christ," in *The Real Jesus and Other Sermons* (Philadelphia: Judson Press, 1926), 1–7. Also see the rest of Francis's book.

The Last Judgment

Murray gave this sermon on November 26, 1978, at Immanuel Church-on-the-Hill in Alexandria, Virginia. The manuscript is located in box 64, folder 1096, Murray Papers.

1. The original manuscript also lists Matthew 25:31–46, although she does not provide the text.

2. This theological doctrine was adopted in 325, during a council meeting in the city of Nicaea. It was meant to assert "proper" and "accurate" thinking concerning the major dimensions of the Christian faith—e.g., who Jesus is and the nature of the Trinity (i.e., the Father, the Son [Jesus], and the Holy Ghost).

3. Works by Langdon Gilkey with which Murray might have been familiar include *Naming the Whirlwind: A Renewal of God Language* (Indianapolis: Bobbs-Merrill,

1970), and *Reaping the Whirlwind: A Christian Interpretation of History* (1976; reprint Eugene, OR: Wipf and Stock, 2000).

Ministry

This sermon was given at the Wisconsin Avenue Nursing Home in Washington, DC, on July 22, 1979. The full text is found in box 64, folder 1098, Murray Papers.

1. Some of Hans Kung's more popular texts with which Murray might have been somewhat familiar include *The Church* (1967; reprint London: Bloomsbury, 2001); *What Must Remain in the Church* (1973; reprint Roermond, Netherlands: Fontana, 1977); and *On Being a Christian* (1974; reprint New York: Doubleday, 1976).

2. This line is from the Episcopal Church's catechism.

3. A former bishop of Massachusetts with whom Murray would have been familiar. He served from 1976 to 1986, which would have covered the years of Murray's training and ministry. He played a significant role in the Episcopal Church's ordination of women in the 1970s.

4. Some of the books by John Macquarrie that Murray might have known include *Principles of Christian Theology* (New York: Scribner, 1966); *Paths in Spirituality* (New York: Harper and Row, 1972); *The Faith of the People of God: A Lay Theology* (New York: Scribner's, 1972); and *Thinking About God* (New York: Harper and Row, 1975).

Sermon Given on December 23, 1979

Readers can find an original copy of this sermon in box 64, folder 1100, Murray Papers.

1. John Macquarrie, *Principles of Christian Theology* (New York: Scribner, 1966), 276–279. See note 4 to "Ministry," above, for additional Macquarrie texts with which Murray might have been familiar.

Sermon Given on June 24, 1979

The manuscript for this sermon does not indicate the title nor does it provide the church where Murray preached it. The manuscript is available in box 64, folder 1098, Murray Papers.

1. A theologian and cardinal in the Roman Catholic Church. Murray may have been familiar with his texts such as *Models of the Church* (New York: Doubleday, 1974).

2. See note 1 to "Ministry," above.

3. See note 1 to "Ministry," above.

The Light of the World

A sermon preached at the Episcopal Church of the Holy Nativity, Baltimore, Maryland, on the Fourth Sunday after Epiphany, February 1, 1981, and at the Episcopal Church of the Atonement, Washington, DC, on the Fifth Sunday after Epiphany, February 8, 1981. See box 116, folder 2083, with a duplicate copy in box 99, folder 1783, Murray Papers.

1. Moorhead Kennedy was a U.S. Embassy hostage in Iran freed in 1981.

2. Martin Luther King Jr., *Where Do We Go from Here: Chaos or Community?* (New York: Harper & Row, 1967), 184.

3. Cyrus Vance was secretary of state (1977–1980) under Jimmy Carter. Edmund Muskie succeeded Vance as secretary of state (1980–1981), and Christopher Warren was deputy secretary of state (1977–1981).

The Prodigal Son

Found in box 64, folder 1099, Murray Papers.

Out of the Wilderness

This sermon was given at St. Luke's Presbyterian Church on July 21, 1974. Murray did not provide the location of the church. The manuscript is in box 64, folder 1089, Murray Papers.

1. Such references include the story collection by Edward Jones, *All Aunt Hagar's Children* (New York: HarperCollins, 2006). There is also the song "Aunt Hagar's Blues," by W. C. Handy, as well as "Aunt Hagar's Children's Blues," by Tim Brymn.

2. This Civil War diary has received considerable attention, and it provides insight into the nature and meaning of the war from the perspective of those with means in the South—the planter class. It covers a four-year period from 1861 to 1865. See Mary Boykin Chestnut, *A Diary from Dixie,* ed. Catherine Clinton (New York: Penguin Classic, 2011).

3. Gerda Lerner, comp., *Black Women in White America: A Documentary History* (New York: Vintage, 1992).

4. I believe Murray is referencing Lear Green, who had herself mailed from Baltimore to Philadelphia in 1854. She was aided in this successful escape by her mother and fiancé. Green is mentioned in William Still, "Escaping in a Chest," in *The Underground Railroad* (Philadelphia: Porter and Coates, 1872), https://www.gutenberg.org/files/15263/15263-h/15263-h.htm.

5. Information on Jackson is available (listed by name) in *Taking the Underground Railroad to Freedom* (Prague: E-artnow, 2017).

6. Now named Bethune-Cookman University, in Daytona Beach, Florida.

7. See "Dr. Bethune's Last Will and Testament," Bethune-Cookman University, https://www.cookman.edu/history/last-will-testament.html. Murray has abridged the quotation somewhat; in the document, it reads, "I leave you racial dignity. . . . Despite many crushing burdens and handicaps, I have risen from the cotton fields of South Carolina to found a college, administer it during its years of growth, become a public servant in the government of our country and a leader of women. I would not exchange my color for all the wealth in the world, for had I been born white I might not have been able to do all that I have done or yet hope to do."

Sermon Given on June 12, 1977

Murray gave this sermon at the Church of the Holy Comforter in Washington, DC. The text is in box 64, folder 1093, Murray Papers.

1. Karen L. Bloomquist has held leadership positions in the Evangelical Lutheran Church in America, as well as serving on the faculty of Wartburg Theological Seminary. Her books include *The Promise of Lutheran Ethics* (Minneapolis: Fortress Press, 1998), and *Liberating Lutheran Theology* (Minneapolis: Fortress Press, 2011).

2. I am unable to find the source for this quotation. The following prayers are at the end of this sermon in the original file:

COLLECT FOR CHRISTMAS

O God, you make us glad by the yearly festival of the birth of your only Son Jesus Christ; Grant that we, who joyfully receive him as our Redeemer, may with sure confidence behold him when he comes to be our Judge; who lives and reigns with you and the Holy Spirit, one God, now forever. AMEN.

FOR ALL SORTS AND CONDITIONS OF MEN

O God, the creator and preserver of all mankind, we humbly beseech you for all sorts and conditions of humanity; that you would be pleased to make your ways known unto them; your saving health unto all nations. More especially we pray for your holy Church universal; that it may be so guided and governed by your good Spirit, that all who profess and call themselves Christians may be led into the way of truth, and hold the faith in unity of spirit, in the bond of peace, and in righteousness of life. Finally, we commend to your fatherly goodness all those who are in any ways afflicted or distressed, in mind, body or estate; that it may please you to comfort and relieve them according to their several necessities, giving them patience under their sufferings, and a happy issue out of all their afflictions. And this we beg for Jesus Christ's sake. AMEN.

Sermon on the Ordination of Women

Murray gave this sermon on January 31, 1976. The manuscript is in box 27, folder 520, Murray Papers. She gave it during the course of her General Ordination Examinations, January 26–February 1, 1976 (Set III 76–142, Part A).

1. See, for example, Carter Heyward, *A Priest Forever: One Women's Controversial Ordination in the Episcopal Church* (Cleveland: Pilgrim Press, 1999), and Paul Avis, *Seeking the Truth of Change in the Church* (London: Bloomsbury/T&T Clark, 2003).

2. This is possibly a quotation from Reverend David R. Stuart ("a pseudonym of an Episcopal clergyman who has requested that he remain anonymous," according to the website Wijngaards Institute for Catholic Research, http://www.women priests.org/classic/stuart.asp). It appears in David R. Stuart, "My Objections to Ordaining Women," in *The Ordination of Women: Pro and Con,* ed. Michael P. Hamilton and Nancy S. Montgomery (New York: Morehouse Barlow, 1975), 44–55.

Has the Lord Spoken to Moses Only?

On May 8, 1977, Murray gave this sermon to the congregation of the Church of Our Savior, Washington, DC. It is located in box 64, folder 1093, Murray Papers.

1. Patricia Martin Doyle, "Women and Religion: Psychological and Cultural Implications," in *Religion and Sexism: Images of Women in the Jewish and Christian Traditions,* ed. Rosemary Radford Ruether (1974; reprint Eugene, OR: Wipf and Stock, 1998), 15.

2. Ibid., 15–16.

3. Julian of Norwich, "Revelations of Divine Love," in *Religion and Literature: A Reader,* ed. Robert Detweiler and David Jasper (Louisville, KY: Westminster/John Knox, 2000), 71.

4. Doyle, "Women and Religion," 27.

Mary Has Chosen the Best Part

Murray gave this sermon from the pulpit of the Good Shepherd Episcopal Church, Silver Spring, Maryland, on July 14, 1977. The text is housed in box 64, folder 1094, Murray Papers.

1. William Wordsworth, "The World Is Too Much with Us," https://www.poetry foundation.org/poems-and-poets/poems/detail/45564.

Healing and Reconciliation

Murray gave this sermon on February 13, 1977, at the Chapel of the Cross in Chapel Hill, North Carolina. It is found in box 94, folder 1637, Murray Papers.

1. On the speech, given on August 28, see "Martin Luther King Jr.," National

Archives at New York City, https://www.archives.gov.

2. This is Murray herself.

Gifts of the Holy Spirit to Women I Have Known

On May 14, 1978, Murray gave this sermon at St. Philip's Episcopal Church in Durham, North Carolina. The manuscript is in box 64, folder 1095, Murray Papers.

Sermon Given on April 22, 1979

This sermon was giving during a service held at the Wisconsin Avenue Nursing Home in Washington, DC, on April 22, 1979. The full text is in box 64, folder 1097, Murray Papers.

1. A reference that could not be verified has been removed here.

Exodus

Murray gave this baccalaureate sermon at the invitation of Cedar Crest College in Allentown, Pennsylvania. The service took place on May 20, 1979. This manuscript is found in box 64, folder 1098, Murray Papers.

1. See the Cedar Crest College website at http://www.cedarcrest.edu/.

2. Ruth T. Barnhouse, "Patriarchy and the Ordination of Women," in *Toward a New Theology of Ordination: Essays on the Ordination of Women,* ed. Marianne H. Micks and Charles P. Price (Somerville, MA: Greeno, Hadden, 1976), 71–89.

3. Patricia Martin Doyle, "Women and Religion: Psychological and Cultural Implications," in *Religion and Sexism: Images of Women in the Jewish and Christian Traditions,* ed. Rosemary Radford Ruether (1974; reprint Eugene, OR: Wipf and Stock, 1998), 38.

4. Quoted in Octavio Paz, *The Other Writing: Postcolonial Essays in Latin America's Writing Culture* (West Layfette, IN: Purdue University Press, 1993), 59.

5. Reinhold Niebuhr, *The Irony of American History* (1952; reprint Chicago: University of Chicago Press, 2008).

Sermon Given on June 6, 1982

Found in box 126, folder 2292, Murray Papers.

1. Phyllis Bird, "Images of Women in the Old Testament," in *Religion and Sexism: Images of Women in the Jewish and Christian Traditions,* ed. Rosemary Radford Ruether (1974; reprint Eugene, OR: Wipf and Stock, 1998), 41–88. Murray is quoting from pages 41–42.

2. Found in James Weldon Johnson, "The Creation," in *God's Trombones* (New York: Viking Press, 1927), 15–21.

3. Phyllis Trible, *God and the Rhetoric of Sexuality* (Minneapolis: Fortress Press, 1978), 22, 201, 63.

4. Joan Chamberlain, *The Feminine Dimension of the Divine* (Asheville, NC: Chiron, 1994), 106.

Servanthood—Eleanor Roosevelt

Based on internal evidence, this sermon was likely given on November 4, 1984. It is found in box 65, folder 1106, Murray Papers.

1. John Donne, "No Man Is an Island," *Meditation XVII: Devotions upon Emergent Occasions,* in Donne, *The Complete English Poems* (New York: Penguin, 1977).

2. Stanley Hauerwas, *Peaceable Kingdom* (South Bend, IN: University of Notre Dame Press, 1991), 123–124.

3. Ibid.

4. Lash's books on Roosevelt include *Eleanor and Franklin* (New York: Norton, 2014), and *Eleanor: The Years Alone* (New York: Norton, 1972).

5. See note 4.

Sermon on Isaiah 6:1–4

Murray gave an initial sermon as a candidate for Holy Orders on the first Sunday in Lent, March 3, 1974, at Emmanuel Church, Boston, her sponsoring parish. A copy is in box 64, folder 1089, Murray Papers.

Let Not Your Heart Be Troubled

On May 1, 1977, Murray gave the following sermon from the pulpit of St. Philip's Episcopal Church in Brooklyn, New York. The manuscript is in box 64, folder 1093, Murray Papers.

1. William Lyon Phelps was a literary critic and scholar who taught at Yale from 1901 to 1933.

Put Up Your Sword

Murray gave this sermon at the Church of the Atonement in Washington, DC, on April 12, 1981. This document is found in box 65, folder 1103, Murray Papers.

Sermon Given on May 2, 1982

Murray gave this sermon at Holy Nativity in Baltimore. It is found in box 65, folder 1106, Murray Papers.

1. On nuclear weapons, see the Union of Concerned Scientists, http://www.ucsusa.org/.

Sermon Given on April 29, 1984

Murray gave this sermon at the Church of the Holy Cross, Pittsburgh. It is found in box 65, folder 1106, Murray Papers.

Nursing Home Sermon

This talk was given at the Wisconsin Avenue Nursing Home in Washington, DC, on October 28, 1979. The manuscript is located in box 64, folder 1099, Murray Papers.

1. Murray referenced Letty Russell often. She would have encountered much of Russell's writing while a seminary student. See, for instance, *Human Liberation in a Feminist Perspective: A Theology* (Philadelphia: Westminster Press, 1974), and *The Liberating Word: A Guide to Nonsexist Interpretations of the Bible,* ed. Russell (Philadelphia: Westminster Press, 1977).

The New Creation

Murray gave this Fourth Sunday in Lent sermon on March 20, 1997, at Reverend William A. Wendt's St. Stephen and Incarnation Church in Washington, DC. It is in box 64, folder 1092, Murray Papers.

1. Texts by Taylor include "The Will of God. IV. In the Epistle to the Hebrews," *Expository Times* 72 (1960–1961): 167–169.

2. His research included *Nature and Grace* (New York: Crossroad, 1988).

3. I assume that this is a continuation of her use of Carpenter's work.

4. Bultmann was a New Testament scholar who taught at the University of Marburg, Germany. His work, among other things, provided a significant way to think about biblical texts in terms of historical-cultural context.

Sermon on Isaiah 9:2, 6, Luke 2:6–7

Sermon delivered at the Feast of the Nativity of Jesus Christ, December 24, 1982, at the Church of the Holy Nativity in Forest Park, Baltimore. It is found in box 65, folder 1106, Murray Papers.

Forgiveness Without Limits

Murray delivered this sermon at the Church of the Atonement in Washington, DC. The service was held on November 11, 1979. The manuscript is in box 64, folder 1100, Murray Papers.

1. Murray mentions Kung's *On Being a Christian* (1974; reprint New York: Doubleday, 1976) in numerous sermons.

2. From "Loving Your Enemies," in Martin Luther King Jr., *Strength to Love* (1963; reprint Minneapolis: Fortress Press, 2010), 43–52.

3. Carl Rowan was a journalist with the *Washington Post,* and James Reston worked for the *New York Times* as Washington, DC, diplomatic correspondent and bureau chief.

Palm Sunday Sermon

Murray wrote the following concerning this sermon: "This sermon is my memorial sermon to my mother, Agnes Fitzgerald Murray, who was buried March 29, 1914, the Sunday before Palm Sunday. I have only one vague memory of her, since I was three years old when she died, but her memory was made fresh and alive for me by my maternal aunts and grandparents who loved her." It was given on Palm Sunday, April 7, 1974, at All Souls Church in New York City. It is found in box 64, folder 1089, Murray Papers.

1. Arlene Silberman was a frequent contributor to *Reader's Digest* and *McCall's.*

2. Flusser taught early Christianity and Judaism within the Second Temple period at Hebrew University. His best-known book, of which Murray likely was aware, is *Jesus* (1965; reprint Pune, India: Varda Books, 2014).

Faith Makes Us Whole

This sermon was delivered on the twenty-first Sunday after Pentecost, October 24, 1982, at the Church of the Holy Nativity in Forest Park, Baltimore, MD. It is found in box 65, folder 1106, Murray Papers.

Sermon Given on August 5, 1984

Found in box 65, folder 1106, Murray Papers.

1. See Romans 8:35–37.

The Meaning of Baptism

Murray gave this sermon at the Episcopal Church of Atonement in Washington, DC, on the first Sunday after Epiphany, January 11, 1981. Reverend Robert B. Hunter was the rector. It is found in box 65, folder 1103, Murray Papers.

1. Murray frequently referenced Kung's *On Being a Christian* (1974; reprint New York: Doubleday, 1976). At one point, in the sermon "Ministry," above, she mentioned owning the book but acknowledged having given it limited attention.

2. See Isaiah 41:1–3.

3. Hodgson retired from Vanderbilt University Divinity School, where he taught theology. Books by Hodgson with which Murray would have been familiar include *Jesus—Word and Presence: An Essay in Christology* (Minneapolis: Fortress Press, 1971),

and *New Birth of Freedom: A Theology of Bondage and Liberation* (Minneapolis: Fortress Press, 1976).

4. Hodgson, *Jesus—Word and Presence.*

5. Murray is drawing from Kung's *On Being a Christian.* I am uncertain as to which text by King Murray is quoting. She was familiar with his work and often pointed to his final text, *Where Do We Go from Here?*

6. Murray provided this information concerning the quotation: Jacques Ellul, 189–190. One book from which it could be drawn is *The Presence of the Kingdom* (New York: Seabury, 1948).

Can These Bones Live Again?

This sermon was delivered on March 12, 1978, as part of the "Women's Day Service" at St. Ambrose Episcopal Church in Raleigh, North Carolina. Reverend Arthur J. Calloway was rector, and the chair of the event was Geraldine Calloway. The manuscript is found in box 64, folder 1095, Murray Papers. Several long quotations that could not be identified were deleted from the sermon. This was done without altering the tone and intention of Murray's remarks.

1. See Psalm 137:1–3.

2. The poem, "Dark Testament," is Murray's own, published in *Dark Testament.*

Thoughts on Dying and Death

This sermon was given on February 26, 1978, during the Lenten season. It is located in box 64, folder 1095, Murray Papers.

1. See Romans 5:3–5.

Man in God's Image

Found in box 88, folder 1523, Murray Papers.

1. I believe Murray is referencing Lewis M. Killian and Charles M. Grigg, *Racial Crisis in America: Leadership in Crisis* (Upper Saddle River, NJ: Prentice-Hall, 1964).

Christian Community

Murray gave this sermon at the Chapel of the Good Shepherd in New York City on May 10, 1977. The manuscript is found in box 64, folder 1093, Murray Papers.

1. Parker taught New Testament at General Theological Seminary in New York City. His books include *The Gospel Before Mark* (Chicago: University of Chicago Press, 1955).

2. Julian of Norwich is mentioned in numerous sermons.

Sermon on Acts 8:5

Murray gave this homily at the Episcopal Divinity School in Cambridge, Massachusetts, on April 28, 1982. It is located in box 65, folder 1105, Murray Papers.

The Prophetic Impulse

On December 12, 1982, Murray gave this sermon at the Church of the Holy Nativity in Forest Park, Baltimore, Maryland. It is in box 65, folder 1106, Murray Papers.

1. Lines from Langston Hughes's poem "Dream Deferred" were edited out here.

2. He was an activist protesting nuclear weapons. He threatened to destroy the Washington Monument as part of his protest and was killed by police.

3. Martin Luther King Jr., *Where Do We Go from Here: Chaos or Community?* (1967; reprint Boston: Beacon Press, 2010).

Atonement

This sermon was given on September 9, 1979, at an unknown location. The document is found in box 64, folder 1099, Murray Papers.

1. Charles W. F. Smith taught New Testament at Episcopal Divinity School in Cambridge, Massachusetts, as well as at Virginia Union Theological Seminary in Alexandria, Virginia. He was on the committee that revised the 1928 Book of Common Prayer. His books include *The Jesus of the Parables* (Philadelphia: Westminster Press, 1948). Murray did not provide details concerning the source for this particular reference.

2. Martin Luther King Jr., *Where Do We Go from Here: Chaos or Community?* (New York: Harper & Row, 1967), 184.

The Holy Spirit

This sermon was given on the Sunday after Ascension Day, May 22, 1977, at Reverend James O. West's Calvary Protestant Episcopal Church, Washington, DC. It is located in box 64, folder 1093, Murray Papers.

Sermon Given on April 3, 1983

Murray gave this sermon at the Easter Day celebration at St. Bartholomew's Church, Baltimore, Maryland. It is found in box 91, folder 1582, Murray Papers.

1. Gunther Bornkamm, *Jesus of Nazareth* (New York: Harper and Row, 1975), 181.

2. Hans Kung, *On Being a Christian* (1974; reprint New York: Doubleday, 1976). Murray noted having this book and referenced it often in her sermons.

Sermon on Matthew 5:20

Found in box 64, folder 1098, Murray Papers.

1. Fosdick was a major figure in the championing of a modern depiction of the Christian faith, including a push against assumptions the Bible is the "literal" word of God. His books include *The Man from Nazareth as His Contemporaries Saw Him* (New York: Harpers, 1949), and *The Manhood of the Master: The Character of Jesus* (Seattle: Inkling Books, 2002).

2. J. Deotis Roberts, *Liberation and Reconciliation: A Black Theology* (1971; reprint Louisville, KY: Westminster/John Knox, 2005), 39.

3. Reinhold Niebuhr, *Moral Man, Immoral Society* (1932; reprint Louisville, KY: Westminster/John Knox, 2013), 64.

4. Roberts, *Liberation and Reconciliation,* 56.

5. This is a reference to James H. Cone's *God of the Oppressed* (1975; reprint Maryknoll, NY: Orbis Books, 1997).

Salvation and Liberation

The Unitarian Society of Germantown, Pennsylvania, was the site of this sermon given on April 1, 1979. The manuscript is in box 64, folder 1097, Murray Papers.

1. Jones's books include *Black Awareness: A Theology of Hope* (Nashville: Abingdon, 1971), and *Christian Ethics for Black Theology* (Nashville: Abingdon, 1974).

2. See Letty M. Russell, *Human Liberation in a Feminist Perspective* (Philadelphia: Westminster Press, 1974), 54.

3. See Gustavo Gutierrez, "Introduction," in *A Theology of Liberation* (Maryknoll, NY: Orbis Books, 1973), xiii–xvii.

The Second Great Commandment

Murray gave this sermon at the Parish of the Epiphany in Winchester, Massachusetts, on November 21, 1976. The full manuscript is found in box 64, folder 1091, Murray Papers. A thematically similar sermon was given on October 14, 1978, and is found in box 64, folder 1096, Murray Papers.

1. See Romans 8:38–39.

2. From the Episcopal Church's Book of Common Prayer.

Reflections on the Special General Convention

This document, dated September 1969, provides Murray's reflections on the Special General Convention as it related to issues concerning women and church ministry. The document is found in box 95, folder 1666, Murray Papers.

1. Roughly eleven presidents, including Franklin D. Roosevelt, Gerald Ford, and George H. W. Bush.

2. James A. Pike was an Episcopal bishop of California who was very involved in racial justice work both within the church and in the larger society.

3. Alice Paul was a major figure in the fight for the Nineteenth Amendment to the Constitution, which prohibits gender discrimination with respect to voting. She was a major player in the fight for women's rights. Betty Friedan's *The Feminine Mystique* (New York: Norton, 1963) was fundamental in starting the second wave of feminist activism.

4. These are United Thank Offering funds. They are collected and used by the Episcopal Church to support various ministries and missions.

5. The House of Bishops and the House of Deputies are the governing bodies of the Episcopal Church. The House of Deputies has roughly nine hundred members (clergy and laity) and meets to conduct its business every three years at General Convention.

What the Protestant Episcopal Church of the USA Could Be Doing the Next Century

This essay is found in box 67, folder 1148, Murray Papers.

1. A reference to Paul Tillich, a theologian mentioned numerous times in sermons contained in this volume.

2. Decter was a controversial writer who published with outlets such as the *Atlantic,* the *National Review,* and the *New Republic.* Her involvements included work as the founder of the Independent Women's Forum—a conservative organization concerned with economic issues and women. Her books include *The Liberated Woman and Other Americans* (New York: Coward, McCann and Geoghegan, 1971).

3. A coloratura is a soprano with the strong ability for singing a particularly melodic style of operatic music. Rooks was a major figure in the study of African American religion as well as the leadership of the United Church of Christ. He was the first African American to serve as president of a predominately white seminary, when he became president of Chicago Theological Seminary in 1974 (until 1984).

4. A chasuble is a sleeveless outer garment worn by an Episcopal priest. A surplice is a loose-fitting garment worn over a cassock.

Law and Religion

Murray gave this lecture at the College of William and Mary in Williamsburg, Virginia, on January 16, 1980. The manuscript is in box 90, folder 1569, Murray Papers.

1. Patricia Martin Doyle, "Women and Religion: Psychological and Cultural Implications," in *Religion and Sexism: Images of Women in the Jewish and Christian Traditions,* ed. Rosemary Radford Ruether (1974; reprint Eugene, OR: Wipf and Stock, 1998), 15–16.

2. Rosemary Radford Ruether, *New Woman, New Earth: Sexist Ideologies and Human Liberation* (1975; reprint Boston: Beacon Press, 1995), 9–10.

3. See Sheila D. Collins, *A Different Heaven and Earth: A Feminist Perspective on Religion* (King of Prussia, PA: Judson Press, 1974), 64.

4. Ruether, *New Woman, New Earth,* 11–15.

5. See Paul K. Jewett, *Man as Male and Female* (Grand Rapids, MI: Eerdmans, 1990), 51–61.

Challenge of Nurturing the Christian Community in Its Diversity
Murray delivered this lecture on March 28, 1979, at the Church of the Atonement in Washington, DC. It is located in box 90, folder 1568, Murray Papers.

1. Canon Lloyd Casson was an Episcopal priest working in Delaware who was involved in issues of social justice. See, for example, Rebecca Moore, Anthony B. Pinn, and Mary R. Sawyer, eds., *Peoples Temple and Black Religion in America* (Bloomington: Indiana University Press, 2004).

2. This is in the foreword to Letty M. Russell's *Human Liberation in a Feminist Perspective* (Philadelphia: Westminster Press, 1974), which is also the source of the previous quotation from Russell.

3. Rosemary Radford Ruether, *New Woman, New Earth* (1975; reprint Boston: Beacon Press, 1995).

4. See Russell, *Human Liberation in a Feminist Perspective,* 140.

Minority Women and Feminist Spirituality
This essay is found in box 87, folder 1508, Murray Papers.

1. Deborah Harmon Hines, "Racism Breeds Stereotypes," *Witness* 65, no. 2 (February 1982): 5–8.

2. This collective was composed of Black feminist thinkers who wrestled with issues of identity and identity formation in light of social justice issues. Its work took place over the years 1974 to 1980. See the Combahee River Collective website, http://combaheerivercollective.weebly.com/.

3. See Gloria I. Joseph and Jill Lewis, *Common Differences: Conflict in Black and White Feminist Perspectives* (Garden City, NY: Anchor Books, 1981).

4. Ibid.

5. Ibid.

6. Jacquelyn Grant's early critique of Black theology is found in "Black Theology and Black Women," in *Black Theology: A Documentary History*, ed. James H. Cone and Gayraud Wilmore (Maryknoll, NY: Orbis Books, 1979), 1:323–338.

7. James H. Cone, *My Soul Looks Back* (Maryknoll, NY: Orbis Books, 1985).

8. Ibid.

9. Ibid.

10. Pence was an activist in Minnesota who worked on issues such as domestic abuse.

11. See Marianne H. Micks, *Our Search for Identity: Humanity in the Image of God* (Minneapolis: Fortress Press, 1982).

The New Feminism

This lecture was given at the University of Arkansas at Fayetteville on March 29, 1972. It is found in box 89, folder 1551, Murray Papers.

1. Barbara Harrison, "Feminist Experiment in Education," *New Republic*, March 11, 1972, 13–17.

2. Rossi was a sociologist whose work focused on the status of women in U.S. society—including the workplace and home. Her books include *The Feminist Papers* (New York: Columbia University Press, 1973; reprint Boston: Northeastern University Press, 1988).

3. Freeman is a feminist scholar and activist whose writings include *The Politics of Women's Liberation* (London: Longman Group, 1975) and editor of *Women: A Feminist Perspective* (1975; reprint New York: McGraw-Hill Humanities, 1994).

Black Women, Racism, and the Legal Process in Historical Perspective

Murray gave this talk as part of the First National Scholarly Conference on Black Women, sponsored by the National Council of Negro Women. It took place on November 12, 1979, at the Shoreham Americana Hotel in Washington, DC. The manuscript is found in box 90, folder 1568, Murray Papers.

1. See, for example, Diane K. Lewis, "A Response to Inequality: Black Women, Racism, and Sexism," *Signs: Journal of Women in Culture and Society* 3, no. 2 (Winter 1977): 339–361.

2. On Bernard, see, for instance, Michael Kimmel and Yasemin Besen, ed., *The Jessie Bernard Reader* (New York: Routledge, 2015).

Coping with Racism and Sexism

Murray gave this talk at Phillips Exeter Academy in Exeter, New Hampshire, during a conference related to women educators in independent schools. It took place June 24, 1983. The document is located in box 91, folder 1581, Murray Papers.

1. See Gloria T. Hull and Barbara Smith, "Introduction," in *But Some of Us Are Brave: Black Women's Studies,* ed. Gloria T. Hull, Patricia Bell Scott, and Barbara Smith (Old Westbury, NY: Feminist Press, 1982), xvii–xxxii.

2. Ibid.

3. See Elizabeth Higginbotham, "Two Representative Issues in Contemporary Sociological Work on Black Women," in Hull, Scott, and Smith, eds., *But Some of Us Are Brave,* 93–102.

4. Gloria I. Joseph and Jill Lewis, *Common Differences: Conflicts in Black and White Feminist Perspectives* (Garden City, NY: Anchor Press/Doubleday, 1981), 38.

5. Constance M. Carroll, "Three's a Crowd: The Dilemma of the Black Woman in Higher Education," in Hull, Scott, and Smith, eds., *But Some of Us Are Brave,* 115–128.

6. Ibid.

7. Rosemary Radford Ruether, *New Woman, New Earth* (1975; reprint Boston: Beacon Press, 1995), 125.

Black Women

Murray gave this address at a dinner honoring Virginia Coffey, a civil rights figure working in Cincinnati. The event took place on September 9, 1977. The address is located in box 90, folder 1566, Murray Papers.

1. See Andrew Billingsley, *Black Families in White America* (New York: Touchstone Books, 1988).

2. For additional information, see, for instance, Milla Granson, Brooklyn Museum, https://www.brooklynmuseum.org/eascfa/dinner_party/heritage_floor/milla _granson.

3. See Greg Hand, "Ohio Was Not Home-Free for Runaway Slaves," *Cincinnati Magazine,* February 18, 2016, http://www.cincinnatimagazine.com/citywiseblog /cincinnati-curiosities-runaway-slaves/. See also John R. Howard, *The Shifting Winds: The Supreme Court and Civil Rights from Reconstruction to Brown* (Albany: State University of New York Press, 1988), 40–41.

4. Gerda Lerner was a pioneer in the establishment of women's history, having developed degree-granting programs at several institutions. Her writings include *Black Women in White America: A Documentary History* (1972; reprint New York: Vintage, 1992), and *The Creation of Patriarchy* (1986; reprint New York: Oxford University Press, 1987).

5. For more information, see *Mary McLeod Bethune: A Biography* (New York:

Doubleday, 1964), and Ashley N. Robertson, *Mary McLeod Bethune in Florida: Bringing Social Justice to the Sunshine State* (Charleston, SC: Arcadia, 2015).

Women on the Move

Murray gave this "devotional talk," as she described it, at the membership campaign kickoff event for the Young Women's Christian Association, National Capital Area, Washington, DC, on March 17, 1977. The speech is located in box 90, folder 1566, Murray Papers. An identical copy is also found in box 118, folder 2098, Murray Papers.

1. *Pauli Murray: The Autobiography of a Black Activist, Feminist, Lawyer, Priest and Poet* (Knoxville: University of Tennessee Press, 1989).

2. Ibid.

3. See Mary Daly, *Webster's First New Intergalactic Wickedary of the English Language of Patriarchal Religions* (Toronto: Women's Press, 1998).

4. Based on her comment concerning terrorism, it is likely Murray was referencing the Hanafi Siege in Washington, DC. During March 9–11, gunmen took control of three buildings in DC. There were two deaths and three injuries.

5. March 16, 1977, p. 34, col. 2.

6. *Washington Post,* March 17, 1777, p. E-8.

Chronology

1. She was born as part of the seventh generation of Episcopalians in the family.

2. In hindsight, she pointed to this as an early sign of her eventual movement into church ministry.

3. Questions in part were answered for her through reading Kahlil Gibran's *The Prophet* (New York: Knopf, 1923), and Gibran, *Jesus, the Son of Man* (New York: Knopf, 1946).

4. This meeting renewed her determination to fight for equality within the church and society more generally.

5. It found nothing in the Constitution nor in the church canons that prevented the ordination of women.

6. She had this status changed to Master of Divinity candidate because the additional time was useful in light of the delayed conversation in the church concerning women in ordained ministry. She was the oldest student and the only Black in her entering class.

7. For 1973 requirements for candidacy, see "An Outline of Canon 2 Title III" and "Guidelines," box 95, folder 1667, Murray Papers.

8. The ordination was performed by bishops who had either retired or left the Episcopal Church, hence the ordination of these women was considered irregular. However, in 1976, during the General Convention in Minneapolis, the church decided to permit the ordination of women. Consequently, these women were eventually "regularized" in 1977.

9. She explained why in a letter dated June 18, 1975. Murray to Vestry of Emmanuel Church, Boston, June 18, 1975, box 63, folder 1071, Murray Papers.

10. Her examinations are in box 27, folder 520, Murray Papers.

11. In terms of her performance, she was in the 56th percentile in Old Testament, 61st percentile in New Testament, 69th percentile in Church History, 49th percentile in Christian Theology, 9th percentile in Ethics, and 49th percentile in Liturgics, and had a total score in the 51st percentile. These percentages correspond to the short-answer section of the examinations and place Murray in comparison to the 267 (at one point the number given is 257) students who took that part of the examinations. The explanation of the percentile rank provided to Murray indicates that most taking the examinations had a percentile rank of 50 percent. The written evaluation of her examinations indicated that her answers did not demonstrate, according to evaluators, information concerning her own spirituality or her inner life and its impact on her sense of ministry. Her answers were general and gave little sense of her personal rationale for ministry. However, her answers were considered good otherwise.

12. This church had been served by her uncle-in-law. She worked there until her graduation.

13. She was one of three women, along with three men, ordained on this day.

14. Murray delivered a paper during the meeting and also served as a commentator at other sessions.

15. The pastoral letter in box 65, folder 1106, Murray Papers, is worth noting in that it outlines the struggle over the possibility of selling the Church of the Holy Nativity's building to the African Methodist Episcopal denomination. The congregation was racially mixed and the church located in what was once an affluent white community. Murray argued that the church must recognize the characteristics that would allow the congregation to survive: (1) multiracial in composition and leadership, (2) progressive in terms of women—such as Murray serving as its priest, (3) progressive in terms of inclusive language, and (4) progressive in terms of the involvement of the laity. This letter was read to the congregation on November 14, 1982. Also of interest is a personal note to the congregation on her appointment. It outlined her duties, as she understood them, and provides perspective concerning

her relationship to the other segments of the local church's leadership. It is in box 65, folder 1106, Murray Papers.

16. The reasons for this are outlined in a letter dated November 27, 1982, to Brenda Roberts Brown, senior warden of the Advisory Board for Church of the Holy Nativity, box 68, folder 1140, Murray Papers.

Selected Bibliography

I am grateful to Stephen Finley, who compiled the initial draft of the bibliography.

Antler, Joyce. "Pauli Murray: The Brandeis Years." *Journal of Women's History* 14, no. 2 (2002): 78–82.

Azaransky, Sarah. *The Dream Is Freedom: Pauli Murray and American Democratic Faith.* New York: Oxford University Press, 2011.

———. "Jane Crow: Pauli Murray's Intersections and Antidiscrimination Law." *Journal of Feminist Studies in Religion* 29, no. 1 (2013): 155–160.

Bell-Scott, Patricia. *The Firebrand and the First Lady: Portrait of a Friendship: Pauli Murray, Eleanor Roosevelt, and the Struggle for Social Justice.* New York: Knopf, 2016.

———. "'To Write Like Never Before': Pauli Murray's Enduring Yearning." *Journal of Women's History* 14, no. 2 (2002): 58–61.

Bryant, Flora R. "An Examination of the Social Activism of Pauli Murray." PhD dissertation, University of South Carolina, Columbia, 1991.

Caldbeck, Elaine Sue. "A Religious Life of Pauli Murray: Hope and Struggle." PhD dissertation, Northwestern University, 2000.

Collins, Patricia Hill. "Pauli Murray's Journey Toward Social Justice." *Ethnic and Racial Studies* 41, no. 8 (2018): 1453–1467.

Dorrien, Gary. "Race, Gender, Exclusion, and Divine Discontent: Pauli Murray and the Intersections of Liberation and Reconciliation." *Cross Currents* 67, no. 2 (2017): 373–399.

Drury, Doreen M. "Boy-Girl, Imp, Priest: Pauli Murray and the Limits of Identity," *Journal of Feminist Studies in Religion* 29, no. 1 (2013): 142–147.

———. "'Experimentation on the Male Side': Race, Class, Gender, and Sexuality in Pauli Murray's Quest for Love and Identity, 1910–1960." PhD dissertation, Boston College, 2000.

———. "Love, Ambition, and 'Invisible Footnotes' in the Life and Writing of Pauli Murray." *Souls* 11, no. 3 (2009): 295–309.

Firor Scott, Anne, editor. *Pauli Murray and Caroline Ware: Forty Years of Letters in Black and White.* Chapel Hill: University of North Carolina, 2006.

Fisher, Simon D. Elin. "Challenging Dissemblance in Pauli Murray Historiography, Sketching a History of the Trans New Negro." *Journal of African American History* 104, no. 2 (2019): 176–200.

———. "Pauli Murray's Peter Panic: Perspectives from the Margins of Gender and Race in Jim Crow America." *Transgender Studies Quarterly* 3, nos. 1–2 (2016): 95–103.

Gilmore, Elizabeth Glenda. "Admitting Pauli Murray." *Journal of Women's History* 14, no. 2 (2002): 62–67.

Haney, Elly. "Pauli Murray: Acting and Remembering." *Journal of Feminist Studies in Religion* 4, no. 2 (1988): 75–79.

Hartmann, Susan M. "Pauli Murray and the 'Juncture of Women's Liberation and Black Liberation.'" *Journal of Women's History* 14, no. 2 (2002): 74–77.

Hiatt, Suzanne R. "Pauli Murray: May Her Song Be Heard at Last." *Journal of Feminist Studies in Religion* 4, no. 2 (Fall 1988): 69–73.

Humez, Jean M. "Pauli Murray's Histories of Loyalty Revolt." *Black American Literature Forum* 24, no. 2 (Summer 1990): 315–335.

Mack, Kenneth W. *Representing the Race: The Creation of the Civil Rights Lawyer.* Cambridge, MA: Harvard University Press, 2012.

Mooney, Regina E. "Transgression as Transformation: An Investigation into the Relationship Between Mystically Religious Experience and Moral Experience in the Lives of Dorothy Day and Pauli Murray." PhD dissertation, Claremont Graduate School, 1992.

Moschella, Mary Clark. *Caring for Joy: Narrative, Theology, and Practice.* New York: Brill, 2016.

Murray, Pauli. *The Autobiography of a Black Activist, Feminist, Lawyer, Priest and Poet.* Knoxville: University of Tennessee Press, 1989.

———. "Black, Feminist Theologies: Links, Parallels and Tensions." *Christianity and Crisis,* April 14, 1980, 86–95.

———. "Black Theology and Feminist Theology: A Comparative View." *Anglican Theological Review* 60, no. 1 (January 1978): 3–24.

———. *Dark Testament and Other Poems.* Norwalk, CT: Silvermine, 1970.

———. *Human Rights U.S.A.: 1948–1966.* Philadelphia: Board of Missions, Methodist Church, 1967.

———. "The Liberation of Black Women." In *Voices of the New Feminism,* edited by Mary Lou Thompson, 87–102. Boston: Beacon Press, 1970.

———. *Proud Shoes: The Story of an American Family.* Boston: Beacon Press, 1999.

———. "Reexamination of the Roots of the Racial Crisis: Prologue to Policy." JDS dissertation, Yale University, 1965.

———. "The Rights of Women." In *The Rights of Americans: What They Are, What They Should Be,* edited by Norman Dorsen, 521–545. New York: Pantheon, 1971.

———. *Song in a Weary Throat: An American Pilgrimage.* New York: Harper and Row, 1987.

———. "'The Spirit of Revolt Took Shape': 1942–1944, A Blueprint for First Class Citizenship." In *Reporting Civil Rights,* vol. 1, *American Journalism, 1941–1963,* compiled by Clayborne Carson, David J. Garrow, Bill Kovach, and Carol Polsgrove, 1:62–67. New York: Library of America, 2003.

———. *States Laws on Race and Color.* Cincinnati: Women's Division of Christian Service, Board of Missions and Extension, Methodist Church, 1951.

———. "Three Thousand Miles on a Dime." In *Negro: An Anthology,* edited by Nancy Cunard and Hugh Ford, 67–70. New York: Frederick Ungar, 1970.

Murray, Pauli, and Henry Badcock. "An Alternate Weapon." *South Today,* Winter 1942–1943, 53–57.

Murray, Pauli, and Murray Kempton. *"All for Mr. Davis": The Story of Sharecropper Odell Waller.* New York: Workers Defense League, 1940.

O'Dell, Darlene. "Sites of Southern Memory: The Autobiographies of Katharine Du Pre Lumpkin, Lillian Smith, and Pauli Murray." PhD dissertation, College of William and Mary, 1997.

———. *Sites of Southern Memory: The Autobiographies of Katharine Du Pre Lumpkin, Lillian Smith, and Pauli Murray.* Charlottesville: University of Virginia Press, 2001.

Panton, Thelma M. "Thy Rich Anointing: The Lives and Ministries of Pauli Murray and Barbara Clementine Harris." *Sewanee Theological Review* 51, no. 4 (2008): 387.

Peppard, Christiana Z. "Democracy, the Verb: Pauli Murray's Poetry as a Resource for Ongoing Freedom Struggles." *Journal of Feminist Studies in Religion* 29, no. 1 (2013): 148–155.

Pinn, Anthony. "Pauli Murray's Triadic Strategy of Engagement." *Journal of Feminist Studies in Religion* 29, no. 1 (2013): 160–164.

———. "Religion and 'America's Problem Child': Notes on Pauli Murray's Theological Development." *Journal of Feminist Studies in Religion* 15, no. 1 (Spring 1999): 21–39.

Rosenberg, Rosalind. *Jane Crow: The Life of Pauli Murray.* New York: Oxford University Press, 2017.

Rupp, Leila J., and Verta Taylor. "Pauli Murray: The Unasked Question." *Journal of Women's History* 14, no. 2 (2002): 83–87.

Saxby, Troy R. *Pauli Murray: A Personal and Political Life.* Chapel Hill: University of North Carolina Press, 2020.

Ware, Susan. "Pauli Murray's Notable Connections. *Journal of Women's History* 14, no. 2 (2002): 54–57.

Williams-Carey, Hunter. "Racism and Sexism: The Dominant Influences to Pauli Murray's Understanding and Defining of Jane Crow." PhD dissertation, Sarah Lawrence College, 2012.

Index

Abernathy, Ralph, 180
abolitionist movement, 305
abortion rights, 279
Abraham (biblical), 73–74, 197
Abyssinian Baptist Church, 347–348
Advent, 253
affirmative action, 310, 318, 322
Alexander, Raymond Pace, 317
Alexander, Sadie T. M., 317, 318
All Saints Day, 156
altruism, 224
Amos (biblical), 86
Anderson, Carol, 100
Anderson, Marian, 21
anger: of Blacks, 107; in Black theology, 13; in the Christian community, 213, 245, 263, 286; at God, 56, 111; of God, 132; of men, 10; of women, 7, 301, 307
Anglican Communion, 99, 100, 263; Black Caucus, 265; Women's Caucus, 265
Anthony, Susan B., 290
Aristotle, 274
Ascension Day, 228
atonement, 22, 223–227, 246
Augustine of Hippo (saint), 273

"Backstairs in the White House" (television drama), 284
Baker, Ella, 351
Baldwin, James, 197
Ball, George N., 227
baptism, 190–193, 219, 221, 229
Barclay, William, 69
Barlow, Irene "Renee," 7–8, 9, 200
Barth, Karl, 276
Bartimaeus (biblical), 183–184

Bates, Daisy, 351
Bathsheba (biblical), 78–79
Bayne, Stephen, 84
Benét, Stephen Vincent, 3
Bennett, Anne McGrew, 82
Berman, Harold, 277
Bernard, Jessie, 322
Bethune, Mary McLeod, 76–77, 340–341, 348
Bethune-Cookman College, 340–341
Bigelow, Page Smith, 100
Billingsley, Andrew, 337
Bird, Caroline, 255
Bird, Phyllis, 121, 271
Birmingham, Alabama, 172
Black community, 300, 340, 341, 342, 344
"Black Feminist Statement," 330
Black liberation movement, 299
"Black Manifesto," 13
Black Union of Clergy and Laity, 259
Black women: alienation of, 296–299, 325–338; coping with racism and sexism, 314–322, 325–334; depressed economic position of, 342–344; different perspectives from white women, 328–330; dilemma of, 331–332; and feminist spirituality, 295–302; health of, 330; historical strength and contributions of, 75–77, 336–344; and the legal process, 315–318; multilayered oppression of, 330–331; myths and stereotypes of, 296–298, 321, 326, 331; practicing law, 318–321; and slavery, 76, 105, 297, 314; and the women's movement, 332–334. *See also* Black community; women
Black Women in White America (Lerner), 75
Bloomquist, Karen L., 82